D1871771

ART-MANUFACTURES OF INDIA

ART-MANUFACTURES OF INDIA

[SPECIALLY COMPILED FOR THE GLASGOW INTERNATIONAL EXHIBITION, 1888.]

BY

T. N. MUKHARJI, F.L.S.,

GYAN

Published by

Gyan Publishing House
5, Ansari Road
Daryaganj, New Delhi-110002
Phone: 011-47034999, 9811692060
E-mail: books@gyanbooks.com

Distribution Network
gyanbooks.com
India, USA, Canada, UK, Australia, France

© Publisher

All rights reserved. No part of this work may be reproduced, stored, adapted, or transmitted in any form or by any means, electronic, mechanical, photocopying, micro-filming, recording or otherwise, or translated in any language, without the prior written permission of the copyright owner and the publisher.

ISBN : 978-81-212-6649-9 (PB)
First Published, 1888

2nd Impression 2022

Printed at: Gyan Press, Delhi.

The book is sold subject to the condition that it shall not, by way of trade or otherwise, be lent, resold, hired out, or otherwise circulated without the prior publisher's written consent.

ART-MANUFACTURES OF INDIA
Author: T. N. MUKHARJI

ART-MANUFACTURES OF INDIA.

[SPECIALLY COMPILED FOR THE GLASGOW INTERNATIONAL EXHIBITION, 1888.]

BY

T. N. MUKHARJI, F.L.S.,

INDIAN MUSEUM, CALCUTTA,

OFFICER IN CHARGE OF THE INDIAN CENTRAL OFFICE FOR THE GLASGOW INTERNATIONAL EXHIBITION.

1888.

Photo-etching. Survey of India Offices, Calcutta, March 1888.

CARVED SANDAL-WOOD PANEL FROM AHMEDABAD.

Scale about ¼

NOTE.

The illustration opposite represents the art of sandal-wood carving as practised in South India, notably in Canara and Mysore.

Comprehensive illustrations of Indian art-manufactures will be found in the *Journal of Indian Art*, published under the direction of Sir Edward Buck, C.S.I., LL.D., Secretary to the Government of India in the Revenue and Agricultural Department, by W. Grigg, Esq., Elm House, Hanover Street, Peckham, London.

ACKNOWLEDGMENTS.

My acknowledgments are specially due to the following gentlemen whose writings on the subject of Indian Art-ware I have largely used in the present work, or who have assisted me in obtaining collections for the Glasgow International Exhibition :—

SIR GEORGE BIRDWOOD, C.S.I., K.C.I.E., LL.D.
SIR EDWARD BUCK, C.S.I., LL.D.
SIR WILLIAM HUNTER, K.C.S.I., LL.D.
SIR MAHÁRAJÁ SOURENDRO MOHAN TAGORE, KT., MUS. DOC., C.I.E.
DR. GEORGE WATT, M.B., C.M., F.L.S., C.I.E.
BABU RAJENDRĀ LALA MITRA, C.I.E., LL.D.
COLONEL J. WATERHOUSE.
A. PEDLER, ESQ.
W. H. JOBBINS, ESQ.
COLONEL D. G. PITCHER, S. C.
A. H. PIRIE, ESQ.
BABU GANGA DHAR GANGULI.
B. H. BADEN POWELL, ESQ., C.S., C.I.E.
J. L. KIPLING, ESQ., C.I.E.
SURGEON-MAJOR T. H. HENDLEY.
SURGEON-GENERAL G. BIDIE, M.B., F.L.S., C.I.E.
J. GRIFFITHS, ESQ.
B. A. GUPTE, ESQ.
H. L. TILLY, ESQ.
T. CHICHELE PLOWDEN, ESQ., C.S.
COLONEL E. B. EUAN-SMITH.
CAPTAIN A. C. TALBOT, S.C., C.I.E.
COLONEL H. POWLETT.
BABU SRI RAM.
MAJOR W. H. C. WYLLIE, C.I.E.
LIEUTENANT-COLONEL W. J. W. MUIR.
J. JOHNSTONE, ESQ.
COLONEL A. LEMESSURIER, R.E., C.I.E.
COLONEL J. C. BERKELEY.

CONTENTS.

VOWEL SOUNDS IN INDIAN NAMES.

a	short sounds	as	a	in	Pall.
á	long "	as	a	in	Palm.
e	"	as	e	in	Pell.
i	"	as	i	in	Pit.
o	"	as	o	in	Pole.
u	"	as	u	in	Pull.

Old spelling has been retained in many well-known names, and no accent has been used on i or u. Long i sounds as "ee" (double e), and long u as "oo" (double o). Most of the names have been spelt in the old style in the map accompanying this book. To facilitate identification, names as spelt in the map have been given within brackets in the Alphabetical Index at the end of the book.

INDIAN CURRENCY.

The rate of exchange is variable. A rupee may, however, be taken at 1*s* 4*d.* [The present (June 1888) rate of exchange is about 1*s* $4\frac{1}{10}$*d.*].

1 Pice = $\frac{1}{4}$ Anna = 1 Farthing.
1 Anna = $\frac{1}{16}$ Rupee = 1 Penny.
1 Rupee = 1 Shilling and 4 Pence.

ART-MANUFACTURES OF INDIA.

INTRODUCTION.

THE following pages contain a brief account of the most important art-manufactures of India. They are intended to give a general idea of such articles to the visitors at the Glasgow International Exhibition. The present collection there is not only a representative one, but also includes many articles of the best and purest workmanship. That it has been possible to get together such an assortment of Indian art-ware within so short time and with such small provision of funds, is largely due to the successful management of the late Colonial and Indian Exhibition. The knowledge which it imparted to the people of Great Britain about the resources of India, and the clever ingenuity of their fellow-subjects in turning out beautiful and original examples of art-workmanship, has now begun to bear some fruit. A large number out of the millions of visitors before whose eyes the Colonial and Indian Exhibition displayed the artistic wealth of India carried back with them a desire to possess specimens of such art, and the large number of such specimens which have through its means been scattered over the length and breadth of the land have created for Indian handiwork a taste of which the value is most important to Indian interests. It is now said that not only in Great Britain, but also on the Continent of Europe, this taste is creating a public opinion that no salôn, however brilliant it may be in other respects, can be considered fashionable or perfect unless it possesses at least a few decorative articles of Indian manufacture. Thus, while on the one hand the kind interest taken in the Indian artisans and their work by Her Majesty the Queen-Empress, by His Royal Highness the Prince of Wales, by the nobility and gentry of England, and by connoisseurs of art both in Great Britain and India, has helped to bring about a true appreciation of Indian manufactures, and to foster a demand for them in Europe; on the other hand the encouragement afforded by the Colonial and Indian Exhibition has created a confidence in the minds of native merchants and manufacturers in the value of exhibiting their works abroad, and a spirit of enterprise is already perceptible among them in their readiness to send their goods to foreign markets on their own account. The feeling of confidence now established by the recent success of the Indian merchants and manufacturers in Great Britain has been the cause of a great increase in the number of private exhibits, so that works of art have been sent to the Glasgow International Exhibition from all parts of the country in addition to those purchased from funds supplied by the Executive Council.

Articles of superior workmanship selected out of this combined collection will be shewn in cases, and will be sold to lovers of art who would prefer to wait till the close of the Exhibition in order to secure the possession of the more perfect specimens. In the present account will be found a general description of such articles, their history, place of manufacture, and the prices at which they are sold. It is needless to state here, that the manufacturers who have sent their goods to the Glasgow International Exhibition cherish a strong hope that the patient, persevering industry, by the aid of which these articles have been produced, will be thoroughly appreciated by the British public.

T. N. MUKHARJI.

CALCUTTA,
30th May 1888.

ART-MANUFACTURES OF INDIA.

I.—Fine Arts.

Paintings and Drawings.

PICTORIAL art is said to have made considerable progress in ancient India. A very high efficiency in the science of painting is attributed to Yakshas and Nágas, who lived in the mythological age, and are described as half-human half-supernatural beings. They could produce "such exact copies that these could not be known from the things painted." In later times, their place was taken by a class of men called *Chitrakars*, or picture-makers, who followed the profession from father to son. Mention is made of their work in various old books. Among these may be cited that in Sakuntalá, a celebrated drama written by Kálidása, one of the greatest of Sanskrit poets who flourished about two thousand years ago.

Sakuntalá was the name of a pretty maiden who lived all her life in the forest-home of her adopted father, a hermit of great sanctity. One day the king of the country came to hunt in the neighbourhood, and seeing this beautiful flower of the forest, he fell in love with her. His love was returned, and the sage was not unwilling that his adopted daughter should wed a sovereign over whose head rested the imperial umbrella of India. So the king came back to his home rejoiced, and presently sent costly jewels for his beloved. But the simple girl did not know how and where to wear these precious things. For she only knew how to make garlands of jasmine and other flowers, or to make a bracelet out of the soft lotus stem. She was sorely puzzled. But happily in the little cottage where she lived there hung from the wall the portrait of a lady with toe-rings, anklets, necklets, and all sorts of ornaments painted upon it. From this picture Sakuntalá learnt how to put on her ornaments.

It may be inferred from the above description that the art of painting was in an advanced state two thousand years ago, and that portraits were executed at the time with care and minuteness. It was even so before this time, when the Buddhist religion was supreme in India. At this period there was a school of painters in the Middle Country, then one in the West in Rajputana; subsequently the Eastern School was founded in Bengal, and the Northern Schools in Nepal and Kashmir, while South India was proud in the fame of its master-painters, Jaya, Parájaya, and Vijaya.

As a matter of fact, not a vestige of the ancient paintings of India exists at the present day, except that executed by the Buddhists on the walls of the Ajanta cave-temples, the excavation of which was carried on for one thousand years, from 200 B. C. to 800 A. D. These cave-temples lie among the wild hilly country of Khandesh, in the Bombay Presidency, which up to a recent date abounded in man-eating tigers and even more ferocious bands of marauding robbers. Perhaps their very inaccessibility saved these valuable temples from the fate which works of a similar nature in the more open country met at the hands of iconoclastic Vandals of India. A connoisseur of pictorial art, and himself a well-known artist, Mr. Griffiths, the Superintendent of the School of Art, Bombay, thus admires these fresco-paintings:—

"The painters were giants in execution. Even on the walls some of the lines, drawn with one sweep of the brush, struck me as very wonderful; but when I saw long delicate curves traced with equal precision on the horizontal surface of a ceiling, their skill appeared to me nothing less than miraculous. For the purposes of art-education, no better examples could be placed before an Indian art-student. The art lives. Faces question and answer, laugh and weep, fondle and flatter; limbs move with freedom and grace, flowers bloom, birds soar, and beasts spring, fight, or patiently bear burdens."

Of another scene, that of a "Dying Princess," Mr. Griffiths states—"For pathos and sentiment, and the unmistakeable way of telling its story, this picture cannot, I consider, be surpassed in the history of art." About the defects of these paintings he remarks:—

"The state of mind in which these paintings originated and were executed must have been very similar to that which produced the early Italian paintings of the fourteenth century. There is the same slight attention to the science of art, the same crowding of figures, the same want of ærial perspective, and the same regard for a truthful, rather than for a beautiful, rendering of a subject."

Another fault of these fresco paintings is the highly conventional treatment of such accessories as buildings, hills, seas, and rivers. Buildings are represented by a thick line over the heads of the inmates, hills are shewn by brick-like blocks, and seas and rivers are recognised by the boats and fishes in them. But such conventional treatment is an exception, while "most of the objects are rendered with a faithfulness and exactness that shew the authors to have been keen and practised observers and masters of execution." Thus very high encomiums have been paid to the only specimen of old Indian painting now extant, and of late years even this has been greatly injured by "bees, bats, and barbarians." With her other glories, the art of painting has vanished from India.

Although the art of painting is against the rules of the Muhammadan religion, and was not therefore always encouraged by the Musalman rulers of India, still pictorial art was not without its patron at a time when every nobleman had in his train a retinue of experts in other art-industries. The Mughul Emperor Akbar was one of its greatest patrons. In the celebrated Persian work called the *Ain-i-Akbari*, which contains a historical account of his administration, and which was written by his order and under his immediate supervision, Akbar speaks pretty plainly about the unreasonable prejudice entertained by his co-religionists against the noble art of painting. He says: "I do not like those people who hate painting. They ought to know that a painter has greater opportunities of remembering God, for however life-like he makes a picture he knows that he cannot give it life, and that He and He only is capable of doing that." Akbar had sixteen great artists at his court, a specimen of whose work has been preserved in the miniature illustrations of the *Razm-námah*. *Razm-námah*, or the History of the War, is an abridgement of the great Sanskrit epic, the Mahábhárata, which the Emperor ordered to be made in Persian in 1582 in order to remove the fanatical hatred prevailing between Hindus and Musalmans which he thought arose mainly from their ignorance of each other. A valuable copy of this work, if not the original manuscript, exists in the Royal Library of Jaipur, containing 169 miniature illustrations, which cost more than £40,000. These are "magnificently drawn and illuminated in the highest style of Persian art." A large number of portraits of Emperors and Governors, executed by unknown artists during the Muhammadan régime, were sent to the Calcutta International Exhibition. Saracenic, or, more properly speaking, the Persian art of painting, has left its impress upon the indigenous painting in the West of India, by bringing into it a large amount of care and minuteness, and eliminating from it much of its traditional conventionality. The style of making flat pictures, largely practised in Lahore and Jaipur, is an example of this mixed art.

That Indian art has undergone considerable decadence since the time when the fresco paintings in the Ajanta cave-temples were executed, is shewn by the pictures made by professional painters of the present day. They are simply coloured "daubs," intended to represent by figures and other accessories the exploits of some mythological hero. No attention is paid in them to symmetry, to perspective, or to an effective adjustment of light and shade.

But we are perhaps on the threshold of a revival of pictorial science in India, not of the old indigenous kind, but of the Art as it is now understood in Europe. The Schools of Art established under the auspices of the Government in the different presidency towns have already wrought a wonderful change in the ideas about painting hitherto entertained by the people. These institutions have become extremely popular. Although the eye and the mind of the Indian people have not yet been sufficiently educated to form a true conception of the refinement and depth of imagination displayed in a European master-production, yet the æsthetic faculty inherent in the Indian enables him to appreciate and admire its beauty and sublimity.

Fresco paintings.—Grotesque figures of men and animals are painted on walls all over the country. The likenesses are very rude, and are generally done with a red ochre called the *Geru*. Soldiers, tigers, and elephants are favourite subjects on which the artists delight to display their skill. Geometrical designs are sometimes employed, chiefly in the decoration of boats. In North India, where architectural decorations are more or less Saracenic in style, the ornamentations are very often floral. This kind of work is executed by the masons, who gently rub the colours on fresh-laid plaster by the aid of a small iron spatula. In Bengal, such fresco paintings are largely to be seen in halls where religious ceremonies are held. An audience hall, highly decorated in this style, exists at Krishnagar, where, in the last century, a Rájá lived, who was recognised as the head of the Hindus of Bengal. In the Panjáb, such artists are constantly employed in the beautification of the Golden Temple at Amritsar, and of religious edifices in other parts of the country. Mild indigenous colours were formerly used for such paintings, but now the brilliant aniline dyes have found their way in this as they have in other industries requiring the use of colour. [See "Decorative Painting applied to Architecture."]

Oil-painting.—This art, as it is understood in Europe, hardly seems to have ever made much progress in India. Very rude oil-paintings are produced in certain parts of the country, notably in Jagannáth. The painters at this holy place take a long piece of cloth on which they lay a paste of black earth, or black earth and cow-dung mixed. When dry, a coating of lac is put upon it. Thus a stiffness is acquired, and the porous quality of the cloth is destroyed. Paint is then applied on this prepared cloth, and figures and accessories made to describe the worship paid to the great "Lord of the Universe," who is represented by a symbolical figure without hands or feet. Paintings of this kind, describing the exploits of other Gods, are displayed by itinerant beggars before the wondering eyes of simple villagers. They carry rolls of such pictures under their arm, which they spread on the ground, and explain to the attentive villagers the various scenes as they are gradually unrolled.

A long roll of painting, shewing the temple of Jagannáth and the ceremonies performed therein, is sold for R40, or about £3.

In fairs and other public places, still more rude oil-paintings are sold in large numbers. These are laid on old pieces of cloth, sized by a paste made of black earth, and fixed on a frame of four pieces of slit bamboos. As soon as the paste is dry, the painter begins to put the colours upon it, and in ten minutes the picture is ready for sale. The subjects chosen are mostly mythological.

The price of such a picture is 1¼ annas, or about 1¼ *d.*

The art of oil-painting is now being taught by European masters in the Schools of Art established in the different presidencies. These schools have turned out a number of good painters who earn their livelihood by making portraits of wealthy Indian gentlemen, as well as by drawing original pictures depicting different phases of Indian life.

An ex-student of the School of Art charges R100 to R300 (£7 to £21) for a life-sized oil-painting. Smaller pictures representing Indian life may be had for R25 to R100.

Paper-paintings.—A large number of water-colour portraits made in the latter portion of the Muhammadan period (1500 to 1800 A. D.) exist in the country, and are in the possession of old native families. The names of the artists are not known. A collection of such portraits was gathered from Dacca and Saháranpur for the Calcutta Exhibition. Dacca, the former seat of Government in Bengal, sent three,—*viz.*, of Nawáb Jaswant Khán, of Nawáb Nasrat Jang, and Nawáb Shams-ud-Daulat. Sahâranpur in the North-Western Provinces sent six pictures, said to have been the property of Nawáb Shaista Khán, one of the Lieutenants of Emperor Auranzeb. These were a portrait of Nur Jahán Begam, a portrait of Emperor Sháh Alam, a portrait of Sultán Murád Bakhsh, a portrait of Hazrat Ibrahim Adam, a battle scene at Haidrabad, and a battle between Emperor Alamgir and Rájá Jaswant Sing. Besides these, there was in the collection a portrait of Shaikh Sádi, the famous Persian poet, and the author of the celebrated Persian work called the *Gulistán*. These paintings are in the Persian style as revived by Akbar.

Mention has already been made of the *Razmnámah*, the Persian abridgement of the Sanskrit epic the *Mahábhárata*. There is a copy of this work in the Royal Library at Jaipur containing 169 full-page miniatures. Six of the most characteristic of these miniatures were copied and enlarged, and these were displayed in the Jaipur Court of the Colonial and Indian Exhibition. Of these, two may be described :—

(1) King Yudhishthira's visit to the lower regions, where the souls of sinners are in torment. He is being escorted by a heavenly guide. He is filled with horror as he witnesses the awful scenes, and he wants to retrace his steps. Immediately a transformation takes place, sweet fields and beauteous paths appear where before all was horror, and the shining Gods come down from heaven to take him to the abode of bliss. King Yudhishthira was made to witness the torments of hell as a punishment for his having failed but for once in his life to speak the whole truth.

(2) A royal banquet four thousand years ago, given by King Yudhishthira to his friends just before the sacrificial horse was let loose, with a placard on its brow challenging the world to seize and detain it. The painting shows a large brick-built house, in the front of which are the court musicians playing on their

instruments. In the outer apartment the male members of the royal family, with Krishna and other friends, are partaking of the feast, while the holy Bráhmans, with the sacred thread hanging from their neck, are busy distributing the various delicacies, the food being eaten out of ornamental plates and cups, and washed down by cool perfumed water contained in goglets called *surâhis* in the modern language of Upper India. On another side a woman of the shepherd caste has brought a basket of earthen vessels containing curd, which a servant of the royal household is taking down from her head. In the inner apartments the royal ladies, bedecked with picturesque garments, and gems of inestimable value, are holding their own feast. Draupadi, the common wife of the five brothers, is there; while Gándhári sits in a corner, sad and sorrowful, with her cheek resting on her hand, and the everlasting bandage on her eyes which she put on on the day of her marriage, because her husband was blind, and she would not enjoy the blessings of vision because her husband could not.

This picture is given as an illustration in the *Journal of India Art*, published under the patronage of the Government of India by Mr. W. Griggs, Elm House, Hanover Street, Peckham, London.

Copies of such pictures can probably be obtained by application to Dr. T. Hendley, in medical charge of the Jaipur State.

Similar miniature pictures on paper are still made by the ivory-painters of Delhi. A picture representing the court of Akbar the Great can be had for R100.

Pictures of the same style are also done at Jaipur. They are painted on card, thick paper, or gold-beater's skin. Dr. Hendley thus describes the industry:—

"Enormous quantities of brightly-coloured pictures of every

grade of merit are produced throughout the State. Almost every noble has a painter in his retinue, and in the town of Jaipur there are several middlemen who deal solely in pictures. The best men naturally live in the capital, and the pride of these are employed by the Prince, receiving retaining fees in the shape of salaries or lands, with the privilege of working for private parties when not wanted in the palace. Many of these posts are hereditary where the son is capable. Jaipur frequently sends men to other States for special work, as, for example, a beautiful palace at Jodhpur was chiefly decorated by an artist from this State. Mythological subjects find very ready sale.

"The most *advanced* artists have taken to clothing the Gods in European costume, with similar surroundings; thus Siva (the Great Destroying Principle of the Hindu Trinity) is shewn sitting in a hall lighted by candles in glass shades, and Krishna (an incarnation of Vishnu, the Protecting Principle of the Hindu Trinity), drives a phæton, which is filled by his friends and attendants. The following are popular sets of designs: Sets of the incarnations of Vishnu and Siva; forms of Durgá (Goddess of Energy); the Sikh Gurus (Preceptors); the Jain Lords or Tirthankars; series shewing the ceremonies performed at every stage of a Rajput's (warrior caste) career; portraits of the Mahárájás of Jaipur; the personified modes of music sets; sets of trades and callings, with different faces (not the same face for each trade as at Benares); portraits of famous men, priests, and women in local costumes. The finest work in outline is done on gold-beater's skin."

The following may be quoted as the price of typical specimens :—

	R
Mahákáli (Goddess of Energy)	21
Portrait of the Rájá of Jaipur	8
Ditto of Rustam, the great wrestler . . .	3
Krishna	4

Pictures like those of Jaipur are made at Bikánir, another Native State in Rajputana. Prices vary from R1 to R100.

Curious water-colours are also executed in Alipura and Datia in Central India. A picture of this kind, representing a tiger seizing an antelope, the whole forming a Persian inscription, was sent to the Colonial and Indian Exhibition.

Water-colour paintings are also carefully executed by one Totá Rám of Lahore. The subjects as usual are mythological. A collection of his pictures exist in the Indian Museum. Among these is a curious painting shewing how Hindu ascetics perform austerities, and gradually evolve a subtle force existing in the human constitution. Another picture, by the same painter, depicts the battle at Kurukshettra, which took place about four thousand years ago. This picture has been executed with great minuteness, and shews a considerable amount of good taste in the arrangement of colours. The following are the prices at which Lahore water-colour paintings are sold :—

	R
The great battle of Kurukshettra . .	80
The Court of Kauravas	70
Kansa being slain by Krishna . . .	40
The Kálinág Mathan	40
Sitá in captivity	30
The Varáha Avatár	30
The Narasinha Avatár	15
The Vámana Avatár	25
The Jagannáth, or the Lord of the World .	7

Ethnological pictures are made at Jhang and Nawashahr, in the district of Jallandhar, Panjáb, and mythological pictures in the native style are painted at Kangra and Kapurthala.

In Nepal, coloured sketches of temples, shrines, Gods and Goddesses are made by a class of Newars called *Chitrakars*. "The drawings are neatly finished, and the colouring shews some taste. There is, however, little or no idea of perspective."

Similar paintings are executed in the towns of Hampa, Sagra, and Anantpur, in the Madras Presidency. A water-colour drawing in red, blue, and gold, representing Krishna seated on a throne, with a pot of butter in one arm, and a milkmaid on each side dallying with him, was sent from Madras to the Calcutta International Exhibition. The accessories in this picture were all pasted on. Price, R132.

Until recently, a superior kind of water-colour paintings was executed in Bengal by a class of people called the *Patuás,* whose trade also was to paint idols for worship. These paintings were done with minute care, and considerable taste was evinced in the combination and arrangement of colours. The industry is on the decline, owing to cheaper coloured lithograph representations of Gods and Goddesses turned out by the ex-students of the Calcutta School of Art having appeared in the market. A painting in the old style can still be had, by order, at a price of R10 and upwards.

The *Patuás* now paint rude "daubs" which are sold by thousands in stalls near the shrine of Kálighát in the neighbourhood of Calcutta, as also in other places of pilgrimage and public fairs. The subjects as usual are mythological, but of late they have taken to making pictures representing a few comical features of Indian life. Such pictures are generally sold at a price ranging from a farthing to a penny. The following is a typical list:—

Goddess Káli	$\frac{1}{2}$ *d.*
Rádhá-Krishna	$\frac{1}{2}$ *d.*
Jagadhátri, the Mother of the World .	$\frac{1}{4}$ *d.*
Goddess of Learning	$\frac{1}{2}$ *d.*
Woman fetching water	$\frac{1}{2}$ *d.*
Milking	$\frac{1}{2}$ *d.*

The students of the School of Art also turn out water-colour paintings in the European style. The head of a religious ascetic, with his beard and beads, is for them a very attractive subject, as also the faces of different castes and different nationalities. They do no tappear to have acquired much proficiency in making scenic pictures. A water-colour painting, executed by a student of the School of Art, is sold at R25 and upwards.

A collection of water-colour pictures was sent to the Colonial and Indian Exhibition by Babu Sarat Chandra Dás, C.I.E. "These paintings were executed by Tibetans, and are in the style of those used for decorating the interior of Tibetan monasteries."

In most of the chief towns of Mysore, the *Chitrakars* practise the art of making water-colour pictures. "The pictures principally represent chiefs, kings, and figures from Hindu mythology." Prices range from R5 for a single figure, 10″ × 10″, to R15 for groups in plaques of 20″ × 20″.

The following account of picture-painting in Burma is supplied by Mr. H. L. Tilly of the Public Works Department :—

"In the last census 1,078 persons were returned as following this profession, of whom more than half lived in the villages. The towns of Rangoon, Moulmein and Bassein, and the districts of Bassein and Henzada, contain the greater number of artists. The profits of painting vary according to the artist's reputation. A portrait painter in Moulmein is said to command as much as R80 to R120 for a single likeness, and the best decorators in Rangoon earn R60 a month. An ordinary artist makes about R30 a month.

"In painting, the materials used are colours in powder bought in the bazar and coming from England (excepting indigo, yellow ochre, and vermilion from Mandalay), charcoal, cotton instead of canvas, a size made of lime and tragacanth, and brushes made by the artists of the hairs from the inside of a bullock's ear, bound together with silk, and glued into quills obtained from the adjutant, cormorant, and pigeon.

"The majority of the Burmans seem to draw by intuition, and those among them who have been trained to any art are masters of the pencil, although they have little idea of perspective or of the balance of light and shade. Although the details are conventional, the general idea is the creation of the workman. It is not therefore surprising that the artists of the country produce wonderfully good pictures of dramatic or mythical incidents, full of life and humour, for in these branches of art conventional attitudes are not out of place. Their portraits, though somewhat like the original, are stiff, and the backgrounds or accessories are absurd, being generally badly-drawn representations of articles of European furniture. Landscape-painting is in its infancy, but the artists are anxious to learn. Altogether pictorial art in Burma is progressing, and the artists are conscious that they have much to learn, so that there is every hope that they will rapidly improve.

"Pictures are drawn on cotton, stretched tightly on a light wooden frame. The cotton is first washed over with size, after which the subject is outlined in charcoal, and, when correct, in red ochre; after that the colours are laid on as required. The background is generally a flat wash of dark colour."

In many parts of Upper India, an ornamental scroll-work is made on paper by the finger-nail, which has been rightly characterised by Mr. Kipling as "one of the numerous examples of futile ingenuity for which India is remarkable." An embossed nail-work, executed by one Miran Bakhsh of Lahore, was sent to the Calcutta International Exhibition. Price, Rs. 15. A picture drawn by finger-nails was also sent from Indor to the above Exhibition.

Glass-paintings.—Until a short time ago mythological pictures were painted on glass in many parts of Bengal. They possessed no artistic merit, and the trade is on the verge of extinction. Similar paintings are executed in other parts of India. A specimen of painting on glass was sent to the Calcutta Exhibition from the Rámpur State in the North-Western Provinces. This was done by two Kashmiri artists in the employ of the Nawáb. In Madras glass-paintings are made at Chandragiri in North Arcot District.

Ivory-paintings.—Delhi is the chief centre of this industry. Miniature ivory-painting is a development of the art of illuminating Persian manuscripts, so much admired and so eagerly sought after in the days of Muhammadan supremacy in India. Portraits of emperors, empresses, and other beauties of the Muhammadan Court, and pictures of the chief buildings in Northern India, like the Táj at Agra, and the Juma Masjid at Delhi, are favourite subjects. The artists also copy in colours photographic portraits. Water-colour alone is used. These miniature paintings are often employed to decorate carved ebony caskets, and are also set in jewellery. The head is either drawn in full front, when it is called *do-chashm* (two-eyed), or in profile, called *ek-chashm* (one-eyed). Mr. Kipling thus speaks of the quality of the pictures turned out :—

> "The introduction of photography is gradually bringing about a change in Delhi miniatures. The artists are ready to reproduce in colour any portrait that may be given to them; and although sometimes the hardness of definition and a certain inky quality of the shadows of some photographs are intensified, much of their work in this line is admirable. The stiffness which used to be their failing characteristic is disappearing; landscape, a branch of art treated in indigenous art with stern conventionality, is attempted in a freer spirit, and it seems not unlikely that a new, and perhaps more fresh and vital, way of looking at nature may be adopted. Supposing this change to be desirable,—a point that is not absolutely certain,—the Delhi work of to-day is strongly marked by the fault of its qualities, the excessive delicacy and minuteness of handing, well expressed by their customary phrase, *ek bál qalm* (a brush of a single hair), the quality of the handling being far more esteemed than sound drawing, good colour, or truth of effect."

All the Delhi artists are Muhammadans who claim Persian descent. They have now established themselves in Calcutta and Bombay, where they sell a large amount of their work. The prices of miniature ivory-paintings range from R10 to R100.

Ivory-painting is executed to a small extent at Benares and Trichinopoly. In the former place a Hindu, called Chuni Lál, follows the profession. The pictures are done in gold and colours in the style of manuscript illumination. The subjects are mythological. Prices range from R20 to R50 a piece. Twelve Benares pictures were sent to the Calcutta International Exhibition (1883), valued at R515.

The work done at Trichinopoly is fairly good. Two specimens of this kind were shewn at the Calcutta Exhibition by one Gopál Swámi Rájá. One of these represented a scene from the great epic Rámáyana. Ráma was shewn here seated with his wife on a throne; on his left were his three brothers, on his right a number of Indian sages, while below were a number of monkeys in a state of adoration, and on the footstool knelt the great monkey god Hanumán, supporting Ráma's feet. The price put on the picture was R57½, or about £4. The second picture represented Krishna, the next incarnation of Vishnu, as playing on his flute under his favourite *Kadamba* tree (*Anthocephalus Cadamba*), with a milkmaid on each side offering him a ball of butter, while a cow was licking his feet. Price, R32. In the same Exhibition were shewn several miniature ivory-paintings sent by one Rájá Gopál of Madras. These were intended to be set in jewellery, and the prices were as follows: 7 sets of ivory paintings for bracelets, R4-8; 2 sets for brooch, R3; 2½ dozens for buttons, R12-8.

Though not a speciality of Jaipur, many of the artists in that place can paint on ivory. They have probably learnt the art from the Delhi painters.

Talc-paintings.—This kind of painting is largely made at Trichinopoly in South India. They are chiefly illustrative of castes and native industries. A book containing a dozen pictures of this kind may be had for R4. Paintings on talc are also executed in Benares, illustrating trades and industries, and the religious ceremonies and festivals of the Hindus. In sets of pictures representing trades one face serves for a series of the various head-dresses worn by different castes. Prices, R3 to R7 per dozen.

Leather-paintings.—At Nossam in the Cuddapah District of the Madras Presidency, circular pieces of leather are hand-painted for use as table-mats. Dr Bidie states that they are "curious and sometimes quaint, but never possess much artistic merit."

Paintings on cloth.—Hand-painted chintzes are made in the Madras Presidency, called *Palampores.* [See "Chintzes."]

Paintings on wood.—Wood-painting is practised in all parts of the country. In Upper India, Muzaffargarh, Delhi, Lahore, Jallandhar, Simla, Benares, Bareilly, and Patna are noted for their painted wooden boxes and toys. It is known as the *kámágari* work, the name being derived from the word *kámán*, a bow, on which this kind of decoration was first used. The bow is still made and painted in this fashion in certain parts of the country. Panels, chests, oval boxes called *kautás*, and other wooden articles are painted in water-colours, on which a varnish is subsequently applied as a protection. Such articles sell from half a rupee to R20. [See also "Decorative Painting applied to articles of domestic use."]

Manuscript Illumination.—Caligraphy as an art was highly admired by the Muhammadans, the peculiar formation of the alphabet used by them specially favouring its free development. Since the days when the Caliphs of Baghdad encouraged arts and sciences, it was the pride of every Muhammadan Court to collect around it not only the most expert artists and the famous poets, but also the best caligraphists. Illumination of manuscripts with pictures, though prohibited by law, is, however, the natural growth of the Persian caligraphic art. Large sums of money were often spent on such work. As already mentioned, £40,000 were paid to the artists by the Emperor Akbar for the illumination of the *Razm-námah*. At the Jaipur Exhibition of 1882, by the side of the *Razm-námah* was displayed a copy of Shaikh Sádi's Persian work *Gulistán*, which was executed within the last fifty years, under the direction of Mahárájá Banni Singh of Alwar, who gave at least R50,000 as salary to the man who prepared the illuminated manuscript. The whole work is said to have cost more than R1,00,000. The border of each page is beautifully illuminated in gold, and on no two pages are the designs alike. A page of this *Gulistán* was shewn at the late Colonial and Indian Exhibition, London. Mr. Kipling thus remarks of other collections :—

"Sir W. W. Hunter writes: 'The Royal Library at Windsor contains the finest examples in this bye-path of art. A noble manuscript of the *Sháh-Jahán-námah*, purchased in Oudh for £1,200 in the last century, and now in possession of Her Majesty, will amply repay a visit.' The house of Firmin Didot of Paris, however, possessed perhaps the largest and most complete collection of examples of this bye-path, which is in fact a broad highway, leading, as has been demonstrated in Europe, to the highest achievements of pictorial art. M. Ambroise, Firmin Didot, and M. P. Barty exhibited, in the retrospective department of the Paris Exhibition of 1878, works which it would now be difficult to match in Persia or India. Recently several leaves of a superb *Sháh-námah*, each leaf a picture, full of most elaborate and perfectly-wrought detail, have been acquired for the South Kensington Museum by Mr. Purdon Clarke. These pictures contain a complete exposition of the architectural forms of Samarkand and Persia. Many similar treasures are still in the possession of native princes, and others belong to wealthy families. The production of such work, notwithstanding its minuteness and finish, must have been immense, for Albert de Mandelso records that Akbar was credited with the possession of 24,000 manuscripts richly bound. Many of these, as invariably in the case of the Kurán, were probably manuscripts illuminated in ornaments merely in gold and colours. But many contained pictures, and one in the

Lahore Museum, marked as having belonged to Akbar, seems to have been an exposition of the miracles in the Bible."

A highly ornamented manuscript in the Páli character has within this year (1888) been procured for the Art Section of the Indian Museum at Calcutta. It is decorated in gold and colours, and has been purchased for R120.

In all the large towns where there are wealthy Muhammadan families, the art of manuscript illumination is still practised by a few men. In Lucknow, Rámpur and Agra, in the North-Western Provinces, it is done by a few Kashmiris. "Prices are fanciful, and fixed by no scale. A good example, such as an illuminated Kurán, would cost about R100."

A large number of such illuminated manuscripts were brought together at the Calcutta International Exhibition (1883). These were lent by the old Muhammadan families in Northern India, and among them were the following interesting illuminated manuscripts:—

(1) A Persian work translated about 250 years ago by Mir Imdád of Persia, said to be the best of Persian caligraphers. The book is profusely illuminated with gold and enamel. (2) *Murakka*, a Persian scrap-book, containing the best specimens of handwriting collected for the Emperor Aurangzeb in the year 1102. Hijra (1681 A.D.) It contains also a number of pictures illuminated with gold. (3) *Katát Ibu Iman*, a poem in Persian, transcribed before the time of the Emperor Akbar and written in a beautifully fine hand by Sultán Ali Mushadi. It belonged to the Emperor Jahángir, and bears a few autograph lines by Emperor Sháh Jahán. (4) *Murakka*, a scrap-book, containing a collection of original portraits by noted Indian artists of eminent men and historical celebrities. The work also contains a number of beautiful Persian manuscripts. Most of these manuscripts and scraps were lent by the Nawáb Bahádur of Murshidabad. A collection was also sent from Sitápur, Mahmudabad, and Rámpur in the North-Western Provinces, and from Tonk, a Muhammadan State in Rajputana. Among the specimens sent from the last place was a work called *Fatuhu-l-harámin*, by Abdur Rahman Jami, copied by Muham-

mad Zahid, by order of Mahammad Tahir Khán Bahádur of Ispahan, in A.H. 955 (350 years ago). This book was first sold for 5,000, next for 1,100, and lastly for 1,700 coins."

To the above Exhibition was also sent a beautiful Tibetan manuscript, written in silver. The most curious specimens of manuscript illumination displayed were, however, the illuminated palm-leaf manuscripts received from Orissa. In this part of Bengal, and in almost all parts of the Madras Presidency, books are still written on the long narrow leaves of the palmyra palm (*Borassus flabelliformis*), which are then stitched together by a thread at one end. Letters, documents, and rent receipts are also written on palm-leaf. The writing is cut into the leaf by an iron style, on which powdered charcoal is then rubbed. The black of the charcoal sinks into the scratches made with the style where it adheres when the leaf is washed leaving other parts of it plain. Manuscripts of this kind are often illuminated, and among such curious objects brought to the Calcutta Exhibition was a work called *Gít Govinda*, of Jaya-Deva, a Bengali-Sanskrit poet of the fourteenth century. The bent form of Krishna with his lute, the grotesque figures of milkmaids, the lowing cows and the sucking calves, and the swaggering attitude of Cupid with his flower-bow, are pictures which received additional interest from the material on which they were drawn.

Engravings and Lithographs.

Engravings.—The only engraving that existed in the country in former times appears to be that of making copper plates for grants of land and other documents, of making seals, and of preparing wooden blocks for calico-printing. Latterly, in imitation of the European art of engraving, rude blocks were made of tamarind and other woods for the illustration of almanacs and village school-books. In Calcutta, at the present time, a few ex-students of the School of Art follow the profession of wood-engraving. Of these, one Gopál Chandra Karmokár is the most skilful, and the work turned out by him would compare favourably with that done in England. Some years ago there was a demand for wood-cuts among the vernacular newspapers, but at the present moment it is on the decline, and the industry is not flourishing.

Seal-engravers exist in almost all large towns, specially those which formed provincial seats of government during the Muhammadan rule. Delhi, the capital of the Empire, is still noted for its seal-engraving. Mr. Kipling remarks :—

"Seal-engraving is an art which, owing probably to the unusual skill of two generations of engravers who worked in the Daraiba, is considered to be a speciality of Delhi. All that can be done in Persian letter-cutting on seals is done here, but there has never been in India any good intaglio cutting as it is understood in Europe. It is curious that races that excel in minute work should have so completely neglected this form of art."

Specimens of seal-engraving of Harnám Singh and Pratáb Singh of Shahabad in the Ambala District were sent to the Calcutta International Exhibition. Mr. Kipling in sending the specimens remarked :—

"The trade of the Mohr-Kand, or signet-cutter, is a common one, but it is almost universally confined to engraving vernacular signatures on blood stone, for the use of those who sign their names by affixing an impression of their seals. The craftsmen mentioned above, however, have carried their practice much further than usual and can engrave crests, &c., in intaglio, both in stone and metal, with great skill, and deserve to be more widely known than they are. One of the curiosities of the Indian art is the neglect in ancient times of cameo and intaglio cutting by artists who excelled in most other forms of art. Greek and Roman intaglios in cornelian are occasionally found on the frontier, but a few rude Mithraic emblems on stone are the only specimens of the art of native origin."

Lithographs.—A large number of lithographic pictures are every year turned out by an Art Studio established in Calcutta by a number of ex-students of the School of Art. These pictures have no artistic merit, most of them being done in imitation of the European style. They have, however, become very popular and are largely purchased by the people all over the country. Until recently colouring was all executed by hand, and not by the latest chromo-lithographic process, and the prices were therefore rather high. Some English chromo-lithographer took advantage of this, and made exact copies of the Calcutta Art Studio pictures in colours, and sent a large consignment for sale in India at one tenth the usual prices. The sale of these English-made pictures of Hindu Gods and Goddesses has now been stopped. Porcelain Gods are now being imported from England.

Lithographic printing work is largely done in Upper India, as type printing is not suited to the running Persian character. The lithographic establishment of Munshi Newal Kishor at Lucknow is the largest in India, from which a vast number of Persian and Arabic works are sent to all Muhammadan countries. Cheap story-books are lithographed in many of the large towns in the Panjáb, "but these are coarsely executed and are seldom good in design."

Photographs.

Photography in its highest form is still in the hands of Europeans. A large number of natives have learnt the art, and practise it as a profession, in the large towns of the different provinces, but as a rule they are unable or unwilling to lay out the necessary capital, and they do not bestow on their work the necessary amount of patience and care. As a consequence, therefore, native productions, with very few exceptions, do not possess such a good reputation as those turned out by the European firms. The best photographs hitherto turned out by a native of India are the Indian views executed by Lálá Din Dayál of Indor. The views of Sanchi Tope near Bhopal are specially excellent. He sells them at R1-12 for a mounted picture 10″ × 12″.

At Calcutta, Messrs. Bourne, Shepherd & Co., and Messrs. Johnston, Hoffman & Co., are photographers of note. The former sent a set of photographs of Bengal scenes to the Colonial and Indian Exhibition, and the latter of Nepal scenes, as well as of its inhabitants and of many of the wild tribes represented in clay models at that Exhibition. A collection of photographs was also sent from the Panjáb by Mr. Bull and Dr. Dickinson, representing Hindu festival scenes and the ordinary street life of Lahore. An album of views in the Central Provinces, chiefly of Hindu temples, was sent to the above Exhibition by Mr. Blees of Jabalpur. A very interesting collection of photographic views was sent to the Calcutta Exhibition by Messrs. Nicholas & Co. of Madras. These, according to Dr. Bidie, "are of considerable archæological interest, and some of them, such as the carved ceiling, must have been very difficult of execution." They are sold at R3 each.

The Mahárájá of Jaipur employs a photographer. Several artists have also been employed by the Jaipur Durbar in colouring photographs, which they do with considerable skill. They were employed to colour the photographic illustrations of the work entitled "The Memorials of the Jaipur Exhibition." This work is from the pen of Surgeon-Major T. H. Hendley, an expert in Indian art, under whose management a very successful Exhibition of art-manufactures was held at Jaipur in 1882.

Sculpture.

Decorations in the old temples, and the figures of Gods and Goddesses scattered all over the country, shew that the Hindus of ancient times made great advance in the art of sculpture. The industry has long since declined, although figures of Gods and Goddesses are still made in many parts of the country.

In Bengal the art has almost died out. It was, however, a very flourishing industry in ancient times, as the stone figures now found in Orissa and Chota Nagpur attest. In Orissa, many of these images were broken and desecrated by a Bráhman convert to Muhammadanism named Kálápáhár. Latterly the sculptors of Dáinhát, a small town in the Bardwán District, annually turned out a large number of images, but the trade has suffered owing to the decline of Hinduism in Bengal. Sculptors form a separate Hindu caste, known by the name of *Bháskars*. Stone figures are still made at Gya, which, however, will be treated in this work under the head of "Stone carving." Such figures are also made in many other places, notably in Jaipur, in Rajputana, Mundasaur in Gwalior, and Dhar in Central India.

Sculpturing in the European style is now taught in the Schools of Art at Lahore and Bombay. Several portrait busts by Mr. J. L. Kipling, Principal of the former School of Art, were sent to the Calcutta Exhibition, and one by Mr. G. F. Pinto, assistant teacher of the same school. A marble bust of Shámal Dás Parmánand Dás, executed by Vála Hirá, an ex-student of the Bombay School of Art, was sent to the Colonial and Indian Exhibition.

Funeral Pyres and Masks.

Funeral pyres and masks made in Burma are classed under "Fine Arts." The former are made and burnt in honour of the dead and the latter used in theatres and village dances. Mr. Tilly thus describes the manufacture of the two objects:—

"*Funeral pyres.*—The materials and workmanship of funeral pyres vary according to the means and position of the relatives of the deceased. A priest is honoured with a lofty seven-roofed spire built over a square base, the whole erection being some 70 or 80 feet high. The frame-work is run up of rude carpentry, the panels being formed of split bamboos woven together, or, in the more substantial parts, of jungle-wood boards. The lower portion is covered by paintings, often grotesque and sometimes 'horrible in their delineations of the tortures of hell.' The upper portion, just below the spire and over the coffin, is enclosed on each side by flame-like wings, gorgeously coloured, and above all rises the fairy-like, seven-roofed spire. This ephemeral structure, although destined to be burnt, is a highly artistic production; the form, colour and details are alike good and suited for the designer's purpose, for when finished it stands in the centre of a flat plain surrounded by other similar erections of lesser splendour around which crowd a huge concourse of Burmans in their gayest holiday attire. The pyre is thus the centre of a mass of splendid colour and gleaming white, and to maintain its place of honour it requires every inch of its towering height, and every aid that the artist's grotesque fancy or mastery of colour can lend it. Effigies of horses, elephants, or mythical animals are sometimes placed around the pyre at the cremation of a priest. They are often very large and are always grotesque. The poor man's bier is made of bamboos covered with paper on which vari-coloured papers are pasted in strips, making out the edges of the patterns. Here also the design is good, the forms vigorous and graceful, and the contrasts of colour excellent.

"*Mask-making.*—Masks are used in the theatres and in some of the village dances. The best masks are made by pasting six or eight layers of paper (made of bamboo) over a wooden block. When dry, the mask is cut down the back, taken off the block, joined together and colours put on. The inferior qualities are made of bamboo-basket roughly woven to the general shapes of the head. The ears, nose, lips, and other excrescences are modelled of clay mixed with chopped straw, and are stuck on to the basket-work and the whole covered with layers of paper as before. The Burmese excel in the delineation of the grotesque, and their masks would certainly bear away the palm, in this respect, from the productions of Europe."

The *Tázziás* which the Shiah Muhammadans make in India on the occasion of the Muharram festival very much resemble in construction the funeral pyres of Burma. They are made of basket-work, adorned by various-coloured paper and gold and silver tinsel. Masks are made in all parts of India and sold at fairs and gatherings. But these have no artistic value, and are only intended as toys for children.

Masks are made of *papier-mâché* in Jaipur, Rajputana. Dr. Hendley states:—

"For many years past miracle plays, representing the appearance of the Man-lion (Narsinha) and the Boar (Varáha), incarnations of Vishnu, have been represented in Jaipur in the beginning of summer. There are several men who devote themselves to preparing masks in papier-mâché of the principal as well as the subordinate characters and persons of all nations, who are placed as representatives of their respective countries in prominent positions to witness the miracles, whereby the Hindu believes the world was twice saved. Besides complete figures, masks are made which are worn by the men and boys who represent the minor deities, and even animals who assist at the ceremony. With the aid of painted cloth and leather, excellent models of elephants and camels are also produced, which can be moved about in the same way as the hobby horses of old English fairs. The faces are very cleverly painted. Birds, reptiles, and beasts of all kinds are also well modelled and coloured."

II.—Decorative Art.

Properly speaking, many articles of Indian art-ware of the present day are purely "decorative" or sumptuary. They are not made for the wear and tear of ordinary use, but are only intended to be put in niches and on mantel-pieces as ornamental curiosities. Such articles will be described under their respective heads of "Manufactures in metal," "Ivory-carving," &c. In the present chapter therefore only art applied to architecture, and articles purely decorative, which do not fall under any of the primary classes to which the art-manufactures of India have been divided in this book, will be treated.

Architectural Designs and Models.

Architectural designs, as an aid to builder's work, are only made by native masons when a costly edifice is taken in hand. In the towns, however, where the land at the command of the builder is limited, a design is first made before the construction of a building is commenced. In Calcutta this is done by men who have been more or less influenced by European education. The preponderance of European influence in the Indian mind, and the want of due appreciation of indigenous art on the part of the Europeans, led to such a discouragement of the native architecture as to make the Indian architects quite indifferent to their own style of work. The educated natives of India associate buildings in the European style with enlightenment and progress, and it is the conservative trading and money-lending classes only which still encourage native modes of architecture. Mr. Growse, C.S., thus remarks on the subject:—

"If the mercantile classes of native society are distinguished by their conservative adherence to ancestral usage, the landed gentry, who are on visiting terms with European officials, cherish equally strong aspirations in the opposite direction. To relieve the monotony of their eventless life, many of them spend large sums of money every year in building, and keep a native architect as a regular member of their domestic establishment. But he is warned that nothing in the Indian style can be tolerated; some Government office in the civil station, or the last new barracks in the nearest military cantonments, are the palatial edifices which he is expected to emulate."

Mr. Growse has been trying to bring about a *rennaissance* of old Indian style of architecture. With this view he trained native masons at Muttra, Bulandshahr, and other places in the North-Western Provinces to furnish him with designs of old edifices.

A number of architectural drawings were sent to the Calcutta International Exhibition from Lahore. Most of these were executed by the students of the Mayo School of Art. The following are examples:—Coloured elevation of the *Chauburji*, decorated with enamelled pottery, and built by Begam Zeban Nessa; gateway of Wazir Khán's mosque; a portion of Wazir Khán's mosque, price R40. Several well-finished drawings were also sent to the Colonial and Indian Exhibition. Among these may be mentioned the copies of inlaid floors from the Hammám, or Turkish Bath, in the Delhi Palace. These drawings reproduced the most important details of the inlaid marble floors of the Bath.

Bombay also sent designs for bas-relief; a view of a marble cenotaph at Bhavnagar; full sized detail drawings of a marble screen, and others of similar nature.

Designs of ornamental details are made at Jaipur,

notably of carved stone-work as applied to buildings. Dr. Hendley states :—

"Rajputana is pre-eminently the country of stone-carving and masons, and the best work is done under the Public Works Department, headed by Lieutenant-Colonel Jacob, the Executive Engineer. The best designs may be seen in the new Albert Hall at Jaipur, now approaching completion. The young men who prepare the designs under the supervision of Colonel Jacob, have spent months in copying on the spot the best examples of the marvellous carvings at Delhi, Fatehpur Sikri, and elsewhere in Rajputana and the adjoining Districts, and then pervaded by the spirit of the originals, have produced new designs of the same school, but without being in any sense of the word copies. In the same way judicious supervision has made the Jaipur sculptors equal in technical skill to any masons in the world, at all events when not employed on the figure."

Dr. Hendley further states that "before beginning a building, a native artist generally prepares a design shewing the arrangement of rooms and more prominent features, but the details are usually worked out as the building progresses, and the ornament, as in mediæval times, is, as often as not, the result of individual taste and effort rather than of slavish mechanical copying of the ideas of a master." In Karauli, and other States of Rajputana, rough designs of similar decorative work are made, each drawing costing R2 and upwards.

In Nepal such work is done by the *Chitrakars,* or painters, under the direction of the masons and builders.

Architectural models are made in many parts of the country, chiefly of buildings of historical celebrity. Among these may be mentioned the famous Tájmahal of Agra, models of which, both in marble and soap-stone, are made and sold to visitors. These vary in value according to material and size. A fine marble model of the Táj can be had for R500. Models in sandstone are made of temples and buildings both at Lucknow and Mirzapur. In Bengal, models are made of Sher Sháh's tomb at Sasseram. Similar models are also made in the Panjáb. The Nabha State sent to the Calcutta Exhibition a model of a summer-house, which was then (1883) in course of construction. A model of the Sikh Golden Temple at Amritsar was sent to the Colonial and Indian Exhibition. The following is a description of the decorations used in this celebrated edifice.

"The *Darbár Sáhib* of the Sikhs at Amritsar owes its English name 'Golden Temple' to the fact that its upper portion is sheathed in embossed copper, gilded. The lower part is covered with marble inlaid in carnelian, jasper, and mother-o-pearl in arabesque patterns, similar to those in the Hammám of the palace at Delhi, and in the Táj at Agra. There are, however, notable differences, for the Sikhs not being bound by any Muhammadan canon to exclude representations of living creatures, introduced birds, fishes, and occasional human figures into the work. In the treatment of the ordinary forms of Muhammadan architecture they were beginning to make changes, and it is possible that they might have developed an interesting style of their own."

Models of buildings are also made in the Bombay Presidency. An example of this work was sent to the Colonial and Indian Exhibition. It was the model of a tomb which was being erected (1886) in white and black marble, at Junágad, to the memory of its late chief.

At Jaipur all the important architectural works to be made in stone are first executed in clay so that the effect might be judged. The men employed work in this material with great facility and skill. Elaborate models of public buildings have also been made to scale in plaster of Paris. The stone-cutters, called *Sitáwats*, of Jaipur, make models of temples and other buildings and send to all parts of India. Models in brass are also made. Dr. Hendley gives the following description of a brass model lately made :—

" A model on a large scale in brass is now being made for a banker at Ajmir, of the city which the God of the Firmament (Indra) is fabled in the sacred books (*Puránas*) to have given to Rakhab-Deo, the first of the *Tirthankars*, or deified Jaina Lords. It represents several large squares, each with four grand gateways and surrounded by shops and houses with large halls and temples crowded with figures. All the details are beautifully carved and finished, and the whole is covered with gold, and some of the gateways are decorated with floral designs in colour. The brass-work alone is to cost R10,000, and the gold laid upon it will amount to R90,000 more. The model is to be placed in a temple, and its owner hopes that when he finally attains *moksha*, or salvation, an abode on a similar scale will be allotted to him in the future world. In this way is buried much of the precious metals in India to reap a heavenly instead of an earthly harvest."

A model of a Jaipur house was sent to the Calcutta International Exhibition. Price, R78. Several models of this kind were also sent to the Colonial and Indian Exhibition by the Jaipur State. Among these may be mentioned the model in brass of the cenotaph of Mahárájá Sawái Jai Singh II, founder of Jaipur; a model of a marble shrine; and the brass model of a temple.

A soap-stone model of the tomb of Mahárájá Bakhtáwar Singh of the Alwar State, in Rajputana, was sent to the above Exhibition. It was done to scale, and the building itself at Alwar is considered an edifice of the pure Hindu style of architecture. Ten models were sent to the same Exhibition by the Mysore State, representing notable structures and ancient remains, and another was a model of the Haidar Ali's Jail for European prisoners of war in the Seringapatam Fort.

Decorative Paintings applied to Architecture.

Mention of this art has already been made under the head of "Fresco-paintings." In Bengal, architectural paintings are executed by common masons *(Ráj-mistris)* in halls called *dáláns*, where religious festivals are held, as well as in sitting rooms. They generally consist of the conventional lotus and geometrical designs, though sometimes figures of birds, other animals, and human figures are introduced. Formerly these paintings were executed on the mud-walls of thatched buildings, called *chandimandaps*, which were almost the only indigenous architectural work of Bengal Proper, for masonry work was very scarce in the last century. The palace at Krishnagar was constructed by a Musalman architect, and the paintings or geometrical designs in it are strictly Muhammadan. Ordinary distemper painting is practised at Delhi, Amritsar, Lahore, and almost everywhere in the Panjáb. Painting on wood in water-colours is largely executed. The ground is first prepared by covering the wood with cloth or with the fibre of *San* (*Crotalaria juncea*), mixed with whiting and glue. Sometimes the fibre is only employed to stop the crevices over the ground thus prepared. Sheets of tin foil are then pasted, and on this metallic ground designs are painted in water-colours, some of which when varnished are transparent. The colour of the varnish is yellow and thus such portions of the tin foil which are left become golden, while transparent blues and other colours are lighted through with a metallic sheen. Mr. Kipling thinks that this "work probably originated from the necessity of closing up the pores of the wood so as to prevent resinous exudations from blistering the work during the summer heats, a precaution which is only partly successful. Doors and ceilings exist of old work which are really beautiful." The ceiling painting at Amritsar and other places is also generally in water-colour protected by a coating of varnish. Linseed-oil, the chief vehicle of European work, though a product of the country, was never used in such painting. It is now coming into use. The only indigenous form of painting in which linseed-oil was used is "on the very odd and out-of-the-way Afridi fabrics known as Peshâwar lac cloths." [See also "Paintings on wood," and "Decorative paintings applied to articles of domestic use."]

Wall paintings are largely employed in Rajputana. Dr. Hendley writes :—

"The beauty of the Jaipur plaster work is unrivalled. The floors of all places, and even ordinary rooms, are covered with polished plaster of the purest white, grey, or red. The walls are adorned with dados in the same material, and these are enriched with ornaments in fresco or distemper in various colours. Nothing could have a cooler or more pleasant effect in a hot climate. Some of the cornices in rooms are exquisitely decorated with figures in colour, as, for example, a series representing the sports of women and children in the *zenana*. A beautiful set of cornice panels, each containing a flower in gold and colour, is now being painted in one of the large halls in the palace by students of the School of Art and other artists.

"It is the fashion in Jaipur, and many other parts of Rajputana, to cover the outer as well as the inner walls of houses with paintings of various kinds, such as battle-scenes, figures of elephants, or mythological subjects, in various colours. This is, after all, the training ground of most of the artists who occasionally produce very striking pictures in this line."

In Alwar, the walls of houses and palaces are painted in different colours, set with pieces of glass of variegated hues, and finally bordered with leaves of beaten gold. Only a few men are engaged in this work, who are mostly in the employ of the State.

In Mysore, arabesque work in gold and bright colours was largely employed in the decoration of walls during the Muhammadan time. Good specimens of such work exist in the Mysore palace. The industry is now on the decline, but similar work can still be made from R5 to R10 per square yard.

In Nepal, figures of Buddhist and Hindu divinities are painted on the walls of temples and houses. Colonel Berkeley, the Resident at Nepal, writes:—

"Gilding is freely used in the decoration of temples, the coverings on which are often painted in the brightest colours. In the large mansions erected in late years by the Gurkha aristocracy in *quasi*-European style, the decorative painting is in the worst possible taste, the brightest green and red wood-work being combined with white-washed walls. The beams, window-frames, and other wood-work of old houses are often painted with patterns in black and white. The pictures of gods, &c., are rude and hideous as a rule, but the decoration of beams and ceilings in black and white is often tastetul."

Decorative Wood-carving, applied to Architecture.

Carved wood-work is largely employed for doors and window-frames. In Bengal, plain wood is now generally used, but carved doors are found here and there in old houses. These are fast disappearing. In Gya there are one or two remarkable pieces of wood-carving on the fronts of balconies of houses; also in Maldah in similar positions. Attempts are being made to resuscitate this work.

In many parts of the North-Western Provinces, notably at Sahâranpur, carved doors of good workmanship are still made. Specimens of such work were sent to the Calcutta International Exhibition from Sahâranpur and Aligarh. Carved façades of wood were sent to the Colonial and Indian Exhibition from Sahâranpur, Farukhabad, Mainpuri, Lucknow, Cawnpore, Muttra, and Agra. A specimen of such wood-work has been sent to the Glasgow International Exhibition (1888) from Lucknow, by Dr. James Cleghorn; price, £50. Another has been sent by Seth Jánki Dás of Farukhabad, the price of which in the place of production is R500. A third has been purchased for the above Exhibition from Farukhabad for R250. The other places in the North-Western Provinces where carved wood-work for architectural purposes is made are Bareilly, Azamgarh, and Bulandshahr.

Wood-carving is extensively produced in the Panjáb; the places most noted for it are Bherá in Sháhpur District; Batálá in Gurdáspur District; Amritsar; Chiniot in Jhang District; Jhelam; Ráwalpindi; Hissar; Lahore and Siálkot. All over the Province ordinary carpenters do the carving, and there is scarcely any large town where this kind of work is not done. The Indian Palace at the Colonial and Indian Exhibition was made by two wood-carvers taken from Bherá. Two Bherá men have again been sent to the Glasgow International Exhibition. The chief specialties of the Panjáb architectural wood-carving is the *chaukát*, or the frame-work of doors and windows, which is highly ornamented. Most of the wood-carvers in the Panjáb are Muhammadans, and the ornaments carved are entirely Musalman. The cheapest wood-carving is done at Bherá. The wood used is *Deodár* (*Cedrus Deodara*), on which foliage and geometric diapers are boldly executed. At Batálá, Amritsar and other places *Shisham* (*Dalbergia latifolia*) wood is used, which is more substantial and costly. Mr. Kipling writes:—

"Wood-carving in the Panjáb is happily still essentially an architectural art, and, excepting at Simla, where in response to a European demand, there is a production of carved articles for furniture and drawing-room decoration, there is but little of the trivial fancy work in which the Indian wood-carver is supposed to excel. On the doors and windows of native houses, the best efforts of the carvers are expended. These are frequently wrought at a distance from the place where they are to be used and are built into the structure at the will of the purchaser. The style is Muhammadan. The ornament is severely conventional, and the introduction of panels of framed lattice work, locally known as *pinjra*, ingeniously dovetailed in geometric designs, gives an Arabic character to the whole. The doorways of Delhi, Lahore, Amritsar, Batálá, and the older towns of the Province, include finer work than those made in modern towns, but the art is still full of vitality. The cheapness of this work at present is one of the most remarkable features, which is due to the fact that most Panjáb carpenters practise ornamental carving from their infancy. As a demand has arisen of late years, the prices have gone up, and will probably rise still higher. But there could be a practically unlimited supply."

Bombay wood-carving, as applied to architecture, was best shewn in the Baroda Pigeon House at the Colonial and Indian Exhibition. Mr. B. A. Gupte thus describes the industry in that Presidency:—

"As far, at least, as Western India is concerned, the art of wood-carving for architectural purposes most assuredly belong to the Gujrátis. It stands to reason to believe that these Gujrátis, who are Jains or Vaishnavas, and who originally belonged to the Buddhist religion, have acquired their art of carving from the early sculptors of the ancient caves or rock temples of India. It also looks probable that the art of carving practised by the Buddhists on the harder material, stone, was transferred to a softer material, wood, during the time of the Muslim rulers of Hindustan, who fostered Indian art by introducing into it less costly and more effective material than that which the natives of the soil were in the habit of using. * * The carved balcony selected for the Calcutta International Exhibition by Captain Temple from Dabhoi, as the oldest work extant, had the cypress tree carved on it, which shows the Muhammadan influence upon architectural carvings. * * The wood-carvers of Dabhoi are very skilful, and it is admitted that the ancient artistic renown of the place is not lost. Fine specimens of wood-carving on doors, cornices, verandahs, balconies, pillars, and brackets of houses are met everywhere in the towns of Dabhoi, Vasu, Sojitra, Pitlad, Pattan, Sidhpur, Vadnagar, and Baroda. The new palace at Baroda which is under construction contains full illustration of the master art the Gujrátis possess."

Architectural wood-carving of the Madras Presidency was well illustrated in the screen made for the Colonial and Indian Exhibition. It was made of Burma teak wood, constructed by a carpenter of Madras, and carved by twenty artisans from the different parts of the Presidency. A very fine doorway of carved *Nim* wood (*Melia Azadirachta*) was also sent from Bellary.

Carved wood-work is made at Nágpur, of which specimens were sent to the Colonial and Indian Exhibition. The screen made for that Exhibition was of carved wood. Central Provinces are deficient in art-manufactures, and, in the opinion of the Provincial officer, wood-carving "is perhaps the only one in which these Provinces can hold their own against other parts of India. It is no uncommon thing to find, even in small villages, houses with carved teak fronts of considerable beauty, and in several towns there are streets with carved wooden frontages displaying very considerable taste and skill. Carved wood plays an important part in Nágpur architecture, and the Marhatta palaces in the vicinity of the city are distinguished by their high verandahs of black teak, often very elaborately carved."

Bold and effective wood-carving is done at Sikar, Fatehpur, Lachmangarh, Jhunjnu, Chiráwá, Nawalgarh, and Singháná and other large towns in the Jaipur State. This work is largely patronised by Jaina merchants for their temples. A highly ornamental screen was made in this style of work for the Colonial and Indian Exhibition.

Carved doors and frames of various patterns are made in Bikánir. The workmanship is good. Price,

R8 to R110 for a door-frame, and R5 to R40 for a pair of doors.

There exist a few wood-carvers of considerable skill in the Indor city. A specimen of their work was sent to the Colonial and Indian Exhibition in the shape of a gateway, with carved figures in imitation of Buddhist art. The best workmen in Indor receive R1-8 per day as wages.

Carved doorways, pillar-posts and other architectural wood-work were formerly made in Mysore. At present there is no market for such work. The daily wages of a wood-carver there is 12 annas.

Specimens of Kashmir architectural wood-carving were sent to the Colonial and Indian Exhibition. These were in the latticed or the *pinjra* style. The carving is made on *Deodár* (*Cedrus deodara*) wood, and the lattice work on the wood of *Pinus excelsa.* The work is very cheap, about one rupee per square yard. The Kashmir screen at the Colonial and Indian Exhibition was of carved wood. It was copied from the verandah of an old wooden mosque. The carving was done under the supervision of Sir Oliver St. John, Resident at Kashmir, by eight carpenters paid at the rate of 5 to 7 annas ($5\frac{1}{2}$ to 8*d.*) a day.

In Nepal architectural wood-carving is the most important of all decorative art found in the country. Pillars, doorways, arches, balconies, windows, and other parts of a building are decorated with highly artistic carvings. Figures of deities, demons, dragons, snakes, and animals of all sorts, also wreaths of flowers and intricate patterns, are worked in elaborate details, the proportions being always graceful and true. The work is expensive, and the industry is therefore fast decaying.

Architectural wood-carving is largely practised in

Burma, chiefly on Buddhist monasteries and temples. The most common descriptions of carving are foliage in bas-relief, foliage carved in a single plane, foliage in two or more planes entwining, figures in bas-relief, figures carved in the flat, and figures sculptured in the round. Mr. Tilly thus describes the Burma architectural wood-carving :—

"With work covering such a large range, it would be wearisome to describe each variety in even a few of the manifold uses to which it is put. The most characteristic work, both of foliage and figures, is to be found at Buddhist monasteries, where the sacred seven-roofed spire, supported on vermillion and gold-plated pillars, rises above a placid figure of Gotama; each line of eave and gable is adorned with a many-pinnacled piece of carving rising up at the corners over the head of a guardian angel. It would be difficult, even with a pencil, to represent the beauties of such carving, of which the principal characteristic is the delicacy of the curves which bound the undulating upper edge of the eaves-boards where the flame-like pinnacles stand out dark in contrast against the receding roof. The lower edge is generally straight, and is marked by a border pattern, while it often drops at the corner into a pendant of open tracery. A good carver will skilfully introduce figures of birds and animals, or the grotesque head of a *Belu*, or wild man, into his work. It is easy to imagine how well such carving lends itself to the decoration of furniture. An Institute of Industrial Arts has been established in Rangoon to develope this industry, and it is hoped that a foreign demand may spring up.

"The designs of the rougher kinds of carvings are drawn in chalk or charcoal on the wood itself, and are chiselled out with great rapidity by the workman. The degree of finish depends on the position the work is to occupy, and the price the patron can afford to pay. For better kinds of work the design is drawn on paper with a pencil and placed on the wood. The larger holes are gouged or chiselled out, and the rougher work done by the pupil, the master finishing it off. The foliage is conventional, but a good workman is exceedingly particular in obtaining easy flowery curves, and in working out every detail, however roughly, in strict accordance with truth and the propriety of the art. Thus, for example, each tendril should spring from the main branch as it does in nature, and no accidental crossing of another branch can serve as an excuse for introducing a spray which might conveniently fill a space which has hitherto been forgotten. Each leaf, bud, or flower has its proper shape, and no vague mixture of the characteristics of another style is allowed. Every figure must be properly placed with suitable branches or sprays to hold or stand upon."

The price of labour for wood-carving in Burma varies from 12 annas to R20 a square foot. Very good work may be obtained for R5. A carved figure or statue 4½ feet high, properly painted, of first class work, may be obtained for R60, and a small unpainted figure of about 6 inches high for R2. A journeyman carver obtains R1-8 a day, and the best master carver gets R2 a day.

Decorative stone-carving applied to architecture.

Upper India and Rajputana are the chief centres of stone-carving for architectural purposes, specially the latter place, where timber is scarce and stone abundant. The whole country is full of magnificent buildings, both ancient and modern, built and adorned with carved stone of exquisite workmanship. The ruins at Chittor, the temples at Ajmir now converted into a splendid mosque, and the celebrated Kutab Minár of Delhi, all attest to the excellence of the Hindu art of stone-carving. The Muhammadans when they came to this country "found themselves," as Mr. Hope rightly observes, "among a people their equals in conception, their superiors in execution, and whose taste has been refined by centuries of cultivation." They forced on them, however, their own bold features of minaret and pointed arch, but borrowed their pillared hall, delicate traceries, and rich surface ornament. The early Muhammadan rulers of Upper India employed Hindu artisans from Rajputana for the erection and ornamentation of their capitals, and these architects soon got influenced by the Saracenic style of building, which they gradually introduced into the construction of palaces and temples in their own country. The famous Tájmahal at Agra, and the palaces, baths, cenotaphs, and mosques at Agra and Delhi all shew the very high excellence to which stone-carving attained in Upper India. The quarries of Makráná, in the Jodhpur territory on the side of the Salt Lake of Sambhar, supplied the white marble for the Táj; while Bhartpur furnished the red sandstone used in the construction of the palace of Akbar at Fatehpur Sikri. Jaipur and Ajmir supplied the coloured marble, and Jessalmir the nummulitic limestones, for the decoration of these edifices.

On the Bengal side, the hilly countries on the west, and Orissa on the south, made considerable advance in the art of stone-carving. The temples, embankments, and ruins in Orissa attest to considerable skill in this industrial art.

In the North-Western Provinces, Agra and Mirzapur are the two places where decorative stone-carvings for architectural purposes are largely made. In Agra stone trellis-work in sandstone is made for from R15 to R18 per slab measuring about 2′ 6″ square. In the same place is also made exquisitely fine work in marble and in alabaster in imitation of the marble screens of the Tájmahal; price about R30 to R40 for a small slab or screen. The following account of the present stone-carving of Agra is taken from the *Journal of Indian Art,* Vol. I, page 96:—

"Another decorative art, tracing its descent from the Augustan age of the Mughul Empire, is the *Jáli* or stone-tracery, executed both in red sandstone and in the crystalline white marble of Rajputana. The *Jáli* is a fine filigree of marble or sandstone fretted into an almost endless network of geometrical combinations. The requirements of the climate of Northern India for some material which should, like glass, afford protection. from the weather and at the same time admit free ventilation, have been satisfied by the elaboration of this unrivalled window tracery. The specimens of carving in soap-stone belong to a modern development of the same hereditary art. The material, which also comes from Rajputana, is a stratite of particularly tough texture and a warm grey tint,—'it stands like leather, though it cuts like cheese.' The floral or arabesque patterns are beautifully sharp and clear, and the boxes, trays, and other articles are admirably suited for drawing-room use. Mr. Keene hopes for a time when this cheap and pretty work may be extended to architectural decoration, at least in the interior of halls and reception rooms, where its introduction, either as cornices or mantel mouldings, would be most effective. He suggests that in India the decoration of a whole drawing-room with soap-stone carving would be hardly more expensive than that of the same walls with English paper-hanging."

Soap-stone is too soft and brittle for use in decorative architecture. A perforated window made of it was however sent to the Colonial and Indian Exhibition from Rewa Kantha in the Bombay Presidency.

It has already been stated that under the guidance of Colonel Jacob the best designs are being collected at Jaipur. Perforated stone screens, called *Jáli*, are largely made at Jaipur. The masons of this place have become so proficient in the work, that they can design and carry out, almost with their eyes shut, an endless variety of tracery either in stone or plaster.

In the Bhartpur State large quantities of perforated lattice-work (*Jáli*), in red sandstone are made. The Bhartpur screen at the Colonial and Indian Exhibition consisted of a carved red sandstone architrave and false arch supported on carved pillars, and surmounted by a perforated sandstone screen. The stone used, though called red, is a light brown or salmon-coloured sandstone from the Rupkat quarries. It is much used in Bhartpur and the neighbouring States, is easily manipulated, and admits of very fine work. The screens, the pillars, and the false arch were made in imitation of the style followed in the State.

Stone trellis-work is carved in sandstone and marble by masons in Bikánir, the price being R20 per square foot for marble, and R10 for sandstone trellis-work. Balconies are carved in red stone in various patterns at Bikánir, Churu, and Sardárshahr; price R60 for a balcony of 3 feet by 5 feet. Doorways are made in sandstone at Bikánir and other large towns in different patterns; value according to size and workmanship, R200 to R1,000. Carved sandstone pillars, with patterns of flowers and other decorations, cost R30 for a pillar of 10 feet long and 3 feet in circumference. Bikánir sent to the Colonial and Indian Exhibition a stone model of a cenotaph and of a banker's house; also carved trellis plaques and windows.

The Alwar screen at the Colonial and Indian Exhibition consisted of panels of white marble, perforated and carved in relief, fitted in a frame-work of black marble and teak wood, and supported upon three beautifully carved white marble pillars. These designs are of pure Hindú style and were taken from the Alwar palace. In the Alwar State there are quarries of white, pink, and black marble; the quality of the white marble is said to be the finest obtainable in India for statuary purposes.

Carved doorways, balconies, archways, and cornices are made in the Karauli State, the red and white sandstone found in the quarries within Karauli being specially adapted for the work. The carved trellis-work screens are particularly handsome, the cost of which ranges from R2 to R4 and upwards per square foot.

Perforated screen-work and tracery, pillars, &c.,

are made in the Dholpur State of red and white sandstone quarried at Dholpur, Bári, and Sir Mathura. Ornamental work, screen-work, and tracery are charged at R1-3-0 per square foot and upwards according to design and intricacy of work. Dressed stone blocks from 10 annas to R2 per cubic foot according to size. Rough dressed stone blocks at 8 annas and upwards, according to size, per cubic foot.

Carved panels and plaques are made at Gwalior, which are executed with great skill and fineness. Some very good stone-carving of perforated work were sent to the Colonial and Indian Exhibition of 1886. Price, R95 for a panel 2 feet square. Carved pillars and other specimens of a similar nature were sent from Indor to the same Exhibition. One of the pillars was an elaborate piece of work, modelled partly in imitation of Buddhist carvings. In connection with the Gwalior stone-carving industry may be mentioned the gateway which was made under the superintendence of Major J. B. Keith, and shewn first at the Calcutta International Exhibition of 1883, and then at the Colonial and Indian Exhibition, London, 1886. This work was elaborated by Major Keith "to assist some 2,000 starving artisans," and he thought "this would be best compassed by illustrating the carving of many periods." Major Keith writes in connection with this gateway:—

"The stone-carving industry is admirably adapted for Australia, where there are neither climatic obstacles nor those involved in a foreign labour market competing with the Home. A skilled workman in Gwalior gets his *6d.* a day, and his English brother in this country *6s.* Ornament in the shape of ecclesiastical furniture, such as reredos and altars, as well as material for interior decoration in ordinary houses, could easily be provided. Any one who compares the carving seen on the New Law Courts with that of the Gwalior Gateway will assuredly declare in favour of the latter. The stone hardens by exposure. There are upwards of a thousand skilled workmen in Gwalior;

mistris or foremen getting from R15 to R60 per mensem; masons from 5 to 8 annas, labourers 3 annas, and boys 1 anna per diem. There are four quarries lying between Dholpur and Gwalior, and seeing that with the lamented death of the Mahárájá Sindhia, the Gwalior Durbar will be under British control for some time, there need be no difficulty in obtaining a concession. Ordinary stone is sold for 2 annas 9 pies per square foot to the ordinary public, and for R9 per 100 square feet to the English Public Works. The beams are sometimes as much as 40 feet in length. Ordinary perforated screen-work is 8 annas per square foot, and floral work 6 annas. The art is purely traditionary, but, like all traditionary arts, is in danger of being starved. A lad barely 12 years of age sits beside his parents, and with a rough piece of charcoal for a pencil, his eye his sole measurement, he will trace an intricate arabesque with the greatest delicacy and fidelity. After this the chisel falls into his hand as if made for it, and he carves in either high relief or low relief the work represented on the Gwalior Gateway."

Plaster work of Jaipur.

Among other architectural decorations may be noticed the plaster-work of Jaipur. Mention has already been made of this work under the head of "Decorative painting applied to Architecture." Sometimes walls and ceilings are decorated in plaster enriched with scales of mica, which impart to them a very cool and satin-like lustre. Plaster decorations in floral or arabesque work are also largely employed. The flowers are raised, and sometimes gilt or tinted. Another favourite mode of decoration in Jaipur is the mirror work, either in silvered glass or talc, in some cases backed with discs of plated copper or with coloured pieces of metal foil. The general effect of such decoration is as if the rooms were adorned with gems, though it is apt to be overdone. The pieces of glass are often set in gilt or silver borders, arranged in various arabesque patterns or in the forms of trees and flowers. Mirrors and portraits in fresco are sometimes interspersed, and often the outlines are formed by plain plaster. Such work is frequently done at the present day. Another mode of decoration prevalent in Jaipur is that with painted glass, something like the Venetian glass mosaic. The design is cut out of a sheet of plaster or metal, and behind the openings thus formed pieces of coloured glass are arranged so as to produce a picture. A second piece of plaster cut in the same way as the first is then placed behind, and the whole cemented together. This is a very ancient use of coloured glass, and has a rich effect when the sun shines through the panel.

Under this head Mr. Kipling mentions a similar kind of ceiling work executed at Amritsar, of which specimens were sent to the Calcutta International Exhibition. Of the ceiling work from Amritsar, and also ornamental moulded work in paper made at the Mayo School of Art in combinations of plaster, Mr. Kipling thus writes :—

"Sometimes the mirrors are discs separately framed, but in another style; small pieces of mirror are framed in arabesque scrolls wrought with great delicacy in white plaster. The mirrors are blown in their globes, which are silvered on the inside and then broken into fragments. There are numerous examples of this fantastic and beautiful but laborious form of decoration in the old buildings of the Panjáb; and in Persia also it is well known. The border of an otherwise good specimen in the collection is disfigured by panels in which Chenille wool work of crude colour has been inserted under the glass—an example of the triviality and vulgarity into which a striving for novelty is apt to lead the native craftsman. The gilt and coloured plaster-work is more serious, and excepting for its tendency to excessive minuteness of detail, there is but little fault to be found with it. The fourth specimen is entirely of wood. This variety is formed of small pieces of wood of geometric forms, such as hexagons, triangles, &c., which are prepared and painted separately and afterwards put upon the ceiling, being held together by strips of raised moulding. The effect is often exceedingly rich, while the work is not nearly so laborious as might be imagined. In Cairo there is a greater variety of pattern than Panjáb can show, where however several fine ceilings have disappeared entirely of late years.

"The ornamental moulded work in paper shewn by the Mayo School of Art consisted of a wainscot in coloured and gilded paper, a screen, and a shield of the arms of Panjáb. The common paper of the country being very fibrous, is particularly suitable for this purpose, and is easily pressed into moulds with a suitable paste, and when dry and fixed, it is nearly as hard as wood."

Thatched Halls of Bengal (Chandi-Mandaps).

The decoration of thatched halls in Bengal, called *chandi-mandaps,* was of a very unique character. These halls were used as sitting rooms and also for holding the different religious festivals, and formed part of every house in rural Bengal half a century ago, when masonry buildings were rare. Large amounts of money were often lavished in the construction and adornment of such thatched halls. The bamboo was cut and split very fine and smoothed with an incredible amount of diligence, so that it "could be rubbed on the eye without hurting." Beams made of Palmyra wood were prepared with equal care. Talc scales were first laid on the bamboo skeleton of the thatch; over these scales was then spread a layer of the plumage of the so-called Indian jay (*Coracias indica,* vern. *Nilkantha*), and finally the thatch was covered with straw. It is said that in time of festivals the best edifices of this kind were covered with cloth to prevent the attention of worshippers being distracted by the sight of so much decorative beauty. Masonry work is now universally preferred in this country, and the construction of the best description of *chandi-mandaps* has fallen into disuse, and in a very short time will be altogether a thing of the past.

Ornamental bricks and Stucco Moulding.

Remarkably good bricks, moulded on the face with figures, groups, and patterns, used to be made in parts of Bengal. A very good example of a building decorated in this way is the Kántanagar temple near Dinájpur. The mouldings are deep, clean, and quaint; in the figures a good deal of life is shewn; and some of the patterns are very beautiful. In Chandernagore a temple is decorated in this way, but the designs and moulding are inferior.

Old stucco-mouldings are found on some houses in Bengal. Those in Dacca are most remarkable for their beauty. With much difficulty a few specimens were obtained for the Colonial and Indian Exhibition from Mohim Chandra Basák of Dacca, as the industry is dying out for want of demand.

Decorative paintings applied to articles of domestic use.

Earthen pots and wooden chests are sometimes painted in water-colours, but, except in the case of *Papier maché* articles, the industry is not important.

Coloured pots.—In Bengal such painting is commonly done on earthern vessels, and is of two kinds. In one class of earthenware, called *Sakherhánri*, the outside surface is decorated with ordinary paints of different colours after the vessel has been baked; while in the other the vessels are painted with a certain kind of earth, called *bil-máti*, and the colour burnt in. The painting is extremly primitive in character. Good specimens of painted earthern pots were however sent to the Colonial and Indian Exhibition from Gya, in which some artistic taste was shewn.

A very beautiful description of hand-painted pottery comes from Sitápur in Oudh. On these floral decorations in different colours are drawn on a green ground with a very pleasing effect. A collection of such painted pots has been sent to the Glasgow International Exhibition. Prices range from 6 annas to R1.

Kámagari work.—In Panjáb decorative painting on articles of domestic use is chiefly confined to *Kámagari* work, already described under the head "Paintings on Wood." Mr. Kipling has furnished the following description of this kind of wood-painting:—

"The decoration of the bow and arrow which till recently were in ordinary use, and which are still made, has given its name *Kámángari,* vulgarly *Kámágri,* from *Kámán,* a bow, to the indigenous scheme of painted decoration in wood. It is invariably water-colour protected by a varnish. Sometimes true gold is used to heighten the effect, and it is occasionally punched and otherwise treated, but more frequently a ground of tinfoil, or of tin levigated, and used like European shell gold or silver, is laid as a preliminary. Over this transparent, semi-transparent colours acquire a sheen, and where the foil left uncoloured, yellow or white varnishes produce the effect of gold or silver. The bows from Multan and other districts show the original and still existent form of the art, and the linen chests and bed-legs from Delhi, its modern practice. In old houses, doors and chests are sometimes found of a simpler and better type of design, and of a more agreeable colour."

[See also "Paintings on Wood" and "Decorative Paintings applied to Architecture."]

Papier-maché.—In connection with decorative painting may be mentioned the *Papier-maché* work. The chief centre of this industry is Kashmir, and the art appears to be of Persian origin. Large quantities of such articles are annually made in Srinagar, chiefly consisting of trays, plates, blotting books, ink-stands, pen-trays, boxes, caskets, miniature boats, and paper-knives. The patterns are bold, and are of the same description as those on the famous Kashmir shawls, which, together with their rich colouring, produce a very picturesque effect. Real gold is sometimes used in the decoration. Mr. Kipling states that "in response to the English demand for 'something chaste,' the rich colouring and bold patterns formerly in vogue have given way to a somewhat sickly monochrome of cream colour and gold." Many of the articles commonly described as *Papier-maché* are however made of wood.

A valuable collection of Kashmir *Papier-maché* has been sent to the Glasgow International Exhibition. The following are the prices of typical specimens at the place of production:—a table R15; a pair of pots, called *Martbán* R15; a ditto, smaller, R1; a pair glove-boxes R6; a writing set, 4 pieces, R18; a pair boats, R2-4; a handkerchief-box, R2-8; a pair card-boxes, R6; ditto, smaller, R1-8; a tray with 12 sides, R10; half-dozen round trays, R10. The names of the makers who supplied goods for the Glasgow International Exhibition are Safdar Mughul, Muhammad Ali, Kázim Ali, and Rahman Khán of Srinagar.

In the North-Western Provinces *Papier-maché* articles are made in Jaunpur, Rámpur, Mandáwar in Bijnor District, and Muzaffarnagar. The industry is however of Kashmir origin. The ware made at Rámpur is very good, and that of Jaunpur fair. The Jaunpur work has greatly improved within the last four or five years. Mandáwar articles have gradually acquired a distinct character. Salvers, cigar-cases, and card-cases are generally made at Jaunpur, teapoys and salvers at Rámpur, and inkstands, pen-cases, trays, and boxes at Mandáwar and Muzaffarnagar.

A collection has been sent to the Glasgow International Exhibition from Jaunpur, Mandáwar, and

Muzaffarnagar. The following are the prices of typical specimens at the places of production :—Jaunpur—a cigar-case, R12-8; an oval tray, R12; a round dish, R3; an envelope-case, R10. Muzaffarnagar—a box, R15; a pen-case, R6-8. Mandáwar—a box, R20; a flower vase, R3; a plate, R3.

Clay Models.

Jadu Náth Pál, his brother Rám Lál Pál, his nephew Bakkeswar Pál, and his relation and neighbour Rákhál Dás Pál are now the only four clay modellers of note at Krishnagar, a town about 60 miles north of Calcutta. The figures made by them have acquired great celebrity, and they have repeatedly gained medals and certificates in most of the International Exhibitions held since 1851. There is considerable delicacy and fineness in their work; the figures are instinct with life and expression, and their pose and action are excellent. The late Mr. Locke, Superintendent of the School of Art, Calcutta, however, found fault with their "unhappy predilection for introducing pieces of real fabrics in the clothing; actual hair and wool in the figures; and in the accessories, straw and grass, &c." In his opinion "this has a tendency to lower their work to the level of ingenious toy-making." But whatever objection there might be in a purely artistic point of view to the practice of putting actual hair, wool, and other accessories on the figures, it cannot be denied that it gives to them a very life-like appearance. Considerable delicacy and ingenuity are often displayed in the preparation and manipulation of these accessories, and some of these are made, not by the modellers, but by other trades and caste-men. For instance, thatched houses are made by professional thatchers called *Gharámis;* baskets are made by *Doms,* a low caste people whose profession is to make baskets; trees and plants are made by men who have acquired a proficiency in this branch of work. Krishnagar modellers belong to the Hindu caste of *Kumárs,* or potters, one of the nine artisan classes of Bengal, whose rank stands just beneath the Bráhmans and Writers. From time immemorial the occupation of this caste has been to make earthen vessels, and the figurative representations of divine manifestations described in Hindu sacred books. These tangible representations of divine attributes are worshipped in Bengal on prescribed days throughout the year. The making of an idol is a fine art by itself, and not only the potter who makes it, but also the rich man in whose house it is worshipped and who holds the festival, feels a considerable amount of pride if the public praise its artistic construction. The potter makes the figures of such idols, the painter colours them, and the *Máli,* a member of the flower-selling caste, adorns them with tinsel ornaments. Then the priest comes and invokes the particular divinity whose figure is made to come down from heaven and accept the offerings prepared by the humble worshipper. After the offerings have been made, and the prescribed time for the deity's stay upon earth has expired, it is again respectfully asked by the priest to go back to its heavenly abode. The idol is then a lump of clay, like the body of a living organism after life has departed from it. It is then consigned into water.

A miniature scene illustrating the great festival of Bengal, *viz.,* the worship of the Goddess Durgá, held every year in September, has been sent to the Glasgow International Exhibition. Durgá, a form of the great Goddess "Energy" that pervades the universe, is represented as having ten hands engaged in killing the "Evil Principle." Her husband, the great Siva, the "Destruction and Reproduction Principle" of the Hindu Triad, occupies a lowly place on the top of the frame-work, for this festival is specially in honour of his consort. She has her children with her. On the extreme right Ganesha, the God of Wisdom, sits grave with his elephant-head, to whom offering is made before all other gods, for he is the God of Success as well. Next to him the lady of the golden complexion is Lakshmi, the Goddess of Wealth, Prosperity, and Good Fortune. Naturally she is highly honoured all over India. Thursday is specially assigned to her, as Sunday is dedicated to the presiding deity of the sun, and Monday to that of the moon. On the extreme left of this assemblage of gods and goddesses is Kártikeya, the God of War, who rides on a peacock. He is a bachelor, and means to remain so all his life [for according to the Hindu Sástras gods are also subject to death and eventual absorption into the Original Cause, the Supreme Being]. Simple village folks say that everything was settled for Kártikeya's marriage, and that the marriage procession actually started for the bride's house. Ere it had gone far, he remembered that he had left something behind at home. So he came back and surprised his mother in the act of eating hurriedly, not with one hand only, as gods and men usually do, but with ten hands, the extra eight having been produced to meet the extreme urgency of the occasion. He pressed his mother for an explanation of this act on her part. With much reluctance she informed him that as daughters-in-law starve their mothers-in-law, she was making the best of the little time now left of her absolute rule over the household. "Mother, if it is so, then I will never marry," said the dutiful son. The Durgá form of the Goddess of Energy has therefore ten hands. This of course is a village story, like that of God and the Tailor, implicitly believed in England a short time ago. Next to Kártikeya, to the left of Durgá, stands on a lotus Saraswati, the Goddess of Arts and Sciences. She has a day specially dedicated to herself in February, when she is worshipped by schoolboys and artisans all over Bengal. On this occasion her figure is not always made, but books, ink-pots, tools and instruments stand for a symbol. Animal sacrifices are made to Durgá, and in the worship of the different manifestations of "Energy." In the scene sent to the Glasgow Exhibition, the sacrifice of a buffalo has been represented.

Krishnagar modelling industry originated from this making of idols for worship. Gradually the gods and goddesses came to be furnished with attendants, and in public worships got up by subscription, more for amusement than for a religious obligation, life-size mythological scenes, scenes from daily life, portrait figures of athletes and other celebrities, caricatures, comical subjects, and figures representing any scandal current at the time, were gradually introduced. The manufacture of toys and miniature figures is a natural growth from this stage of the industry. But it is said the modellers owe to Dr. Archer the notice which Europeans now take of their work. As mentioned before, Krishnagar models and scenes were sent to the different International Exhibitions since 1851, where they always formed objects of great admiration and curiosity. In the Amsterdam International Exhibition of 1882, an interesting feature of the Indian section was a row of native shops with life-size figures. This novel scene was repeated at the Colonial and Indian Exhibition, and the place where it stood was always densely crowded with visitors. At this Exhibition were also shewn a large number of life-sized ethnological models, illustrating the different aboriginal tribes who still lead a savage life among the jungles and mountain fastnesses of India. This work of modelling the tribes from nature was first commenced during the Calcutta International Exhibition, when typical specimens were brought to Calcutta, and their figures made in clay by Jadu Náth Pál, under the supervision of Dr. Watt, C.I.E. Jadu Náth Pál has no equal in India in this kind of work.

Seventeen life-size ethnological models have been sent to the Glasgow International Exhibition. The following short description of some of the tribes will shew on what kind of work this new art of ethnological modelling is now being employed :—

Khámti.—The Khámti tribe reside in Assam on the North-East frontier of India. They and the other races inhabiting this quarter are of Mongolian origin. The Khámtis were once a very powerful people, having conquered the whole of Assam and a large part of the easternmost section of Bengal. Those that settled down in the Assam valley have long been converted into Hinduism, but the Phakiáls, Kanjangs, and other sections of the race still retain the costume, customs, and religion of their ancestors. Of all the races in the North-East frontier of India, the Khámtis have made the greatest advance in knowledge, arts, and civilisation. They are Buddhists by religion, and possess an established church of their own. A large portion of the people can read and write. They live in large houses built of timber, with raised floors and thatched roofs. Their temples are elaborately carved. In addition to their sacerdotal duties, the priests beguile themselves by carving in wood, bone, or ivory in which "they evince great skill, taste, and fecundity of invention, carving in high relief twisted snakes, dragons, and other monsters with a creditable unity and gracefulness of design." Their chiefs also work but with a more valuable material. They work in gold, silver, and iron ; forge their own weapons and make their wives' jewels. The women make embroidery, well-wrought bags for their husbands, and bands for the hair and other pretty things. The Khámtis practise polygamy, but the supremacy of the first wife is always maintained. A large chopper-like weapon, called the *Dáo*, and a shield made of buffalo-hide are the only offensive and defensive weapons of a Khámti. But many of them now carry muskets or fowling pieces.

Mishmis.—This tribe resides on the high mountains that separate the Brahmaputra valley from the plateau of Tibet. They possess large flocks and herds, specially that of the hill-ox called *Mithun.* A Mishmi reckons his wealth, first, by the number of his wives, and next by the number of animals he possesses. He buys his wives with his animals, the price of a wife ranging from a pig to twenty heads of oxen. They are a short, sturdy race of fair complexion. They largely trade with the British villages in Assam, where they bring the Aconite root, the medicinal plant called the *Coptis teeta*, and musk bags of the musk deer. The Mishmis are still a very wild race, and little advanced in arts and civilisation. Their religion is equally primitive, simply consisting of demon propitiation on the occurrence of illness or any family misfortune.

Daphlás.—This race belongs to the Abor group of tribes, who occupy another section of the Eastern Himalayas that separate the Brahmaputra valley from Tibet. They have the same type of Mongolian physiognomy as other races of Assam. Their religion is worship of spirits, to whom they make offerings as a protection they are supposed to give to themselves, to their cattle and their crops. They practise polygamy whenever they can afford it, but polyandry is far more common. Mr. Dalton thus relates a case of Daphlá elopement:—

"A very pretty Daphlá girl once came into the station of Lakhimpur, threw herself at my feet and in most poetical language asked me to give her protection. She was the daughter of a chief, and was sought in marriage and promised to a peer of her father who had many other wives. She would not submit to be one of many, and besides she loved, and she eloped with her beloved. This was interesting and romantic. She was at the time in a very coarse travelling dress, and assured of protection she took fresh apparel and ornaments from her basket and proceeded to array herself, and very pretty she looked as she combed and plaited her long hair and completed her toilette. In the meantime I had sent for 'the beloved' who had kept in the background, and alas! how the romance was dispelled when a dual appeared! She had eloped with two young men!!"

Nágás.—The Nágás are the most important of all the Assam tribes. They inhabit the hills between Assam and Burma, and are divided into many branches. They are a brave and a hardy race, and often good-looking. But a custom is prevalent among many of the Nágá clans to allow matrimony only to those "who have made themselves as hideous as possible by having their faces elaborately tattooed. The process of disfiguration is carried to such a length, that it gives them an unnatural darkness of complexion, and that fearful look which results when a white man blackens his face." They build very substantial houses, those for notables being very large, sometimes 250 to 300 feet in length, on the front, and in the inside of which are numerous trophies of the chase and memorials of feasts. In a separate house, dedicated to the collection of more bloody objects, are arranged human skulls in shelves like books, the records of recent achievements, and baskets full of fragments of skulls, the memorials of the bloody deeds of their forefathers. A Nágá is not allowed to tattoo himself until he has taken a human scalp or a skull, nor is he considered an acceptable suitor to the hand of a young bride unless he can present her with such a "gory token of his love." Nágás have no temples or priests, but they sacrifice to sylvan spirits.

Mikirs occupy the hills east of the Brahmaputra They are a peaceful people, and are good subjects of the British Indian Government.

Gáros live further west, in the mountainous country called the Gáro Hills, which are now included within the British territory. The national character of the Gáros is very highly spoken of by Colonel Dalton :—"They are lively, good-natured, hospitable, frank and honest in their dealings, and are noted for their love of truth." The Gáros have taken some of the Hindu ideas about supernatural matters and have given them their own wild aspect. The following is their account of the Creation :—

Rishi Salgong is the head of the gods who lived in heaven. He eloped with a heavenly beauty named Mainon, and came and lived in Tura, the principal village in the Gáro Hills. They had a son, who is the father of fire, and all the heavenly luminaries; and a daughter named Donjongma, who is the mother of mankind.

Also at the same time there appeared an egg in the world, self-begotten. Out of it sprang a lovely female, called Nashtu, who began to fill the earth with animals and vegetables. First issued streams of water from her womb which were the origin of all the rivers; next came an alligator, and then she produced grasses and reeds. She next brought out the first animal, called *Matchidobo*, which is seldom seen by men, and he who sees it dies. Then came fish of all kinds, frogs, snakes, trees, buffaloes, geese, a daughter, and a priest, who perhaps married the daughter. For she had a son who married Dorjongma mentioned at the end of the last paragraph, and also three daughters, who are respectively the mothers of the three races of human beings, *viz.*, the Bhutiás of the Himalayas, the Gáros, and the Firingis (English).

The Gáros therefore claim relationship with the

English, but they disdain to have anything to do with their neighbours, the Bengalis, who are "of unknown origin." The Gáros have priests who perform sacrifices; foretell events by examining the entrails of animals; cure diseases by incantations and offerings to gods; cultivate land, and go to war. Nothing is more savoury to a Gáro palate than the flesh of a dog, which he rears for food along with kine, goats, swine, fowls and ducks. Cats are not despised. Unmarried young men in a Gáro village live separate from the females in a place called the "Bachelor's Hall," but there is no restriction on innocent intercourse between the sexes, and they freely mix with each other in the labours of the field and other pursuits. It is the custom of the Gáros for a young lady to propose for the hand of a suitable young man, and not the reverse, as prevails in Europe. It would be the height of immodesty in a young man to court a young girl, and any such infringement of the national custom would be summarily and severely punished.

The above are only a few typical specimens of the various aboriginal races modelled by Jadu Náth Pál, the Government modeller. Besides those mentioned above, models of a Karen of Burma, Santál, Kol, and Bhuyá of Chota Nágpur, and Banwalla, Bawalla, and Laguli of the North-Western Provinces have been sent to the Glasgow International Exhibition. A complete collection of such models is deposited in the Indian Museum at Calcutta, and copies have been sent for the Imperial Institute as well as to many of the Continental Museums. Copies can be had on application to the Secretary to the Government of India in the Revenue and Agricultural Department, Calcutta. Price R40 for each model, exclusive of arms, dress, and other appurtenances.

Rákhál Dás Pál is the best artist in miniature scenes,

but he charges a very high price. The scene sent to the Glasgow Exhibition representing the sacrifice mentioned above is made by him. He also made other scenes for the Glasgow International Exhibition, the most interesting among them being the one illustrating a tea garden in Assam. He has also made the scenes representing a marriage, a marriage procession, the car festival of Jagannáth, the landlord's court, and the smoking of opium.

Bakkeswar Pál, and his father Rám Lál Pál, have made for the Glasgow International Exhibition the "Swinging Festival," now prohibited by Government because of the torture to which fanatics and others subjected themselves on such occasions. They have also made the "Collector's Court," "the Extraction of date-palm sugar," and "a Theological Discussion among the Bráhmans of Nadiya." The palm tree made in the "Sugar Extraction" model is particularly good. Bakkeswar Pál has acquired a special proficiency in making models of Bengal fishes. A collection of such fishes has been sent to the Glasgow International Exhibition. The imitation is perfect.

Collections of clay models of fruits and vegetables have also been sent to the above International Exhibition. These have been made by Nibáran Pál of Krishnagar. He has also made the small miniature figures representing different trades.

Prices of scenes, miniature figures, and models are as follows:—Tea Garden scene, R1,200; Durgá Pujá scene, R175; Marriage and Marriage Procession, R375; Landlord's Court, R150; Smoking of Opium, R40; Car Festival, R360; Sugar-cane Irrigation, R20; Theological Discussion of Bráhmans, R40; Collector's Court, R375; a Village School, R50; Swinging Festival, R180; Oil-Pressing, R25; Ploughing, R15; Extraction of date sugar, R20; a collection of fishes,

R300; miniature figures representing trades and professions, R9 to R12 per dozen; a collection of vegetables, R100.

Figures and models of various kinds of fruit are made at Borayá in Bardwán, Darbhángá, Hatwá, and Chaprá, but these are vastly inferior to those made at Krishnagar, Lucknow, or Poona.

Similar figures, scenes, and models of fruits and vegetables are made at Lucknow in the North-Western Provinces. The Lucknow modellers are specially good in models of fruits and vegetables, and, as a rule, they can turn out much cheaper articles than the Krishnagar artists. Lucknow figures are without those defects complained of by Mr. Locke, *i.e.*, the modellers there do not use actual hair, wool, pieces of clothing, and other accessories for the decoration of the miniature figures, but make them in clay, which gives them more durability, though not the same life-like character as those of Krishnagar. Small figures coloured in imitation of terra-cotta made at Lucknow are particularly good. Lucknow scenes and figures, however, generally want that unique expression which is a characteristic feature of the Krishnagar models. The scenes sent from Lucknow to the Glasgow International Exhibition will give an idea of the kind of work that can be performed there, at a cheaper price than what is charged at Krishnagar:—

Thuggi.—A miniature scene representing *Thugs* murdering an equestrian Rajput traveller. The *Thugs* were professional murderers, who considered it a religious duty to counteract over-population in this world by putting to death all men they could lay their hands upon. They looked upon themselves as agents of the great Goddess of Destruction created specially for this object, like death and disease, snakes and tigers, crocodiles and sharks, and various other enemies that constantly prey on humanity. For this perilous devotion to her service, the great Goddess permitted them to take whatever belonged to the victims, their necklets and bangles, cash and wearing apparel, and horses and pack-bullocks. The Goddess still more favoured her adherents in times gone by, when she sent her heavenly attendants to remove the dead bodies of the victims; but since an unlucky curiosity tempted a *Thug* to look behind how this was effected, she ceased to do them this service. As India is a country where division of labour speedily adjusts itself to a scientific nicety, the refusal of the Goddess to dispose of the corpses gave rise to a separate trade which was at once taken up by a low-caste people who took the name of *Logáis*, and who followed the camp of the *Thugs*, dug the graves long before the intended victims were murdered, and buried them when all was over. The *Thug* murdered by strangling his victim with a handkerchief, on one end of which was tied a copper coin, the weight of which made the handkerchief rapidly swing round his neck. When strangulation by handkerchief was not easy, a string with a noose at one end was used, as in the scene in which the equestrian traveller is being murdered. In the other *Thuggi* scene, murder by handkerchief is shewn. The *Thugs* committed their crime on the sly, by getting into the good graces of travellers, gradually gaining their confidence and making them go along with them until they had arrived at some convenient place where they could murder and plunder them without any reasonable chance of detection. *Thugs* never openly attacked the travellers, for that kind of work belonged to *Dacoits*, also worshippers of the great Goddess, but nevertheless for whom the *Thugs* had the greatest contempt. *Thuggiism* has now been practically suppressed.

Another very interesting scene sent from Lucknow

is the one in which a woman is shewn performing the rite of *Sati*, or burning herself in the funeral pyre with the body of her husband recently dead. This practice has been prohibited for the last sixty years. In former times, not only newly-made widows immolated themselves in this way, but men also burnt themselves in pyres they constructed with their own hands. The Bráhman who followed Alexander the Great did so before the whole Greek army. The Hindus believe in the transmigration of the soul, and liken the body to a suit of clothes. When it gets worn out, they wish for a new suit to be better able to perform the duties of *life*.

Among other scenes sent from Lucknow to the Glasgow International Exhibition may be mentioned "the cremation" as practised in Upper India, a "marriage procession" of the trading or the *Baniá* caste, "irrigation by swing basket," "irrigation by lever," "well irrigation by leathern bags," and "irrigation by Persian wheel." A large number of figures and models of fruits and vegetables have also been sent by private exhibitors. A very good model of a village was made by the Lucknow artists for the Colonial and Indian Exhibition. This model represented very fully the village life in the North-Western Provinces in all its details.

As mentioned before, Lucknow articles are cheaper than those made at Krishnagar. The two scenes representing the practices of the *Thugs* cost only R30; *Sati*, R30; cremation, R30; and the marriage procession, R40. Miniature clay figures made at Lucknow are sold for R9 to R24 per dozen. Hirá Lál, Priá Dás, Mátá Din, and Bhawáni Dás are the noted clay modellers of Lucknow. The following are typical specimens of small figures:—an ascetic, R2; a washerwoman, R2; a tobacco shop, R3; a monkey-man,

R3; a water-carrier R2; a Panjábi, R1-5; an old man, R5.

Figures and models of various descriptions of fruit are made at Delhi and Ambala. The Ambala figurines resemble those of Lucknow, being the work of a man who originally came from that place. Delhi models are not so good. But excellent models of poisonous snakes are made at Delhi by a potter, named Hirá Singh. These are made in *terra-cotta* and coloured in water-colours from the plates in Sir Joseph Fayrer's *Thanatophidia*. A collection of such models of snakes is kept in the District offices for the identification of poisonous serpents, for the destruction of which there is a fixed rate of reward. Models of snakes made by Hirá Singh are deposited in the Indian Museum, Calcutta, as a work of art. A series of terra-cotta figurines, sketched in clay from living models, illustrating the working people of the Panjáb, were sent to the Colonial and Indian Exhibition. These were mostly made by Mr. G. P. Pinto of the Mayo School of Art, Lahore.

Models of a superior kind are made at the School of Art, Jaipur. They resemble Lucknow work. A life-size model of a religious mendicant has been sent from Jaipur to the Glasgow International Exhibition. The modelling is well-executed. Dr. Hendley has furnished the following interesting account of the mendicant:—

"Gobind Dás, aged 40 years, Swámi of the Rámánandi sect, resident of Muttra District, applied for treatment at the Mayo Hospital at Jaipur in September 1887. He gave the following account of himself. About six years ago he purchased for R5 a small wooden bedstead which was covered with strong iron nails, and practised sleeping upon it for one year at Dhur Mahádeo temple at Muttra. He then went to Brindában, where he stayed for a month. After that he journeyed for six months to Barkki Gangá and Sironji. He remained at Sironji a year, and after that at Lucknow for a year and a half. He stopped next for a year at the Triveni Ghât, which is at the junction of the Jumna and Ganges at Allahabad, and then journeyed *viâ* Lucknow, Agra, Bhartpur, Mohwa, Rangarh, and Bandikui to Jaipur. He spent some time in different parts of Jaipur, and for the last fortnight had remained in Jahán Bazar, or principal street. He stated that over-indulgence in good food, smoking *charas*, or Indian hemp, exposure to rain, and pressure of the iron nails had at last made him sick. He was suffering from dropsy and other disorders, and desired earnestly to return to Muttra to die. He parted with his bed for a small sum and left Jaipur." The model is made of *papier-maché*.

Large quantities of miniature clay figures are made at Poona in the Bombay Presidency. The Poona Municipal Corporation estimates the value of the annual outturn at R10,000. About forty years ago, three men named Bapuji Supekar, Jingar, and Kalu Rám Gavandi, first opened shops at Poona for the sale of these figures. The present modellers are Tátiá Vevhári, Sitárám Joshi, Dáji Náráyan, Sukh-rám Seth Sonár, Raghopant, and Mároti Gurav. Poona figures resemble those made at Krishnagar, both in their superior finish and in the practice of using pieces of cloth for dresses. A good collection of the Poona manufacture consisting of about 30 figures can be had for R60. The collection of Poona figures sent to the Colonial and Indian Exhibition was very interesting. They were "distinguished for their truthful modelling and life-like representation of the large variety of races inhabiting the Bombay Presidency, each race having its dress and turban distinct from another."

Figures of camels, horses, cows, and other familiar animals and birds are made at Surat, a collection of which was sent to the Colonial and Indian Exhibition.

In the Mysore State, models of fruits, vegetables, and reptiles are made at Chennapollam. The imitation is not perfect, but the colouring is good. A cluster of fruit with leaves costs R5.

Models are made at Tonk in Rajputana. A model of a bullock-tonga, with a pair of bullocks, was sent from this State to the Colonial and Indian Exhibition.

A collection of clay figures representing native trades, as well as figures of gods, was sent to the above Exhibition from Gwalior.

A very inferior kind of clay figures as toys for children are made all over the country. Figures of gods and goddesses are generally made, and are very largely sold at public fairs and places of pilgrimage. Their prices are very cheap, from a farthing to a penny.

Similar toys are also made of lac. Sometimes considerable skill is shown in their manufacture. Ilámbázár in Bengal is a place noted for such lac models. A collection of lac toys, consisting of models of fruits and animals, was sent to the Calcutta Exhibition from Gushkará in Bardwán ; price six annas each.

Of late the manufacture of plaster of Paris figures has been introduced into the country, chiefly by Italian artists employed in the Schools of Art. The ethnological models, originally made in clay, are now cast in plaster of Paris. A collection of busts made of this material was sent to the Colonial and Indian Exhibition from Bombay. These were modelled by a native of India, named Valla Hirá.

A very curious collection of heads, modelled in *papier-maché*, has been sent to the Glasgow International Exhibition. These are made at Jaipur, and are intended to illustrate the different Hindu castes found in Rajputana, and the turbans they wear. The heads are copied from life models and are very characteristic. They have been painted in water-colours. The turbans made of pieces of cloth, are mostly coloured or printed, and are tied into exactly the same shape as they are done by the different tradesmen in Rajputana. A collection consisting of 144 heads cost R195, or R1-5-0 each in the place of production.

III.—Musical Instruments.

The Hindus of old made considerable advance in the art of music, and brought it under the domain of science and gave it a symmetrical form. Swaraswati, the Goddess of Learning and Art, presides over this branch of science, and the sage Nàrada was an adept in the art of music. As with other Hindu sciences, the art of music experienced great decadence in later ages, and many of the old books on the subject have been lost. This happened before the Muhammadans came into this country, and it underwent still further deterioration during the early years of Musalman rule, owing to the new conquerors being strictly forbidden by their religion to cultivate music. The Musalmans are only allowed to beat a drum called *Dàf* at marriages and other ceremonies, apparently for the purpose of giving publicity to the event. But the sweets of music were very soon found to be too tempting for Muhammadans of culture and refinement, and as early as 1285, in the reign of Emperor Kaikobad, one Amir Khasru discovered the high standard of Hindu music, as compared with the system known in Arabia. Notwithstanding the religious prohibition, he carefully studied the subject, and zealously adopted the Hindu style, and since that time Indian music had no more ardent followers than its Muhammadan conquerors. Akbar the Great collected around him the most expert musicians then existing in the country, among whom the name of Tán Sen is still a household word in all parts of India. As regards the division of the scale or gamut, there does not appear to exist any very great difference between the European and Hindu systems of music. In the

Hindu music, the octave, is recognised with seven full notes which are called *grámas*. These are named *Sharaja*, *Rishava*, *Gàndhāra*, *Madhyama*, *Panchama*, *Dhaibata*, and *Nishàda*, the eighth being considered a repetition of the first. All the Sanskrit writers agree in saying that originally there were only six *Ràgas*, or primary tunes, five being created by the deity Mahádeva, and one by his wife Pàrvati. These *Ràgas* gradually came to be invested with a mythological garb, and are now considered as polygamous living spirits, for each has numerous sub-tunes for its wives. So far as musical instruments are concerned, the Hindus do not now possess anything like the highly developed instruments used in Europe. But in the manufacture of the instruments they have, considerable ingenuity and skill are often displayed, and they are often decorated with ivory, silver, and other materials, hence these have been classed as art-manufactures. Dr. Bidie makes the following remarks on Hindu musical instruments and Hindu music:—

"With the Hindus music has always been a favourite art, and the popular deity Krishna is generally represented as playing on a flute. Much ingenuity has also been devoted in India to the invention of musical instruments, and these possess a particular interest at the present day, inasmuch as some have remained unaltered for centuries. Beginning with the simpler forms belonging to the rude hill tribes, and proceeding onwards to those in use amongst the more civilised population of villages and cities, we find a most interesting variety, capable of affording much information as to the characteristics of the national music. From this point of view they have hitherto received little or no attention, and a rich field of research therefore remains for the investigation of the ethnologist and the musician. As regards Hindu music, some of the older airs are rich in expressive melody, and one reason why the higher class of them does not appeal to European taste lies in the peculiarities of the scale. According to Carl Engel, 'the Hindus divide their musical scale into intervals smaller than our semitones. They adopted 22 intervals called *Sruti*, in the compass of an octave. The *Sruti* may therefore be compared to our chromatic intervals. But from an old treatise written by Soma, it is evident the common scale of the Hindus had much the character of the pentatonic order of intervals.' In the construction of musical instruments, the natives of India have called into requisition a great variety of substances. The chief of these are reeds, bamboos, gourds, wood, iron, brass, shells, bone, ivory, gut, bladder, and skin. The principal places of manufacture in the Madras Presidency are Tanjore, Malabar, and Nilgiri."

In Bengal musical instruments are chiefly made at Calcutta, Murshidabad, Dacca and Bishnupur; in the North-Western Provinces at Lucknow, Benares, and Rámpur; and in the Panjáb at Delhi, Amritsar, and Lahore. A complete collection of musical instruments can be obtained for about R1,000.

The following description of the instruments have been partly furnished by Sir Mahárájá Sourendro Mohan Tagore, Doctor of Music:—

Stringed Instruments.

Kachchhapí Viná.—A very classical stringed instrument, popularly known as the *Kachuá Sitár.* It owes its name to the shape of the gourd, which is flat like the back of the *Kachchhapa* (tortoise). The present name "*Sitár*" (literally "three wires") was given to it by Amir Khashru (a poet and musician of the 13th century), on account of the number of wires with which it was then mounted. The wires now used in it vary from five to seven. The instrument is said to have been the favourite of Saraswati, the Goddess of Music. Very good *Sitárs* are made at Dacca. It is sometimes made of ivory.

"This instrument, called *Chittari* in South India, has in that part of India a length of 4 feet 2 inches, width $1\frac{3}{4}$ inches, and depth $9\frac{3}{4}$ inches. Originally no doubt the body of this instrument was of gourds, some of which are ribbed, and the dug-out wooden body now used is adorned with a series of ribs radiating from the posterior single peg, to which all the strings are attached, over the convexity of the instrument, and again converging at the base of the neck. The instrument known as the guitar in Europe, is evidently copied from this one; and curious to say, the Italian name of it is *Chittara*, while the Spanish designation is *Guitarra*, and the French *Gaitare*. There can be no doubt that the whole of these names are derived from the same root or word. The strings are of wire, and seven in number. Of these, six are of equal length and pass over the general nut up to the turning pegs, but the seventh, at a short distance up the finger-board, passes through a metal peg, and then turns up to a turning peg in the side of the neck. The finger-board has numerous frets, made of ligatures of twine passing round the neck" (Bidie).

In the Panjáb, there are several kinds of *Sitár*. "In form these instruments are not inelegant. The body is gourd-shaped, and exceedingly bulging; in fact, consisting of the half or section of a large gourd, with a flat face, the shoulder sloping off into the long wooden handle. The instruments are often prettily and elaborately inlaid with ivory, or else painted in gold and colours and varnished. The varieties of *Sitár* are the *Madhyam Sitár*, the *Chargah Sitár*, and the *Tarabdár Sitár*. The favourite form of *Sitar* is the *Madhyam*. This is the instrument introduced at Delhi by Amir Khasru. The *Madhyam Sitár* has the handle long and hollow, or deeply concave, but faced with a thin piece of *Tún* wood (*Cedrela Toona*). The frets are of brass, and grooved in the middle, so as to retain the cat-gut belt which holds the fret to the handle, but admits of its being moved up and down to the position proper for the music to be performed. The frets are 16 in number, that is, prepared to produce on the first string two octaves; in compass a large instrument is sometimes made with twenty-one frets or three octaves. The *Sitár* has commonly five strings, but sometimes six. The first string, called *Madhyam*, is of thin steel wire, obtained from Delhi or Bareilly; the others are two of brass, and the third of steel wire. The three last are the drone, or accompanying, and always open, strings being tuned to the key-note, fifth or *panchama*, and the lower octave of the key note; if there are six strings, the key-note is doubled in unison; if seven, the third is given as well as the fifth, thus giving the whole chord.

Chargah Sitár is like the *Madhyam*, has four strings, and no frets, but permanent marks on the handle indicating the position of the fingering. *Tarabdár Sitár*, or sympathetic *Sitár*, has the handle slightly concave, and under the frets, and under the playing wires, a set of very thin steel wires are extended, tuned to the ascending notes of the gamut. The pegs which hold these strings are at the sides of the handle, those holding the playing strings at the head. The *tarb* of purely sympathetic strings, vibrating and producing a shrill twang in unison, and by sympathy with the corresponding note struck on the upper strings. The admirers of the sympathetic Pianoforte of modern times will perhaps be surprised to note so very ancient a recognition of the principle (Baden Powell).

Kinnari Víná.—The hollow of this instrument is, in some specimens, made of eggs, and in others of precious metals. In construction, tuning, &c., it resembles the *Kachchhapí Víná*, though smaller in size. This instrument was in former times used by women, and is said to be the origin of the *Kinor* of the Jews.

In Madras *Kinneri* consists of a wooden bar with the ends ornamented with griffins' heads, &c. Two gourds painted in floral patterns are fixed below the bar. The strings are of wire, two in number, and supported by a bridge. There are five frets for fingering. Length 3 feet 1 inch.

Mahati Víná.—This is the most classical, and perhaps the most difficult, of the musical instruments of the Hindus. Its invention is ascribed to the pious sage Nárada, who used it to accompany his hymns to the Deity. It consists of five main-wires and two side-wires, the latter being used for the purpose of giving an artistic accompaniment to the performance. This instrument is said to be the mother of several varieties of stringed instruments used in ancient and modern Europe. The instrument is popularly called in India the "*bin*," a corruption of the term "*víná*."

In the Madras Presidency the body of this instrument is hollowed out of fine old jackwood with belly of the same material, and is protracted into a long neck like that of a guitar, but has a gourd at the upper end fixed below to increase the sound. The strings are of wire, and seven in number. Four of them are mounted, as in the guitar, over a bridge and are furnished with a number of frets. Three of the strings run along the sides of the neck and have an arched bridge of metal; and the scroll is adorned with a golded griffin's head. Length of instrument 3 feet 6 inches, depth of body 9 inches, width 11¾ inches. (Bidie.)

In Upper India the *Bin* consists of a long hollow bar or keyboard, flat above, and concave below: on this the wires rest, and it is supported on either end by a large gourd. It is the best sounding of all the stringed instruments played by aid of the fingers and the *Mizráb* or the wire guard. It has six strings and moveable frets; the first string alone, which is played with the frets, called *Báj*, the other six strings are strung at some distance off the *Báj*, so as to have room for the play of the finger. The second and third are of steel wire, the fourth of brass, the fifth of steel, and the sixth of steel also, but with fine brass wire coil upon it. This string is called *Larz*. The *Bin* has also the sympathetic strings called *Tarb*, whose screws are on the side of the handle. They are nine in number, *i.e.*, eight notes of the gamut and one below: thus the second string of the upper set being tuned to middle C (*Sharaja*), the lowest note of the *tarb* will be B natural, corresponding to the second C above, and so up the scale. The *Bin* is frequently made of a very large size, with proportionately stout wires, and can then produce a loud sound: it is used more for instrumental music than accompanying the voice. It is not to be confused with a sort of *pipe* also called *Bin*. (Baden Powell.)

Nádeswara Víná.—A very modern instrument, being a combination of the *Kachchhapí víná* and the violin. The instrument is tuned and played upon like the *Kachchhapí*.

Shauktika Víná.—A variety of the *Kachchhapí Víná*. The hollow of the instrument is made of mother-o'-pearl.

Surbáhár.—This is an enlarged variety of the *Kachchhapí Víná*, devised about 60 years ago by Ghulám Muhammad Khán, a noted musician of Lucknow. The instrument is specially adapted for the playing of the *álápa*, *i.e.*, the expression of a melody in all its phases.

Tritantri Viná.—A variety of the *Kachchhapí Viná.* The hollow of the instrument is flat, and in some specimens made of wood.

Prasaraní Viná.—This is a modern instrument, constructed on the principle of the *Kachchhapí Viná,* but without side-wires and with a subsidiary finger-board. It is mounted with three wires, respectively tuned as the F, C, and G of the lower octave.

Sursringára.—This instrument is a mixture of the *Mahati, Kachchhapí,* and *Rudra viná,* devised by the celebrated *Bin*-player, Piyár Khán. The instrument is, like the *Rudra viná,* played against the shoulder of the player. It is mounted with six wires, and to its narrow end is attached a hollow gourd to increase the volume of sound produced.

Rudra Viná.—Now known as *rabáb* among Muhammadan musicians of Persia and Afghanistan, and *rubeb* among those of Arabia. It is mounted with six strings made of cat-gut, and is said to be the prototype of the mandoline, Spanish guitar, and other instruments of a similar construction. The instrument has no frets arranged over the finger-board. It is much used in Upper India.

Sarod.—An instrument much used by musicians of the North-Western Provinces of India. It was formerly used in out-door royal processions. Like the *Rudra viná,* it is mounted with cat-gut strings, which are, however, tuned on a different principle. Unlike the *Rudra viná,* it is mounted with side-wires, varying in number from seven to eleven.

Alábu Sárangi.—A very old instrument, called by some European writers on Hindu music the "Indian violin." The surface of the instrument is like that of the violin, and there is a hollow gourd under it.

The instrument is known among Muhammadan musicians as *Kamarchá.*

Mina Sárangi.—So called on account of the figure of a fish (*mina*) attached to the end of the hollow. In all other respects it resembles the *Esrár* or *tayús.* The back of this instrument ought to be made of one entire piece of gourd, but this being rare, a wooden back is frequently used.

Nádataranga.—This is a large stringed instrument, producing a deep bass sound, and used in the native orchestra. A modern instrument, constructed on the principle of the *Esrár*, of which it is merely a large variety, without the side-wires.

Sárangi.—This instrument is generally used to accompany dancing and light songs, and is peculiarly adapted to the female voice. The *Sárangi* is mounted with four cat-gut strings and side-wires of brass, the number of the latter varying at the will of the player. Rávana, the monster-king of Lanká (Ceylon), is said to have been the originator of instruments of this description.

"*Sárangi* is the common fiddle used by dancing girls. It has a thick short handle, almost as broad as the body, and is, like it, hollow. The body is also hollow and faced with parchment; it is chamfered, or pared away at the sides towards the middle. The strings are of cat-gut, four in number, and attached to screws with large knots fixed in the handle, two in front and two at the sides. There are also eleven or thirteen *Tarb,* or sympathetic strings, which are fixed to screws or pegs, arranged in two rows; these pass through the body of the handle and project at the side. The end of the wires are introduced through small holes in the surface. The sound of this instrument is very harsh and disagreeable." (Baden Powell.)

Sursanga.—The instrument is merely the *Esrár* without the side-wires. It is a modern invention, said to have been made by Sebarám Dás, of Bishnupur, in the district of Bánkurá, Bengal.

Swaraviná.—Popularly called the *Surbin.* The instrument is classical, and somewhat resembles the *Rudra viná* in appearance. The *Surbin* is mounted with four strings, and is capable of producing three octaves of sound.

Sarabath.—On the Madras side a stringed instrument is used, called *Sarabath.* It has a drum-like body, made of one piece of wood hollowed out. Though at first sight it appears cylindrical, " it is found to be traversed by two holes at the base of the neck, and to be cut so as to form thin wings or scrolls. The bottom of the drum-like body is closed with a thin piece of wood, and the belly with parchment. The neck emerges from the body in a deep bracket-like piece, and the actual neck from the nut to the upper fret is only about 8 inches long. The finger-board is inlaid with etched ivory, and the neck behind covered with bright, blue cloth with gilt figures on it. Viewed as a whole, the instrument has in shape some resemblance to the figure of a bird, more specially as the neck ends in the gilded head of a bird. There are six tuning pegs, and the same number of cat-gut strings, but four of them are closely arranged in pairs and could hardly be played except as pairs." This instrument appears to be a modified form of the next one, the *Táus* of Upper India.

Táus or Mayúri.—The instrument derives its name from the figure of a *Mayur* (peacock—Persian *Táus*) which is attached to the hollow. The addition of the figure constitutes its sole difference from the *Esrár.*

Mr. Baden Powell describes it as "a long-handled instrument, of which the body is in the form of a peacock, whence the name. The upper part of the body is covered with strained parchment, and the lower part highly coloured, gilt, and varnished to resemble a peacock. The handle, which is very long, is hollow, but faced with a thin slip of *Tún* wood. It carries 16 moveable brass frets. Along the left side of the key-board or handle a small bar of wood is attached, which carries 16 pegs, which hold 16 sympathetic steel rings (*Tarb*), which are arranged slightly diagonally, so as to come down to the bridge of the instrument, which supports the four main strings on the upper edge, and the 16 *tarb* strings through 16 small holes in the centre of it. The four strings are arranged as usual: one, alone at the right side, which is changed by fingering to produce the melody; the other three tuned to the key-note, fifth and octave form the bass or drone accompaniment; the four strings are made, the first three of steel, the fourth of brass wire. All are of equal length and attached to four large pegs, two in front, and two at the side of the extreme end of the handle, but as the second string produces a shriller tone than could be got by having the full length and tightening the screw, it is shortened by a small ivory peg through which it passes just below the fifth fret. The instrument, which I have heard played with considerable skill, is played with a bow fitted with a number of black horse hairs and stiffened with rosin; the hairs of the bow are not arranged flat as in an European violin bow, but in a bunch, with a piece of wood at one end, which can be adjusted to tighten the hairs. When once set right they are tied down with string, there being no screw arrangement as in the European bow."

Mahá Tumburá.—A large variety of the *tumburá*. Generally used in native orchestras.

Machanga.—A very classical instrument, somewhat resembling the head of a trident. The instrument has to be held with the teeth, by the left hand, while the wire is generally tapped with the forefinger of the right. Only one note is produced, the pitch of which can be regulated by the use of wax, or of a paste of flour over the wire.

In South India it is called *Morjung*. "It is an iron instrument identical with the Jew's harp, except that the tongue projects $1\frac{1}{2}$ inches behind, so as to give greater facility for holding it in the mouth. The French name of the instrument is *Trompe*, and the Scotch *Trump*, both evidently identical. The English name of Jew's harp is probably a corruption of the French *jeu-trompe*, or *joy-trumpe*. Although only a toy, yet it is capable-of wonderful musical performances, and various marvellous performers on it have from time to time appeared in Europe. Some of these used two or more instruments, 'each having a fundamental tone of its own, and consequently different harmonies.'" (Bidie.)

Tumburá or Tumbura Víná.—So called after the celestial musician Tumburá, who invented it. The instrument is at present mounted with four strings, which serve the purpose of an unvarying accompaniment to vocal music. The object of the *Tumburá* is mainly to indicate the key-note adopted. The instrument has been in use in various countries, in the east and west, from ancient timesu nder different names, and with varieties of construction and modes of tuning.

On the Madras side it is called *Thamburi.* "It is a sort of guitar. The body is semi-globular, made out of jackwood, and both it and the long neck are inlaid with ivory decorated with floral patterns, etched and filled in black and red pigment. Length 4 feet 4 inches, width 1 foot 2½ inches, depth of body 10½ inches. It has four wire strings, and the same number of tuning pegs, which are artistically shaped and adorned with ivory etched. The belly is convex, and the bridge of dark wood,. and to keep the strings clear of the sharp convexity behind the bridge, they are ingeniously passed through bone heads. Originally the body of *Thamburi* was a gourd, and the instrument has been used by the Egyptians and Abyssinians from remote times."

Ananda Lahari.—An instrument mostly used by singing-beggars. It consists of one cat-gut, the variety of sounds produced by which is due to the different degrees of tension to which it is subjected.

This is called *King* in Upper India, where it consists "of a single wire stretched over two small bridges resting on either end of a stick or bamboo, which passes through a small half gourd at either end, like our basket stick: the face of the gourd is left open." (Baden Powell.)

In South India this instrument is called *Thunthona*, and "may be regarded as in some measure a sort of *Trigonon*, with a small drum added to increase the resonance. It is chiefly used by beggars to accompany their recitations, and the pitch can be lowered or raised by means of the tuning peg." (Bidie.)

Sárindi.—A rude form of the Sárangí, and known to be an ancient instrument; now generally used by up-country people.

Ektárá.—Used exclusively by religious mendicants for accompanying pastoral songs. The instrument is mounted with one string. This and the following instrument are largely used by the Vaishnavas of Bengal, who go about villages singing songs.

Gopijantra.—Used exclusively by religious mendicants for accompanying pastoral songs. The instrument is mounted with one string, the different sounds being produced by the compression or otherwise of the fingers with which the lower part of the instrument is held. *Gopijantra* is a favouite musical instrument of the *Vaishnava* sect in Bengal, called the *Báuls*, who go about villages singing songs about the transitoriness of mundane happiness and urging the people to practice devotion for their future welfare.

Chártárá.—A four-stringed instrument, three of brass and one of steel. It is played with a wooden stick or plectrum, called *Java.*

Kanún—The psaltery, or a sort of harp. The strings, made of steel, are twenty-three in number, to include three octaves.

"They are fixed by moveable screws at the upper end. It differs from our harp in principle of construction, inasmuch as the strings which are fixed to the sounding board, are thence carried, not diagonally upwards to the curved upper beam, but horizontally to a beam opposite the sounding board. There are 28 strings."

Tid or *Tad.*—A rude instrument made of *Deodár* (*Cedrus deodara*) wood. It has four strings and is played with a bow. Chiefly used in the Panjáb.

Dotárá.—A two-stringed instrument like the *Chártárá*, but possesses a thicker and shorter handle.

Chikárá, a fiddle, used by mendicants in the Panjáb. It has three strings, made of bunches of black horse hair, and there are five sympathetic strings.

Kamánchi, a large fiddle, mostly in use among the Kashmiris.

Wind Instruments.

Bánsi.—The Indian flute, made of bamboo wood. The invention of the instrument is ascribed to the Hindu Deity Krishna, who is said to have been very fond of it. It is called *Pullangolal* in South India.

Sarala Bánsi.—The Indian flageolet. The instrument has to be held straight before the mouth when played upon.

Laya Bánsi.—Like the *Sarala Bánsi* the instrument has to be held straight before the mouth, but it has to be blown into from one extremity of the lips.

Alghoza, a sort of flageolet made of bamboo, and slightly shaped like a funnel. Used in the Panjáb.

Nairi.—A sort of clarionet, made of wood, very much like the *Surna* of the Panjáb and South India. Used in Kashmir.

Benu.—The Benu is a popular instrument with the people of Orissa. A classical instrument, about 4 feet 6 inches in length, and made of bamboo wood.

Kalama.—So called, because of its likeness to the *kalam* (pen).

Alkuja.—A whistle made of bamboo, used in South India.

Magavine.—A small oboe-like instrument, made of hard wood, used in South India. The reed in this, as in most other reed instruments, is usually made out of the pointed end of the flowering spathe of the cocoa-palm, and is therefore thick and stiff and harsh in tone compared with reeds made from cane. Sometimes, both in the north and south, sections of the leaf of Palmyra palm are used in making reeds. The *magavine* has eight finger-holes in front, all of the same size, and one behind. The upper end is made in a way that leads me to suppose that some mouth-piece originally belonged to it, and the lower end is ivory mounted. (Bidie.)

Karna.—A large instrument like an oboe, used in South India. It is made out of one piece of black wood, and without the usual metal bell. Like the above, it has eight finger-holes in front and one behind, and the reed is made of palmyra leaf. The length of the instrument is 18 inches, and the diameter of the bell-mouth 4 inches.

Nagasarum.—A South India oboe-like instrument, made of black wood, and brass-mounted. The upper end, which carries the reed, is made of brass, and the reed is made from the spathe of the palm; length 22 inches. The bell is made of brass, turned, and is 3½ inches wide. There are eight finger-holes in front, and two more near the lower end of the tubes on each side.

Surna.—Another variety of South Indian oboe, with seven finger-holes in front, and one behind. It is made of one piece of black wood, and is 11¾ inches long and 3 inches wide at the lower end; reed made of palmyra leaf. Also found in the Panjáb.

Panchama-oththu.—A South Indian instrument, consisting of a wooden tube covered with leather and with brass mountings; bell with etched figures; Length 13¼ inches, diameter of bell 3½ inches. Reed made of palm spathe. There is only one finger-hole, and the instrument is used as a drone.

Oththu or Sutho.—A wooden tube covered with leather, with only one finger-hole, and brass mounted. Length 1 foot 10½ inches, diameter of brass bell 3¾ inches. Reed made of palm spathe, used as a drone. (Bidie.)

Shánáyi.—As played in the *Nahabat*. The *Nahabat* is an Indian brass band played on festive occasions and marriage processions. The musicians are invariably made to sit on an elevated position, generally over gates or triumphal arches, &c. This band had its origin in the Muhammadan period, and is still in use. The Shánáyi, called *Sharná* in Persian, is said to have been a favourite instrument with the Mughul Emperor Akbar Sháh.

Thiruchinnam.—A thin brass trumpet used in South India.

Kombu.—An "S"-shaped brass trumpet, resembling in shape the ancient Scandinavian horn, and is used on various ceremonious occasions.

Sringa.—The Indian horn. The instrument is said to have been a favourite of the Hindu deity, Siva.

Rana Sringa.—An instrument formerly used in military bands. It is now used in religious processions.

Turi.—The Indian trumpet; used on occasions of war, and also with the *Nahabat.*

Sharnao.—A bag-pipe, or set of pipes, fitted with an inflated goat skin; used in the western hills of the Panjáb.

Thuththi.—A rude kind of bag-pipe used in South India. The bag is made of a small goat's skin, the blow-pipe being inserted in the place of one foreleg, and the chanter in room of the other. The other natural openings of the skin are closed by internal ligatures.

"Instruments of the nature of a bag-pipe are of very ancient date and very widely diffused, having been used by the Hebrews, Greeks, Romans, Arabs, Persians and Hindus, and by most Celtic and Slavonic races. To the ancient Romans it was known as *Tibia utricularis*, and is said to have been a favourite instrument with Nero. Forms of it are still known and used in Italy, France, Germany, Russia, and Poland, and in the eastern countries already specified. It was also at one time a popular instrument in Lincolnshire and Northumberland. It is alluded to by Chaucer, and Shakespeare mentions it on several occasions, as in Henry IV, Part I. It has long been cultivated in Ireland, and the drones in the Irish pipe are furnished with keys. It is the national instrument of the Highlands of Scotland, and its music has cheered the Highlander on to victory in every field on which British bravery has been conspicuous. It was the duty of the Highland piper in the field to cheer the clansmen on the march, to lead the van into battle, to alarm them when in danger, to collect them when scattered, to recall the heroism of their ancestors, and to incite them by passionate strains to imitate their example. In peace, the bag-pipe cheered the festive board, gave life and merriment to the wedding, and at death poured out the wild wailing notes of the coronach as the body was carried to the grave. The Hindu instrument is a very barbarous one, and capable of playing only in few notes. The reed is made of a piece of cane with a vibrating tongue cut on one side, and there are five holes in the chanter, some of which are partially closed with wax." (Bidie.)

Sankha.—A very ancient instrument made of conch shell, formerly used on warlike, festive, and religious occasions, now only on the latter. It is blown through a small hole made at the spiral end. This instrument might, not inappropriately, be called the father of wind instruments. In days of yore, *Sankhas* of various descriptions were in use, such as the *Páncha-janya* (used by Krishna), *Devadatta* (used by Arjuna), &c. The *Sankha* is also used in Buddhist temples. The instrument is sometimes called by Europeans the "conch trumpet." In some shells the spiral end is encased in brass, which has a mouth-piece like a trumpet. The other end of the shell is also brass-mounted, and has a large floral expansion, in shape something like the tail of a mythical bird often seen on temples.

Gomukha.—Another kind of conch, somewhat resembling the mouth of the cow, whence it derives its name.

Barataka.—A large-sized conch, made of the *kauri* shell.

Tubri.—Called Tiktiri in Sanskrit, and *Bin* in Upper India. A rude instrument with double tubes used by snake charmers.

It is called *Majidi* in South India, and consists of a bottle-gourd with a blow-pipe at the smaller end, and thin flagelot-like tubes inserted into the bulbous end. The lower ends of the tubes all open into one brass bell. The centre tube has nine finger-holes in front, the three lower of which are shut with wax. The tube to the right has no finger-holes. Inside the gourd there is a reed for each tube, made by cutting a vibrating tongue in a kind of grass or reed. The centre tube is the chanter, or performing tube, and the side ones drones, which are tuned to the chanter by means of the wax-stopping in the finger-holes. The parts of the instruments are fastened together by means of a black wax. (Bidie.)

Instruments of Percussion.

Mandirá.—The sound of this instrument is produced by two cups made of bell-metal, striking against each other. The *Mandirá* is used to measure out the time in a musical performance. It is called *Jora* or *Kainai* in Upper India.

Khattáli.—The castanets of the Hindus. The instrument consists of two steel bars. Large cymbals are called *China* or *Jhani* in Upper India.

Ghantá.—A ringing bell used at the time of worship.

Talli.—A small bell, worn round the neck.

Mridanga.—A drum, an ancient instrument, said to have been invented by the Hindu Deity Brahmá.

The *Mridanga* is intended to accompany classical forms of songs and hymns. It is sometimes played with the *Mahati Viná, Rudra Viná*, &c., &c.

Pakhwáj.—A large barrel-shaped drum, but much more elongated. The parchment ends are therefore smaller in diameter.

Dholaka.—The *Dholaka* is generally used to accompany songs sung in operatic and other performances.

Bányá and Tablá.—The *Bányá* is played upon with the left hand, and the *Tablá* (sometimes called the *Dáhiná*) with the right. This pair is a modern invention, the idea being taken from the *Mridanga*, the left end of which is represented by the *Bányá*, and the right end by the *Tablá*.

Dhák.—A large drum formerly known as *Dhakká*, and used in the war field, but now the instrument is used on occasions of religious festivities, such as the

Durgá Pujá, *Charak Pujá*, &c. The right hand side of the instrument is played upon with two sticks, the left hand side is not touched at all.

Dhol.—A large drum, but smaller than the *Dhák*. It is struck with sticks, used, like above, in ceremonies and festivals. It is called *Thaval* in South India.

Nakárá.—A kettle-drum.

Dhausse.—A military kettle-drum carried on horse back.

Naubat.—A very large kettle drum carried on camel's back in Upper India.

Pombai.—Of South India, consists of two oblong shaped drums lashed together. One is played by beating with the fingers, and the other by rubbing a stick covered with leather laced with rope.

Gonthalam.—Of South India, consists of a pair of kettle-drums turned in the shape of flower-pot out of the trunk of a tree.

Gidikatti.—A pair of miniature kettle-drums like the above.

Udukkai.—A brass hour-glass-shaped drum, covered with bladders and laced with twine, used in religious ceremonies. A smaller sort is used by jugglers and men with performing monkeys.

A similar instrument is called *Dug-dugi* in Bengal, and *Mandil* in Upper India. It is a barrel-shaped drum of turned wood.

Khol.—Chiefly used to accompany the *Kirtana* and other religious songs.

Dindimi.—A smaller variety of the *Khanjani*.

Jhanjh, Khanjani.—The instrument is supplied with two small cymbals, which make a jingling sound when it is struck upon. Called *Khanjni* in Upper India, and *Kanjir* in South India.

Táshá.—A tambourine, consisting of a sort of basin of pottery-ware, covered with goat-skin, and played with sticks. It is worn suspended from the neck of the performer.

Dairá.—A large tambourine without bells.

Dáf.—A sort of tambourine used by low-caste people. It is a circular wooden frame, the front being covered with parchment, and the back by a net-work of cat-gut or goat-gut, leaving a round hole in the centre.

Daurá.—A small drum used by labourers and itinerant showmen.

Tumkanári.—A drum used by the Kashmiris. "It consists of an earthen pot, narrow at the bottom and wide at the mouth, shaped in fact like a flower-pot; the mouth is closed with parchment or skin, and the instrument is held under the left arm, and drummed on with the right hand." (Baden Powell.)

Nyastaranga.—The *Nyastaranga,* a trumpet-shaped instrument, has to be placed upon the vocal chords, sounds from which produce by vibration a clear reedy note upon the instrument. It is believed that an instrument of this description is scarcely to be met with in any other part of the world than India. It is known in Sanskrit as the "*Upánga,*" and is extensively used by Hindus in the North-Western Provinces, and particularly at Muttra and Brindában.

Jaltaranga.—A number of porcelain cups of different sizes, more or less filled with water, according to the sound required. The cups are then touched with a stick, and in this way two or three octaves are produced.

Kartál.—Two pieces of hard wood, played like the "bones" of the Negro singers. It is called *Tikri* in South India.

Santur.—A steel triangle, similar to that used in Europe in bands.

IV.—Jewellery and Personal Ornaments.

Indian women being as fond of jewellery as their sisters in other parts of the globe, the maker of gold, silver, and brass ornaments has been an important member of the village commune from time immemorial. The dress of native women, which leaves a larger part of the body bare than in colder climates, admits of an elaborate personal adornment by means of ornaments. Want of pecuniary means does not stand in the way of satisfying this vanity, for ornaments are made of all sorts of materials, from the cheapest bangles made of lac, glass, or brass, to the most valuable gold necklaces, thickly studded with pearls and diamonds; and thus the wearer has before her a large assortment from which to choose, according to the means at her command. Although the love of personal adornment has been in some cases carried to an absurd length,—so that it is often painful to one unaccustomed to such sights to behold a peasant woman labouring in the field loaded with a heavy weight of bangles and anklets, made of solid brass, without any pretension to being artistic or ornamental,—still some of the cheap trinkets are so well made as to deserve to be classed within the domain of art. The Indian workman displays his good taste, which seems to be inherent in his nature, wherever he has a chance of doing so. He cannot cut or chase ornamental designs on hard bell-metal articles without raising the price to a point beyond the means of the class for whom they are intended; but he is free to exercise his ingenuity on the softer lac, and, indeed, bangles made of this material in many places display great taste in the combination of colours and tinsels. As want of decoration and finish in the brass ornaments is due to the stern necessity of making them cheap, there is other reason why Indian gold and silver ornaments often lack that neatness of execution which is a characteristic feature in European articles of a similar description. To lay by some money as a provision for a bad day is perhaps a more cogent object with the head of a family in possessing gold or silver ornaments than personal adornment. Hence massive solid articles of soft pure gold are preferred to flimsy ornaments made of hard alloyed gold but of superior workmanship. An Indian seldom purchases gold or silver ornaments, but he orders the goldsmith to make these for him from gold or silver which he supplies himself, the wages of the maker being paid at the time-honoured fixed rate on the weight of the metal used. Such a system does not encourage superior workmanship. But still Indian jewellery is not devoid of art or of delicacy of finish. Mr. Maskelyne in his Report on jewellery in the French Exhibition of 1866 remarked:—

"It is said that even that delicate and most sensitive instrument of touch, the hand of the Hindu, is not sufficiently sensitive for fashioning the finest sorts of Indian filigree, and that children alone are employed in the manipulation of such a spider-web of wire. Of fabrics so delicate, nothing is to be seen among the jewellery at Paris,—indeed the best of the Indian filigree, and that by no means worthy of its source, is to be found among the articles exhibited under the goldsmith's class. It is to be remarked of this elegant and primitive—perhaps very earliest—form of ornament in precious metal, that it had probably reached its limits for delicacy and design at a very archaic period, and has made no real progress in recent times; that, in fact, the early Greek filigrainer worked with as much facility and delicacy as the Hindu artisan of our day, who inherits the skill and the methods he uses by the direct descent of an immemorial tradition. But there are other forms of the goldsmith's art scarcely less venerable than that of the filigrains, possessed of great native beauty, and which also have survived in India, through the long roll of centuries, as the Zend and

Sanskrit languages have survived there, the inheritance of families or clans. Those forms of art are perishing one by one: as the family in whom it may have been handed down becomes extinct or lets the thread be broken, each of these hereditary industries of India moves on with time to its extinction."

We have in India the most primitive methods of personal adornment in the wild aboriginal races as well as its highest development among the more civilised Hindus and Muhammadans. Bones of animals, tusks of wild boar, plumage of birds, shells, and seeds of gaudy colours still afford an endless supply of personal ornaments to the savage tribes of the Indian forests, while on the other hand the skilful *Murassiá-kár* set with unrivalled ingenuity precious stones on massive golden jewellery for the use of the high and the rich. Old books and old statues shew that costly ornaments were in use in India from prehistoric times. *Rig-Veda,* the oldest book in the world, mentions ornaments worn by the gods. Rudra, a Vedic deity, is described as "shining with brilliant gold ornaments" and wearing "an adorable, uniform necklace." The demons described in the same book had plenty of "gold and jewels," and kings and sages prayed to the gods for valuables of that kind. Kakshivat, the sage, prayed for a son "decorated with golden earrings and jewel necklace." This was many thousand years before Christ. But the discovery and introduction of gold, silver, and other shining metals did not altogether throw into disuse the ornaments of a primitive age. Up to a very recent date no Hindu wife would consider herself pure unless she had on her wrists bracelets made of conch-shells. A brief religious ceremony was always performed to welcome this valuable ornament before it was actually put on. The shell bracelet was respectfully put on a plate, and an offering was made to it of vermillion, green blades of grass, and rice, and food was given to the man who brought it for sale. Shell-bracelet was a favourite ornament of the great Goddess of Energy. A song is recited by religious mendicants in villages describing a family quarrel between her and her husband, the ascetic deity presiding over Destruction, who once, owing to his poverty, could not afford to satisfy the wish of his wife to have a new set of shell-bracelets! An iron bracelet has also come down to us from our mothers of the pre-historic age. Every wife is bound to wear this on her left wrist on pain of bringing ill-luck to her husband. She puts it off only on the death of her husband. Rich people now encase this iron bracelet in gold.

Ancient Ornaments.

Old Sanskrit books describe the following ornaments worn by the Hindus in ancient times:—

Ornaments for the Head.

The arrangement of hair was an object of great solicitude in ancient India, and Dr. Rájendra Lála Mitra has given a very interesting account of it in his book entitled "The Indo-Aryans." To decorate the head and the hair first with feathers of birds and garlands of flowers, and then with ornaments made of shining metals, was a natural outcome of that passion for artificial embellishment inherent in the female constitution. Pearls and gold chains and crowns, coronets and tiaras were used from remote times, and such ornaments were known by the following names—

Málya.—A gold garland in imitation of that in flower.

Garbhak.—There is now a difference of opinion about the nature of this ornament. According to some it was merely a golden hair-pin, according to others a sort of chain to tie up the hair.

Lalámak.—A sort of wreath, made of three rows of gold leaves, with a star in the centre studded with gems. Precious stones were set on the two sides, and it had a fringe of pearls.

Apir.—A wreath worn where the hair is parted.

Bálapásyá.—A string of pearls twisted round the hair.

Pári-tathyá.—Called *Sinthi* at the present time; made of gold and studded with precious stones; worn where the hair is parted, with pendants hanging on the forehead.

Hansa-tilak.—A golden imitation of the leaf of the *Pipal* tree (*Ficus religiosa*), often studded with gems, worn just above the forehead.

Dandak.—Shaped like a bracelet, made of beaten gold leaf twisted round. Sometimes pearls were set upon it. It gave out a jingling sound when shaken.

Churá-mandan.—A gold ornament made in imitation of the lotus leaf (*Nelumbiun speciosum*). It was worn just above the last-named ornament.

Churiká.—Made of gold in imitation of a lotus flower; it was worn behind the head.

Lamban.—This was an assemblage of tiny gold flowers which hung from the head behind. Its present name is *Jhálá.* Pearls were attached on each side of the gold flowers, and emeralds and other precious stones were put in the middle.

Mukut.—Crown, formerly worn only by kings and queens. Precious stones were profusely inlaid in it. Brilliant feathers of birds were often attached on the top. A modified form of it has now been introduced in Bengal. It is made of gold.

Ornaments for the Ear.

Muktá-kantak.—A string of pearls joined together by a very thin wire of gold. It is still in use in many parts of the country.

Dwirájik.—A gold ring with pearls on each side and a precious stone in the middle. Its present name is *Birbauli.*

Trirájik.—Like the above, but it had pearls in the middle.

Swarna-madhya.—Like the above, with golden ornamentation in the centre.

Bajra-garbha.—An earring with a diamond in the centre, with pearls on the sides, and precious stones hanging between the pearls. It is called *gimdá* at the present day.

Bhuri-mandal.—Like the above, with pearls on each side, and diamonds between the pearls.

Kundal.—Made of gold, terraced like a flight of stairs, and inlaid with diamonds. Very much worn by the ancients; still in use in Upper India, and worn both by men and women.

Karnapur.—A flower-shaped earring. Varieties of it known by the names of *Karnaphul*, *Champá*, *Jhumká*, *Jhámpá*, &c., are now in use.

Karniká.—Also called *Tálpatra, Tárpatra*, or *Tálbar*, an ornament in imitation of palm leaf (*Borassus flabelliformis*). It is not now in use; but palm leaf covered with lac is still worn on the ear.

Srinkhal.—Literally a chain, generally made of gold. Still worn in Upper India.

Karnendu.—Or the "moon of the ear," worn on the back of the ear.

Lalátiká or *Patra-páshyá.*—A small plate made of gold, jewelled in the centre. Until recently it was in use in Bengal and was known by the name of *Páshá.*

Necklaces.

Prálambiká.—A long necklace hanging down to the navel.

Urahsutriká.—A pearl necklace hanging down to the navel.

Devachchhanda.—A pearl necklace of one hundred strings.

Guchchha.—A pearl necklace of thirty-two strings.

Guchchhárdha.—A pearl necklace of twenty-four strings.

Gostan.—A pearl necklace of four strings.

Ardha-hár.—A pearl necklace of twelve strings.

Mánavak.—A pearl necklace of twenty strings.

Ekávali.—A pearl necklace of one string.

Nakshatra-málá, literally a "chain of stars." A pearl necklace of one string of 27 pearls.

Bhrámar.—A one-stringed necklace of large pearls.

Nil-lavaniká.—A pearl necklace of five, seven, or nine strings, with sapphire pendants.

Varnasar.—A pearl necklace of five, seven, or nine strings, with diamonds in addition.

Sariká.—A necklace of nine or ten pearls fitting close to the neck.

Bajra-sankaliká.—A necklace of nine or ten pearls with a sapphire tassèl at the back.

Baikakshik.—A necklace that hangs from the neck in a curved way like the sacred thread of a Bráhman.

Padak.—Amulets of various shapes; gold, or gold and jewelled. If suspended from the neck by a golden thread it is then called *Bandhuk.* Still in use in all parts of the country.

Arm Ornaments.

Keyur.—An armlet, with the head of lion or other animals; jewelled; something like the *Bázuband* of the present day. If without tassel, it was called *Angad.*

Panchaká.—Beads of different shapes stringed together into an amulet. Its present name is *Poinchi* or *Ponchi.*

Katak.—A square jewelled gold amulet.

Bracelets.

Balaya.—A bracelet still used all over the country.

Chur.—A flattened bracelet made of gold wire. Still largely in use.

Ardhachur.—Bracelet of less width than the above; still worn.

Kankan.—Serrated bracelet; still in use.

Finger Rings.

Finger rings were used in India from very ancient times. The Bráhmans of old, who lived in the forest and were very poor, used to wear rings made of *Kusa* grass (*Saccharum spontaneum*). This practice has come down to the present day, for similar rings are still worn when any religious ceremony has to be performed: otherwise the water offered to the gods or to the manes of ancestors will not be accepted. The Bráhmans of Bengal still wear on the fourth finger a ring made of a mixture of eight metals. The Hindu law prescribes a gold ring for the index finger and a silver ring for the fourth finger. Rings are mentioned in various old books. In the *Mahábhárata* it is mentioned in connection with Drona's introduction into the royal family of Hastinápur, near Delhi. The story runs as follows:—

Drona was a poor Bráhman, who had a son, whom he sent to a school where boys belonging to wealthier families also received their education. After school hours the boys used to play and talk of the various delicacies they ate at home. One day the wealthier boys mentioned milk, which Drona's son never heard of; for his father was a sage and they all lived on fruits and vegetables. He ran home and asked his mother for milk, and not getting it, he began to cry. Drona's wife in order to pacify the child macerated some rice in water, which she gave him to drink, saying that was milk. Rejoiced, Drona's son next day went to school and triumphantly told his playmates that he had tasted milk. "Where did you get it, your father has no cows, nor money to buy it?" enquired the boys. "Oh, my mother made it at home!" said Drona's son. Then on further cross-examination it was found out that he had no real milk. The boys then clapped their hands and laughed, upon which he returned home and cried bitterly for the humiliation he experienced at school. This went to Drona's heart, and he made up his mind to go to the king of Panchála for some cows. Now, this king was his schoolmate and his great friend, who once promised to give him half his dominions. Now, however, he would not even know him, and on Drona's insisting on his being his friend, he ill-treated him and turned him out of the palace. Droṇa then meditated revenge, and he thought this could be best accomplished if he succeeded in making the rulers of Hastinápur espouse his cause. So to Hastinápur he went, and sat near a well sad and silent. By some lucky chance the princes of the royal family came playing there, and in order to ingratiate himself into their good graces, Drona amused them by throwing his ring into the deep well and taking it out again by some method described as the *Ishiká*. He then told the boys to go home and tell their guardians what he had done. This led to Drona's being appointed tutor to the princes, and since that time his boy had plenty of real cow's milk. When the princes grew up, they declared war against the king of Panchála, whom they defeated and severely punished for insulting their master and a Bráhman.

Mention of engraved finger-rings is also made in the *Rámáyana*. Sitá, the wife of Ráma, prince of Oudh, was abducted by Rávana, the ten-headed giant of Ceylon. Ráma sent Hanumán, a monkey, to search for her. When Hanumán arrived at Ceylon he introduced himself to Sitá by saying, "Madam, I am the messenger of Ráma. Look, here is his ring engraved with his name." It is also mentioned in *Sakuntalá*, the drama previously mentioned. The following are the different kinds of rings mentioned in Sanskrit books :—

Dwi-hirak.—Rings with a diamond on each side and sapphire in the centre.

Vajra.—A triangular finger ornament, with a diamond in the centre and other stones on the sides.

Ravimandal.—A ring with diamonds on the sides and other stones in the middle.

Nandyávartta.—A four-sided finger ornament studded with precious stones.

Nava-ratna or *Navagraha.*—A ring on which the nine most precious stones have been set. The nine precious stones in Sanskrit are called :—*Hirak, Mánikya, Baiduryya, Muktá, Gomed, Bidrum* or *Prabál, Marakata, Pushpa-rág,* and *Indranil ;* or the Diamond, Ruby, Cat's-eye, Pearl, Zircon, Coral, Emerald, Topaz, and Sapphire.

Bajra-beshtak.—Ring of which the upper circumference is set with diamonds.

Trihirak.—Ring with two small diamonds on the sides and a big one in the centre.

Sukti-mudriká.—Ring made like the hood of a cobra snake, with diamonds and precious stones on the upper surface.

Mudrá or *Anguli-mudrá.*—Ring with name engraved upon it.

Ornaments for the Waist.

Kánchi.—A single gold chain.

Mekhalá.—Gold chain of eight strings.

Rasaná.—A clasp of 16 chains joined together on one end.

Kaláp.—Ditto of 25 chains.

Kánchidám.—A gold band, four fingers wide, with tassels and clinks.

Anklets and Ornaments for the feet.

Pádachur.—A hoop made of gold, with precious stones.

Páda-kantak.—Four-sided three-ribbed gold band with grains inside for clinking.

Páda-padma.—An ornament of three or five golden chains, often studded with jewels. It is now made of silver and known by the name of *Charan-cháp* or *Charan-padma.*

Kinkini.—Anklet made of gold, with grains inside, which clinks. Now known by the name of *Ghungur.*

Mudriká.—Made of gold, coloured red. It also clinked.

Nupur.—Small bells stringed together with grains inside. It surrounded the feet on all sides. Now only worn by dancing girls, and made of inferior metals.

Modern Ornaments.

As stated before, ornaments are very largely worn by women all over the country. Almost all the gold that is annually imported into the country and a large portion of the silver are used up for the manufacture of such ornaments. In India, both gold and silversmith's work is done by the same class of people, known by the caste name of *Swarnakár*, *Sonár* or *Sekerá*, *i.e.*, worker in gold. Such work was until recently the monopoly of this caste, but of late many blacksmiths, cultivators, and other castes have adopted it as their trade. Neither of the two men sent to the Glasgow International Exhibition is a goldsmith by caste. One, the "chaser," belongs to the cultivating caste of Bengal; the other, the "maker of shapes," is a writer by caste, but being born deaf and dumb, his guardians thought fit to put him as an apprentice under a goldsmith. As a result of European civilisation, lucrative professions, which from time immemorial were set aside for different castes, are now being invaded by other castes, and trade, which hitherto formed a definite land-mark in the caste system of India, will be no longer so in a short time. Any such breach of caste rules was met with severe punishment fifty years ago. Nevertheless the caste-system will exist in India for a long time to come, so far at least as religion, marriage, and other social ceremonies are concerned.

Four sub-divisions of labour have taken place in the jeweller's work:—(1) The *Swarnakár or Sonár*, who hammers down the metal into a plain form, or casts it in a die, or beats into shape in a cold mould. If it is to be ornamented with patterns, then it goes to (2) *Nakáshi-wálá* or *Chaterá*, *i.e.*, embosser or chaser. If jewels are to be set, then it goes to (3) *Murassiákár* or *Kundansáz*. If it is to be enamelled, it goes to (4) *Minákár*. Of late another trade has sprung up—that of "diamond-cutting." Almost every large village has its *Sonár*, who makes plain ornaments, but the *Nakáshi-wálás* live only in towns. Sellers of precious stones formerly lived only in the old capital towns, like Delhi and Lucknow, but now they have opened shops in Bombay and Calcutta. Enamellers are still few in number, Jaipur being the only place noted for its enamelled jewellery.

Bengal Ornaments.

The following is a list of the ornaments at present worn by the women in Bengal:—

Ornaments for the head.

Sinthi.—A long gold chain put on the middle of the head where the hair is parted until it reaches the brow, where it ends in a jewelled pendant. Two other chains issue from the point just above the pendant, run along the border of the hair above the forehead, and terminate on each side behind the ear. These minor chains have smaller pendants or pearl tassels.

Jinjir.—Gold or silver chain to wrap round the hair. Gold, silver, or silk lace is often used for this purpose.

Kántá.—Hair-pins; sometimes simply gold or silver sticks, but often topped with gold or silver flowers, butterflies, &c. These are known by various names, such as *Nakskatra-phul* or the star flower, *Pánkátá* or the betel-leaf pin, &c.

Chiruni.—A comb made of gold worn on the head as an ornament.

Ornaments for the Nose.

Nose ornaments do not appear to have been in fashion in ancient times, for no mention is made of them in the old books, nor it is known since when they came into use. It is now going out of fashion in

Bengal. The following nose ornaments are still worn more or less in many parts of the Province:—

Nath.—A large gold ring with pearls and stones, worn on the left side of the nose.

Nákchhábi.—A stud worn on the left side of the nose.

Mákri.—A thinner and smaller ring, worn either on the left side or through the cartilage of the nose.

Besar.—This is made in different ways, but it is generally a flat piece of gold shaped like a half moon. It is hung from the cartilage of the nose.

Nolok.—A small gold ring with a oval reddish pearl. It is hung from the cartilage of the nose, and is a favourite ornament with young girls.

The cartilage of the nose is pierced when the girls are very young, only a few months old. The nose of male and female infants of mothers whose children do not live is pierced when only a few days old, into which an iron, silver, or gold ring is inserted. This is said to have the effect of preserving the child from early death. The idea is probably taken from the practice of putting a string through the nose cartilage of bullocks in order to keep them under sufficient control.

Ornaments for the Ear.

Dhenri.—An ornamented gold stud worn on the lobe of the ear.

Mákri.—Rings worn all over the ear.

Mách.—A fish-shaped ornament sometimes attached to the above.

Páshá.—A flat circular piece of gold, ornamented, worn through the lobe of the ear.

Jhumká.—A flower-shaped ear-ring, made in imitation of an *Abutilon* flower.

Karnaphul.—Literally the "flower of the ear"; as the name implies, a flower-shaped ornament worn through the lobe of the ear.

Kánbálá.—An ear-ring with pearl pendants worn on the upper part of the ear.

Kán.—A gold ornament shaped like the ear itself, on which rings are attached. It is worn covering the ear.

Birbauli.—A broad ear-ring with studs.

Chaudáni.—A large ear-ring.

Pipulpátá.—An ear-ornament shaped like the leaf of *Ficus religiosa.*

Dul.—An ear-ring with a long pendant of some kind of precious stone. Similar ear-rings are now imported from Europe with glass pendants of different colours.

Champá.—An ear-ornament shaped like the flower of *Champá* (*Michelia champaka*).

There are many other ornaments for the ear. Ear ornaments are getting out of fashion in Bengal, for they make a hole in the ear lobe which is not liked nowadays; only the lighter kinds are sometimes used. Formerly Bráhman lads used to wear for a short time a gold ear-ring after the "ear-piercing" (*Karnabedh*) ceremony, but now even this is seldom done.

Necklaces.

Kanthmálá.—A necklace made of elongated gold beads.

Mohan-málá.—A necklace of gold beads, embossed.

Pánch-nali.—Necklace of five strings of small gold beads.

Sát-nali.—Necklace of seven strings.

Dáná.—Necklace of one string of larger beads.

Matarmálá.—Necklace of gold beads shaped like peas.

Hár.—Necklace of various patterns, such as *Tárá-hár* (star-pattern); *Hele-hár* (snake-pattern); *Kám-rángá-hár* (in imitation of the ribbed fruit of *Averroha bilimbi*); *Dará-hár*, (rope pattern); *Got-hár* (chain-pattern).

Champákali.—Literally "buds of *champá*" (*Michelia champaka*). A series of golden buds strung into a necklace.

Chik.—A broad diamond-cut necklace that sits tight on the throat.

Hánsuli.—A gold collar. The *Hassi* of up-country.

The other ornaments for the neck are similar to those used in Upper India, of which a list has been given in a subsequent page.

Armlets and Bracelets.

Mardáná.—An ornament made of gold beads strung together, worn above the wrist.

Jabdáná.—Literally "Barley grain." Bracelet of beads made like barley.

Chál-dáná.—Literally "Rice grain." Bracelet of beads made like rice.

Murkimáduli.—Bracelet made of gold beads shaped like parched rice covered with unrefined sugar, as sold in the bazar.

Palákánti.—Bracelet made of coral and gold beads strung in alternation.

Churi.—Bracelet made of gold wire. A highly wrought ornament.

Misri.—Bangles, with ornaments like the crystals of sugarcandy.

Ratan-chur.—A highly wrought gold plate, which is placed on the upper side of the palm, attached by five gold chains to the five gold rings on the fingers.

Báuti.—A solid bracelet with patterns, made of gold, silver, and baser metals; now going out of fashion.

Báunri.—A kind of bracelet.

Poinchi.—The *Ponchi* of Upper India; bracelet made of gold beads. Formerly also made of silver and baser metals.

Khoye-no.—Bracelet made of silver, consisting of beads shaped like parched rice.

Bálá.—This kind of bracelet is the most important of all the bracelets worn in Bengal. It is made of gold, silver, and baser metals and is worn by all classes of the people. It is often jewelled or enamelled. Heads of tigers, alligators, and other animals are often made at each end of the bracelet.

Ananta.—A golden hoop, embossed, worn on the arm.

Tágá.—Ditto, plain.

Kankan.—A thin kind of bangles, generally made of silver. This has found favour among Europeans.

Damdam.—A twisted form of thin bracelet.

Labanga-phul.—A bracelet made of gold beads shaped like cloves.

Nárikel-phul.—A bracelet made of gold beads shaped like the flower of the cocoanut palm.

Karpadma.—Literally the "Lotus of the hand," an ornament for the palm.

Gajná.—A flexible bracelet like that used in Upper India.

Ras-no.—A flexible bracelet like that used in Upper India.

Tár.—A hoop made of gold, worn on the arm, chiefly by children.

Báju.—A flattened amulet for the arm, of various shapes, often ornamented and studded with jewels.

Hátmáduli.—A drum-shaped amulet to contain charms and medicines, worn on the arm. Also worn by men.

Táwiz.—Originally an amulet; but now a highly wrought ornament, made of pieces of gold of a zigzag shape.

Jasham.—An armlet made of a number of drum-shaped amulets strung together.

Waist Ornaments.

Chandra-hár.—Made of gold or silver chains, with a moon-like tablet in the middle. It is worn as a necklace in Upper India.

Surya-hár.—A modified form of the above.

Got.—A thick chain made of gold or silver.

Chábi-chhikli.—A thin chain for keys.

Biche.—A chain made like a centepede.

Byáng.—A waist ornament of gold or silver beads shaped like a frog. Worn by children.

Batphal.—Waist ornament for children of beads shaped like the fruit of *Ficus indica.*

Nimphal.—Waist ornament for children of beads shaped like the fruit of *Nim* (*Melia Azadirachta*).

Bor.—Waist ornament for children, of round shaped beads.

Komorpátá.—Waist ornament for children of zig-zag shaped pieces of gold or silver.

Anklets and Ornaments for the Feet.

In Bengal gold ornaments are not worn below the waist, for gold is considered as the metallic representation of *Lachhmi,* the Goddess of Wealth. In Rajputana and other parts of India it is however worn as anklets and other ornaments for the feet. The following ornaments for ankles and feet are in use in Bengal.

Bánkmal.—A curious shaped hoop made of silver, worn on the ankles. It has almost gone out of fashion except in the wild and less Europeanised Districts.

Gol-mâl.—A round anklet.

Joren-mal.—A twisted form of above.

Páinjor.—An ankle ornament made of chains and pendants, called *Pahzeb* in Upper India.

Gujri.—Anklet worn above the *Páinjor.*

Pancham.—Anklet worn above the last.

Charan-padma.—An ornamented tablet with chains worn on the upper side of the feet.

Benki.—An anklet worn by children.

Ghungur.—Anklet made of beads with grains inside to make it clink.

The other ornaments for the feet are like those in use in Upper India. Various kinds of rings for the fingers and toes are also worn, but these do not require a separate description.

Ornaments worn by men.

In India jewellery has been worn by men from time immemorial. The practice is however getting out of fashion with the progress of European civilisation. In Bengal it has almost altogether ceased to exist, and except by very young boys, ornaments are rarely now worn by the male sex. They are however still worn by men in Upper India. The following list of modern ornaments worn by men is taken from Mr. Baden Powell's "Panjáb Manufactures."

Head Ornaments.

Sarpech—Jighán, the jewelled aigrette worn in front of the turban.

Kút-biládár.—An oval pendant worn over the forehead.

Kalgi.—Plume in jewelled setting.

Turah-i-marwárid.—Tassels of pearls worn on the turban.

Mukut.—A head-dress worn by the Hindus at weddings, &c. *Mukut* is the crown formerly worn by kings and queens.

Ear Ornaments.

Bálá.—Large thin rings. They have a pearl or so strung on the gold wire of which they are made.

Murki.—Smaller ear-rings of the same shape.

Zanjiri.—A chain worn with the *bálá* to keep it up.

Dúr (gold).—A small ear-ring with three gold studs on one side.

Birbali.—A broad ear-ring with three studs.

Durichá.—An ear-ring with pendant tassel.

Necklace and Neck Ornaments.

Málá.—A necklace of large beads hanging down long and loose.

Kanth, Kanthi.—(Worn by women also.) This fits rather close to the neck; the pendant may be omitted.

Nám.—An amulet, round or star-shaped, suspended from a twist of coloured silk thread fastened round the neck by tying at the back.

Táwiz.—A square amulet, jewelled or otherwise.

Takhti.—A flat square plate engraved with figures, &c.

Hainkal.—A chain of twisted silk, from which depend, by little golden loops, various coins, amulets, &c., all round.

Zanjiri.—A set of chains.

Chandramá.—A large gold flat medal suspended by a single ring on a silk chain or cord.

Bracelets.

Ponchi.—Worn on the wrist. A series of strings of shells or small gold elongated beads.

Kangan or *Kará* or *Gokhru.*—A bracelet of stiff metal, worn bent round the arm; when the edges are serrated, it is called *Gokhru.*

Upper India Ornaments.

The following list of female ornaments worn in Upper India is taken from Mr. Baden Powell's "Panjáb Manufactures."

Head Ornaments.

Sisphúl, Chaunk, or *Choti-phúl.*—A round boss worn on the hair over the forehead; it is cut or indented so as to resemble a gold flower like a chrysanthemum.

Phul.—A boss like the above, only smooth, hemispherical, and set with jewels; it is worn on the top of the head—one or two are worn at pleasure.

Mauli.—A long chain made of rows of pearls separated by jewelled studs, about 8 inches long, hanging from the head on one side.

Sir Máng.—A chain and pendant worn on the head by the Hindus.

Bodá.—An ornament of silk and silver plaited into the hair of children.

Ornaments worn on the Forehead.

Dámni or *Dáuni.*—A fringe hanging over the forehead on either side of the face. Some of these are richly jewelled.

Kutbi.—Variety of above.

Sosani.—Variety of above.

Tiká or *Kashká.*—Small ornament worn on the forehead (pendant).

Chánd-biná.—A moon-shaped pendant.

Táwit.—Small amulets worn on the head.

Jhumar.—A tassel-shaped ornament or pendant. Mostly worn about Delhi.

Guchhi Marwárid.—A cluster of pearls.

Bindli.—Small tinsel forehead ornament.

Barwátá.—Tinsel stars worn over the eyebrows.

Ear Ornaments.

Báli or *Goshwárá.*—A set of rings worn all round the edge of the ear.

Báli Bahádurí.—It has a large pointed stud in the centre.

Karnphul, Bhedu, and *Jhumká.*—All forms of tassellike ornaments, made with silver chains and little balls, fringe of silver chain work, &c.

Pipal-wáttá, or *Pipal-pátá.*—Like a *Murki*, but has a drop or pendant to it ending in a fringe of little gold *Pipal* leaves.

Kantálá.—A similar ornament; has a stud besides the pendant.

Bálá-khhungridár.—A heavy fringed ear-ring.

Bálá kátoriwálá sádá.—An ear-ring, mostly plain.

Khalil.—Small ear-ring.

Jalil.—Like the above, only the central stud is jewelled.

Phumni.—Silk and tinsel tassels.

Máchh-machhlián.—A small gold figure of a fish worn as an ear-ring.

Tid or *patang.*—A locust-shaped jewelled pendant; along the crescented lower edge hang a row of gold *Pipal* leaves.

Tandaura, *Dedi.*—A huge star-shaped jewelled stud.

Mor Phunwár.—A pendant of jewels; being a rude imitation of the figure of a peacock.

Nose Ornaments.

Nath.—A large nose-ring, one side of the ring being ornamented with a belt of jewels or a few pearls, and gold spangle ornaments, &c., hung on to it.

Bulák.—A small pendant either worn hung to the cartilage of the nose, or else strung on to a *Nath.*

Latkan.—A sort of ornament of pendants put on

to the thin gold ring called a *Nath* and hanging from it.

Morni.—A small pendant for the above, shaped like the spread-out tail of a peacock.

Laung.—A small stud let into the flesh of the nostril on one side, generally of gold, with a pearl or turquoise on it.

Phuli.—A small ring with a single emerald or other stone of an oval shape as a pendant.

Bohr.—A jingling pendant of gold *Pipal* leaves.

Machhlián be-sir.—Headless fishes.

Teeth Ornament.

Rekhán.—Made of gold and worn on the *teeth*, a stud of gold or silver fixed into the front teeth.

Necklaces and Neck Ornaments.

Chandan-hár.—A collar or necklace of a great number of chains.

Málá or *Hár.*—A plain necklace of pearls or gold beads, &c., hanging down long.

Champákali.—A necklace like a collar with pendants. The pendants or rays are either plain metal or set with stones.

Jugni.—A single jewelled pendant, hanging from a necklace.

Mohrán.—A gold *Mohur* or coin hung by a silk necklace.

Haul-dil.—A sort of amulet of jade; not square

as a *Táwiz* always is, but cut in curves round the edge.

Saukan-mohrá.—A small gold medal or large coin suspended by a single ring on a silk chain or cord.

Hassi or *Hass.*—Like a torquea. A ring or collar of silver, thick in the middle, and thin at either end.

Galáband.—A jewelled collar.

Mohan-málá.—A long necklace made of large gold beads, with an interval of gold twisted thread between each bead.

Itrdán.—A square jewelled (or plain gold) pendant, attached to a silk chain, at the back of a small box-like vinaigrette to contain *Itr* or perfume.

Kandi.—A chain of silk carrying amulet cases.

Silwáttá.—An amulet case shaped like a small gold pillow or bolster, with two rings attached to suspend it.

Arm Ornaments.

Bázuband.—A broad belt-like ornament generally mounted on silk and tied on the upper arm.

Nau-ratan.—Like above; the ornament consisting of a band of nine gems set side by side, and bound by silk ties.

Táwiz.—An amulet worn on the upper arm.

Anant (The endless).—A large thin but solid ring of gold or silver, used chiefly by Hindus.

Bhawatta.—A square gold ornament, worn on the upper arm.

Bracelets.

Ponchian kutbi.—A bracelet made of gold or silver beads, shaped like rats'-teeth (*Chuá-danti*), or like grains of cardamoms (*Iláchidáná*).

Kangan or *Kará Zanáná.*—A bracelet of stiff metal, worn bent round the arm, made specially for women.

Bánká.—Thick gold bracelets. Hindus wear them.

Gokhru.—Bracelet of stiff metal with edges serrated.

Gajrá.—A flexible bracelet made of square gold studs mounted on a silk band.

Churi of sorts, *e.g.*, *Kantákhárat*, *Chaurás*, *Kanganidár*, &c.—They are made of a flat ribbon of gold or silver; bent round.

Báin.—Long silver *sleeve* or tube worn on both arms, like a lot of *churis* fastened together.

Band.—An armlet, broad and heavy.

Jhankangan.—Small hollow bracelets, with grains introduced into the hollow to rattle.

Finger Rings.

Angushtri.—A ring set with stones, called also *Mundri* or *Anguthi.*

Chhallá.—The *chhallá* is a quite plain hoop or whole hoop ring (with or without stones), being gold or silver, but the same all round. Worn also on the toes.

Angushtárá or *Anguthá.*—A big ring with a broad face, worn on the great toe.

Khari panjángla.—A set of finger rings of ordinary shape.

Sháhálami or *Khári.*—A ring of long oval shape.

Birhamgand.—A broad ring.

Anklets.

Pahzeb.—Various ankle ornaments made with chains and pendants of silver, which clink together when the wearer walks.

Chánjar.—A large hollow ring, which rattles when the wearer walks.

Karián-pair or *Khalkhal.*—Large thick bands worn on the anklets.

Khungru.—A ring or ankle of long ornamental beads of silver, worn on the feet.

Zanjiri.—A set of chains with a broad clasp, called also *Torá.*

Ornaments of South India and Bombay.

The above will give an idea of the kind of personal ornaments used in India. Ornaments of the same kind, or of a more or less modified form, are used in South India. A large collection both of old and modern jewellery was sent to the Colonial and Indian Exhibition from the Madras Presidency. Of these, the most curious were the gold ornament to cover the *queue* of plaited hair falling from the back of the head, which is worn by Bráhmans only, and other gold and silver ornaments worn on the top of the head. The gold ear-studs worn on the distended ear lobes were no less interesting. The collection also included a splendid assortment of necklaces, wristlets, waist-chains, anklets, toe-rings, armlets, &c. Besdes the *Swámi* jewelry to be mentioned hereafter, the favourite patterns in Madras are those in imitation of flowers. The most common patterns for bracelets are *Kalanji* and *Erukkam*, the latter being an imitation of the curious-shaped flower of *Calotropis gigantea*. Brooches are made of various patterns, such as the *tiger claw*, the *armadillo* with leaves and flower-drops, *peacock, pagoda, drum, cocoanut, custard fruit, plantain bunch, butterfly, elephant-muster, &c.* Necklaces are made of *Chakram, Rudráksham, butterfly*, and *rose* patterns. The local names for different patterns of neck ornaments are—*Kundasharam, Arambumani Korva, Kumbala-tháli Korva, Ulkettu, Nágapatháli Korva, Elachá-tháli Korva, Pálachu Korva, Sháropali, Kuvala-tháli Korva, Gnali, &c.*; of ear-ornaments are—*Kundalam, Koppu, Sátha Kádiláthu, Thaká, Sátha-thaka, &c.*

In the Colonial and Indian Exhibition, among other things Bombay sent a pair of gold anklets (*Phulsankla*), a large ear-ring inlaid with precious stones (*Toti*) worn by Rájput ladies; gold ornaments for the hair (*Chamari*); gold ornaments worn at the ends of fingers and thumb during marriage ceremonies; and a gold necklace (*Champákali*). This collection of jewellery was obtained from the Bhavnagar State. In Bombay the different patterns of head ornaments are known by the name of *Mud, Chandrakor, Phul*, and *Ketak*; ear-ornaments by *Káp, Tongale, Bugdya, Kánbáliá*, and *Báliá*; nose-ornaments by *Nath*, as in Upper India; necklaces by *Chunpatti, Motyáchepende, Vajratik, Kantha, Pot, Tándali-pot, Thusi, Sari, Chapekali málá*, and *Harpar revdi málá*; armlets by *Velá, Tulbandi, Bájuband, Gajre, and Kankne*; wristlets by *Patalias*; *Got, Bángdya* (bangles), and *Todhe* (chain for wrists); rings by *Angthi, Salle, Mohorechi angthi*; and *Khadyachya angthya*; waist zone by *Kamar-*

patta; anklets by *Válá, Todhe, Painjan;* toe-rings by *Ranajodvi, Jodvi, Phule, Gend,* and *Masolia.*

Ornaments of Central India and Rajputana.

Gold necklets of a peculiar kind are made at Sambalpur, an out-of-the-way district lying on the extreme east of the Central Provinces, and is 220 miles distant from the nearest railway station. The necklets made here are rough in execution, but are interesting as the handiwork of a place so remote from road or railway communication. They are largely worn by Bráhman youths and are supposed to possess the virtues of an amulet.

As in most other branches of Indian art, Jaipur has a great reputation for its jewellery. The ornaments made are those in use in Upper India. In connection with this subject Dr. Hendley remarks:—

"The forms of Indian jewellery are as endless as is the demand for it. In prosperous times all classes invest their savings in this manner, and no girl can become a bride without, for her position in life, a really considerable outlay on ornaments for her person, which serve as her dowry, and as a provision for her family in times of need. Sooner or later however her gold or silver are sure to be sold or find their way to the melting pot, and thus it is the most ancient forms are found in the base metal ornaments which are worn by the poor, specially by the *Banjárás* or wandering grain merchants, for the material of which they are made has no great intrinsic value."

Rings, necklaces, armlets, and *Sirpech* or head ornaments are made at Bikánir. Fairly good work is done when jewellery and arms are set with precious stones; prices vary from R200 to R10,000. Gold and silver bangles and silver head ornaments and anklets are also made. Prices of bangles vary from R25 to R100 for silver and R200 to R1,000 for gold.

Hollow bangles and brooches of gold and silver are made at Alwar, having various patterns cut upon them, and are much admired by Europeans. A silver bangle ordinarily costs R9 and a silver sword brooch R4.

Silver ornaments from Chhatrapur and Indor were sent to the Colonial and Indian Exhibition. The most effective ornaments made are bracelets dovetailed together, and others of basket work. A set of silver ornaments as ordinarily worn by native women cost about R700. Exquisitely light and fine rings of gold and silver are made at Jhánsi in Gwalior territory.

Himalayan Ornaments.

In the Himalayas, where, owing to the cold, a greater part of the body has to be kept covered with thick clothing, there is not much scope for ornaments. But still the head is adorned with a cap ornamented with silver moon-like pendants, the ear is covered with large round rings and studs, and around the neck is a profusion of necklaces, the first one fitting tight, the successive ones lengthening more and more until the last hangs down to the waist. Besides gold and silver, beads of glass, amber, and coral are used in making these necklaces, and turquoise, which come from the high regions just beyond the mountains, are also highly valued.

A very interesting set of ornaments was sent to the Calcutta International Exhibition from Darjiling. Among these were a gold locket and chain necklace (*Jántá*) made in Sikkim by Kancha Sonár; another gold necklace of a different pattern called *Towai;* a gold head flower, called *Phul;* a pair of gold ear-rings called *Tokicha;* another of a different pattern, round and flat, worn in the lower portion of the ear, called *Tariwar;* a silver necklace called *Tik;* a silver coin necklace called *Hari;* a pair of silver bracelets called *Chura,* and many other ornaments of quaint designs. The designs of Nepalese ear-rings, head ornaments, &c., are also peculiar, and not seen elsewhere.

Assam Ornaments.

Ornaments made in Assam are curious in form and design. These are mostly made in the Khassia and Jaintia Hills, at Barpetá in Kámrúp District, and at Sylhet. The following account of Assam jewellery has been furnished by Mr. H. Z. Darrah, the Director of Agriculture of that Province.

Khassia and Jaintia Hills Jewellery.—The best known articles of Khassia Hills jewellery are the coral and gold necklaces so largely worn by the more wealthy of the Khassia women. These necklaces consist of alternate beads (about the size of small marbles) of coral and gold held together by a thread passing through a hole in the centre of each. The coral is real and comes from Calcutta. The gold beads are shells of gold filled up with lac. The value of a necklace varies from R50 to R200.

Barpetá Jewellery.—A peculiarly fine species of gold filigrain work is made at Barpetá in the Kámrúp District. The articles are chiefly bracelets and necklaces—the latter being specially beautiful. The gold is sometimes imported direct from Calcutta, but is often obtained by melting down Muhammadan coins brought (to save weight) instead of rupees, by the elephant traders of Rangpur and Purnia.

Sylhet Jewellery.—The gold and silver ornaments

made at Sylhet are copied largely from Manipur. The art is almost entirely in the hands of the Manipuris, of whom some fifty are engaged in the trade. The gold used is always pure, but a large number of the articles consist of half gold and half silver. The ornaments most commonly made are the following:—*Kankan.*—A kind of bracelet usually worn in pairs one on each wrist. The inner surface is usually silver, the outer gold, with elaborate devices of flowers, wreaths, crowns, &c. These are ingeniously worked by hammering the gold on a suitable iron spike. The ends meet in the form of a circle, but are not joined. The bracelet yields to pressure like a ring of steel, so that it can be put on and taken off with facility. A pair of *Kankan* generally requires two *tolás* (260 grains) of gold and an equal quantity of silver. *Kháru.*—A kind of bracelet very similar to a bangle; made sometimes of gold, and sometimes of silver, and sometimes of both combined. A pair is generally worn on each arm. *Sonápoki.*—A kind of necklace, formed generally of 21 beads. Each bead is a small rounded cone-shaped shell of gold with a base of silver. The interior is filled with lac. Two small rings of gold at opposite sides of the bead afford the means of uniting them to each other with thread and thus of making a necklace. Each bead usually contains about 6 grains of gold. *Bethguta* or *Gulluguta.*—A kind of necklace worn usually by children, the *Sonápoki* being generally confined to women. It differs from the *Sonápoki* only in the shape of the beads. Each bead resembles a cube with the angles truncated, and is a shell of gold filled with lac. *Báju.*—A gold armlet usually worn by women and boys.

Burma Ornaments.

Gold and silversmith's work, including filigrain, setting of precious stones, &c., is extensively carried on in Burma. The census of 1881 gave the number 7,272 as persons engaged in this kind of work including dealers in precious stones, in gold and gold leaf, and those doing lapidary work. The number refer to those Districts which were known as British Burma. The following account of the industry has been furnished by Mr. H. L. Tilly of the Public Works Department:—

"The best workmen are naturally attracted to the large towns, where they obtain high wages; but every village greater than a hamlet has its goldsmith and silversmith, and more than half the workmen of the province are thus scattered abroad away form the centres of population. The most excellent work is produced in Rangoon and after that in Moulmein, Shwegyin, Prome, and Thayetmyo.

"The workmanship of the Burmese artisans are chiefly confined to necklaces (*Dalizans*), ornaments for the hair, ear-plugs, chains, hair-pins, buttons, and bracelets. These are of filigrain work, with which are associated small pieces of solid gold either beaten out into the petals of a leaf or cut like a diamond to form the flashing centre of a rosette or a sparking pendant. In this case the burnished gold retains its proper colour, but in all others it is dyed red with tamarind juice, a barbaric custom to which the Burmese tenaciously cling. The reason given is that no other metal but gold will assume this particular ruddy colour when treated with tamarind juice; it may in fact be regarded as the Hall-mark of Burmese jewellery.

"The goldsmiths show great skill and, what is rarer amongst the Burmese, great patience and industry in making their filigrain work. For they have first to draw the wire from solid gold, and they then laboriously construct the delicate pieces of which the work is finally formed. The *Dalizan* or necklace is perhaps the prettiest of all Burmese ornaments, and in silver it is sought after by Europeans. It is composed of a collar about half an inch high, from which hang rows of peacocks, rosettes, crescents, &c., linked together and gradually narrowing towards the lower edge.

"Ornaments for the hair are of two kinds,—those made of sprays of leaves and those made by attaching conventional ornaments to a curved bar by spiral springs. In both kinds a peacock or a pheasant is introduced in the centre, coloured pieces of glass and sometimes precious stones are set in the leaves, and the whole piece vibrates with every movement of the head.

"Chains and round necklaces are formed by plaiting flat pieces of gold in various ways and soldering on to the faces small knots and grains. This kind of work is perhaps the best in design and finish of any made by Burmese goldsmiths.

"Most of the gold used is obtained by melting the English sovereign. Chinese gold leaf coming through Upper Burma is employed when a purer gold is required. The leaves are about three inches square and are of three qualities, the best being said to be quite pure. A small quantity of pure gold is also obtained from the Shan States and Bangkok, a very soft variety, having a slightly green colour. Gold leaf is sent out from England in small quantity.

"To dye an ornament red it is scrubbed with a wash made of gunpowder 1 part, salt ½ part, and alum 1 part. Add water and boil for half an hour. The mixture cleans the gold and prepares it for the dye, which is made of tamarind, sulphur, salt, and water."

The proportions are only known to the master goldsmiths. The ornament is boiled in the above composition for about an hour. Mr. Tilly continues:—

"As every Burmese woman has at least one article of gold jewellery, there is a large demand, and the goldsmiths would drive a good trade were it not that each pupil, directly he has learnt a smattering of the business, sets up on his own account. The charge for gold work varies with the delicacy of the workmanship required. The ordinary charge is the price of the gold plus R3 a *tical* for workmanship; very excellent work may be obtained for R6 a *tical;* and the most exquisite that the artists of Burma can produce cost R10. The latter work is for design and finish equal to that of Bond Street, but it is difficult to find workmen who are equal to producing it."

Setting of precious stones.

As stated before, precious stones are set in jewellery by the wealthy classes. The principal stones used are diamonds, rubies, onyxes, carnelians, emeralds, turquoise, jadestone, serpentines, agates, jaspers, marbles, &c. The work of setting stones is performed by the *Murassiákár* or *Kundansáz*. After the goldsmith has finished his work the article goes to the enameller to be enamelled on the back, and then it comes to the setter of jewels. Delhi is the head-quarters of this industry, and Mr. Kipling makes the following remarks on the subject :—

" Another speciality of Delhi is the incrustation of jade with patterns of which the stem work is in gold and the leaves and flowers in garnets, rubies, diamonds, &c. For examples of the best of older work we must now go to the great European collections, where are objects of a size and beauty seldom met with in India. The mouth-pieces of *Hukkas*, the hilts of swords and daggers, the heads of walking-canes, and the curious crutchlike handle of the *Gosáin's* or *Bairági's* (religious ascetic) staff, also called a *Bairági*, are, with lockets and brooches for English wear, the usual application of this costly and beautiful work. Each individual splinter of ruby or diamond may not be intrinsically worth very much, but the effect of such work as a whole is often very rich. The *Murassiákár* or jewel-setter was formerly often called upon to set stones, so that they could be sewn into jewelled cloths. For this purpose, as when the stone was to be incrusted upon another, as with minute diamonds or pearls on large garnets—a common Delhi form —or on jade, he works with gold foil and a series of small chisel-like tools and fine agate burnishers. The open work claw settings, which leave the underside of a stone clear, have been copied from European work. There is no dodge of the European jeweller, such as tinted foil backing for inferior stones, or fitting two splints of stone to form one, that is not known to the Delhi workmen. These and many other devices they have *not* learnt from Europe, for they are tricks of the trade common to all countries."

The setting of precious stones as an industry was introduced into Calcutta by Delhi workmen about fifty years ago. These men took some blacksmith boys of Dacca as apprentices, who in time became experts in the art and superseded the up-country workmen. Several members of this caste have now established themselves in Bombay as jewel-setters. In Calcutta itself the industry is not in a very prosperous state. Two large collections of ornaments set with precious stones were lent to the Calcutta Exhibition by the Mahárájás of Dumráon and Betiá.

Necklets and other ornaments are made of garnets, agates, and other stones. Such ornaments will be treated under the head of "Lapidary's" work.

Ornaments for European Use.

The Assam and Burmese jewellery have attracted European attention. Among other places, ornaments for European use are chiefly made at Dacca, Cuttack, Lucknow, Delhi, and Trichinopoly. These are almost all made of silver, of European shape with Indian patterns.

In Cuttack the work is all filigrain, and is made of pure silver. This is first purified by melting sixteen parts of silver with one part of lead. It is then cast into bars or sticks by being run into moulds. The next process is to beat the silver into plates, which are then drawn into wire. Patterns are then formed by taking the wire one by one, and carefully arranging them on a sheet of mica, on which they are fastened by a peculiar cement. Thus held the different parts are then united by soldering. The last process is that of cleaning and finishing, which gives the Cuttack work such a delicate snowy appearance. The following are the names of different patterns made at Cuttack and their local prices:—Lily bangle, R18;

lily necklace, R19; lily bracelet, R16; lily brooch, R4; lily earring, R2-8; diamond bangles, R13-8; diamond brooch, R4; leaf brooch, R4; leaf bangle, R20; butterfly brooch, R4; butterfly necklace, R20; butterfly bracelet, R17; butterfly earring, R2-5. A half ball set, consisting of a necklace, bracelet, brooch, and earring, would cost R32; a set of tape pattern ornaments would cost R34. A complete collection of Cuttack jewellery can be had for about R300.

The ornaments made at Dacca are also filigrain work, and the process of manufacture is the same. Formerly a superior kind of filigrain work, called *Mandilá*, existed at Dacca, but the industry died out shortly after the arrival of the English, and no specimens of that work can now be obtained. The present style of work was introduced into Dacca only about seventy years ago, and is largely followed by members of the blacksmith caste, called *Karmakár*. Shell-cutters (*Sánkháris*) and weavers (*Tántis*) also follow the profession, but as a rule articles turned out by them are inferior in workmanship and quality. The following are the prices of Dacca silver ornaments adapted for European use:—Necklaces from R12 to R20; bracelets from R12 to R22; brooches from R3 to R10; crosses from R2 to R10; butterfly from R1-8 to R4; beetles from R2 to R10; hairpins from R1-8 to R5: flowers R3 each; ear-stars R1 per pair; earrings R2 to R3.

In the North-Western Provinces, the best jewellery for European use is made at Lucknow. A specialty of Lucknow is that known as diamond-cut silver ornaments. Facets are cut and burnished, which, when in the form of stars, bear at a distance a strong resemblance to the flashing of a diamond. The price of typical specimens of Lucknow jewellery is as follows:—Bangles, diamond-cut, per dozen, R13;

bangles, fish pattern, R19; bangles, zig-zag pattern, R14; bangles, moon pattern, R19; bangles, snake pattern, R9 per pair; necklace, R17; stars for ribbon, R4 to R6 for a set of 5; pendants, R2 to R3 each; brooches, R2 each; hairpins, R2 to R3.

The following information about Delhi jewellery has been furnished by Mr. Kipling:—

The chief characteristics of the best Delhi jewellery are the purity of the gold and silver employed, the delicacy and minuteness of the workmanship, the taste and skill displayed in the combination of coloured stones, and the aptitude for the imitation of any kind of original on the part of the workmen. Its faults are occasional flimsiness and a gaudiness which is perhaps too harshly judged by comparison with the sober and massive style now in fashion in Europe. The competition of the present day also has caused a falling off in the purity of the metal. In addition to the purely native ornaments, Delhi produces also many articles for European use, such as gold bracelets of various kinds mounted with miniature paintings, mat pattern, &c., crescent and quarterfoil-shaped filigree brooches, necklaces, belts, rings, set with precious stones, studs, solitaires, and indeed every kind of ornamental jewellery. Mr. Kipling further remarks elsewhere:—

"As to the objects produced, there is scarcely anything called jewellery that cannot be imitated at Delhi; and the continual passage of tourists has created a demand for several varieties of native work not strictly belonging to the locality, as well as for articles of English style. Massive rings with one precious stone set in strong open work, and almost as well finished as those in a Bond Street window, are now as frequent as the rings with several stones which are perhaps more like the true Delhi notion. Many of these are tastefully arranged and skilfully mounted. The embossed silver work of Madras, with Dravidian figures in relief, known as *Swámi* jewellery, is more coarsely imitated. In the best Madras examples the figures are entirely hand-worked, but they are often made at Delhi by die-stamping, afterwards chased. Filigrain has always been used as an accessory to more solid work, and now the lightness of Genœse or Cuttack articles is sometimes attempted. Silver and silver gilt wire woven into a kind of matting pattern is applied to belts and bracelets. All the varieties of watch chain are imitated and some adaptations of native chains have been done.

"The patterns of necklaces worn in the hills are now regularly wrought at Delhi. In gold, suites of amethyst, topaz, turquoise, and other stones are made. The gold framework is sometimes twisted or of *babúl* work. This last is one of the oldest and most characteristic forms. The name is taken from the pretty and sweetly-scented *Babúl* or *Kikar* (*Acacia arabica*) flower, which is a ball of delicate yellow filaments. It is also called *khár-dár*, or thorn work. Convex forms, as the centres of brooches, the fringing balls set round miniatures, &c., are studded over with the minute gold points, each of which, with a patience and delicacy of hand that defy European imitation, is separately soldered to the thin plate base. Good, soft gold alone is used for the points, while the base is of slightly inferior metal. The articles are finished by being placed into a sharply acid bath, which produces a clear mat-gold bloom, that does not long survive wear and tear. Major McMahon says that various castes wore ornaments of this sort before its suitability for objects of English use came to notice.

"A bolder form of similar work is called *Gokhru*, and is based apparently on the bur (the caltrap of Indian and also of mediæval European warfare—a ball studded with spikes thrown to impede the progress of cavalry, is also called a *Gokhru*). This is worn by *Ját* men as an ear-ring, and the same treatment is applied to women's bracelets. Among other patterns produced by soldering small details on a base may be mentioned a rose pattern of minute flowers. This is common all over India, but is perhaps most perfectly done in the red-stained gold ornaments of Burma.

"The miniature paintings of Delhi are frequently set in gold cable twist patterns as bracelets, necklets, and brooches. Small plaques of Pratábgarh enamel, a semi-translucent green incrusted with tiny gold-chased patterns of figures and animals, are also, with true and false avanturine, mounted in a similar way. The almost invariable feature of Delhi work is a thin shell of gold incrusted with better gold, or with stones of some kind, and afterwards filled with hard lac. The enamel work is often spoiled by being done on gold too thin to withstand without distortion the heat of the enamel fire."

The price of Delhi jewellery made of gold is as follows :—A pair of flexible gold bracelets, mat pattern, R200; one gold necklace, R175; one gold bracelet, rose pattern, R65; one jewelled locket, R40. But it is difficult to give a fair indication of the price, as it depends on the quantity and quality of materials used and the nature of the workmanship. A peculiar kind of necklaces made of thin silver beads is made at Pánipat in the Karnál District. These are sold for R10 to R30 each.

In the hill districts a great variety of fanciful silver necklaces is made, which are sometimes combined with coral and amber, and more frequently with coins or small enamelled pendants.

Madras jewellery has now acquired a great reputation all over the world, specially those made at Trichinopoly, with grotesque mythological figures, known as the *Swámi* pattern. The shape of the articles are European, only the patterns are Indian. Jewellery made in Travancore, Cochin, Canara, and Vizagapatam also attracted some attention at the Calcutta International and the Colonial and Indian Exhibitions. The prices of *Swámi* jewellery at the place of production are as follows:—Bracelets, R15; necklace, R20; brooch, R5; ear-rings, R4. The principal places in which jewellery is manufactured, in the Madras Presidency, are Madura District, Chingleput District, Karnúl, Salem, Anantpur, South Canara, Madras, Kistna, Malabar, Godávari, Cuddappah, Vizagapatam, and Tanjore.

Swámi jewellery is also made at Bangalore in Mysore and exported in little quantities. Over and above the price of silver the cost of workmanship charged is from half to one rupee per *tolá* (180 grains) of silver.

Enamelled Jewellery.

Minákári or the art of enamelling was known in India from very early times. The art now is not in a very flourishing state, except at Jaipur. It is however still practised on gold at Jaipur, Alwar, Delhi, and Benares; on silver at Multan, Bháwalpur, Kashmir, Kangra, Kulu, Lahore, Haidrabad in Sind, Karáchi, Abbottabad, Núrpur, Lucknow, Kach, and Jaipur; on copper in Kashmir, Jaipur, and many other places. But the work done on gold at Jaipur is the best in the world. "The colours employed rival the tints of the rainbow in purity and brilliancy, and they are laid on the gold by the Jaipur artists with such exquisite taste that there is never a want of harmony; even when jewels are also used they serve but to enhance the beauty of the enamel." The Jaipur enamel is of the Champlevé variety, *i.e.*, the outlines are formed from the plate itself, and the colours are deposited in depressions of it. The following account of Jaipur enamel is taken from a paper contributed by Dr. Hendley to the *Journal of Indian Art*:—

"There are two kinds of encrusted enamels—the Cloisonné or filigrain enamel, and the Champlevé, in which the outline is formed by the plate itself, while the colours are placed in depressions hollowed out of the metal to receive them and are made to adhere by fire. The design is prepared by the *Chitera*, or artist, generally a servant of the master jeweller, who also keeps books of patterns, some of great age, from which customers can make a selection, generally with a very good idea of the result to be obtained in metal. The *Sonár*, or goldsmith, then forms the article to be enamelled, and afterwards passes it on to the *Gharai*, the chaser or engraver, who engraves the pattern. These men are not Sikhs, but ordinary members of the goldsmith or carpenter sub-castes of Hindus. The engraving is done with steel styles, and the polishing is completed with similar tools and agates. The surface of the pits in the gold is ornamented with hatchings, which serve not only to make the enamel adhere firmly, but to increase the play of light and shade through the transparent colours. The enameller or *Minákár* now applies the colours in the order of their hardness, or power of resisting fire, beginning with the hardest. Before the enamel is applied, the surface of the ornament is carefully burnished and cleansed. The colours are obtained in opaque vitreous masses from Lahore, where they are prepared by Muhammadan *Manihárs*, or bracelet-makers. The Jaipur workmen state that they cannot make the colours themselves. The base of each colour is vitreous, and the colouring matter is the oxide of a metal such as cobalt or iron. Large quantities of cobalt are obtained from Bhagor, near Khetri, the chief town of a tributary State of Jaipur, and are used in producing the beautiful blue enamel. All the colours known can be applied to gold. Black, green, blue, dark yellow, orange, pink, and a peculiar salmon colour, can be used with silver. Copper only admits of the employment of white, black, and pink, and even of these the last is made to adhere with difficulty (this applies to Jaipur copper enamels). In the order of hardness and of application to the metals, the colours are as follow:—White, blue, green, black, red. The pure ruby red is the most fugitive, and it is only the most experienced workmen who can bring out its beauties. Moreover, the Jaipur artist alone succeeds in giving the transparent lustre to this colour which so charmed and surprised the jurors of the earliest great international European exhibitions. The enamel workers at Alwar, an offshoot from Jaipur, are sometimes fairly successful, but the Delhi jewellers, who turn out a great deal of inferior enamel, only produce a red with an orange or yellow tinge."

Various ornaments of gold enamel work are made at Jaipur, such as charms, armlets, anklets, bangles, and necklaces. Almost all the better kinds of native jewellery are enamelled on the back, and usually also on the edges and between the gems in front. A gold bracelet of crocodile pattern would cost about R100. A gold bracelet of crocodile pattern set with diamonds would cost about R200. A pair of ear-rings would cost about R18; a fish ring, R6-8; mango-shaped lockets from R15 to R75; necklaces, plain or set with gems, from R200 to R1,200; a hair-pin, R10; a breast-pin, R12. Scarf rings, brooches, and other articles are also made. The mango-shaped locket, called *Kairi*, is very much admired. Hindus and Muhammadans use it to keep scents. Bracelets made for Europeans are oval in shape and are carefully enamelled both on the inner and the outer surface. "The necklaces are generally a series of plaques united by chains or links of gold, and are reversible, the back being constructed of medallions of Pratábgarh or Ratlám enamels. Necklets, rosaries, and watch chains of enamelled balls are also made. As the plaques used as brooches afford good surfaces for enamelling, the designs upon them are bolder than usual."

About sixty years ago, the art of enamelling was introduced in Bengal from Delhi, but it did not take root, and as an industry it has now entirely disappeared from the Province. A specimen of Patna enamel work was sent to the Calcutta International Exhibition, but no information was supplied.

Mr. Baden Powell, in his book on "Panjáb Manufactures" (1872), mentions Benares as a place which stood next to Jaipur in the art of enamelling. No specimen was, however, sent to the Calcutta or to the Colonial and Indian Exhibition. Very little enamelling is now done here. What is made is prepared only by order. Enamelling is also executed to a limited extent in Lucknow and Rámpur, but the artists confine their efforts to enamelling plate rather than jewellery.

In the Panjáb enamelled ornaments are made at Delhi, Kangra, Multan, Bhawalpur, Jhang, and Hazara. Delhi work is the most important. Some of the Delhi work is almost equal to that made at Jaipur. It is chiefly employed, as at Jaipur, to decorate the backs of jewelled ornaments of gold, a bright translucent red enamel being always preferred. The enamelling of Multan, Jhang, and Kangra is generally of a dark and light blue colour, the blue vitreous enamel being the most common. Mr. Kipling states:—"Red and yellow are not so often seen, and the colours, though true vitreous enamel, are opaque. It might be described as *Champlevé* in so far as that the enamel is laid in hollows between raised lines of metal. These are, however, produced by hammering the silver plaque into a steel *thappa* or die and not by graving out. At Bhawalpur, objects of large size are produced, and they have one or two translucent colours. In Hazara the only colours are a crude green and sometimes yellow on silver." The art, it is said, was introduced into Multan by one Noulu, some 400 years ago, since which time it has undergone considerable improvement. Necklaces, bracelets, and other ornaments made of silver are enamelled in dark and light blue, black, red, and an inferior yellow. These are sold by weight at from R1-4 to R2 per *tolá* of 180 grains. Similar articles, but of quaint and curious shapes and patterns, are made in Kangra, which are enamelled blue, green, and yellow. Mr. Kipling states :—

"The silversmiths of Kangra are skilful in the application of vitreous enamel to small articles of silver used as ornaments. Finger and toe-rings, necklaces in great variety, and ornaments for the brow, head, and ears, connected by chains, are decorated in dark blue and green enamel. The patterns sometimes include figures drawn with the Polynesian rudeness which seems characteristic of all modern hill work, but there is a distinct and not unpleasing character in the work. An old Kangra pattern of anklet, now seldom made, is a series of birds of very archaic design in enamelled silver, connected by silver links. The silversmiths are also said to imitate, with considerable dexterity, the most elaborate specimens of European ornaments."

A gold and silver neck ornament, called *Timniya*, partly enamelled, made at Jodhpur, attracted some attention at the Colonial and Indian Exhibition. Its price varies from R20 to R200, according to weight. It is made of different shapes, and is worn by every Hindu woman in Marwar.

A little enamelling work is also done at Bikánir, which is chiefly employed on the head ornaments of women, necklaces, swords, daggers, &c. Cost of enamelling articles, R2 per *tolá* of 180 grains. At

Alwar enamelling is done to a limited extent, but the work is good.

A very fine species of enamelling on gold is done at Jorhát in Assam. The colours are blue, green, and white, and the effect is strikingly beautiful. The ornaments produced are lockets, ear-rings, bracelets, and necklaces. The sale is not extensive, and is only confined to the Assamese. The ornaments are often set with precious stones.

A kind of imitation enamel is wrought in Indor and Ratlám. Studs, brooches, necklaces, bracelets, &c., are made. Opinions differ about the mode of manufacture, which is a family secret. But the work is said to consist of "thin gold leaf cut into fine and elaborate designs, and laid on glass of various colours. It is frequently bordered with silver or gold filigrain, and is very effective in appearance." Price, set of studs R2; brooches from R5 to R25; bracelets from R20 to R40. [For a further account of the art of enamelling see "Enamelled Ware."]

Ornaments made in inferior metals.

In Bengal, North-Western Provinces, and practically all over India, heavy personal ornaments made of brass and bell-metal are largely worn by low castes and aboriginal tribes. These mostly consist of ornaments for the neck, the hands, and the feet. Of these the following are well-known ornaments: *Hánsuli*, a neck ornament already described under gold and silver jewellery. *Pairi*, heavy ornament for the feet. *Kará*, anklets. *Batesi*, wristlets worn on both hands from the wrist up to the elbow. *Kháru*, a broad bracelet.

Personal ornaments of base metals are made at Madras, Madura, and Kistna Districts in the Madras

Presidency. They are made of copper or some other cheap metal, and the designs are varied and often pretty. From an ethnological point of view they are of great interest, and they are also suggestive from an artistic point of view.

Such articles are largely made in Jaipur, and some of the castings are wonderful examples of skill and ingenuity. For example, a bracelet of elaborate interlacing gold links is cast in one piece by means of a clay mould and wax. The oldest and best forms are found amongst the poor, because they are not so easily taken by novelties, and their ornaments, if broken up, would be worth less than as they are.

Mock Jewellery.

Imitation of gold and silver jewellery is made in all parts of India. The practice of imitating jewels and jewellery has been carried on from ancient times, as shown by the incident related in the old Drama, the "Toy Cart," quoted both by Sir George Birdwood and Dr. Rájendra Lála Mitra. The incident refers to a question raised about the reality of certain jewels produced in a Court of Justice, and Wilson in his "Hindu Theatre" thus translates the passage :—

Judge.—Do you know these ornaments?

Mother.—Have I not said? They may be different, though like. I cannot say more; they may be imitations made by some skilful artist.

Judge.—It is true, Provost, examine them; they may be different, though like; the dexterity of the artist is no doubt very great, and they readily fabricate imitations of ornaments they have once seen in such a manner that the difference shall scarcely be discernible.

In Bengal brass jewellery is often gilded with gold and silver and is largely worn by low castes.

When new they cannot be distinguished from the real articles without a very close examination. All gold and silver ornaments worn here are imitated in this way, a collection of which would cost from R50 to R200. A brass-gilt collection of such ornaments was sent from Poona to the Colonial and Indian Exhibition to illustrate the gold and silver ornaments worn by Marhatta women.

Large quantities of mock jewellery are made at Delhi. Mr Kipling remarks :—

"Large quantities of sham jewellery made of brass, coloured glass, and plain glass with tinted foil behind it, are sold. These preserve the native forms of ear-rings, bracelets, and head ornaments, and are often very pretty. Year by year, however, a larger number of European imitations are imported; notably large brass beads in open work rudely counterfeiting filigrain. It is not always easy to say in such things where Germany or Birmingham ends and Delhi begins, for the stamped tinsel settings are combined with wire, silk, and beads in a most ingenious way, till the completed ornament resembles those made in good materials of real native work. There is no affectation, however, about the ornaments - cast in zinc for very poor people, where the workmanship, though following the forms of silver and gold, is rough and costless as the material. A considerable amount of taste is displayed in the stringing and arrangement of small coloured glass beads. From one shop the writer purchased 32 necklaces of different patterns, some in beads, others made of seeds and suitable for religious ascetics, others of lac, coated with yellow foil, with coins, also in lac, hanging to them, and others in wood. No two were alike, and the price asked for the 32 was two rupees. To a native purchaser it would have been less. Nowhere else can so much bravery be bought at so cheap a rate; and from the proverbs quoted by Dr. Fallon in his Dictionary, about Delhi dandyism, it would appear that cheap finery is a 'note' of the place."

Glass and Lac Bangles.

Glass and lac bangles are made all over the country. They are of various colours and are of various patterns.

The best glass and lac bangles are made at Gházipur, Benares, Lucknow, Delhi, and other towns in Upper India. Glass bangles are sometimes coated with lac, on which tinsel and bits of coloured glass are set. In Bengal, the best descriptions of glass bangles are made at Hájipur, Patna, Bhágalpur, and Murshidabad. A forehead ornament, called *Tikli*, made of painted glass, is worn by the Behar women. In the Bombay Presidency glass bangles are made at Shivapur near Poona by four establishments of Lingáyet Káchári*s*, employing about 25 to 30 men. Formerly they obtained the raw glass from Haidrabad, but at the present time they get sufficient quantities of broken bangles which they use. Similar bangles are also made at Chinchni in Thánná District, where 30 to 40 Musalmans are engaged in the industry. About twenty years ago, one Alibhái Ghulám Mohi-ud-din introduced the art of manufacturing a better kind of glass bangles. The price of a dozen bangles ranges from 4 to 8 annas. In Madras glass bangles are made in many places. Dr. Bidie writes :—

"The chief seats of the industry in the neighbourhood of Madras are the Kalahastri and Venkatagiri *taluks* of North Arcot, and large quantities of the crude glass prepared there are exported to Rangoon and elsewhere. The process followed in its preparation in these places is a very simple one. A kind of saline efflorescence *soudu-man*, which in some places is abundant on the surface of the soil, is collected and placed in pots containing about six Madras measures each. Sixty of these are built into a large clay furnace and baked for some time until the contents have been fused into white frit, called *gazu rai*. During the process the *soudu-man* loses half its bulk and the crude frit is turned out in the shape of hemispheres. The *soudu-man* is a natural carbonate of soda which contains sufficient siliceous matter to make the *frit*. To give it colour the *gazu rai* is powdered and mixed with various metallic substances. To produce a blue glass or *nilam rai*, a blue powder, probably sulphate of copper, is used; for green or *paccha-rai*, copper filings; for blue-red, *utha-rai*, a black stone from Conjeveram called *nalla-rai*, and for red, *sonne rai*, a stone known as *chembadi rai*, also from Conjeveram. When coloured, the glass is broken and fused once more and then sold.

In Assam lac ornaments "are principally made at Karimganj in Sylhet. Bracelets are almost the only articles turned out. The body of the bracelets is a compound of lac and clay, but the ornamentation consists of pure lac, previously coloured red, yellow, or blue, laid on in thin narrow stripes. The colour being brilliant, the bracelets have a showy effect."

In Delhi, "lac bangles, incrusted with spangles in stamped orsidue and with beads, are made in large numbers. Some are coated with tin, ground and applied as a paint, and then covered with a tinted varnish, a method of obtaining a metallic glimmer through colour which is characteristic of many Indian forms of decoration. The lac bangle trade is almost entirely in the hands of women."

Lac jewellery consisting of bracelets, necklaces, &c., are made at Rewa and Indor, those of Rewa being specially handsome in design and skilful in workmanship.

Shell Ornaments.

As stated before, bracelets made of conch shell have been in use in India from time immemorial. Such bracelets are called *sankha* in Sanskrit and *sánkhá* in vernacular, and are made of the *Maza rapa* of Lamark, *Turbinella rapa* and *Voluta gravis* of Sir E. Tennant. The bracelets are made by cutting the shells into small annulets, which are dyed with lac, and decorated with gold foil, beads and other ornamentations. The bracelets turned out, however, are extremely rude and wanting in finish. Only fifty years ago the wearing of shell bracelets was universal in Bengal among the Hindus, but now they have gone almost entirely out of fashion except in the out-of-the-way Districts. The wearing of shell-bracelets was considered a religious obligation by the Hindus of Bengal, and even now a set is always presented to the bride by her father on the occasion of her marriage. On such occasions ivory bangles are substituted for shell bracelets in Upper India. Dacca has, however, come forward to supply the modern taste by turning out delicate bracelets and bangles of different patterns. A collection of such ornaments has been sent to the Glasgow International Exhibition. The local names of different patterns and the prices are as follows :—*Báshá-rekhi* bracelet, R1-2 per pair; *Kárnish-dár, i.e.*, bordered bracelet, R1-2 per pair; *Bácháddr Khayeshá* bracelet, R1 per pair; *Khayeshá* bracelet, 14 annas per pair; *Jaltaranga* or wavy bangles, R1-2 per pair; *Diamond-cut* bangles, R1-2 per pair; *Rangil* or coloured bangles, R1-2 per pair; *Makar-chehárá* or alligator-headed bracelet, R1-2 per pair, &c. Shell bracelets are also made at Sylhet. In Eastern Bengal they are still worn by all Hindu women, except the widows. [See also "Ivory, Horn, and Shell Manufactures."]

Ornaments made of Ivory, Horn and Wood.

Chains, armlets, crosses, and other ornaments are also made of ivory, horn, and wood. A fine pair of ivory armlets was sent to the Colonial and Indian Exhibition from Sáran in Bengal. Ivory bangles and other personal ornaments are also made at Murshidabad, Cuttack, Amritsar, Siálkot, Multan, Páli, Indor, and other places. An ivory ornament for the ear, called *Karna-changa,* worn by the Tipperas, a hill tribe on the north-east frontier of Bengal, was sent to the Calcutta International Exhibition. The following remarks on the manufacture of ivory bangles in Upper India are taken from an article contributed by Mr. Kipling to the *Journal of Indian Art*:—

"The ivory bangle, it has been remarked, is usually a mere ring. The writer has never seen a specimen of open work or other carving, a mode of treatment that seems suitable to the material and well within the powers of the Indian artisan. The traditional usages of caste have probably a controlling effect. In the Panjáb, on the occasion of a marriage, the *Mámá*, or maternal uncle, of the bride is expected to present her with a set of ivory bangles coloured red, green, or black, and ornamented with tinsel spangles, or lines with minute scratched circles, as may be the peculiar fashion of the caste. The higher castes wear these only during the first year of wedlock, after which they are replaced by bangles of silver and gold or other materials. The women of some Hindu castes, however, always wear ivory. In nearly all cases the nature of the material is so disguised by colour it would appear that some cheaper substance might be made to serve eqally well. In parts of the North-Western Provinces ivory is not used for bangles, but they are common throughout the Panjáb, in the greater part of the Bombay Presidency, in Sind, in the Central Provinces, in the Western States of Rajputana, and in parts of Bengal. The ancient town of Páli, a station on the Jodhpur branch of the Rajputana Railway, on the old trade route between Bombay and Delhi through Ahmadabad and Ajmir, maintains a specialty in bangle turnery which, according to native report, it has enjoyed for centuries, and absorbs the greater part of the ivory that is sent northward from Bombay. This is another instance of the curious tendency of Indian crafts to be localised in out-of-the-way places, in a way that is not easily accounted for. There are at Páli whole streets of ivory bangle-turners. Their wares are produced in sets of graduated sizes, covering the arm from the shoulder to the wrist, with an interval for the elbow, and they are worn almost universally in the Western Rajput States."

A collection of four armlets in ebony and ivory was lent by the Mahárájá of Hatwá to the Calcutta International Exhibition. Ornaments of buffalo horn are made at Monghyr. A collection consisting of a necklace, a brooch, and four snake bangles was purchased for the above Exhibition.

Ornaments of ebony wood and the wood of the areca or betel-nut palm (*Areca Catechu*) are made at Monghyr. These are chiefly for European use. A collection of such ornaments has been sent to the Glasgow International Exhibition. A set of these ornaments would cost about R1-8 to R2-8 at the place of production. Necklaces and other ornaments are also made of various seeds and wood, of which the following list has been compiled from Dr. Watt's Dictionary of the Economic Products of India:—

Abrus precatorius, the Crab's-eyes or *Rati* seeds.—The fact of this red shining seed with its black eye-spot being used for rosaries suggested the specific name *precatorius*. They are strung together along with shells and black seeds in necklaces, and are also largely used in the decoration of boxes, baskets, &c.

Adenanthera pavonina, the Red-wood or *Rakṭa-kánchan*.—The brilliant scarlet seeds of this tree are larger than the preceding, flattened and devoid of the black eye-spot, otherwise they are very much alike. They are strung and worn by the women in many parts of India.

Adhatoda Vasica, the *Bákas* of Bengal and *Arusá* of Upper India.—The wood of this plant is made into small beads resembling those made from *Ægle Marmelos*, *Cajanus indicus*, and *Flacourtia ramontchi*.

Ægle Marmelos, the *Bel*.—Beads are made from the rind as well as from the wood. Strung with the fibre of *Agave americana*, they are worn by the Sudras to denote that they are not Muhammadans.

Æschynomene aspera, the *Solá*.—Prepared pieces of pith are sometimes worn by the aboriginal tribes as ear-ornaments. Garlands of beads of the pith of

Solá, coloured and tinselled, are used to decorate idols and worn by brides and bridegrooms.

Aquilaria Agallocha, Eagle-wood.—Beads made of this odoriferous wood are occasionally seen.

Areca Catechu, Betel-nut palm.—Beads are made from the nut: they are rarely worn entire, but are turned into fancy shapes. Rings and ornamental articles are made of betel-nut at Jaipur. Ornaments are made of wood in Monghyr.

Bamboo.—A ring of specially-prepared bamboo is placed in the ear-perforation by the Taukul Nágás of Manipur.

Borassus flabelliformis.—The leaves are cut up into neat bracelets and worn by Santál girls. Lacquered palm leaf is worn as ear-ornaments in South India.

Cajanus indicus, the *Arhar.*—The wood is made into small beads.

Canna indica, the Indian shot, or *Lál-sarbo-jayá.*—The black seeds of this plant are sometimes strung as beads along with the red crab's-eye seeds.

Caryota urens.—The dark-coloured oval seeds of this palm are used as buttons, and by the Muhammadans are sometimes strung as beads.

Coix lachryma, Job's tears.—There are two principal forms of this grain, one almost round and either white or black. This form is sometimes, though less frequently, used for ornamental purposes than the next, but it constitutes an important article of food amongst the hill tribes on the eastern frontier of India. The second form is tubular, about half an inch long. This is extensively used for decorative purposes, the dresses worn by the Karen women being often completely covered by pretty designs of this grain. It is also used by the Nágá and other Assam tribes in the construction of ear-rings and other simple and elegant articles of personal adornment.

Corypha umbraculifera.—The *Bazarbatú* nuts imported into Bombay; also exported from North Canara by Arabs from the Persian Gulf who trade along the Western Coast. These are worn as beads by the Hindu devotees.

Cotton-wool, in large bundles, often two or three inches in diameter.—Cotton-wool is worn in ear-perforations by the Northern Manipur Nágás, and also certain classes of the Nágás proper. Similar tufts are also used in decorating the hair. As a modern degeneration it is by no means an unusual thing to find two or three empty cartridge cases placed in the ear instead of the cotton decorations—the brass ends being turned forward.

Diospyros, sp.—Gamble says that the Burmese use the wood for ear-rings. Ornaments for European use are made of *Diospyros melanoxylon* wood at Monghyr in Bengal.

Elæocarpus ganitrus, or *Rudráksha.*—The five-grooved and elegantly tubercled nuts are worn as a necklace by the followers of Ṣiva. It is considered a religous duty for them to wear a necklace of this kind. It is also supposed to have a beneficial effect on the health. Considerable importance is attached to the number of faces on the nuts. Imitations of these nuts are made in eagle-wood. The *Rudráksha* necklets have of late found great favour among European ladies, and a large collection of them has been sent to the Glasgow International Exhibition.

Elæocarpus lanceolatus, the Utrasum beads.—These are said to be imported from Java.

Elæocarpus tuberculatus.—As with the two preceding, the nuts of this tree are used as beads.

Enonymus grandiflorus, the *Siki* nut.—These are strung as necklaces.

Enonymus fimbriatus.—The red seeds are strung into ornaments for the head.

Gyrocarpus Jacquini, Zaitun.—The seeds are made into rosaries and necklaces.

Linum usitatissimum, the common flax.—Mr. F. Duthie, Superintendent of the Botanical Gardens at Sahåranpur, states that "some necklaces said to be composed of sections of the stems of this plant were sent to him from Calcutta."

Nelumbium speciosum, the Sacred Lotus or *Padma.*—Designs of this flower are frequent in Hindu and Buddhistic sculptures, an inverted lotus forming the dome of all Buddhists and Jain temples. It is sacred to *Lakshmi,* the Goddess of Wealth. The dry nuts are strung as beads.

Ocimum basilicum, the Sweet-scented Basil.—The wood is used like the preceding.

Oryza sativa.—Chains made of unhusked rice were sent to the Calcutta International Exhibition from Gushkará, a village in the Bardwán District.

Putranjiva Roxburghii.—The black nuts of this plant are made into necklaces and rosaries and are worn by Bráhmans and put round the necks of children to ward off diseases caused by evil spirits; hence the name *putra-jiva,* life of a child.

Reeds.—Pieces of reeds are worn in the ears by some of the Assam tribes. They are also used to enlarge the ear-perforations, being bent like the letter N or W.

Santalum album.—Beads made of sandal-wood are strung into necklaces, Large quantities of such necklaces are sold to Muhammadan pilgrims at Ajmir.

Symplocos spicata.—The *Búri* of Sylhet.—*Roxburgh* says the seeds of this plant are very hard, about the size of a pea, and resemble the minute pitcher; when perforated they are strung like beads and by the people are put round the necks of their children to prevent evil.

Tamarix articulata.—The *Farás.*—The wood is made into small ornaments.

Vateria indica.—The Indian copal tree.—The resin is made into beads, which very much resemble the true amber.

V.—Manufactures in Metal.

Metal manufactures are perhaps the most important of all Indian art-ware. Such articles have been made in this country from very ancient times. In the *Rig-Veda,* supposed to be the oldest book in the world, golden cups are alluded to. Twashtá, the Vulcan of the Hindu mythology, acquired great celebrity for his skill in making metallic articles, but he was surpassed by the Ribhus in the art of making "sacrificial vessels of wood and metal, and on one occasion Twashtá is said to have sought to slay his rivals, and on another to have applauded their design, and admired the brilliant results of their skill." Vessels made of gold, silver, and inferior metals are frequently mentioned in comparatively modern works. Dr. Rájendra Lála Mitra states:—"In a mediæval work, the *Káliká Purána,* plates of gold are described to remove excesses of the three humours, and promote the strength of the vision; those of silver, favourable and inimical to bile, but calculated to increase the secretion of wind and phlegm; those of bronze, agreeable and intellectual, but favourable to undue excitement of blood and bile; those of brass, wind-generating, irritating, hot, and heat and phlegm destroying; those of magnetic iron, most beneficial in overcoming anasarca, jaundice, and anæmia; those of other stones or clay are inauspicious; those of wood wholesome, invigorating, and poison-destroying." Coming down to later times, *viz.*, the Buddhist period, we find metallic vessels in universal use, as they are at the present day.

Most of the household utensils in India are at the present time made of metal. They take the place of porcelain, glass, and silver plate in a European household. As a matter of course rich men can alone afford to have gold and silver plate. The manufacture of household articles in precious metals is therefore limited to only a few places, but that in brass and copper forms an extensive industry practised all over the country. The uses to which brass and copper are put are almost endless, and the shapes and patterns of vessels made of them are often very elegant, sometimes grotesque and curious.

Such shapes had their origin in shells of fruits like those of the gourds, leaves of trees like those of the lotus and lily, and bones and horns of animals used for household utensils in primitive times. The original articles made of gourds, leaves, &c., are still in use. We hold them sacred, and employ them for religious purposes. Our religious ascetics, who devote their life in reading the sacred books and making pilgrimages all over India, still use the gourd shell (*Kamandala*) for their water-vessel, eschewing its harder and stronger imitation in brass. We still make platters and cups of leaves, on which we occasionally eat our food, and the water poured out of a hollowed rhinoceros horn is the most acceptable to the gods and the manes. Thus conservatism here, as elsewhere, has made a compromise with age, knowledge, and progress. Bit by bit it has had to give way, and to reluctantly allow the development of the leaf platter into stone platter, stone platter into clay platter, clay platter into wood platter, and wood platter into copper platter. By this time, however, its patience was well exhausted; and when the early Aryans in their exploring rambles through the Himalayan slopes discovered copper and hailed it as an appropriate substance for the manufacture of useful articles, conservatism found in it a more substantial ground than that afforded by wood, clay, or stone to resist any further onslaught upon its time-honoured habits. It refused to move any further, and set its face strongly against any fresh discoveries. Yet, when gold and silver came into the Aryan world *their* claims could not be ignored, and not only an exception was made in their favour, but, as in other countries, they got the first and second place among the metals known to man. Copper, however, is still held as the purest of all inferior metals, and until recently all the sacrificial vessels were entirely made of copper. But for ordinary household purposes the Hindus have long since given preference to the gold coloured brass, and vessels made of it have now come into use in religious ceremonials in many parts of India. Its purity has been further established by its immunity from defilement by the touch of a low caste man. But the difficulty of keeping brass clean and shining soon became rather a laborious task to the early Hindus, and they had therefore to discover a method of toughening it, better to resist the climatic influences of a hot country like India. The result is the *kánsá* or *phul*, a form of bell-metal or white brass, composed of four parts of copper to one of tin. Brass usually contains three parts of copper to one of zinc. It is extensively used in the manufacture of plates, cups, and drinking glasses. Bell-metal is, however, an article of which the purity is rather questionable, for it easily gets defiled by the touch of a man from whose hands you cannot take water with safety to your caste. Muhammadans in India as a rule prefer copper vessels, which they get tinned. The household articles generally made of brass are sacrificial utensils, cooking pots, water vessels, plates, cups, and drinking glasses, spittoons, smoking bowls, betel-holders, betel-nut cutters, scent-sprinklers, lamps, antimony-holders, bird-cages, bells, inkstands, pen-cases, &c.

Gold and Silver Plate.

As stated before, golden cups are mentioned in the earliest of Hindu books, *viz.*, the *Rig-Veda*. Later books also offer abundant evidence to shew that golden plates were in use in India from very early times. The custom followed in ancient India of making presents in large golden trays is well rendered by Sir Edwin Arnold in his Light of Asia in describing the rejoicings that took place at Kapilavastu on the birth of prince Siddhártha :—

> "Moreover, from afar came merchant men,
> Bringing, on tidings of his birth, rich gifts
> In golden trays—goat shawls, and nard and jade,
> Turkises 'evening sky' tint, woven webs."

It is not known whether any old specimen of gold or silver work now exists in the country. The chief repositories of such articles, *viz.*, the palaces of the princes and the temples of gods, have in later times passed through so many vicissitudes, that most of the plates and jewellery must have found their way to the melting pot. Even if any article has by chance escaped this wreck of time, its date cannot be easily ascertained in a country where history has usurped the privileges of poetry. According to Sir George Birdwood, the oldest example of a really ancient work is a gold casket found within a Buddhist tope near Jallalabad. The casket contained some copper coins, which shewed that the monument was built about fifty years before Christ. Sir George Birdwood thus describes the gold casket :—

"The upper and lower rims of the casket are studded with Balas rubies, in alternation with a raised device resembling the *srivatsa*, or curl on the breast of figures of Vishnu and Krishna ; and between these jewelled lines, the whole circumference of the casket is divided into eight niches enshrining four figures represented twice over. The niches are formed by a series of flat pilasters supporting finely-turned arches, circular below and peaked above, between which are figures of cranes with outstretched wings. The whole executed in the finest style of beaten (*repoussé*) goldsmiths' work."

The gold casket belongs to the India Office Library and has been lent for exhibition in the Indian Section of the South Kensington Museum.

The manufacture of gold and silver plate must be an industry of a very limited extent. The abolition of native Indian courts has no doubt told heavily on the trade, and its revival cannot be hoped for until the heavy import duty levied in England upon such articles is removed.

Most of the jewellers in Bengal can imitate gold and silver plate of any form or pattern, but the demand for such work is small, and except at Dacca and Cuttack they are not made unless specially ordered. The filigrain work of Dacca and Cuttack is celebrated for its fineness and delicacy. It is made in the same way as filigrain jewellery described in a previous page. The articles made are generally scent-holders, rosewater sprinklers, card-cases, *Hukkas* (smoking bowls), &c. The cost of labour is high, and equals, or in the case of specially good work exceeds, the price of the silver. Trays, plates, drinking glasses, and other articles of a similar nature are made of beaten silver. A filigrain betel-box, with pendants, a scent-holder, and a rosewater sprinkler would cost about R800. Two scent-holders, consisting of an ornamental centre-piece with a receptacle on the top for the scent, were sent from Cuttack to the Calcutta International Exhibition, on which the price put was R3,078. A card-case from the same place would cost about R25; a basket R55; a cigar-case R84; a tray R68, &c. Silver articles are also made at Murshidabad. A curious pipe was sent from this place to the Calcutta International Exhibition. It had a small flower at its apex, which revolved as each puff of smoke was drawn. A pair of curiously shaped ewers was sent to the same Exhibition from Darjiling. The work was Tibetian and the ewers were used in Buddhist religious services for holding flowers. Sir George Birdwood in his "Industrial Arts of India" states that at Chittagong "the manufacture of vessels in gold and silver is a growing industry; but the gold and silver smiths there can only execute plain work to pattern, and do not seem to have any designs of their own." No specimens of Chittagong work were, however, sent either to the Calcutta International Exhibition or the Colonial and Indian Exhibition. The industry therefore must be of an insignificant character. Silver and gold plate and jewellery of both European and Indian patterns are now extensively made in the suburbs of Calcutta. The trade has only been lately established by men who, in addition to their native education, received a training in the European jewellers' shops at Calcutta. A novelty in silver work is the silver fish, neatly and ingeniously made in many places in Bengal, notably at Kharakpur in the Monghyr District, Darbhángá, Ránchi, and Bod in the Hill States of Orissa. It is used as a scent-holder, and the local price is R7 each. A collection of silver fish from Kharakpur has been sent to the Glasgow International Exhibition.

In the North-Western Provinces, Lucknow and Rámpur are the two principal places where gold and silver plate is made. The articles turned out are generally of the same description as those manufactured at Dacca and Cuttack, but of late they have taken to making things for European use, like tea-sets, plates, saucers, salt-cellars, sugar-basins, and milk-pots. The style of work is different here, and there is a considerable variety in the designs. Some of the work is in plain silver, and some is ornamental. In some the ornaments are engraved, while in others they are beaten out (*repoussé*). Silver gilt articles are also made at Lucknow. Sir George Birdwood states that "Lucknow was once famous for its vessels of mixed gold and silver, but since the abolition of the native court of Oudh, their production, as of all the other sumptuary arts of this once royal and renowned polytechnical city, has steadily declined." A collection of Lucknow silver work has been sent to the Glasgow International Exhibition. The names of patterns commonly known at Lucknow are the hunting pattern, jungle pattern, Kashmir pattern, rose pattern, snake pattern, snake and *Swámi* pattern. A silver betel-case, with nut-cutter, cups, spoon, &c., would cost about R60; a silver goblet R50 to R60; a silver drinking glass R50; a mug of hunting pattern with arches, R22; ditto of jungle pattern, R16; a bowl of hunting pattern, R78; a tea-pot of jungle pattern, R76; a sugar-basin, R20; a cream jug, R15; a toilet bottle, R21, &c. A little silver plate is made of Rámpur pattern in the District of Sitápur; but it appears to be an imitation of European work, turned out by a local goldsmith at the desire of the wealthy landlord of the place. Silver fish is made at Faizabad and Hámirpur: that made in the former place has a golden head. Silver toys representing animals are made at Gokul in the Muttra District. These articles are used as scent-holders.

In the Panjáb, articles of a similar nature like those made in Bengal and the North-Western Provinces are made at Delhi, Kapurthala, Jallandhar, Amritsar, and Lahore. Mr. Kipling states:—

"There is said to be only one exclusively silversmith at Delhi who regularly produces objects of any size. The ordinary silversmiths who are to be found in every village and town confine themselves principally to ornaments and are frequently quite as much money-lenders as artificers. Large objects are made for native courts frequently by a workman, who, after the old feudal fashion, is a State servant. There is not much demand for plate in the European sense, and when it is wanted in the form of trays, plates, cups, *hukkas*, *chhilams*, household utensils, and temple ornaments, the work is often undertaken by a *Taliyár*, who habitually works in copper, and who works at a cheaper rate than the silversmith proper."

Mr. Baden Powell does not speak very highly of the Panjáb silver vessels. He characterises them as rude and wanting in finish. He further states:—

"The silver vessels in use in rich men's houses are the ugliest things imaginable; all that is wanted is to have pure silver, dull, white and heavy. Polishing silver, and the contrast of bright and frosted silver, is unknown and hardly appreciated."

But he praises the great delicacy and ingenuity displayed in "chasing, ornamenting, and engraving patterns on the various articles." The articles made at Amritsar are of the Kashmir style; in fact they are mostly made by Kashmiris settled in that city. A silver ink and pen case in this style of work was sent to the Colonial and Indian Exhibition. A silver box with lock and key and a silver chair made at Amritsar were sent to the Calcutta International Exhibition. In the Lahore Exhibition was shown a silver casket, ornamented with flower, done in a sort of *repoussé* work. The only other place, besides Amritsar, which contributed specimens of silver ware to the last two great Exhibitions, *viz.*, the Calcutta and the Colonial, is Patiálá. To the first it contributed two silver gilt water-vessels valued at R132; and to the Colonial and Indian Exhibition it contributed a pair of similar articles. These ewers are of Hindu pattern, used like the Musalman *Aftábá* for drinking water and domestic purposes. To the Lahore Exhibition of 1870, Lahore, Ludhiáná, Kapurthala, and the Hill States sent many silver articles, but evidently the ware made in those places was not considered of sufficient importance to be displayed in the last two Exhibitions mentioned above. But still, the articles which Kapurthala exhibited at Lahore must have been very curious. They consisted of dates imitated in silver, and a series of vessels of glass covered with silver work. Mr. Baden Powell stated that only two men knew how to make this kind of work, one of whom resided at Kapurthala and the other at Amritsar. "The stems of the glass and the rim are covered with silver gilt and flowered (not filigree work), and the bowl with a covering of silver net, made of fine wire. Drinking cups and vases are made in this way."

Kashmir is famous for its parcel gilt silver ware. The patterns consist of small sprigs of leaves hammered out in relief all over the vessel. Sometimes the ground is silver and the sprigs are parcel gilt: it is then known as the *Gangá-Jamuná* pattern. This *Gangá-Jamuná* is a favourite pattern with Indian artists, which they love to introduce into all sorts of manufactures. It got its name from the two rivers Gangá (Ganges) and Jamuná (Jumna), which between them enclose a tract of land in Upper India known by the name of Doab or "Two-Waters." The colour of the waters that the Ganges carries down to the sea is described in the books as white, while those of its tributary the Jumna deep blue. Hence when on the same article patterns of two colours meet or run side by side, the vessel is described to be of *Gangá-Jamuná* pattern. The vessel which the Kashmir artisans generally made was the *Suráhi*, a water goblet of very ancient and extremely elegant form. Plates, goblets, cups, and other articles are now produced. Sir George Birdwood thus describes Kashmir silver work:—

"The best known is the parcel gilt silver work of Kashmir, which is almost confined to the production of the water-vessels or *suráhis,* copied from the clay goblets in use throughout the northern parts of the Panjáb. Their elegant shapes and delicate tracery, graven through the gilding to the dead white silver below, which softens the lustre of the gold to a pearly radiance, gives a most charming effect to this refined and graceful work. It is an art said to have been imported by the Mughuls, but influenced by the natural superiority of the people of the Kashmir valley over all other orientals in elaborating decorative details of good design, whether in metal work, hammered and cut, or enamelling, or weaving. Cups are also made in this work, and trays of a very pretty four-cornered pattern, the corners being shaped like the Muhammadan arch. Among the Prince of Wales' Indian presents there is a tray with six cups and saucers in 'ruddy gold,' which is an exquisite example of the goldsmiths' art of Kashmir. There is also in the Prince of Wales' collection a remarkable candelabrum, in silver gilt, from Srinagar, shaped like a conventional tree, and ornamented all over with the crescent and flame device, and hanging fishes, its design being evidently derived through Persia from a Turkoman original. The candelabra seen in Hindu temples constantly take this tree form, without the addition of the symbols of the sky and ether; and trees of solid gold and silver, representing the mango or any other tree, and of all sizes, are common decorations in Hindu houses."

A very fine collection of Kashmir silver work has been sent to the Glasgow International Exhibition. It is generally sold by weight, the local price being R1-4 per *tolá* of 180 grains. The same men who make enamelled copper articles also make the silver ware. The two men at present noted for this kind of work are Ahmadju and Habibju of Srinagar.

Chanda in the Central Provinces was formerly famous for its gold and silver work. Sir George Birdwood, in his book on "Industrial Arts of India (1880)," stated that the articles have lost much of their fame, "owing to the decreased demand for their wares under British rule. The District still, however, possesses good goldsmiths and silversmiths, whose work is marked by the strongest local character." The industry seems now to have entirely perished, for not only were no specimens sent to the recent Exhibitions, but no mention of it has been made by the Provincial officer in his report to the Government of India on the art-manufactures of the Provinces.

Naturally, like Kashmir and Kach, Rajputana, with its native courts, affords great encouragement to the manufacture of gold and silver plate. A very fine collection of such work was sent from Tonk to the Jaipur Exhibition, to which the Jury awarded the first prize, for, as they said, they "were good in design as well as in execution," and also because they were "the best and most characteristic present." The collection consisted of open work caskets, a large scent-holder, with numerous receptacles for perfumes arranged like flower-buds on a tree, betel-holders, rosewater sprinklers, and other articles kept in the houses of wealthy men in this country. Some of these articles have been described as "of plain silver, embossed or pierced in bold floral or geometrical designs," while the greater part of them "were also parcel gilt, and the judicious and artistic manner in which the gold was employed greatly increased the beauty of the plate, and was well calculated to produce a rich effect in the conditions under which it is usually seen, namely, in a *Durbar* or public assembly, where minute examination is impossible." Many of the articles would, however, bear a closer examination, as they were well finished and the designs were beautifully executed. The workmen who made the Tonk plate were all Hindus, residents of Chabrá, Pirawá, and Sironj. Gold and silver plate made at Jaipur "is noted more for its massiveness, with occasional grace of form, than for the elaboration of its surface ornament." Jaipur has now under its employ an artisan from Alwar named Nand Kishor, who received his education at the Government Engineering College in Rurki. He has introduced a new style of surface decoration, *viz.*, of engraving figures on the plate in such a way as to imitate in metal the clothing of human beings, natural fur of animals, and the feathers of birds. But in the opinion of Dr. Hendley, "such work, clever as it is, is unsuitable to silver, though on gold perhaps it is more excusable, as the value of the latter metal would prevent frequent use and therefore much cleaning." Larger articles, such as thrones and staves of canopies, are made at Jaipur in precious metals. At Bogru, a town in the Jaipur State, silver plate is made on a moderate scale, by a local goldsmith. A handsomely designed cup, with a cover ending in a spout, carried off the second prize at the Jaipur Exhibition. The Mahárájá of Alwar has a number of silversmiths in his employ, who turned out several specimens of filigrain and chased work for the Colonial and Indian Exhibition. As usual, the articles made are tumblers, cups, saucers, tea-pots, *Hukkas*, betel-holders, and other things suitable for a nobleman's house in India. Processions with figures of men and animals, carriages, and other accessories are often beautifully engraved on the silver tumblers and cups, the designs of which are generally admired. For silver articles the charge for workmanship is eight annas per *tolá* (180 grains). Gold articles of a similar description are made for the State by goldsmiths in the pay of the Chief. Patan, a town in the little State of Jhallawar, has a reputation for its crane-shaped rose-water sprinkler. Such scent-distributors are very tastefully made here: they contain from 12 ounces to 2 pounds of silver, and are sold by weight, the ruling price being R60 per ℔. Perfume boxes, betel-nut trays, tumblers, cups, *Hukkas*, and smoking bowls with covers and silver chains hanging from them are also made at Patan, and sold by weight at the same rate of price. Nor is the little State of Bikánir, though seated among the sands of a howling desert and remote from the roads and railways of modern Indian civilisation, any way behind in this sumptuary art, for which Kach on one side and the sister States of Rajputana on the other have acquired a celebrity among the wealthy classes of India. On the other hand, her very inaccessibility attracted towards her a large number of peaceful merchants, who left their homes in the north and south to escape the extortion of the later Muhammadan kings and the pillage of the Marhattas bent upon destroying the Musalman empire in India. The wealth they brought with them or which they now remit from the distant cities where they trade at the present day, contributed largely to the development of this and other art-manufactures of Bikánir. Excellent examples of Bikánir silver work thus occupied a prominent place both at Jaipur and in the later Exhibition in London. Among the collection shewn in the former Dr. Hendley specially noticed an *Abkhorá* or drinking vessel, which was covered with an embossed floral design, and also a salver of silver *niello*, in which the black outlines of the engraved pattern formed a strong contrast with the shining white of the silver ground. Illustrations of both these articles have been included in the *Journal of Indian Art*. Besides the objects mentioned above, silver is often employed in the manufacture of images, shrines of temples, trappings and harness of elephants, camels, and horses, maces or *chobs* which peons carry as insignia of the high position of their masters, bedstead legs, swinging cots, and other articles whereever it is possible for wealth to make a display.

Work almost similar to that made in Upper India

and Rajputana is done at Gwalior, Rámpurá in the Indor State, and Dhar, Alipurá, and Chhatrapur in Central India. The articles made at Gwalior and Rámpurá have a great reputation for their superior design and fineness of execution, those of the latter chiefly consisting of silver *repoussé* work ornamented with gold. Dhar makes an ingenious rose-water sprinkler in the form of a bird, which can be had for R60.

But no part of India is more celebrated for its work in precious metals than Kach in the Bombay Presidency. The interest lately created among Europeans in the art-manufactures of India has enhanced the demand for such articles, and the industry would have a great future before it if ever the Government of England could be induced to abolish the import duty on gold and silver plate. The increase in the demand has not produced in this case the usual degeneration in the design and execution of the articles turned out. This is probably due to the fact that those who can afford to pay the price of silver can also afford to pay for good workmanship. The same rule does not apply to brass, wood, or stone upon which travellers pounce in order to carry with them a simple *memento* of their visit to the continent of India. They want something cheap with the reputation of having been cut and carved by the dusky hands of men who live in this fabled land. They care little for that which has received a vivid impression upon it of the oriental mind, that intuitively conceives the correct lines of beauty and patiently guides the dexterous hand to bring them out in a concrete form. Dholka, Viragram, Ahmadabad, Junágad, and other places in Gujrát were formerly famous for their plate, but Kach has now taken them all under its wing; and whether such articles are made at Bombay, Poona, or Ahmadnagar, they all go by the name of "Kach silver ware." A large collection of this ware, consisting of salvers, mugs, milk-jugs, card-cases, &c., has been sent to the Glasgow International Exhibition. Over and above the price of gold or silver, the charge for workmanship prevailing in Kach is from a quarter of a rupee to two rupees per *tolá* (180 grains) for gold, and from two annas to eight annas per *tolá* for silver.

In the Madras Presidency gold and silver wares are made at Dindigul, Palai in Madura District, Godávari, Tanjore, Tirupati in North Arcot District, Cochin, and Vizianagram. Articles in solid silver are also made in the Madras School of Art, from which a candlestick designed after the manner of a native Hindu lamp, a water-vessel in solid silver, chased and ornamented, and a spoon, with a bowl supported by parrots, the stem ending with a five-headed snake overshadowing the *Lingam*, were sent to the Colonial and Indian Exhibition. A card-case, a scent-casket, and a bouquet-holder of filigrain work, a betel-nut box with fluted and embossed ornamentation, and a shallow silver bowl with fluted sides and chased centre, were sent to the above Exhibition by the Mahárájá of Cochin, while the Prince of Vizianagram contributed elephant seats (howdahs) and trappings for elephants and horses used on ceremonious occasions. Among the presents made to His Royal Highness the Prince of Wales while he was in India was a shrine screen, of old Madras pierced and hammered silver, which in Sir George Birdwood's opinion "is a wonderful example of manipulative dexterity."

There is some originality in the form of trays, scent-holders, betel-boxes, water-goglets, cups, and other articles made by the gold and silver smiths of Mysore, and they display a considerable amount of delicacy and ingenuity in chasing, ornamenting, and engraving the patterns. For superior workmanship in silver, the wages equal the value of the metal used, and in gold one half its value. Among the presents made to the Prince of Wales was a beautiful golden tray, the rim and cover of which "are elaborately enriched with embossed flowers and leaves; while the bottom is left plain, excepting the well-proportioned border, and a centre panel of flowery geometrical design, which is enchased, so as not to interfere with its necessary flatness of surface." Scent-bottles and caskets of filigrain work are made at Travancore, and silver wire is often employed for the decoration of cocoanut shells. Zelgandal and Aurangabad are the only places in Haidrabad noted for their silver ware. The articles are made in filigrain work.

Burma silver work is gradually attracting the attention of the outside world. The following account of it has been taken from a report furnished by Mr. Tilly to the Government of India:—

"The silver work of Burma is much thought of by *connoisseurs* all over the world, and under the guidance of Europeans it is being improved, while the national characteristics are zealously preserved. The work is hammered, embossed, chased, and carved, and sometimes cut into open tracery, but it is all made in exactly the same way. It can be applied to any shape, and European patterns are often covered with the Burmese work; but the native demand is entirely for articles of simple shape, such as large round bowls without cover or legs, betel-boxes, small oval lime-boxes, and such like. More intricate shapes were made for use in the palace at Mandalay. The Burman artist treats silver in the right way, obtaining the greatest effect that the nature of the material allows. The work is either simply embossed and chased, or, in addition, the background may be cut into open tracery and a burnished lining placed within. This will be better understood after reading how an ordinary bowl is made. The purchaser when giving his order pays for the silver of which the bowl is to be made, and the rupees are melted down in a crucible over a charcoal fire. If, however, the work is to be very good, better silver is bought and is purified over a flaming fire in a flat burnt-clay saucer. Work is paid for by weight and can be obtained at from eight annas to one rupee eight annas per rupee weight; the worst work is dear at eight annas, for it is then equivalent to ordinary Indian work, which is said to cost much less, but the best or master-silversmith's work is decidedly cheap at one rupee eight annas, and the artists will not give it willingly."

In Burma plain polished cups are also sometimes made of a mixture of half gold and half brass. It produces a beautiful colour, which is said never to vanish.

Enamelled Ware.

The art of enamelling as practised in India has already been described under the head of jewellery. Jaipur occupies the pre-eminent place in this branch of Indian art-manufactures. It is an old industry in this beautiful city of many beautiful handicrafts. The oldest example of Jaipur enamel is the crutch staff on which Mahárájá Mán Singh leaned when he stood before the throne of the Emperor Akbar at the close of the sixteenth century. "It is fifty-two inches in length, and is composed of thirty-three cylinders of gold arranged on a central core of strong copper, the whole being surmounted by a crutch of light-green jade set with gems. Each of the thirty-two upper cylinders is painted in enamel with figures of animals, landscapes, and flowers. The figures are boldly and carefully drawn by one who had evidently studied in the School of Nature; the colours are wonderfully pure and brilliant, and the work is executed with more skill and evenness than anything we see at the present day." Of modern articles of note may be mentioned the round plate presented to the Prince of Wales. It took four years to complete it, is the largest specimen of the work made, and, according to Sir George Birdwood, "is in itself a monument of the Indian enameller's art." It is said that the enamel workers at Jaipur were originally brought from Lahore by Mahárájá Mán Singh. Their religion and their dependence at the present day on the Panjáb for colouring materials, Dr. Hendley thinks, confirm the tradition. Besides personal ornaments, cups and plates of gold are enamelled, and although silver enamel of good quality is frequently made, the artists do not like to work in this metal as "the difficulties of fixing the colours and the risks are much greater than when gold is used." As stated before, the form of enamelling practised at Jaipur is what is known as *champlevé*. Sir George Birdwood in his "Industrial Arts of India" thus describes the different forms of enamelling:—

"There are three forms of enamelling followed. In the first the enamel is simply applied to the metal as paint is applied to canvas, and in the second, translucent enamels are laid over a design which has been etched on, or hammered (*repoussé*) out of the metal. Both these are comparatively modern methods. The third form of enamelling by encrustation is very ancient, and is known under two varieties, namely, the *cloisonné*, in which the pattern is raised on the surface of the metal by means of strips of metal or wire wedded on to it; and the *champlevé*, in which the pattern is cut out of the metal itself. In both varieties the pattern is filled in with the enamel. In all forms of true enamelling the colouring glaze has to be fused on to the metal. There is indeed a fourth form of enamelling practised by the Japanese. They paint in the pattern coarsely, as in the first form, and then outline it with strips of copper or gold, to imitate true *cloisonné* enamels."

The principal enamellers in Jaipur are Hari Singh, Amar Singh, Kishan Singh, Ghumá Singh, Shám Singh, Ghisá Singh, Ambá Singh, Gokul and Harsukh Singh. Hari Singh and Kishan Singh are considered the best artists.

Kashmir stands next in importance in the art of

enamelling. The industry has achieved considerable development in the course of the last few years, and Kashmir enamelled work in silver, copper, and brass are now sold by all dealers in Indian art-ware in Bombay, Calcutta, and other places. Water vessels (*Lotá*), gourd-shaped vessels (*Tumbi*), goglets (*Suráhi*) and other ornamental forms, including the *Kángri* or chafferette shape wicker work, are generally made. For copper, different shades of blue are the most favourite colour, red and yellow being less common. On the silver work a light-blue colour is used. The colours are not transparent. As is usual with Kashmir artisans, they have adapted to this work the traditional shawl patterns or their modifications. Gilding in gold is usually combined with enamelling. Enamelled utensils are sold by weight; the price of silver being R1-4 per *tolá* (180 grains) and that of copper 2½ annas to 4 annas per *tolá*. The principal manufacturers of note are Ahmadju, Habibju, and Nabiju.

Betel-boxes, spice-boxes, *Hukkas*, and other small articles are enamelled at Delhi. The Delhi work is not much inferior to that of Jaipur. Enamelling is also done to some extent at Multan, Jhang, Bháwalpur, and Kangra. Mr. Kipling states that "occasionally a *gilás* or tumbler-shaped vessel, or a cup and tray of copper or silver, or a pipe mouthpiece, are enamelled at Jhang or Multan in the opaque colour peculiar to these places; but there is not a regular production." Bháwalpur makes a peculiar kind of silver vessel, called *Mokhabbá*. It is a covered dish which is highly ornamented with chasing, enamelling, and gilding. A slightly translucent blue enamel is peculiar to Bháwalpur. Bháwalpur sent a very fine collection of enamelled ware to the Jaipur Exhibition. It consisted of a water-bottle, price R85; a tumbler, R87; a scent-phial, R17; an antimony-holder, R16. These articles have been described as "parcel gilt silver enamel, coloured dark-blue and enamelled green. The patterns are chiefly conventional flowers in parcels, scrolls, and geometrical diaper work. The general effect was rich and handsome. This work does not require frequent firing. It is probably of the same origin as the Multan enamel." The art of enamelling in Kangra is chiefly devoted to personal ornaments. Small wine cups in enamelled silver were formerly made for Native Chiefs. They are still made to a limited extent. The Kangra enamel is remarkable for its excellence of blue. A little enamelling of the Kangra style is also done in Kulu, chiefly on articles of jewellery.

In the North-Western Provinces, Benares has long been famous for its enamel in gold. The industry is on the decline, and is now only done to order. A little enamelling is also done at Lucknow and Rámpur. The prices of such articles vary from R25 to R1,000. A splendid example of Lucknow enamel, in the shape of a *Hukka*, was sent to the Calcutta International Exhibition. A similar example of Lucknow work was sent to the Jaipur Exhibition by the Rewa State. It was made of silver, the blue and enamelled grounds contrasting beautifully with the flowers of white spinel.

An imitation green enamel is made at Pratábgarh in Rajputana. The process of manufacture is not known, as it is a secret jealously kept by two or three families who practise the art. Sir George Birdwood thinks that it is done "apparently by melting a thick layer of green enamel on a plate of burnished gold, and, while it is still hot, covering it with thin gold cut into mythological or hunting or other pleasure scenes, in which amid a delicate network of floriated scrolls, elephants, tigers, deer, peacocks, doves, and parrots are the shapes most conspicuously represented. After the enamel has hardened, the gold work is etched over with a graver so as to bring out the characteristic details of the ornamentation. In some cases it would seem as if the surface of the enamel was first engraved, and then the gold rubbed into the pattern so produced in the form of an amalgam, and fixed by fire." No exact information exists as to the process of manufacture. The industry is chiefly devoted to the manufacture of flat plaques of different shapes, which are sold to other artists, and utilised "either as separate ornaments or as backings for enamelled brooches or bracelets, which can thus be worn with either side outmost." Similar *quasi-enamel* is also done at Ratlám in Central India, the colour there being blue, while that of Pratábgarh is green.

In connection with the art of enamelling may be mentioned the *Niello* work of Burma, of which the, following account has been furnished by Mr. Tilly:—

"Many of the silversmiths of Burma are proficient in this art, though few are fond of it, because it entails working over a hot furnace and in sulphureous fumes. The design appears as if drawn in silver outline on a black ground. The articles made are cups, lime-boxes, plates, knife-handles, and are all quite smooth with a good polish. The black enamel used is made of lead 2 parts, silver 1 part, and copper 1 part. The materials are melted in a fierce fire and sulphur added at discretion. The object to be treated is made in silver about $\frac{1}{8}$ inch thick, upon which the design is drawn and engraved. The lines of the drawing are left alone, but all other parts are punched in and the edges cut sharp with a small chisel. The *Niello* prepared as above is finely powdered and mixed with borax and placed in all the hollows. The work is then placed under an iron cage in a fierce charcoal fire, where it is fused. It is then filed smooth, polished with sand-paper, then with charcoal dust, and finally burnished like silver work. There is a larger demand for *Niello* work than those few artists who make it can supply, and in consequence the price is higher than it ought to be. The best man, Maung Pô of Shwegyin, charges R3 for workmanship on one rupee's weight."

Encrusted Ware.

Under this head may be classed the celebrated Tanjore metal work, the art in which consists of soldering, wedging, or screwing on silver patterns and figures of Hindu deities on copper vessels. The figures are made in the famous Madras or *Swámi* style, and the white figures in high relief on red copper ground produce an effect at once bold and striking. This and the other equally admired metal industries of Tanjore are thus described by Dr. Bidie :—

"Ornamental work in copper and silver, brass and silver, and brass and copper is made at Tanjore. It is of three kinds, namely, brass graved, brass encrusted with copper, and copper encrusted with silver. Sometimes the brass and copper variety has also figures in tin introduced. In the graved brass-work the first rude impressions are made with a die, and by hammering. The work is then completed by cutting away the brass in the space between the figures, and giving it a granulated appearance with the graver. Finishing touches are also given to the figures. A *lotá* of the common globular shape is usually the subject of this kind of adornment, and the ordinary pattern embraces pannels round the bilge with figures from the popular pantheon and chaste conventional floral designs. Examined closely the figures are seen to be coarsely finished, but the general effect at a little distance is excellent. In the copper and brass ware the vessels are made of brass and covered with figures of copper, which are fixed on the base metal by hammering and a sort of dovetail union. After the copper crusts are put on and worked into shape, the figures are finished by the graver and a chisel. The designs on this ware are of the same character as those on the brass-graved vessels, but the figures are in bolder relief. The encrusting of copper ware with silver figures is a modern adaptation of the older art of covering brass with copper figures, and the silver is attached to the copper by the same kind of junction as that employed for fixing copper on brass. But as the metals are more valuable, greater trouble is taken to secure a better finish, and an examination of the silver figures in first class work shows that more graver and less die or chisel work is used than in the case of copper or brass. The designs consist, as usual, of mythological figures and floral decorations, which, although in some cases rather crowded, have yet an excellent general effect. In fact, profusion of ornament and intricate details are characteristic of all Hindu work, from the embellishment of a temple to that of a *lotá*, and, in the case of the Tanjore ware, age improves its appearance by deepening the hue of the copper, and toning down the colour of the silver. At Tirupati, North Arcot District, various patterns are stamped on the brass, and into these figures thin plates of copper or silver are pressed, and apparently fixed by hammering the edges of the brass over the other metals, so as to make a sort of dovetail. In fact, it is a rude kind of damascene work. The pieces of copper and silver thus used are introduced into the designs in a very irregular way, and the details of the figures, which are generally mythological or floral, are usually worked out by punched lines in imitation of engraving. The result is a certain barbaric splendour, but the general effect is *bizarre* in the extreme. The ware is chiefly made to be sold to the thousands of pilgrims who proceed to the famous shrine of Tirupati, and as they want something striking for their money, the designs do not usually receive much attention."

Damascened or Koftgari Work.

Sir George Birdwood describes "Damascening as the art of encrusting one metal on another, not in *crustæ*, which are soldered on or wedged into the metal surface to which they are applied, but in the form of wire, which, by undercutting and hammering, is thoroughly incorporated into the metal which it is intended to ornament. Practically, damascening is limited to encrusting gold wire, and sometimes silver wire, on the surface of iron, or steel or bronze." As its name implies, the industry originated at Damascus, where it underwent its highest development in the hands of the early goldsmiths. It was, however, brought to India directly from Kabul and Persia. Kotli Loháran near Siálkot and Gujrát, both in the Panjáb, are the two chief seats of this industry, but the art is also practised at Lahore, Jaipur, Karauli, Alwar, Datiá, &c. It is also practised to a small extent in Multan, where it was introduced about two hundred years ago by one Muhammad Murád. The use for which it was originally invented was the decoration of arms and armour, and the glory of the art has departed with that of the mighty warriors of old who fought with shields and swords, buckles and breastplates, and maces and matchlocks. The art has therefore got antiquated, but happily the makers have turned it to the ornamentation of articles for ordinary use, chiefly in a European household, and in the manufacture of such things as well as of shields, arms, and armoury which Europeans purchase as curios, *Koftgari* work in India still maintains its precarious existence.

Mr. Baden Powell thus speaks of the industry:—

"I have already explained that originally arms and armour were the only things in demand, but now, in times of peace—Othello's occupation gone—the workmen have nearly all settled in the Gujrát and Siálkot Districts, and make inlaid work on caskets, vases, pistols, combs, brooches, bracelets, and so forth.

"*Koftgari* is done by first drawing out the pattern on the steel surface with a hard steel needle or *silai*. This leaves a line sufficiently deep to catch the very fine wire laid on. The wire is of pure gold, drawn through a steel *jandri*. The wire is then hammered into the iron according to the pattern and lines already drawn, the whole is then heated and again hammered, and the surface is polished with a white porous stone; where the soft gold is required to be spread, the rubbing and hammering are repeated with greater force. The gold used is pure and very soft."

A large collection of arms, as well as articles of ordinary use have been sent to the Glasgow International Exhibition by private exhibitors on their own account. The work is of various patterns, the most favourite being the *Gangá-Jamuná* described in a previous page. In the true *Koft*, called *Tahnishán*, the designs are deeply cut in grooves into which the gold or silver wire is inlaid, and hammered in while the metal is hot and then burnished. This is, however, expensive, and "hence to meet the demand of the needy, and of the tourist, who likes a good deal for his money, the workman makes his gold adhere to outlines which have been prepared with a file, and for the common kinds of work is even satisfied with using gold leaf." In this kind of cheap work the ornaments are not only superficial, but "the gold is inferior, and the design wanting in character, and too diffuse."

The manufacturers often take a great pride to form, by a skilful inlay of the wire, verses from the Kurán, spells, poetical passages, and prayers for good fortune and prizes at an Exhibition. Thus a shield may contain an Arabic spell worn as a talisman by good Musalmans for protection from all evils and cure for diseases which flesh is subject to. Verses like the following from the *Gulistán* might also be frequently seen :—

> Jahán ái barádar na mánad bakhsh;
> Dil andar Jahán Afri band o bas.
> Makun takiyá bar umr duniyá o pusht;
> Kih bisiár kas chun tu parward o kusht.
>
> "O brother, the world is transitory, therefore put your faith in the Creator; do not rely upon life and the world, for many like you lived and died."

The following are the names of the principal artisans who sent their goods to the Glasgow International Exhibition and the value of their articles :—Ismail Mistri, R430; Khurshid Ahmad and Faiz Ahmad, R1,287; Muhammad-Din, R210; Sharif-Din, R405; Sultán Bakhsh, R378; Ghulám Husain, R157; Qázi Ghuláb-Din, R345; Ramján Mistri, R265; Muhammad Husain, R200; Satr-ud-din Mistri, R311; Imám-ud-din, R540; Nizám-ud-din Mistri, R305, Ala-ud-din Mistri, R345; Chirág-Din Mistri, R340; Fazl Karim, R240; Ahmad Yar, R186;

Khod Yar, R415; Fateh-Din, R301; Fazl-Din, 346; Karm Ilahi, R675; Ibrahim Mistri, R376; Sharf-Din, R230; Alah Muhammad, R230; Talab-Din, R165; Ghulám Muhammad, R563; Sultán Muhammad, R362; Mahtab-Din, R222; Kutab-Din, R181; Nabi Bakhsh, R290; Háji Abdur-Rahman, R693; Nazar Muhammad, R1,350; Sharf-Din, R490; Miyán Nathu, R455; Ján Muhammad, R336; Muhammad Bakhsh, R620; Kutab-Din, R329; Buddha Mistri, R609; Badr-ud-Din Mistri, R205; Háji Karim Bakhsh, R257; Háji Muhammad Yar, R1,585; Umr-ud-din, R345; Muhammad-Din, R612; Muhammad Sharif, R820; Abdul Aziz, R819; Fateh-Din, R1,315; &c., &c.

The next place of importance where damascened work is largely done is Jaipur. Knives, scissors, and betel-nut cutters are decorated in *Koft* work at Alwar. But there is only one man who is engaged in this kind of work, and he is employed by the State. At Datiá sword-hilts, paper knives, paper weights, and other articles of similar nature are inlaid with gold wire.

At Perambular in the Trichinopoly District of Madras, water-bottles made of brass are sometimes inlaid with patterns of zinc; but as a rule the work is coarse and clumsy.

In Burma, silversmiths occasionally do a little damascening either of silver or gold on blackened copper, or silver and brass on iron. The copper is blackened by melting with five per cent. of gold and a little sulphur.

Bidri-Ware.

Another style of damascened ware is what is known as the *Bidri* work. This peculiar art derived its name from the town of Bidar, its original home, which, according to tradition, was founded by a Hindu king of the same name, four centuries before the Christian era. The place lies about 75 miles to the north-west of Haidrabad, within the dominions of the Nizam. Bidar was long the capital of a Hindu kingdom of the same name, and after its subversion by the Muhammadans it continued to be the seat of Government under the Bahmani Dynasty of the Musalman sovereigns of Deccan. It is said that one of the Hindu kings of Bidar invented the manufacture of *Bidri* ware, who used the articles to hold flowers and other offerings which he daily presented to his household gods. Considerable improvements were introduced into the manufacture by his Hindu successors; but it attained its present state of excellence under the Muhammadans, who, wherever they went, not only gave great encouragement to the indigenous manufactures, but also imported from other parts of India, as well as from the chief seats of Musalman civilisation in Western Asia, new arts and industrial crafts. Like many other handicrafts of India, it declined with the downfall of the Muhammadan Empire, although it attracted the notice of men like Dr. Heyne, Dr. Buchanan Hamilton, Captain Newbald, Dr. Smith, and others. Its decline as an industry was so complete that, in the *Oudh Gazetteer*, the most comprehensive work on that province yet published, no mention is made of *Bidri*-ware among the manufactures of Lucknow, although for more than a century it flourished most in the capital of Oudh. Much has been done to encourage and promote this manufacture, so far as the European market is concerned, by the Department of Agriculture and Commerce in the North-Western Provinces. The exertions of the Department were greatly aided by the International Exhibitions held at Melbourne and Calcutta, where

Indian art-ware occupied a prominent place, by the local exhibitions at Simla, Calcutta, and Jaipur, where *Bidri*-ware found an extensive sale, and by the Colonial and Indian Exhibition of London (1886).

The most ordinary articles of *Bidri*-ware are *Hukkas* or smoking bowls, *Suráhis* or water-goglets, *Pikdáns* or spittoons, *Pándáns* or betel-cases, *Abkhorás*, or drinking cups, flower-vases, tumblers, plates, trays, &c. *Hukka* is the general name for the various kinds of appliances which the natives of India employ to smoke a prepared tobacco called *Guráku.* In many places the cocoanut shell is employed for the purpose, an imitation of which is made of wood, brass, or tin in North India, where, owing to the dryness of the climate, the actual shell does not last long. The two forms of *Hukka—Gurguri* and *Farsi*—are generally made of silver or baser metals, in the decoration of which great ingenuity is often displayed. These two forms of smoking bowls are generally oval in the middle, with a flat round base having a hole on the top into which the lower end of a tube, made of hollow reed and ornamented with coloured cloth and lace, is tightly inserted, and which serves the purpose of a pipe by which the tobacco is smoked. The water-goglet, called *Suráhi*, is an article of extremely elegant shape, and is in great demand, but seldom put to any practical use. *Pikdán* or spittoons are made of various shapes and sizes, but are generally flat, with a wide mouth. The *Pándán*, or betel-case, is an article indispensable to well-to-do Indians, who keep in it the leaves of *Piper Betel*, sliced areca nut, limes, cardamom, and other spices, which natives of eastern countries chew with or without tobacco leaf. The *Abkhorá* is a small water-vessel with a wide mouth. For European use flower-vases, tumblers, cups and saucers, plates of various sizes, trays, salt-cellars, and other articles are made.

At present, the four chief seats of *Bidri* manufacture are Bidar itself, Lucknow in Oudh, Purnia and Murshidabad in Bengal. The mode of manufacture is very nearly the same in all the places. The manufacture of *Bidri*-ware is carried on under a system of division of labour, the different processes being generally performed by three classes of people, *viz.*, the moulder, the carver, and the inlayer. The moulder prepares the alloyed metal, casts the vessel, and turns it to its proper shape by his lathe. The carver engraves the patterns on the surface of the vessel, and the inlayer designs the patterns, inlays the ornament of gold or silver, and finally colours and polishes the article. As stated before, the four notable seats of *Bidri* manufacture are Bidar, Lucknow, Purnia, and Murshidabad. In Haidrabad the industry is still an important one, as it commands an extensive sale owing to the practice prevalent in the State of presenting a set of *Bidri*-ware to the bridegroom in time of marriage. "No dowry is considered complete, among the better class of Muhammadans, unless a complete set of *Bidri*-ware, from bed-legs to a spittoon, is included. The high prices often render it necessary for the father of a family to begin his collection years before his daughter is marriageable."

It is not known when the art was brought into Lucknow and Purnia, but its manufacture at Murshidabad dates from the commencement of the present century, when it was introduced by one Mir Iláhi Bakhsh. This Iláhi Bakhsh had an apprentice named Lachhmi, whose son Munna Lál introduced many improvements in the manufacture, and at the time of his death, forty-five years ago, left the industry in a very flourishing condition. But the District authorities state that it is now slowly perishing for want of encouragement. At present, the manufacture is almost entirely in the hands of Muhammadan artisans, who are eight in number, including a female named Ladu. At Bidar, the trade is in the hands of Hindus of the Lingáyet sect. At Purnia four families of the Hindu brazier caste (Kánsáris) are engaged in moulding and turning *Bidri*-ware, who live at Bellori, a village four miles from the civil station of Purnia. The rest of the processes is performed in the old town of Purnia by several Hindu castes, such as the *Sonárs* (goldsmith), *Dhanuks* (labourers), and *Sunris* (wine-sellers), as well as by Musalmans. At Lucknow the trade is in the hands of Muhammadans, who employ the braziers to cast the mould and artisans to perform the rest of the work. In 1881 there were 13 men engaged in *Bidri*-manufacture in the town of Lucknow, who turned out ware of the estimated value of R4,000. Next year the number of manufacturers increased to 31, and the value of the work to R4,500. The patterns are generally of a floral description, more or less natural at *Bidar* and conventional in Upper India. In Purnia, the ornaments are sometimes of a Chinese character, which Sir George Birdwood supposes to have been introduced by way of Sikkim or Bhutan. In Lucknow, the figure of a fish is frequently introduced among the floral decorations to suit the taste of the Muhammadan gentry of the place. This device had its origin in the fact that the late kings of Oudh, occupying the foremost rank among the nobility of the Delhi Empire, delighted in parading their "Dignity of Fish" (*Máhi-murátib*), which consisted of the privilege of carrying before them in all state processions the representation of a fish, made of metal and borne upon a pole, with two circular gilt bells attached to it. This mark of distinction was formerly bestowed only on nobles of the highest order, and the last occasion on which an Emperor of Delhi exercised the privilege of conferring this honour was when

Sháh Alam bestowed the dignity on Lord Lake. The kings of Oudh displayed this dignity not only in its legitimate form, but employed the fish as an emblem of their high position in arts as well as in decorative architecture, and the figure of a partly natural partly conventional fish has found its way among the patterns with which the *Bidri* manufacturers of Lucknow adorn their ware. Two kinds of ware are made in Purnia: the best called *Gharki*, in which the patterns are deeply set and well finished; the other called *Karná-bidri*, in which the patterns are plainer and inferior in finish. A modified form of *Bidri*-work, called *Zarbuland*, is made at Lucknow, in which the patterns are slightly raised and not set even with the surface as in the ordinary *Bidri*-ware. This is an imitation of the encrusted copper and brass-ware, specially those of Tanjore in South India, in which the white silver designs stand in relief on the red or yellow ground of the copper or brass vessels. The process followed in the manufacture of *Zarbuland* ware is nearly the same as that for the ordinary *Bidri*, except that instead of excavating the patterns for the reception of the gold and silver plates, the ornamental designs are raised above the surface and chased. Occasionally gilt silver, instead of the genuine article, is used in covering the patterns of *Zarbuland* work.

The following may be stated as the prices of typical specimens of *Bidri*-ware :—

Bidar manufactures.—Teapoy R195, spittoon R125, wash-hand basin R55, *Suráhis* R16 to R30, flower vases R22 to R45, trays R5 to R24. *Lucknow plain manufactures.*—*Hukka* R6 to R85, drinking glass with cover and plate R42, spittoon R25, plate R8 to R50. *Ditto Zarbuland manufactures.*—Goblet R14, betel case R20, spittoon R35, *Hukka* R6 to R20, wine glass R4, cup with cover and saucer R40, drinking glass with ditto R30, plate R22. Murshidabad and Purnia chiefly make *Hukkas*, the price of which is about R30. A *Suráhi* made in Purnia was priced at R11.

Brass and Copper Vessels.

Brass and copper vessels are used in India for domestic purposes instead of porcelain, glass, and silver ware. Brass consists of copper and zinc, but a kind of bell-metal having copper and tin for its component parts, called *Phul* in Upper India and *Kánsá* in Bengal, is also largely employed in the manufacture of plates, cups, and drinking vessels. Ordinary domestic utensils are not decorated, as, in consonance with the Hindu idea of purity, these are required to be scrubbed with earth or sand before being washed each time they are used. Hindus generally use brass vessels for ordinary purposes; Muhammadans prefer tinned copper. Brass, copper, or bell-metal vessels may be classed as sacrificial utensils, cooking utensils, plates, cups, and drinking vessels, and miscellaneous articles.

Sacrificial vessels differ in different parts of the country, not only in shape, but in the metals in which they are made. On the Bengal side they are generally made of copper, while in other parts of India brass is largely employed. Bell-metal is not considered pure enough for such purposes. Vessels used for purposes of worship consist chiefly of a water-vessel, shaped like the long petal of a plantain flower, and is called *kosá*. A small spoon of exactly the same shape is kept along with it: it is called *kusi*. A basin with a high rim, called *Támrakunda,* in which the idol is bathed; large plates to keep flowers and other offerings, called *Pushpa-pátra* or *Tát;* a stand to place the idol when being worshipped, called *Garur-prishtha;* a brass basket with a handle to keep flowers, called *Sáji*; small cups to hold sandalwood paste and other minor offerings; a single or many-mouthed lamp which is waved before the idol; these and many other small knick-nacks form the worshipping utensils which are made of metal. The images of deities themselves are also made of brass and other metals, and considerable ingenuity is often displayed in their manufacture. A collection of such gods, specially of the old patterns if available, must be very interesting to Europeans. These sacrificial vessels are often decorated with floral designs and figures of divinities. Ornaments are often profusely lavished on the *Lotá* or *Chambu*, a water-vessel, and the *Sinhásan* or throne on which the image is kept. A detailed decription of a brass *Lotá* is given in the *Journal of Indian Art* (I, p 72) by Mr. Rivett-Carnac, from which the following extract is made :—

> "These gracefully-shaped vases, of which a specimen is given in the engraving, are chiefly to be met with in Benares, though they may be occasionally found in the bazars of other large cities. Until quite lately their significance had passed unnoticed. It is true they were known to be engraved with what were supposed to be *Das-Avatár*, or ten incarnations of Vishnu; but a hasty glance at the grotesque figures was all that was vouchsafed them, and the value of the vases lay more in their rich colouring and delicacy of outline than in any merit accorded to them on account of their ornamentation. One of the first was procured some ten years ago in Benares; a party had been made up to explore the bazar, and we came upon these objects, then unknown. This first *Chambu* was of beautiful workmanship, composed of alternate copper and brass diagonals and squares, each square or diagonal enclosing an engraving of one of the ten incarnations."

In the above extract is incidentally mentioned the first notice which Benares ware received from Europeans. Most kinds of ornamental brass work now made in India had their origin in religion, and their headquarters were in places of pilgrimage, where large numbers of pilgrims flocked from all parts of India and took away a number of such vessels as *mementos* of their visit to the holy shrines.

The following are the principal sacrificial implements sent from the Bombay Presidency to the Calcutta International Exhibition (1883):—

Chauki.—A brass stool used in worship.

Kamal.—A stand for idols, named from its resemblance to an open lotus flower, which it is meant to represent. This is also made of other patterns, by fixing it on mythological birds and four-footed animals.

Dholhára—Contains the Sivà *pancha yatan* in a cradle-shaped swing, which is worshipped by all Hindu married women, during the whole of the month of Chaitra (April), being the first month of the Sálivàhan era.

Abhishekh-pátra.—A cup with a hole in the bottom through which water falls on the idol placed below.

Támhán.—Used for washing idols.

Samai.—Open lamps placed one on either side of the stands for holding the idols.

Niranjan.—Used for burning butter before the idols.

Pyále.—Cups with plates, one for keeping the sugar which is offered at the end of the worship, and another for keeping the *panchámrit* (five nectars) or the five products of the cow, with which the idols are washed before they are bathed with plain water.

Udabatticke Ghar.—A pair of stands for holding the incense sticks (*udabatti*) which are kept burning before the idols.

Ghantá.—A bell rung at the end of the worship.

Arghya.—An ablution cup, from which the sacred water is poured in making the offerings.

Halakárti.—A pair of incense-burners, on which a few grains of rice are placed. Over the rice is placed a piece of camphor and ignited.

Adni-Shankháchi.—A tortoise-shaped stand for the conch (*shankh*) shell worshipped prior to commencing worshipping the idols.

Pyálá with *Tabakdi.*—A cup and plate for washing idols.

Salonkhya.—The stand on which is placed the symbols of Siva and Párvati.

Sampushta.—A box in three pieces for keeping the idols for the night after the evening worship. Is also used as a convenient case for idols when the owner is travelling.

Sandhechi Pali.—The ablution spoon used during the performance of *Sandhyá* and other religious ceremonies.

Gangájali.—It is the vessel in which the sacred water of the Ganges (after which it is named) is kept and worshipped along with the idols. The small head forming the stopper is symbolic of the Ganges.

Dabi Kápráchi.—A box for keeping camphor which is burnt before the idols.

Dabi, Halud Kunkwáchi.—Boxes, one for the yellow and the other for the red turmeric powders. These powders are sprinkled over the idols during worship.

Dabi Sakharechi.—A box in which the sugar required for the ceremony at the end of the worship is kept.

Panchárti.—A lamp in which clarified butter is burnt before the idols.

Pujá-pátra.—Used for carrying to the temple flowers, sandalwood paste, and other ingredients used for worship.

Tulasi Vrindávan.—A flower-pot for maturing the sacred *tulasi* (*Ocimum sanctum*) plant.

Pávák.—It is a Gujrát shape, and is used by the Gujrátis as a support to the thigh while taking meals in a squatting position.

Khandil.—A hanging lamp with a chain. The chain is passed through an iron ring, fixed to the upper beam of a door-way frame and the hook at its end is fitted into the largest of the links. One lamp thus placed in a door-way is sufficient to light two adjoining rooms.

Karanda (*Kunkvácha*).—Box for keeping red powder which is applied by native women—both married and unmarried, not widows—to their foreheads. It has two compartments; in the lower is placed the red powder, made by mixing turmeric, carbonate of soda, and lemon juice, in certain proportions; and in the upper is fixed a mirror to the lower lid, and a small box to the upper lid for keeping bees'-wax, with which the red powder is made to adhere to the forehead.

Cooking pots are not decorated. They are always rough and plain. Of these may be mentioned the *Deg*, a large vessel made of copper and tinned. Food is cooked in it chiefly by the Muhammadans in feasts and festivals, when a large number of people have to be fed. The smaller form of it is called the *Degchi*, which is suitable for ordinary household purposes. *Hánri*, *Bokno*, *Bantloi*, &c., are forms of brass cooking pots. A large jar to hold water, called *Ghará*, is used all over the country. It is of various shapes and patterns, and is either cast in a mould or hammered into shape. A very curious brass article has lately come into use in Bengal in the shape of a rice-washer. The article formerly made to serve this purpose was a thickly woven bamboo basket work, of which its present brass form is an imitation. Pans, spoons, and other small articles are made of brass for use in the cook-room.

Plates, cups, and drinking-vessels are almost endless in their shape, size, and pattern. Plates go by the name of *Tháli*, *Tashtari*, and *Rekábi* in Upper India, cups are called *Katorá* or *Báti*, and drinking-vessels are *Aftábá*, *Garuá*, *Badná*, *Abkhorá*, *Gilás* (a corruption of glass), &c. *Suráhi* is a goglet to hold drinking water. It was originally an earthen vessel and its shape is a very ancient one. *Suráhi* is a favourite subject with the decorative metal-manufacturers for ornamentation.

Of miscellaneous objects made in brass or copper may be mentioned the *Hukka*, or the smoking bowl, the scent-holders, and the *Pándán* or a receptacle to keep betel leaves and the spices chewed with it. These articles are very often ornamented, as they do not require to be constantly scrubbed, like those which come in touch with cooked food.

The following account of the metal-manufactures carried on each part of India has been taken from the reports supplied by the Provincial officers.

In Bengal vessels of brass and bell-metal are made in many places, those of Khánkrá near Murshidabad and Jhanjharpur near Darbhángá being considered the best. The other places noted for such manufactures are Calcutta itself, Kánchannagar in Bardwán, Rájsháhi, Kishanganj in Purnia, Islamabad in Dacca, Bánsberiá in Hugli, and Cuttack. Patna makes a peculiar kind of brass tea-urn which is in constant demand among the better classes of Hindus and Muhammadans. Brass articles are for the most part plain, being simply moulded and beaten into the required shape, and have no claim to be classed as art-manufactures, although in some a rough attempt is made at decoration with lines, dots or figures of deities and animals. They are sold by weight, the price varying from half a rupee to two rupees a pound, according to the quality of the metal and the labour spent in the manufacture. The Khánkrá vessels are prized for their fine shape and the polish given to the articles.

In the North-Western Provinces household utensils are largely made at Sultánpur in Oudh and Umlipatti in the Azamgarh District, besides the ornamented ware manufactured at Benares, Lucknow, Moradabad, Jhánsi, Lalitpur, and Gorakhpur. Besides what is known as the Benares ware, this sacred city is noted for its sacrificial and domestic utensils, toys and figures of deities. Good and novel shapes of the common articles are obtainable in many small towns.

The most important of the North-Western Provinces brass and copper manufactures are, however, the Benares brass ware, the Moradabad brass ware, and the Lucknow copper vessels. All these three manufactures have advanced in rapid strides into European favour during the last few years, and at present no dealer in Indian art-manufactures considers his stock-in-trade complete without a good collection of these articles, specially of the first two.

Benares ware.—In the variety of the designs, in the

excellence of the cast, and the rich colouring which gives to the articles a gold-like lustre, Benares brass ware has not been surpassed by any other town in India. The ware is now largely sold not only in India but all over Europe. Plates, water-goglets, trays, cups, *Lotás*, salvers, shields, betel-holders, and various articles are made in this style of work. The brass is first moulded into the required shape and then the patterns are engraved. Mr. Rivett-Carnac thus describes the work of bringing out the patterns:—

"The workers in brass have no tracing or pattern. They may be seen any day in Benares with a brass vessel steadied between their feet, a small hammer in one hand and an iron graver in the other, working out without a moment's hesitation the figures and symbolisms, or the foliated designs, appropriate to the vessel in hand. Not a line drawn on the surface of the brass is there to guide them; still the workman's hand never hesitates, and the incessant tap, tap, of the hammer is deafening as it resounds from all sides. Small boys may be seen trying their 'prentice hand on some simple design, seated beside the old men in spectacles who have long acquired the skill necessary to the carrying out of the more elaborate conventional renderings of the Hindu pantheon. What the bard and the story-teller were to the people in the days when all history was oral and handed down from father to son—that the Benares engraver is to the present day in regard to pictorial religious art. His old archaic art ballads and tales are there stored away in his brain, to be repeated over and over again with scarcely a variation. The audience he recites to love no change: the gods their fathers had engraved on their brass or copper vessels are the gods they know and recognise. The symbols of their old faith they require unchanged from the hand of the graver, and thus, ever to the rhyme of the tap, tap, of the hammer, are quaintly traced on the shining shimmering brass or copper the same lines, carving and weaving beneath an attentive gaze into a pictorial representation of what may be called the Hindu Nibelungen Lied."

The price of a typical collection of Benares ware may be put as follows:—A brass pitcher, R14; a *Suráhi*, R10; a jug, R5; a bowl, R14; a tray R10; a *Lotá*, R6. Benares also makes large quantities of images of deities both in brass and copper as well as in mixed metals and sometimes in gold and silver.

Moradabad ware.—Moradabad brass ware is, like the Benares ware, universally admired. Its origin has no connection with religion, and it seems to be an art developed if not originated by the Muhammadans. The manufacture was not in a very flourishing state before the year 1876. In that year the Agricultural Department of the North-Western Provinces, then presided over by Sir Edward Buck, persuaded a hotel-proprietor at Allahabad to open a stall for the sale of Indian manufactures to Europeans going to England, who generally made a halt here. The elegant shape of the vessels with their rich floriated patterns standing out in their gold or silvery brightness on a black ground soon attracted the attention of the European visitors, and their sale went up by leaps and bounds. As in the Benares ware, the brass is first moulded into the required shape of the vessel, and then the patterns are chiselled out. There are two styles of work, *viz.*, the *Sádá* and the *Siyah-kalam*. In the *Sádá* the brass is first tinned over and then the patterns are engraved or cut out in floriated patterns so as to expose the brass. The patterns are thus yellow, which in contrast with the white ground acquires a golden lustre. In the *Siyah-kalam* work the ground of the vessel is graved out, bringing out in relief the floriated patterns. The depression in the ground is then filled with a black composition of lac, leaving the scrolls a golden yellow. Red and green lacquers are at present used as a variety for both the ground and the patterns, but this work is always associated with inferior design and execution. According to some authority, " the oldest and best of Moradabad work is marked by bold and simple outlines, not overloaded with detail; the modern tendency is to deprave the artistic effect by too minute enrichment and too complicated tracery." But it must be remembered that in all hand-made articles the profusion of ornaments with their delicacy and minuteness excites the admiration of the purchasers. The taste for effect varies, but the patience, perseverance, and ingenuity of the maker are always appreciated. The articles generally made at Moradabad are plates, *Suráhis*, drinking vessels, flower vessels, cups, &c. The price of a typical collection will be as follows:— An *Aftábá*, R33; a shield, R16; a jar, R17; a tray, R18; a flower vase, R9; a *Suráhi*, R12.

At Lucknow, salvers, betel-boxes, scent-holders, and other articles are made of brass and copper pierced. They differ in shapes from those of the Benares ware and are more suited for Muhamadans than the Hindus. A collection of this kind of work has been sent to the Glasgow International Exhibition. The price of a typical collection will be—a betel-box R16; a tray, R39; a round box, R7; a *Husandán*, R31; an ornamented brass syringe, R10.

Articles of brass inlaid with copper are made in various places in the North-Western Provinces, particularly at Benares, Jhánsi, and Lalitpur. Prices up to R10 a piece.

Lamps of peculiar shapes are made at Gorakhpur and Muttra. Price of a lamp varies from R10 to R15.

Hasanpur in Sultánpur District and Umlipatti in Azamgarh are noted for their bell-metal manufactures. The utensils made are plain or ribbed. A plain *Lotá* of Azamgarh would cost R3-2; a ribbed one, R9-6; a plain *Abkhorá*, R2-8; a ribbed one, R3; a plain cup, R1-4; a ribbed, R1-6. A Hasanpur *Lotá* would cost R2; a cup and saucer, R6; an *Abkhorá*, R1-6.

Besides lamps Muttra is also famous for its images of gods and goddesses, specially of Rádhá and

Krishna. Muttra and the neighbouring town of Brindában are the scenes of the early exploits of Krishna, an incarnation of the Great Protector in the Hindu Triad. Thousands of pilgrims every year flock to these holy places, who carry away with them as *mementos* of their visit the brass images of the gods and goddesses as well as figures of horses, peacocks, and other animals. Prices vary from R1 to R10.

Images of mixed metal are made at Hámirpur. They are on a larger scale than those made at Muttra, and are more elaborate and pretentious in their work. Prices up to R15.

In the Panjáb, brass articles are made in almost all the principal towns. Mr. Baden Powell states:—

"Metal vessels in a native household supply the joint place of porcelain, glass, and silver plate in a European family. Hindus use brass vessels, and Musalmans generally copper vessels except in the case of small drinking cups, &c. There is hardly any one so poor, but he has not some brass pots, if no more than the *Lotá* in which he boils his porridge, drinks his water, and holds water to wash in. The wealthier a man is the better off is his house as regards his vessels. In the kitchen of a big house, the array of brass vessels, cooking pots, and water-holders, all scoured bright with earth every day or oftener, is quite formidable. The native gentry use silver drinking cups and some other articles of silver, but the staple article is brass or copper. I believe, however, that glass and crockery are coming more and more into use, even among those who do not ape foreign manners at all. The lamps employed in a great house where European candles and lamps have not found their way, are huge brass candelabra with a broad dish below and a number of branches for little lamps filled with oil and having a wick in the spout of the oil-holder. Brass vessels are sold by weight, so much being allowed extra for workmanship. They are nearly always made of imported sheet brass and copper."

The following are the names of vessels used in the Panjáb and other parts of Upper India:—

Lotá.—A small brass pot, round, contracted towards the mouth, and having just towards the neck a short lip all round.

Kaul or *Katorá.*—A rather flat drinking cup, supposed to resemble in shape a lotus flower (Kaul, Kanval).

Abkhorá.—A drinking pot more or less like a *Lotá*, or shaped like a vase, sometimes made with a handle, cover, and spout. Those with spouts are called "*Abkhorá tutidár.*"

Gilás.—A straight drinking cup shaped like a tumbler, with or without a cover. The name is a corruption of the word "glass" in the colloquial sense of a drinking glass.

Baltoá.—A large vessel for holding water—a brass bucket, with or without rings at the side. Hindus use a *baltoá* to boil a large supply of food for distribution at a feast.

Dol or *Dolchí.*—A round vessel to hold or draw water with, sometimes made of iron; Hindus use it.

Gangá Ságar.—A large brass ewer with a spout for holding water.

Degchá.—A large cooking pot, broad-mouthed and round, with a lip; used by all classes.

Degchi.—A smaller size of the same shape.

Garwá.—A vessel for drawing water and holding it for drinking purposes; used by Hindus. *Garwi* is a smaller size.

Tháli.—A flat plate.

Parát.—A flat brass tray with a rim.

Tabalbáz.—A brass bowl used to hold curds, &c.,

at feasts; the name is derived from the kettle-drum used for hunting to frighten the game, it being of the same shape.

Silfchi or *Chilamchi.*—A basin for washing the hands in.

Aftábá.—A brass ewer from which water is poured.

Patili.—A small cooking pot with a cover, used by Musalmans.

Tumbiyá.—A drinking cup shaped like a gourd shell.

Suráhi.—Water goglets of brass or zinc.

Inkstands, tobacco-pipes, and tea-pots, of curious shapes and designs, are made in the Panjáb Himalayas.

Amritsar, Pesháwar, Delhi, Jagádhri, Riwári, Hushiárpur, Daská, Gujránwálá, and Pind Dádan Khán are the places most noted for their manufactures in non-precious metals. Copper vessels engraved and tinned are made at Amritsar. These are in the Kashmir style; in short, the industry is introduced by a colony of Kashmiris settled in this town. The articles mostly made are circular dishes and *Samavar*, or the copper tea-urn with a heating arrangement. Panels of *repoussé* copper-work boldly embossed in patterns of foliage, in imitation of similar work used in the decoration of the Golden Temple, are wrought by the chasers of Amritsar, who also work in silver on occasions. A large copper panel about 2′ 6″ square, covered with foliage in relief of excellent execution, costs only R24. At Jandialá in the Amritsar District there is a considerable manufacture of plain brass wares, which are brought into the town of Amritsar for sale. The brass-casting is well done, but the work is not ornamented to such an extent as at Riwári and Jagádhri. The prices are regulated by weight. There are a few braziers in Amritsar who do brass-casting as well as those of any other place.

Samavars, Aftábás, trays, salvers, and other utensils of a similar description are manufactured at Peshawar. The patterns are of Persian origin, and in that they differ from the Amritsar ware.

Delhi is famous for its huge cooking pots, called *Degchás*. "In the Lahore and other copper bazars, visitors are invariably offered 'real Delhi *Degchis*,' and most of the smiths from other places admit that they are not so skilful with the hammer and stake as those at Delhi. In shaping a circular vessel of changing diameter, they find it necessary to solder pieces on, while a good Delhi coppersmith shapes the whole without joint from one piece. Nests (*Ganj*) of *Degchis*, with cleanly defined edges fitting closely into each other, are the usual articles made, and they are often admirable specimens of plain hammerwork. Brass articles consisting of plates, cups, trays, &c., are often tastefully ornamented by the brazier (*Chaterá*) with foliage in low relief. There is a considerable production too of small fantastic toys in brass roughly made, but often ingenious and pretty."

At Jagádhri in the Ambala District, lamps and cooking utensils of all sorts are largely made. Some of these are exceptionally well executed, specially the lamps, with branching arms touched with colours on the leaves.

Cooking utensils, cart-bells, and *Hukkas* are produced at Riwári. The bulk of these are coarsely-made things for every-day use, but fancy articles, "involving chasing, engraving, and parcel tinning, are also produced and exported to various parts of the

Panjáb and Rajputana." In accordance with modern custom the practice of tinning the articles is gaining ground.

At Bahádurpur, near Hushiárpur, brass vessels are largely made, and exported to the hills. It is said that they find their way as far as Ladákh. The finish is exceptionally good.

Cups are made at Daská in Siálkot District. Although well executed, there is nothing to distinguish the work done here from that of other places in the Panjáb. A cup made of bell metal sells at 7 annas.

Degchis and other cooking vessels are produced at Gujránwálá; the work is good but in no way differing from that of other places.

Chased brass work is made at Bháwalpur. Bháwalpur cups are noted for their superior finish.

At Phagwárá, near Jallandhar, plain brass work of excellent finish and character is largely manufactured. Plates, cups, and other articles made here are exported to various parts of the Panjáb.

On the use of metal-ware in the Panjáb, Mr. Kipling makes the following remarks:—

"Brass is the Hindu material *par excellence,* and though it is preferred plain for household purposes, as being more easily cleaned, as Hindu usage ordains, it is sometimes richly chased or ornamented. The Muhammadans use copper vessels mostly. But to this rule there are many exceptions. Muhammadans on the frontier, following Persian customs, eat from glazed earthenware, and are said in the large towns to be gradually adopting English and Chinese earthenware and porcelain—a most desirable consummation from the English pottery manufacturer's point of view, for there are no pottery materials in Northern India capable of being made into good earthenware."

Kashmir is famous for its engraved copper ware, a collection of which has been sent to the Glasgow International Exhibition. Of late these articles are extensively sold to Europeans and consist of *Suráhis*, *Lotás*, trays, plates, claret jugs, salvers, tobacco jars, tea services, &c. A typical collection would be as follows :—tray, R8; *Aftábá*, R20; bar jug, R9; flower vase, R4; bowl, R5; *Suráhi*, R6; powder box, R5; Ladákh coffee pot, R5. The articles are sold by weight, the prevailing price at the place of production being R2 per pound. The principal manufacturer is Lassu of Srinagar. Mr. Kipling gives the following description of the Kashmir copper ware :—

"The Kashmir patterns are minute and founded mostly on shawl designs. The ware is generally equally covered with deep chasing. Many of the objects are sent to England to be electro-plated or gilded, but a few are plated in this country: sometimes the surface is tinned and the engraved ground is filled in with a black composition simulating *Niello*. The chief native use in Kashmir and Central Asia, where the art probably originated, is for the *Chagun* or tea-pot, a jug-like vessel with the spout attached along nearly its whole length, for the *Aftábá* and *Chilamchi* or water ewer and basin. The European articles are made in response to the demands of tourists, and are of recent origin. A good *Aftábá* costs from R15 to R30. The prices of other articles are regulated by weight."

In the Central Provinces brass utensils were largely made in many places, specially at Bhandárá, Lodhikherá in the Chhindwárá District, Timorni in the Hoshangabad District, Mandlá, and Sambalpur. They consisted of plain ordinary household utensils, like similar articles made in other Provinces, without any pretension to artistic merit, but were much sought after on account of their neatness and durability. But the industry has much declined within the last ten years. It is said that previous to that time there were at Bhandárá alone upwards of two hundred working firms, whereas now there are only fifty or sixty. "The decline of the trade dates from the extension of the railway to Nágpur, since which brass ware has been imported from Bombay. The imported goods are cheaper than those locally made, though not perhaps so durable, but they command a ready sale. The importation of rolled brass sheets has also greatly affected the brass-workers of Bhandárá in this way, that formerly many of them were employed in smelting and beating out the metal into sheets: now this occupation is gone, since the sheets are imported ready made, and all that remains to be done is to convert the brass sheets into vessels by shaping and soldering. There are still, however, some workmen in Nágpur and Bhandárá who possess some skill in brass graving and can turn out specimens in the style of those made at Benares, though of vastly inferior merit. The Deputy Commissioner of Chhindwárá writes in a similar strain of the brass-workers of Lodhikherá, where brass-working as a special skilled handicraft has died out since the opening of the railway to Nágpur. Brass lamps of curious design, but of very rough workmanship, are made at Jakerá in the Damoh District."

Ordinary household utensils are largely made at Jaipur. They are plain, but highly polished. Of these, Jaipur smoking bowls, called *Gargarás* or *Gurguris*, are noted all over Upper India. Of late Dr. Hendley has introduced the manufacture of brass trays and other articles with arabesque designs from old Indian patterns in *repoussé*. These are made by several exceptionally skilful workmen. In fact, the Jaipur men can imitate anything given to them. The patronage of a liberal court, which has always been noted for its encouragement of art, has led to many good workmen from different parts of India settling there. Salvers and vases of Hindu shapes engraved with mythological figures, soap-boxes, betel-boxes, &c., pierced with floral and geometrical patterns, are made at the School of Art and in the Bazar. Plates and *Lotás* are also made in the School of Art with designs of mythological or hunting scenes scratched upon them. A beautiful hunting scene was thus depicted on a large plate shewn at the Colonial and Indian Exhibition. A wide plain, covered with rank tall grass, among which stood clumps of palmyra palms, lay stretched at the foot of a line of low hills. On the top part of the plate might be seen a herd of deer on the verge of the distant horizon. Some of the deer were grazing, others ruminating, while young kids gambolled at the side of their mothers. Two huge antlers, which stood close by suddenly looked suspicious as if they had just got a faint scent of danger, but had not yet been able to make up their mind about the certainty of their apprehensions. Things, however, had taken a more tangible form in a different part of the scene. A band of huntsmen had come upon another herd of deer. With bended bows and that Rajput swagger in the face, which three centuries ago was a terror, not only to the effeminate races of the eastern Provinces, but also to the bold overbearing people of the Sulaiman Range, they were making a havoc on the retreating flock. The lower part of the plate depicted one of those perilous adventures which occasionally fall to the lot of brave huntsmen in an Indian jungle. On one side of the scene, a tiger was about to spring on a beater, who unhappily had gone too far ahead of his comrades and of the main hunting party riding on elephants. In another part, a tigress was on the point of making a direct attack on the beaters, who were defending themselves with their swords, a weapon on which a true-hearted Rajput always placed the greatest reliance.

Lamps of some excellence are also made with bold designs in which figures are often introduced. Sacrificial implements are also manufactured. *Suráhis* or water goglets and *Hukkas* are made in zinc and enriched with brass bands, plain or engraved, at Chirowa and Jhunjhun. Bells and gongs in mixed metal are also made. A very good collection of Jaipur brass-ware has been sent to the Glasgow International Exhibition. These consist of coffee-pots, trays, figures of animals, &c. The following are the prices of typical specimens:—A Yarkand coffee-pot, R13; a tea-kettle, R18; a brass tray, Delhi pattern, R7; a boat-shaped brass bowl, R7; small brass tray R3; an elephant, R1-4; a tiger, R2.

At Bikánir water-bottles are made of pewter with brass neck and stopper. They are also made of mixed metals. Such water-bottles sell from eight to ten annas per lb. in weight. Besides ordinary household utensils, *Katordán* or brass boxes to keep jewellery are made at Bikánir.

At Dág in the Jhallawar territory brass bedsteads are largely manufactured which have a great reputation in that part of the country. Other articles of note made in Jhallawar are bronze stirrups, brass inkstands and ink-trays of an antique style, rose-water sprinklers, and ornaments worn by the lower classes.

In Karauli, in addition to the ordinary *Lotás*, plates, and other domestic utensils a special kind of *Hukka* bowl is made. This consists of brass covered with a coating of quicksilver and worked in a peculiar and effective manner.

Hukkas, called *Kallis*, are made at Dholpur, which are ornamented. Cups, mugs, plates, and other household utensils are also produced in this State of Rajputana. As in other places, these things are sold by weight, the price being thirteen annas per pound.

A peculiarity in the brass-manufactures of Marwar

(Jodhpur) is the *Lotandiyá,* the vernacular name of a rolling lamp made of brass, sometimes of iron. This lamp is so constructed that it will roll on the ground without upsetting the oil-box or the light being put out. A lamp of this kind has been sent to the Glasgow International Exhibition from Jaipur. A modified form of this lamp can probably be used with advantage on board steamers and sailing vessels. The price varies from R1 to R5. The other specialties of Marwar are *Katordán,* used as a jewel box and for keeping food, price R1 to R10 according to size and finish; *Tironchi* or tripod, used as a water-stand, price R1 to R1-8; *Kanti* or jewel scales, made at Nagaur, used for weighing jewels, and exported to other parts of India.

The brass *Itr-dáns* or rose-water sprinklers of Tonk were noted in former days, but the makers are now dead, and their successors can only turn out a very coarse kind of work.

In Central India, Tehri, Ujjain, Indor, Ratlám, Chhatrapur, Datiá, Rewa, and Charkhári, have some reputation for their brass manufactures. Curious figures of horses, elephants, and other animals as well as images are made at Tehri. Ujjain makes white metal *Lotás* and utensils, as well as old and curious brass images. Indor is noted for its sacrificial implements, a miniature set of which would cost R7-12. Brass pinnacles for domes are made at Ratlám. The work is good though plain. Price about R10 for a pair of pinnacles 1½ feet high. Brass lamps and locks are made at Chhatrapur and Datiá. A perforated rolling brass lamp, like the *Lotandiyá* mentioned above, was sent from Chhatrapur to the Colonial and Indian Exhibition. A kind of safety lock made in these places has the peculiarity of containing in itself a double-barrelled pistol. Peasant jewellery is made both at Chhatrapur and Rewa. The designs of some of the Rewa jewellery are very handsome. Price of a pair of anklets R2. Charkhári makes old and curious brass chess-men.

Domestic utensils are made of bell-metal and brass in most of the towns in the Madras Presidency. Bell-metal utensils are largely made at Bellary, Kasargod in South Canara District, Malabar, and Vizagapatam. Anantpur, Bellary, Salem, Madras, Madura, Malabar, Godávari, Cuddapah, Vizagapatam, and Tanjore are noted for their brass utensils. The articles made are chiefly *Lotás*, called *Chambus* in South India, which are plain or chased and often of very elegant shapes; plates, cups, and lamps. Dr. Bidie states that some of the plates made at Tirupati, a place of pilgrimage in the Madura District, "are of very elegant designs, the core being fluted and margins serrated and of lace-like pattern." Since the introduction of kerosine oil, the manufacture of brass lamps in the old style is dying out. At Tirupatur and Madura in the Madura District carvings on metal are carried on to some extent, and the town of Kistna is noted for its metal engravings. Ordinary copper utensils for household use are made at Kistna, Salem, Madras, Madura District, Malabar, Godávari, Cuddapah, Vizagapatam, and Tanjore, *i.e.*, the same places where brass manufactures of a similar kind are largely turned out. Tin utensils, consisting principally of drinking cups, lantern frames, and boxes, are made at Salem, Vizagapatam, and Tanjore. They are, however, very rude and possess no artistic merit. Lead utensils are made at Salem and Tanjore. At Bellary pewter utensils are made. These are much esteemed owing to the belief that food and water kept in them have a cooling effect on the human system.

The following account of brass and copper manufactures in the Bombay Presidency has been supplied by Mr. Gupte :—

"Brass and copper pots, drums, chains, lamps, &c., are made for domestic purposes in most of the principal towns of the Presidency. A large trade is carried on in these wares in Bombay, Násik, Poona, Sholapur, and Hubli. But Násik and Poona are specially known for their copper and brass wares, which are much used by the Hindus. The Násik vessels are preferred to those of Poona owing to their superior finish. Násik being a place of pilgrimage, many Hindus visit it for religious purposes, and when they return to their homes, they generally take with them a number of copper and brass pots as presents to relations and friends. At the 'Thread' and marriage ceremonies among Hindus of higher classes, a set of copper, brass, or silver drinking pots and cups are given to the boy who is to wear the sacred thread or to the bridegroom. A great demand is thus created annually, and the industry is well supported."

Mr. Gupte further writes—

"Poona brass and copper workers, of whom there are 3,000 to 4,000 in that city, have of late commenced imitating Násik wares to a small extent. Rough pots used for culinary purposes and brass figures are largely made at Poona, the annual outturn amounting to about £250,000. At Amod, in Kaira, there are about twenty-five to thirty workers in brass, whose outturn amounts to about two hundred pounds sterling a year. At Shikárpur and Lárkháná, in Sind, a large trade, amounting to £12,935 a year, is carried on, the workers being Muhammadans and Hindus.

"As copper and brass vessels are in general use among the natives, workers in these metals are found in most of the larger towns of the Presidency. The dealers at Násik and Poona are generally Marhatta or Deccan Kásárs by caste. Besides the dealers, there are three sets of workmen who earn their livelihood as workers in brass and copper—(1) *Támbats*, makers of large articles; (2) *Kalaikárs*, makers of small articles; and (3) *Charkiválás*, workers on the lathe or polishers.

"The *Támbat* or maker of large articles takes a sheet of brass or copper which he lays on the floor, and on it he traces with a compass the shape of the article to be made and cuts it out with scissors or a chisel. The metal is then softened in the fire and hammered first on a hollow stone anvil, and as it assumes a hemispherical shape it is hammered on a bent iron bar anvil, and again softened and hammered three or four times till it is beaten into shape. Each vessel is generally made of two pieces, a lower and an upper, separately beaten into shape and soldered with brass, borax, and chloride of ammonium. The men work in bands of five or six, dividing the labour between them, some making the rough shape, some shaping the neck, others forming the lower portion of the vessel, and the rest giving the whole a rough polish. The polishing given to cooking utensils is a rough scrubbing, with a mixture of powdered charcoal and tamarind pulp, followed by a further beating with a small hammer till the whole surface is covered with little facets.

"Another set of workers in brass at Násik and Poona are the *Kalaikárs*, tinners, who are Pánchâls by caste. The Násik *Kalaikárs* are said to have come from Bidar. Their proper craft of tinning copper and brass pots has of late failed them. They owed their position as specialists to the belief that the heating of chloride of ammonium brought on a household the wrath of the gods, but this feeling has to a great extent passed away, and as tinning is a very simple process, the need of a special class of workmen has ceased. These *Kalaikárs* differ from *Támbats* by casting pots as well as beating them into shapes, and by making small, instead of large, articles.

"The lathe-worker polishes the vessels on a lathe. The process is simple. The vessel is fixed to the lathe with resin wax, and the wheel is turned by a labourer; the polisher sitting close to the vessel, presses against it a sharp-pointed tool, called *rándhá*, which he rests on a small iron guide-bar, and which, as the pot whirls round, scrapes its outer surface. Except one man, who has a coppersmith's shop, the polishers are all skilled labourers without any capital, each earning on an average from 16*s.* to £1-10*s.* a month. One *Kalaikár* at Násik, named Gyanu, who casts pots, has imported an English lathe: his work is truer and far superior as regards finish to that produced on the native lathe, and his articles consequently command a better sale and fetch higher prices. At Poona there are half a dozen English lathes at work."

In his description of the Baroda Court at the Colonial and Indian Exhibition published in the *Journal of Indian Art*, Mr. Gupte further states:—

"Vizanagar brass-ware is much prized in Kathiawar and Ahmadabad. At Dabhoi and Kadi good brass and copper work is done, but the *repoussé* work on brass plates done in the city of Baroda is very creditable."

Baroda repoussé work very much resembles the Benares ware.

A sort of *renaissance* of copper and brass work has now commenced in Bombay. Panels or plaques, the designs of which have been taken from the Ajantá caves, are now made of hammered copper in the School of Art, Bombay, under the direction of Mr. Griffiths. Similarly windows are made of perforated brass work, being a revival of the old work found at Ahmadabad. Two windows of this kind were sent to the Colonial and Indian Exhibition, the designs of which were taken from those in the Ráni Sipri and Sháh Alam mosques at Ahmadabad.

Domestic vessels, idols, lamps, mythological animals, figures of birds, &c., are made of brass, copper, or mixed metal in Mysore. They are mostly rough articles without any finish or accuracy, circles out, lines never true, and marks of the file and burnish visible. Colonel LeMessurier, however, states that good work can be had if liberal wages are paid. The best workmen are the Jains, and the chief seats of manufacture are Sraváni, Belagola, Nágamangala, and Magadi. Brass jewellery is also largely made in Mysore; the price of an entire set would be about R26. Mysore sacrificial implements are mostly old and curious, as no innovation is permitted. They are only made to order and the demand is small.

Brass utensils consisting of *Lotás,* bowls, drinking vessels, bells, lamps of different kinds, figures of deities, and sacrificial implements are largely made by the Newars in Nepal, chiefly at Patan. Of these "the designs of some of the lamps are extremely quaint and artistic. The pagoda-like temples are hung with little bells, to the clappers of which are attached broad leaf-shaped pieces of brass; these are set in motion by the wind, and a continual tinkling is kept up.

Besides these, two classes of bells are largely manufactured. One made in brass is in use in Hindu temples; the other of mixed metal is used by Buddhists. The tone of both kinds is generally clear and musical."

Drinking and cooking utensils of brass, copper, and mixed metal are made all over the Province of Assam. "The material used is either brass or bell-metal (a compound of brass and copper). The latter is melted and cast into moulds. *Lotás* and drinking tumblers are the articles usually produced. Brass vessels are made from sheet brass, which is cut and beaten into the required shape. The manufacture is almost confined to Marias, a Muhammadan caste found all over Assam."

In Burma, images of Gotama, large and small, bells for pagodas, open and closed cattle bells, and flat crescent-shaped gongs used for religious purposes are the principal manufactures in brass and mixed metals. Speaking of that part of the Province recently known as British Burma, Mr. Tilly writes:—

"Five hundred and sixty-four persons were returned as engaged in these trades in 1881. Makers of small brass goods were scattered over the country, while the image-makers and bell-founders were met with only in Rangoon, Prome, and Hanthawaddy. The only important manufactures in brass are the castings in that metal of images of Gotama, bells, and gongs. A rough solid core of the image to be cast is first made in clay somewhat freely mixed with sand and paddy husk. A composition made of bees'-wax 10 parts, resin $7\frac{1}{2}$ parts, to which is added earth oil, is melted down and in its liquid state thrown into a large shallow basin of water, and on cooling forms a layer of uniform thickness on the surface. The composition is then plastered on the clay core, and with the aid of knives and chisels is carved into the desired shape in all its detail. The composition is now in its turn covered entirely, with the exception of a hole on the crown of the head, with a rather thick layer of clay without any attempt to adhere to the lines of the model. When the outer layer of clay is perfectly dry, the model is heated to allow the composition to melt and run out from a small hole provided for the purpose at the foot of the model. When it has all run out the hole is closed with clay and the molten metal, supplied from furnaces close at hand, poured in at the crown of the clay mould. The casting is then left to cool for a day or so, or longer according to its size, when the outer and inner mass of clay is removed. The image is next finished off with files and sand-paper, and polished with steel burnishers. The flat triangular gongs are made in an open sand mould, which has been formed with a wooden pattern. Cattle bells are made by melting out a wax mould, the clapper being placed in the core. Brass work is sold by weight; an image 18 inches high by 12 inches at the base takes 10 or 12 days to make and costs R50, of which the price of materials absorbs R38, leaving R12 for the labour. A moulder's earnings seldom average more than R25 a month. Images are made of brass consisting of copper in proportion of 60 per cent. and tin 40 per cent., or for a better quality, copper 53·4 per cent., tin 40 per cent. and zinc 6·6. For large bells an alloy of one copper and three-fourths of tin is used; for cattle bells ten copper and three-and-a-half tin, and for round gongs an alloy of one copper and quarter tin."

In many parts of India iron and tin are largely used for various sorts of household utensils. Of these, the most important are the frying pans, water buckets (*Dols*), tongs, basins, bowls, spoons, &c.. Pans are now imported from England. None of these articles possess any artistic merit. In Madras, however, a considerable industry was carried on in carved steel work in former times, but the art has all but died out at the present day. Dr. Bidie states that—

"some of the old work was most elaborate and worked out with great fidelity and patience. The style of ornamentation is markedly Dravidian, consisting chiefly of monsters ingeniously poused and grouped and of arabesques."

Naravi and Kosaragod in South Canara District and Malabar, Vizagapatam, and Tanjore are the places where such articles are manufactured. A peculiar kind of iron tripod, called *Tironchi*, is made of iron at Jodhpur. This is a very beautiful folding water-stand,

and was much admired at the Calcutta International Exhibition. Price R1 to R3.

It is extremely difficult to procure old specimens of metal work, for when brass and copper wares get old they are exchanged for new ones. The old ones are taken up by braziers and copper smiths, melted, and made into new vessels. Even if an old article is obtained, it is difficult to find out its authentic age except by guess-work. The only specimen known of ancient metal-ware of an authentic date is a *Lotá* in the Indian Museum, about which Sir George Birdwood writes :—

"The most interesting of all known *Lotás* is one in the Indian Museum discovered by Major Hay in 1857, at Kundla in Kulu, where a landslip had exposed the ancient Buddhist cell in which this *Lotá* had been lying buried for 1500 years; for it is attributed by oriental scholars to the date A.D. 200—300. It is exactly of the shape now made, and is enchased all round with a representation of Gautama Buddha, as Prince Siddhártha before his conversion, going on some high procession. An officer of State, on an elephant, goes before; the minstrels, two damsels, one playing on a *Viná* and the other on a flute, follow after; in the midst is the Prince Siddhártha, in his chariot drawn by four prancing horses, and guarded by two horsemen behind it; all rendered with that gala air of dainty pride, and enjoyment in the fleeting pleasures of the hour, which is characteristic of the Hindus to the present day."

Electro-plating is carried on in most of the large towns, but the industry is still in its infancy. Re-electro-plating of old articles is done by several native artisans at Calcutta. At Agra in the North-Western Provinces electro-plated flasks, tumblers, and tea-pots are made. These are ingenious in construction and made in such a way as to fit several articles of common use into one case. Salvers and betel-boxes are made at Lucknow and Rámpur. In the Panjáb, dishes, spoons, forks, cups, *Hukka* mouth-pieces, goblets, wine-glasses, tea and coffee pots, iron hinges, temple domes, and elephant *Howdahs* are electro-plated. But the industry is a very small one. The art of electro-plating in the European method is known only to a few persons. At Delhi, Lahore, and Amritsar it is easy to get metal wares re-plated with very fair success. At Jaipur a considerable business is done in plating, by the School of Art, and its pupils established in the town.

Arms and Armour.

The classification of weapons used in different ages, generally adopted by writers on the subject, is not applicable to India. Side by side with the highest civilisation, we had in this country at all times races in the utmost depth of barbarism. This want of homogeneity in the population of the Indian continent and the great disparity among the different classes in the arts of civilised life were at no time more conspicuous than at the present moment. Carts made of split bamboos or rough pieces of wood, which have been used for thousands of years, still feed the railway trains with goods brought from a long distance, and postal runners still run across jungles and along narrow village footpaths to deliver the mail bags to a most elaborate Postal Department in communication with all parts of the world through its telegraphs, special trains, and mail steamers. The same man-eating tiger in the forest of Central India might have experienced the effects of an arrow shot from the bamboo bow of the Bhil, as well as of the conical bullet from a rifled gun in its latest improvements. In India stone never entirely superseded wood, horn, or the bone, nor bronze the stone, nor iron superseded the bronze. The freshest discoveries and the newest inventions all worked along with things existing from time immemorial. Thus at a time when writers of old could classify the missiles known to them into (1) those hurled by machines; (2) those hurled by the hand; (3) those hurled by force of spell; and (4) those that could be hurled and retracted, like the lasso and the boomerang; bamboo clubs and slings were still in use as they are to-day, notwithstanding all the guns and pistols ever invented by man.

As in other countries, so in India, the oldest and the most important of national weapons is the bow, which was made either of wood, horn, or metals. Bamboo and rattan cane or the wood of *Sál* (*Shorea robusta*) and other close-grained timbers were used. The horns of buffalo and deer were also considered suitable materials for the manufacture of a bow. Bows were also made of iron, copper, silver and gold. According to the *Rig-Veda*, "the arrow puts on a feathery wing: the horn of the deer is its point: it is bound with the sinews of the cow."

Arrows of later times were of course pointed with iron. Quivers were generally made of hide or basket work and sometimes of metallic plates. Besides shooting the arrows, the bow was also formerly used in casting stone or earthen pellets. Slings were used for the same purpose. Fire-arms are frequently mentioned in old books, and there is no doubt that at least some terrible destructive agency like the Greek Fire was known to the Hindus. Two Sanskrit books have lately been discovered in which a full description has been given of guns and gunpowder as known to the ancient Hindus. In one of them, called *Sukra-niti*, the description of fire-arms, as translated by Dr. Rájendra Lála Mitra, runs as follows :—

"135. The tubular weapon is of two kinds, large and small.

"136. The tube is five spans long; its breach has a perpendicular and horizontal hole; at the breech and muzzle is always fixed a sesam bead for aligning the sights.

"137. The breech has at the vent a mechanism which, carrying stone and powder, makes fire by striking. Its breech is well-wooded at the side, in the middle is a hole half an inch broad.

"138. After the gunpowder is placed inside, it is firmly pressed down with a ramrod. This is the small gun which ought to be carried by foot soldiers.

"139. In proportion as its outside (bark) is hard, its hole is broad, its ball is long and broad; the ball reaches far.

"140. A big tube is called (that gun) which obtains the direction of the aim by moving the breech with a wedge; its end is without wood; but it is to be drawn on cars, &c.; if well welded it gives victory.

"141. Five weights of saltpetre, one weight of sulphur, one weight of charcoal of *Calotropis gigantea, Euphorbia nerifolia,* and other plants, end is prepared in such a manner that the smoke does not escape.

"142. If all this is taken after having been cleansed, is then powdered, and mixed together, one should squeeze it with the juice of *Calotropis gigantea, Euphorbia nerifolia,* and *Alium sativum,* and dry in the sun; having ground this like sugar, it will certainly become gunpowder.

"143. There may be six or even four parts of saltpetre in the gunpowder used for tubular arms, but the parts of sulphur and charcoal remain as before.

"144. The ball is made of iron, and has either small balls in its inside or is empty; for small tubular arms it should be of lead or of any other metal.

"145. The tubular projectile weapon is either of iron or of another metal; it is every day to be rubbed clean, and covered by gunners.

"146. With a similar, greater, or less proportion of charcoal, sulphur, and saltpetre, of realgar, of orpiment, and likewise of graphite,

"147. Of vermillion, also of powder of magnetic iron oxide, and of camphor, of lac, and of indigo, and likewise of the pine gum (*Pinus longifolia*),

"148. Experts make gunpowder in many ways, and of white and other colours.

"149. By the application of fire they throw the ball coming from the tube at the mark.

"150. One should clean the tube first and then put gunpowder, carry it down with the ramrod to the bottom of the tube till it is tight.

"151. Then put a good ball, and place gunpowder on the vent, and by setting fire to the powder at the vent discharge the ball towards its mark."

Javelins, spears, lances, discus, and various other weapons to throw by the hand were known to the ancient Indians, as well as the lasso and the boomerang. The Indian boomerang is described as "having a knot at the foot, a long head, and is a hand broad. Its middle part is bent to the extent of a cubit, it is sharp, black-coloured, and two cubits long. Whirling, pulling, and breaking are its three actions, and it is a good weapon for charioteers and foot-soldiers." Dr. Oppert states that it is still in use in South India and that it is made of wood or iron and sometimes of ivory. He writes:—

"The general belief is that the boomerang is a weapon peculiar to the Australians; but this is by no means the case. It is well known in many parts of India, specially in its Southern Peninsula. The Tamulian, Maravar, and Kallar employ it when hunting, and throw it after deer. In the Madras Government Museum are shewn three boomerangs, two ivory ones, which came from the armoury of the late Rájá of Tanjore, and a common wooden one, which hails from Pudukota. The wood of which the boomerang is made is very dark. I possess four black wooden and one iron boomerang, which I have received from Pudukota. In the arsenal of the Pudukota Rájá is always kept a stock of these sticks. Their name in Tamil is *Valai Tadi*, bent stick, as the stick is bent and flat. When thrown a whirling motion is imparted to the weapon, which causes it to return to the place from which it was thrown. The natives are well acquainted with this peculiar fact."

Of non-missile weapons of ancient India may be mentioned the clubs, maces, swords, daggers, and battle-axes of various shapes and sizes. Of defensive weapons the most important was of course the shield made of hide, generally of rhinoceros hide, hard wood, basket work, and iron and copper. Shields were elaborately ornamented with metal and horn inlay in scrolls or with figures of animals and men. Helmets, plate armour, and chain mail were known from the time of the *Rig-Veda*. The military caste of India, the *Kshatriyas*, has the word *Varman* or "mail-clad" for its surname. Besides metallic armour, leather and quilted coats were also used.

Coming down to later times we find that Indian weapons were famous all over Asia. Sir George Birdwood writes :—

"Indian steel has been celebrated from the earliest antiquity, and the blades of Damascus, which maintained their pre-eminence even after the blades of Toledo became celebrated, were in fact of Indian steel. Ctesias mentions two wonderful Indian blades which were presented to him by the king of Persia and his mother. The Ondanique of Marco Polo's travels refers originally, as Colonel Yule has shewn, to Indian steel, the word being a corruption of the Persian *Hundwanig*, *i.e.*, Indian steel. The same word found its way into Spanish in the shapes of *Alhinde* and *Alfinde*, first with the meaning of steel, and then of a steel mirror, and finally of the metal foil of a glass mirror. The Ondanique of Kirman, which Marco Polo mentions, was so called from its comparative excellence, and the swords of Kirman were eagerly sought after in the fifteenth and sixteenth centuries by the Turks, who gave great prices for them. We have seen that Arrian mentions Indian steel as imported into the Abyssinian ports; and Salmasius mentions that among the surviving Greek treatises was one 'on the tempering of Indian steel.' Twenty miles east of Nirmal, and a few miles south of the Shisha hills, occurs the hornblende slate or schist from which the magnetic iron used for ages in the manufacture of Damascus steel, and by the Persians for their sword blades, is still obtained. The Dimdurti mines on the Godávari were also another source of Damascus steel."

The manufacture of arms in India is dying out.

Its days are past. Bows and arrows, swords and daggers, matchlocks and pistols are no longer of any use, with the universal peace now reigning in India. They have become antiquated and are superseded by the latest inventions in Europe. Still their manufacture would have been continued some time longer for the purposes of hunting wild animals and for pageantry, but the Arms Act has almost destroyed the demand for them. Small quantities of arms are still made in all parts of the country, specially in the Native States, where the Arms Act is not in force. Of these a large portion is sold to Europeans as curiosities.

In Bengal, Monghyr and the town of Banpás in the Bardwán District were formerly famous for their swords, matchlocks, and other arms. The industry has now practically died out in both the places. Recently a Delhi arms and armour manufacturer, named Dál Chand, established himself at Calcutta. He has sent a large and a valuable collection to the Glasgow International Exhibition of both old and new arms obtained from all parts of India. His customers are almost all Europeans. Matchlocks, bows and arrows, spear heads, hunting knives, and other arms are still manufactured in a few places in the North-Western Provinces, chiefly in Najibabad in the Rohilkhand Division, and also in several towns of the Jhánsi Division for sale in the Native States bordering on Bundelkhand. Sword blades and rifles are made at Rámpur, the chief town of a small Native State. This place is famous for the skill of its iron and steel workers and for the temper of its sword blades. Swords, shields, daggers, and chain armour are also made at Agra. Sword blades are procured from elsewhere and mounted here. Price up to R200 for a sword. Sir George Birdwood in his "Industrial Arts of India" (1880) stated that "swords of good temper are still made at Pepani, in the Hardoi District of Oudh." The Provincial officer, however, in his report to the Government of India, does not name the place as one where arms are now manufactured.

In the Panjáb, Kohát, Ludhiáná, and Peshávar are noted for their matchlocks. Swords and knives are also made at Peshávar; swords, daggers, and *Kukris* or small swords used by the Gurkhás, are made at Bherá; swords, daggers, helmets, shields, and chain and plate armour are manufactured and decorated with damascened work at Siálkot; shields are made at Lahore; and *Guptis* or sword-sticks at Hissar. No blacksmith is allowed to make arms without a license. Although there is still a demand for arms among the retinues of the Native Chiefs, the principal purchasers of such articles are now the Europeans.

Arms are made at Jaipur, chiefly small articles for sale to European tourists. There is a great demand for old weapons among the visitors, and these are consequently manufactured for them in whole or in part, *i.e.*, as Dr. Hendley explains, "a modern production may be made to look ancient, or a venerable and useless blade may be fitted into a new handle." Shields are largely manufactured, and Dr. Hendley states that the market has recently become overstocked with them. Shields made of *papier-maché* at Uniara in the south-east of the State are gilded and painted with quaint hunting and battle subjects and then varnished.

Arms are made in other parts of Rajputana. Matchlocks and percussion cap guns are made at Bikánir and are sold at R3 to R10 per gun. Sword-hilts, daggers, knives, shields, bows and arrows, sword-sticks, spear heads, guns, and pistols are made at Jhallawar. Sword-hilts are ornamented with gold and silver work in bas-relief, the price of each being

R20 and upwards according to quality of work. Arms made by the armourer in the pay of this State, named Jiwan Mistri, are fine specimens of workmanship and they won an honourable mention in one or two Exhibitions. Sirohi is famous for its swords, of which the hilts are generally worked with silver and gold. The price of a sword varies from R2 to R200 according to the strength of the steel and the quality of workmanship. Alwar turns out swords, daggers, and spear heads. Superior kinds of swords are made at Alwar by one Muhammad Ibrahim. In some he inserts pearls; such swords are highly admired as curiosities. Daggers made at Alwar are also of curious shapes and contrivances. Some are double, that is, one goes inside the other. Some when pressed at the top open out into a forked shape shewing three teeth. The workmen are all in the service of the State. Swords, spears, daggers, matchlocks, and other ordinary weapons of the country are manufactured by the local smiths of Karauli. Some very fair imitations of breech-loading guns have lately been turned out from the workshops of this State. Bundi smiths used to be noted for their arms, specially matchlocks and daggers. These are made plain as well as ornamented. Price of a plain matchlock R25, of an ornamented one R35, and of a plain dagger R10. Shields are made at Sháhpur; the price of one is R38 including cost of boss and grip.

In Central India, Gwalior weapons are of good workmanship, particularly swords and matchlocks. Ordinary weapons are made at Dhar, Indor, Dewas, and Ratlám. These mostly consist of matchlocks, swords, daggers, battle-axes, &c. Swords made at Gwalior, Panná, and Datiá have often damascened hilts, gold on steel.

Nágpur city was formerly famous for its swords

and daggers of pretty workmanship. The steel was brought from the valleys of the Narbadá and the Tápti. The industry is now extinct, and the only artisan left has taken to the manufacture of cutlery. Panágarh, Katangi, Jakerá, Barelá, and Tenderkherá in the Central Provinces were formerly noted for their gun-barrels and sword blades.

On the Madras side a few swords and other weapons are made at Karnúl, Kistna, Salem, and Malabar. But there is very little demand for such articles and the industry may now be said to be practically extinct. Sir George Birdwood mentions Kudwur and Vizianagram as places where good swords, spears, and daggers were manufactured, and those in the latter place superbly mounted for use in pageants.

Swords and daggers, or as they are called Kurg knives (*Pitche Katti*), are made in Kurg. They are worn tied on the waistband by the people of Kurg as an ornament. The blade is of inferior steel, but the handle is usually made of silver or ivory. The sheath is made of bamboo or blackwood, and is heavily mounted with silver. The silver used in the handle and sheath often costs R10. Gold is occasionally used in the ornamentation, costing an extra sum of R35. A massive silver chain, with silver tassel and chatalaine and a smaller chain, depends from the sheath, which costs R25. *Uda Katti*, as the Kurg sword is called, is a powerful weapon, but now chiefly used for killing pigs, of which the mountaineers of Kurg are very fond. The blade is, however, made of inferior native steel and the handle is generally made of horn. The spike at the back is generally made of brass, occasionally of silver. The sword is without a sheath and is two feet long and four or five inches broad. The belt, made of red cloth mounted with silk and embroidered in gold with silk cords, is fastened on the spike behind. Only ten artisans are employed in making these weapons, who annually turn out articles to the value of R1,000.

Arms were formerly made at Tumkur for sale all over Mysore. Colonel LeMessurier, however, in his report to the Government of India makes no mention of the industry.

In the Bombay Presidency Kach silversmiths have long been famous for their skill in decorating arms in all sorts of *repoussé* gold and silver. Mr. B. A. Gupte writes:—

"The manufacture of Indian arms is now confined almost entirely to supplying the demand created by collectors of curios and European visitors to India, who use them for decorative purposes by displaying them on the walls of their entrance-halls, dining rooms, &c. Modern arms of quaint and varied shapes copied from the standard patterns in use from time immemorial are principally made in Kach." His Highness the Rao of Kach has supplied the Glasgow International Exhibition with a collection of arms consisting of a number of battle-axes, knives, daggers and swords.

Shields are made in Ahmadabad, and Kadi in the Baroda territory, of which an account will be found under the head of "Leather Manufactures."

In Nepal, bows and arrows are still used in some parts of the Tarái for hunting purposes. But such arms have now become obsolete. A curious weapon, called *khorá*, made of rhinoceros hide, was formerly used in warfare. "It is a carved *talwar* (sword), the extremity of the blade widening, so as to somewhat resemble the blade of an axe." It is now used in beheading buffaloes for sacrifice. The animal's head is taken off by one blow. The *kukri* is the national weapon of the Nepalese. It is a large knife with "a short handle and an incurved blade, widening in the middle and drawing to a point at the end." It is universally worn by the hill tribes, often along with a couple of small knives. In the Military arsenal of the State, breech-loading rifles, rifled mountain guns, bayonets, and other arms of modern warfare are manufactured. The sheaths of *kukris* and swords are occasionally ornamented with good filigrain work, either in gold or silver.

In Assam and Burma, the long heavy sword or bill called the *Dáo* is largely manufactured. This is used by the tribes on the North-East frontier both for purposes of agriculture and other household work as well as in warfare. In Chittagong it is "manufactured by the Maghs, has a long blade, widening towards the top, which is square, and fitted straight in the handle."

Cutlery.

Knives, scissors, bill-hooks, vegetable cutters, betel-nut cutters, and various other articles of cutlery are turned out by village blacksmiths in all parts of India. Knives and scissors are, however, now imported from Europe, chiefly from Birmingham and Sheffield, and Rodgers' blades have a great reputation all over India.

In Bengal, Banpás, a village in Bardwán, was formerly noted for its cutlery, and the blacksmiths of that place, numbering about 600 families, have still a great reputation for the superior quality of their handiwork. Of late, one Premchánd Mistri of Kánchannagar, in the same District, has succeeded in turning out knives and scissors almost equal to those of European manufacture. But they are hand-made in the old primitive method, without the aid of any kind of machinery, and although the prices are low at present, they can hardly hope in the long run to compete with machine-made articles. Curious and sometimes highly artistic knives with silver or bone handles are made in Sikkim. At Senhát, in the District of Nadiyá, sacrificial knives and bill-hooks are manufactured. Ornamental handles for knives and swords are made at Patna. Superior articles of ordinary use are made in the Hájipur Sub-Division of the Sáran District. At Lawapur, a village within that jurisdiction, there is a well, the water of which is said to impart unusual strength to iron and steel. Betel-nut cutters of a peculiar kind are made at Dinájpur. Rangpur makes a very superior kind of sacrificial swords, called *Khánrá.* Cutlery for European use with handles of deer-horn are now produced at Ránchi.

In the North-Western Provinces, knives, betel-nut cutters, scissors, &c., are made at Meerut, Shájahánpur, and Lalitpur. Some of these are in imitation of European goods of the same description, and they are curious as shewing how far native workmen can copy by hand the machine-made manufactures of Europe.

In the Panjáb, *sarautás* or betel-nut cutters of fanciful forms are produced at Karnál, "the handles being of brass with quaint projections in which small mirrors and pieces of coloured glass are fixed. A good one costs R2 or R3. Scissors made here are similarly ornamented, the handles being made of brass with bits of coloured glass rudely simulating jewels set therein. A pair of scissors cost about six annas." These articles are prepared for export, and are sold in almost all large towns in Upper India. Many-bladed pocket knives with hooks, screw-drivers, scissors, &c., tobacco-cutters, and dinner cutlery are made at Nizamabad in Gujránwálá District. Mr. Kipling writes :—

"Nizamabad in the Gujránwálá District is known for its cutlery. The tourist is frequently offered at hotels and Dâk Bungalows such things, which are calculated to display the ingenuity of the maker rather than to serve the convenience of the purchaser. The finish and polish of the articles, though not perfect, is better than the quality of the steel, which, although tough, is deficient in hardness and is often scarcely to be distinguished from good iron. A very rude form of penknife with immoveable blade and turned up point in a wooden handle seems to be the only article of Nizamabad make that finds a large sale."

A large collection of table cutlery, consisting of knives and forks, has been supplied for the Glasgow International Exhibition by private exhibitors named Imám-ud-din, Muhammad Din, Khuda Bukhsh, and Alla Jowaya of Bherá. The handles of these articles are made of false jade. Stone handles of various kinds are also made at Bherá for swords and daggers. On the subject of Bherá cutlery Mr. Kipling writes:—

"It is not easy to determine whether the stone-handled cutlery of Bherá should be classed under the head of lapidary's work or cutlery. The same artisan practises both trades, that is to say, he forges and finishes the blade and fashions the false jade or serpentine hilt of the *Peshkabz* or of the hunting or deer knife. Old files of English manufacture are sometimes forged into daggers and knives of good quality. But country iron is generally used."

The blacksmiths of Gujrát (Panjáb) make daggers, knives, betel-nut cutters, scissors, and other articles of cutlery for the *Koftgars* or damasceners. They sell very little independently.

In Rajputana, knives, betel-nut cutters, and other articles of cutlery are made at Jaipur, Bikánir, Jhallawar, and other places. A neat little instrument, called *Pinchá*, containing knife, scissors, and a cork-screw, is made at Nagaur in the Jodhpur territory.

In Central India, penknives are made at Ratlám and betel-nut cutters at Chhatrapur.

As stated before, the single manufacturer of arms now left at Nágpur in the Central Provinces has given up his old trade and taken to making cutlery. He has found it more profitable to make knives of European pattern than to adhere to native designs. Mr. J. B. Fuller, in his report to the Government of India, says that the things made by this man bear an excellent local reputation. According to the same officer native cutlery of some little merit is manufactured at Jobrá in the Damoh District. This place was formerly noted for its arms.

In the Madras Presidency, one family in Salem has long been famous for the superior quality of knives, hunting knives, and hog spears it made. Articles of a similar description are also prepared at Kistna and Malabar.

Wire-drawing.

Spangles, tinsels, ribbons, thread, and wire of silver and gold are made in many of the principal towns, specially those that were seats of Government under the Muhammadans. These are used for embroidery and for the decoration of wearing apparel. Silver and gold tinsel wire are of many kinds, both plain and fancy, and are known under the names of *Sulmá, Tilá, Mukesh, Gokhru,* &c. Gold and silver lace are called *Gotá* or *Kinárá.* Gold and silver thread is called *Kálábatun,* which is used in embroidery. Tinsel spangles are called *Sitárá.* All these articles are made of silver, or an alloy of silver and copper. The silver is first made into a round bar tapering at the end, somewhat like a candle, and covered with a thin narrow plate of gold. It is then called a *Kandlá.* On the subject of covering the silver bar with gold Mr. Baden Powell, from whose work on "Panjab Manufactures" most of this account of wire-drawing has been derived, writes :—

"The quantity of gold put on is more or less according to the colour and quality of the tinsel ultimately required; if but little gold is put on, the tinsel will be of a pale yellowish colour; if plenty, it will be of rich gold-red. The tensile capacity of the gold is wonderful, for however fine the bar may be drawn out, the gold surface always remains. The fine wire used for making thread must be produced by drawing out the *Kandlá* to thousands of times its original length, and yet the gold surface and also the colour of the gold never changes; if the *Kandlá* is thinly gilt and pale in colour, so is the wire, and if the *Kandlá* is dark red, so is the tinsel."

The silver ingot is made into *Kandlá* by a class of men called *Kandlá-kash*. It next goes to the wire-drawer, called *Tár-kash*. By the aid of a single apparatus he forces the gold-plated bar (*Kandlá*) through a series of holes on a stout steel plate, each succeeding hole being narrower and finer than the one before, so that when the *Kandlá* has passed through the last hole it is reduced to the thinness of an ordinary small wire. The wire thus formed is made into coils and it is now called *Veri*. The *Veri* then goes to the *Katayá* or fine wire-drawer, who draws the wire still more fine by a still more simple apparatus. The fine wire now formed is called *Tand*, *i.e.* "pulled material." "Four gages of *Tand* are made: (1) the coarsest for making spangles; (2) *Mukesh-ki-tand* for making *Mukesh* used in embroidery; (3) *Kinári-ki-tand* for making *Kinári* and *Gotá* (gold border and edging); (4) *Wattan-ki-tand* or *Tilá-ki-tand*, the finest of all, for making *Tilá*, the thin kind of tinsel used for manufacturing gold thread, for *Sulmá*, and for weaving *Chuni-bádlá* and the thinnest and lightest gold wire fabrics." The fine wire now goes to the *Dabkai*, who flattens it out into *Tilá*, *Mukesh*, *Gokhru-mukesh*, *Mukesh-bati-hui* for ribbon and lace-making, according to order and according to the fineness of the wire. The flattening is done by hammering. The *Mukesh* is the flattened fine wire, much used "for a gold ground work, being sewn on edge over edge." *Sulmá* is a very fine flattened wire and the prettiest form of gold tinsel. Spangles (*Tárá* or *Sitárá*) are made of the thickest wire by first flattening it and then cutting it into small pieces with a pair of scissors. *Kálábatun*, *i.e.*, gold or silver thread, is made by twisting the flattened wire on to a fine red silk. For the manufacture of silver wire and silver tinsels the silver bar (*Kandlá*) mentioned above is not covered with a gold plate. False wire and false tinsels are made of copper, gilt. Lahore, Delhi, Agra, Benares, Murshidabad, Ahmadnagar, and Burhánpur are the principal places where gold and silver wire is made. Mr. J. B. Fuller in his report to the Government of India thus describes the industry as carried on at Burhánpur in the Central Provinces:—

"Silver gilt wire of Burhánpur is a relic of the days when it supported a Muhammadan Court, and still possesses a considerable reputation. The wire is drawn from bars of silver called *passas*, which are made of a uniform size—six inches in length and 60 *tolás* (*tolá* = 180 grains) in weight. The *passas* are made up, and the wire partially drawn out under Municipal supervision, and a duty of R 1-8 is levied on each *passa*. The purity of the material is ensured by this arrangement, and the Burhánpur wire has maintained a reputation for quality superior to that of wire made at other places in the Bombay Presidency. On the other hand, it has rendered it impossible to meet competition by lowering the price of the wire, and the sale of the Burhánpur manufacture is said to have been affected by the import of cheap imitations from other places.

"Each *passa* receives a gilding, on the thickness of which the price of the wire in great measure depends. The weight of gold used to gild a *passa* varies from 8 to 42 *máshás* (*máshá* = 15 grains). The *passa* is drawn out to a length of 700 yards in the Municipal enclosure, and in this form it is taken home by the wire-drawers. It is subsequently drawn to an astonishing fineness, the degree of which varies with the class of work to which the wire is to be applied. Thus a *passa* from which *kálábatun* (gold and silk twisted thread) is to be manufactured is drawn out to the length of 72,000 yards, while if it is to be used in making flattened wire for braiding (*gotá*) it is only drawn out to 48,000 yards. The process of wire-drawing consists in pulling the wire through a series of holes of decreasing size in an iron plate, the wire being fastened to a wheel, which is turned by a winch. The number of *passas* which have been drawn into wire each year since 1868 has been accurately registered. The results are summarised as follows:—for five years, 1868-69 the average number of *passas* made each year was 2,879; ditto 1873-78 *passas* 2,987; for 1879 *passas* 2,527; for 1880 *passas* 2,865; for 1881 *passas* 3,114. The manufacture does not therefore shew any signs of declining."

Iron, steel, and copper wires are made in many places, chiefly for musical instruments. In Bengal, Keunjhar, a hill state, has a reputation for iron and steel wires used for stringed musical instruments, called *Sitár* and *Tumburá* or *Támburá*. In the North-Western Provinces they are chiefly made at Rámpur.

VI.—Art-manufactures in Wood.

Wood-carving.

Wood-carving in ancient times.

An account of wood-carving has already been given under the head of "Decorative Wood-carving as applied to Architecture." The art is also employed in making smaller articles of household furniture. In ancient India the simplicity of Aryan life gave very little scope for a high development of the art of wood-carving. Still the carpenter was not an insignificant member of the village community. He was called the *Sutradhar* or the "holder of line," and he not only made chariots for the warriors, but also was by profession a driver of chariots both in peace and in war. He was therefore often in the thick of the battle, and unarmed as he was the repugnance to kill an unarmed or an insufficiently armed man, that regulated the conduct of Indian warriors of old, did not extend to his benefit. Thus in the sanguinary combats, so graphically described in the *Mahábhárata* and other Sanskrit epics, almost the first thing which a warrior did in entering the lists was to cut the head of the charioteer with a crescent-shaped arrow. Carpenters are mentioned in the *Rig-Veda*, and in the time of Manu they were sufficiently numerous to be recognized into a separate caste in his Institutes. Besides chariots, the carpenter (who also does the work of the joiner in India) was required to make from very early times bedsteads, thrones, and wooden seats of various forms and patterns. Both the *Brihat Sanhitá*, and the *Silpa Sástra* (work on art) give full directions as to the season and manner of felling a tree, seasoning the wood, and manufacturing the different articles required. The tree was directed to be cut down when the circulation of the sap had stopped. Trees growing on "burial, burning, or consecrated grounds, or at the confluence of large rivers, or by the road-side, also those which have withered tops or an entanglement of heavy creepers on them, or bear thorns, or are the receptacles of many honey-combs and birds' nests," are pronounced unfit for the manufacture of bedsteads. Bedstead legs were often carved, the lowest part of which was usually made into the shape of a lion's paw. They were often mounted or inlaid with gold, jewels, and ivory. Thrones were made of many shapes in former times, and each pattern had a distinct name. The name of a throne in Sanskrit is *Sinhásana*, meaning a "lion-seat." Dr. Rájendra Lála Mitra in his "Indo-Aryans" writes:—

"The name of the throne *Sinhásana* is supposed to have been derived from the images of the lion (*Sinha*), which originally formed its supports; but the secondary meaning of a state-chair or throne soon set aside the derivative meaning of a lion-seat, and such solicistic words as *Padma-Sinhásana*, 'lotus-lion-seat,' *Gaja-Sinhásana*, 'elephant-lion-seat,' like the Yankee 'neck handkerchief,' got into currency from very early times. The objects ordinarily selected for the decoration of the legs were images of lotuses, conch-shells, elephants, geese, lions, pitchers, deer, and horses. The thrones were named differently according to the forms in which the legs were carved. Thus a throne made of *Gambhár* wood with mountings of gold and rubies, having the sides festooned with carvings of lotus flowers, and the feet shaped like lotus buds, was named the 'lotus-throne.' It had a lining of scarlet cloth and for supports of the frame-work eight to twelve human figures, each twelve fingers long. A throne made of the above-named wood with silver and crystal mountings, white lining, and carvings of shells on the frame and the feet, was called the 'conch-shell-throne,' *Sankha-Sinhásana*. It had twenty-seven figured supports. A throne made of jack wood, with gold, amethyst, coral, and lapis lazuli mountings, scarlet cloth lining, and carvings of lines of elephants on the frame, and of elephant heads at the feet, was called an 'elephant throne.' In the same way, the 'goose-throne' (*Hansa-Sinhásana*) was so called from having figures of geese carved on the frame and on the feet. It was made of *Sál* wood mounted with gold, topazes, and agates, and lined with yellow cloth. It had twenty-one human figures for supports. The 'elephant throne' was made of sandalwood, mounted with gold, diamonds, mother-o'-pearl, and lined with white cloth. It had, as its name implies, carvings of elephants on the frame and on the feet, and twenty-one human figures for supports. The 'pitcher-throne' (*Ghata-Sinhásana*) was made of *Champak* wood, and mounted with gold and emeralds; it had lines of pitchers carved on the frame, lotus buds on the feet, and blue cloth for lining. Its figured supports numbered twenty-two. When the throne happened to be made of *Nim* wood (*Melia Azadirachta*) mounted with gold and sapphires, carved with lines of deer on the frame, and deer heads on the feet, and lined with blue cloth, it was called a 'deer-throne,' *Mriga-Sinhásana.* And when it happened to be made of the *Haridrá* wood, mounted with gold and diverse kinds of jewels, lined with various coloured cloth, and carved with figures of horses, and horses' heads at the feet, it was called a 'horse-throne' (*Haya-Sinhásana*). It had seventy-four human figures for supports."

Sofas, chairs, benches, and teapoys were also made in ancient India. The ends of the legs were often carved into the form of lion's paws or eagle's claws, and the ends of bars often terminated in an alligator head, the pattern being known as *Makara-mukha.*

Modern Wood-carving.

At the present time bedsteads, stools, and plank beds, known as the *Takhta-posh*, are largely made for native households. European furniture is also fairly imitated by the native carpenters.

In Bengal almost the only place where carved furniture of note is made is Monghyr. The wood used is the Indian ebony (*Diospyros melanoxylon*) found on the western hills, on which ivory and horn are sometimes inlaid. The industry is now stationary. Cabinets, writing boxes, pen-trays, cribbage boards, and other articles of household furniture are made. Toys and personal ornaments suitable for European use are manufactured of ebony as well as of palm and areca-nut wood. A set of ornaments, consisting of a necklace, a pair of bracelets, a pair of ear-rings, and a brooch costs from R1-8 to R2-8. A cabinet would cost R25, a writing box R22, a box for keeping tea R4, a work-box R5, an envelope case R5, a watch-case R2-8, a walking stick R4, a tray R3, a pair of snakes R1.

Wooden toys, painted in colours, are made at Patna. These toys are now brought to Calcutta for sale. Specimens of wood-carving obtained from Gya were sent to the Colonial and Indian Exhibition, which were pronounced to be of superior workmanship. A jewel box, carved, and ornamented with copper *repoussé* work was sent from the School of Art, Calcutta.

Tables, chairs, and other household furniture for European use, but more or less in native style, are made at Bareilly, Bijnor, Bulandshahr, Aligarh, Farukhabad, Sahåranpur, Ghåzipur, and other large towns in the North-Western Provinces. At Bijnor, the wood used is the so-called Indian ebony, while *Shisham* is employed in other places. At Amroha, a peculiar and very ingeniously constructed folding bedsteads are made. Price up to R50. A carved table has been sent from Lucknow to the Glasgow International Exhibition, price R50; and another has been sent from Aligarh, price R40. Salvers, picture-frames, brackets, and other household knick-nacks are made at Sahåranpur and Budaun. The work is somewhat similar to Swiss or Scotch work. Budaun articles are not much ornamented, but are chiefly confined to plain work for domestic use. Sahåranpur articles are ornamented with floral designs and are very cheap. They have of late attracted European attention and are sold in large quantities to European tourists. A soft white wood called *Dudhi* (*Wrightia tomentosa*) is used. A collection of Sahāranpur white wood manufactures have been sent to the Glasgow International Exhibition. Prices of typical specimens may be stated as follows:—A plate, R2-8; a picture-frame, 10 annas; a pen-tray, 4 annas; a toilet box, R1-4; a work-box, R2-12; a bracket R3; a watch stand, 9 annas. Looking-glass frames, candle-sticks and toys are made at Agra. The best kinds are of walnut wood, and the inferior kinds are made of mango wood. The latter is often painted to make it look like walnut wood. Wooden toys, bowls, cups, and oval boxes, painted in colours, are made at Benares, which are largely sold to pilgrims.

The most important wood-carving, in small work, carried on in the North-Western Provinces is that done at Naginá in the Bijnor District. It is in Indian ebony, on which floral designs are delicately cut out with the chisel. Boxes, pen-cases, ink-stands, book-covers, and other articles are thus beautifully ornamented. The industry has greatly developed in late years, and a large number of people is now engaged in the trade. In the more elaborate and expensive work the black is often relieved by silver and mother-o'-pearl mounts, but it is a question how far this extraneous and new style of ornamentation preserves the integrity and the artistic merit of the original work. A large collection of Naginá wood-carving has been sent to the Glasgow International Exhibition, as private exhibits by Abdulla and Murád Bakhsh. A collection of Naginá work would cost about R300. Prices of typical specimens may be stated as follows:—Table, R90; bracket, R18; book-stand. R16; plate, R14; box, R16; book-cover, R40; inkstand R6, paper-knife 12 annas.

In the Panjáb, book-cases, chiffoniers, small tables, arm-chairs, couches, and wall brackets are made at Simla. Mr. Kipling writes :—

"A trade in furniture carved in walnut wood has grown up of late years in Simla. The workmen are mostly Sikhs from the adjacent plains. The fret saw cutting, which once enjoyed a slight popularity in Europe, is imitated, and Swiss brackets, clocks, &c., carved in wood, have furnished some models. Besides these trivialities, some objects in a better style have been occasionally produced."

Easy chairs, camp chairs, and tables made at Gujrát (in Panjáb) have recently acquired some reputation. The same authority writes :—

"The most characteristic form of the trade at Gujrát is the manufacture of chairs and camp furniture. The large and cumbrous, but undeniably comfortable, easy chair known as the Capperina chair, from its introduction by a District Officer named Capper, and several forms of camp chairs, are the best known. The trade is an increasing one, as the work is fairly strong and well-finished, and the prices moderate. The wood used is *Shisham*. Furniture is so little used by natives of India that it is simply produced to the order of Europeans. A native rich man's house is often well furnished with carpets, hangings, *masnads*, &c., but ornamental furniture is unknown save to those who have adopted the European style. Tables, chairs, low wood octagonal chairs and the *takhta-posh* are only in use. These are produced everywhere in the Province, Delhi, Hushiárpur, Jallandhar, Lahore, Kasur, Amritsar, and Bherá, in the Sháhpur District, produce such things specially."

Cheap chairs with arms of *Shisham* and *Tún* wood (*Cedrela Toona*) are made at Kartárpur in the Jallandhar District. Delhi has its specialty in carved sandalwood and ebony boxes set with oval Delhi miniatures and bound with silver or plated brass. These sell according to size and number of paintings, from R2-8 to R25 each.

In Kashmir carved walnut chairs are occasionally made to order for Europeans, which are finished in the plains or in England. It is supposed that the abundance of excellent walnut wood in Kashmir might make this a profitable industry.

In Jaipur common furniture for native use, such as *chaukis* or square small seats or tables on low legs, boxes, &c., are made at Shekháwati. Folding bedsteads are made at Singháná near Khetri, and some rather boldly-carved bedstead legs have been done in the town of Jaipur. Curious articles of betel-nut, called *kárungar*, are manufactured at Jaipur. These consist of little figures of animals and reptiles, rulers, walking sticks, &c., carved out of pieces of betel-nut, which are joined together when necessary. Toys and other articles of carved wood are made at Dholpur. A cradle, called *Hindorá*, made of wood, carved, coloured and gold-gilt, used for swinging Hindu gods, are made at Jodhpur and exported to Bombay, Gujrát, and other places. The prices of these cradles vary according to the material used, size, and finish, from R20 to R2,000. *Sinhásans* or thrones for deities are also made at Jodhpur. At Ajmir there are some clever carpenters who can imitate the most intricate design and can make any kind of furniture, carriages, &c. They generally work in *Bábul* wood (*Acacia arabica*), which is the only wood procurable in the District.

In Central India wooden toys are produced at Rewa and Gwalior. Sandalwood articles are made both at Rewa and Alipurá. Vases, cups, and other ornamental articles, painted in pretty designs, are made at Ratlám. The other articles of importance manufactured at Gwalior and the principal towns in Central India are carved boxes, ebony smoking pipes, and folding tables.

Furniture is made at Madras, Salem, Anantpur, Malabar, Cuddapah, Vizagapatam, and Tanjore. The designs and usually the ornamentations are mostly copied from European articles, but the imitation is often very fair. At Tirupati, a place of pilgrimage in the North Arcot District, mythological figures are carved in red wood (*Cæsalpinia Sappan*) and sold to pilgrims who visit the sacred hill at that place. These figures, although rough in finish, are executed in a free bold style. *Lotás*, plates, and cups are also made of this wood, which is obtained from the Balapalla jungles in the Cuddapah District. At Trevandrum in Travancore very spirited and well executed designs are carved on diminutive cocoanut shells. A large collection of cocoanut shell articles was sent to the Colonial and Indian Exhibition from this place. These consisted of entire cocoanut shells with lids, cocoanut shells inlaid with silver, tea-pots with tray, sugar-basins, cups and saucers, figures of deities, and other articles made of cocoanut shells, carved, and often inlaid. Similar articles are also made of the hard shell of the *Bel* fruit (*Ægle Marmelos*). The same work, but of inferior merit, is done at Mandasa in Ganjam District and South Canara. At Trichinopoly, Coimbatore, and Tanjore models of temples are carved out of the soft *Solá* pith (*Æschynomene aspera*), those made at Tanjore being the best. Though faithfully executed and look like ivory from a distance, they are, however, very brittle, are easily destroyed by damp, and are liable to the attacks of insects.

Benches were formerly made in Nepal, and were built into the wall and so carved as to correspond with the balconies and windows. Smaller articles of Nepal wood-carving have, however, attracted some attention of late, specially figures, which are quite unique in character. Stands for small figures of deities, figures of Lámás used as stands for incense burnt in time of worship, small boxes, and *kukri* handles are articles generally carved out of wood in Nepal.

In the Bombay Presidency wood-carving is now principally carried on in Ahmadabad, Surat, and Canara. At Ahmadabad there are 800 families of carpenters, but yet the industry has greatly declined compared to what it was in former times. Mr. B. A. Gupte has kindly supplied the following account of the present state of wood-carving industry in the Bombay Presidency:—"The art of wood-carving was almost extinct in Ahmadabad, the only articles made being a few samples of elaborate flower-stands, picture-frames, card cases, &c., in blackwood, for the European visitors to that city, but by the enterprise of Mr. Lockwood de Forest, an American gentleman, a revival has taken place. He has started an establishment for the construction of carved furniture and panels, which are exported to New York by his local agent and manager, Mr. Maganbhái Hattising. About 60 to 80 carvers are employed, who are paid from one to three shillings a day. In addition to employing the best carvers available in Ahmadabad, men have been brought from Kadi, Patan, and Surat. The carvers from Patan are, as a rule, clever. Two cabinets, one bracket, four picture-frames, one flower-stand, and one inkstand have been purchased for the Glasgow International Exhibition, as examples of modern Ahmadabad work. Billimora, in the Baroda territory, possesses 15 to 20 families of carvers, and one Sorabji Jámásji of that town has contributed to the Glasgow International Exhibition a large collection of his manufactures. Wood-carving in teak wood for architectural purposes is still largely carried on at Surat, and there are several workshops in which doors, shutters, ceilings, and windows may be bought ready-made. The work is characterised by considerable freedom and boldness of execution—a treatment most suitable to the size of the objects decorated. A considerable trade in wood-work is also carried on at

Surat in the shape of toys, which consist of figures carved in wood decorated by painting or gilding and then varnished. At Násik, the sacred city of the Hindus, on the banks of the Godávari, which is famous for its old carved timber houses, the art of wood-carving is all but extinct. In 1883 only one carver could be traced, and the window he carved for the Calcutta International Exhibition was found to be as good as the original in the Hingle's *vada*, from which building a sample was selected by Mr. Griffiths, Superintendent of the Bombay School of Art, for being reproduced. The lotus forms the most prominent feature of the house decoration of Násik. There is not a beam, door, window, bracket, or cornice which does not show a treatment based on the form of the sacred lotus. The ancient name of the city is Padmávati, or the city of the lotus, ascribed to the flower-shaped or rather star-shaped tract formed by the confluence of the six tributaries of the Godávari which intersect the town on all sides. The writer presumes that the name 'The city of the lotus' must have influenced the imagination of the artisans who carved the columns, cornices, brackets, and beams found all over the city. That the Indian lotus is the basis of the Corinthian columns of Greece has been amply proved by Thomas Maurice in his 'Indian Antiquities,' volume III (pages 70, 150, and 243), published in 1801. Furniture is manufactured chiefly in blackwood and sometimes in teak. The use of furniture in native houses is of modern date, having been adopted from the Europeans. Demand for good furniture is solely created by the latter, and the bulk of the articles manufactured is for their use. The East India Art Manufacturing Company in Bombay, under the management of Mr. Winbridge, the School of Industry at Ratnagiri, the establishment of Mr. de Forest at Ahmadabad, and a number of native workshops are all actively employed in constructing art furniture of superior design and finish, which has resulted in superseding the clumsily fitted and badly finished old Bombay blackwood furniture."

Carvings on cocoanut shell are practised to a small extent at Sáwantwádi and Canara. Specimens were exhibited at the Colonial and Indian Exhibition.

In Haidrabad (Deccan) wood-carving is done to a small extent at Kamám and Zelgandal. The work is inferior, chiefly toys or figures of animals of grotesque forms and unnatural colours, often not bearing the slightest resemblance to the animals they are intended to represent. The toys are first carved roughly in wood, then shaped with a compound of cowdung or saw-dust, and tamarind pulp or glue. Among the collection obtained for the Colonial and Indian Exhibition was a white pigeon, with tiger-like stripes in ultramarine!

Sandalwood Carving.

The principal places where sandalwood carving is carried on are Canara, Surat, Ahmadabad, and Bombay in the Bombay Presidency; Travancore, Trichinopoly, Haladgi, Raidrug, Tirupatur, Madura, Udiyaghir, Karnúl, Coimbatore, Kistna, and Godávari in the Madras Presidency; and Soráb and Sagar in Mysore. The carvings are most elaborate and minute, sometimes representing patterns of intricate foliage and flowers, but often mythological scenes ornamented with geometrical and floral designs. The *frontispiece* at the beginning of this book represents a slab of sandalwood carving executed in Canara. The slab is fitted into a framework of ebony, the borders of which are boldly ornamented with a beautiful scroll work running up and down all round. The scene represents the deities in heaven in all their celestial glory. On the top, the central figure is Vishnu, the Great Protector of the World, with four hands, his body adorned with the most precious stones, among which is the *kaustabh*, the inestimable jewel obtained by churning the ocean. From his navel rises a lotus, on which sits the four-headed Brahmá, the Creator of the Universe. Vishnu sits at ease under a canopy formed by the hood of a five-headed snake, probably the serpent deity, *Básuki*. On his left is his consort, Lakshmi, the Goddess of Wealth, rubbing his feet. On the right, the monkey-god, Hanumán, is in the act of paying his homage, while angels fly in heaven and gods and demi-gods stand or sit on all sides, in a state of adoration. The middle part is dedicated to Siva, the Great Destroyer in the Hindu Triad. He sits on his favourite bullock, with his consort Párvati, the Goddess of Energy, on his left, and Ganesha, the God of Wisdom, on his right, surrounded by other gods and goddesses as in the above. The lowest part of the tablet represents a celestial battle between the Goddess of Energy and the Buffálo Demon called Mahishásura. The carving is done in high relief. Speaking of sandalwood carving, Sir George Birdwood writes in his "Industrial Arts of India":—

"The Surat and Bombay work is in low relief, and the designs consist almost entirely of foliated ornament; the Canara and Mysore work is in high relief, the subjects being chiefly mythological; and the Ahmadabad work, while in flat relief, is deeply cut, and the subjects are mixed, floral and mythological; for instance, Krishna and the Gopis, represented not architecturally as in Canara carving, but naturally, disporting themselves in a luxuriant wood, in which each tree, while treated conventionally, and running into the general floral decoration, can be distinctly recognised. A line is drawn below the wood, and through the compartment thus formed a river is represented flowing, as on Greek coins, by an undulating band, on which tortoises, fishes, and water-fowl are carved in half relief. The best Canara carving comes from Kompta, and the best Mysore, which is identical in every respect with that of Canara, from the town of Soráb in the Shimoga District."

Mr. Gupte writes that—

"at Surat there were besides the carvers in teak and black wood, 800 Parsi sandalwood-carvers and inlayers, many of whom at the beginning of this century migrated to Bombay, where they opened shops on the Kalbadevi Road for supplying work-boxes, glove-boxes, card-cases, watch-stands, chess-boards, paper-knives, &c. Several of these Parsi settlers have educated their children, who have left the business and become clerks or brokers."

In the Madras Presidency sandalwood carving is carried on in Travancore and South Canara. The Travancore carving is bold and very naturalistic in style. The other places where the art is practised, though on a limited scale, are Trichinopoly, Hadalgi, Ráidrug, Tirupatur, Madura, Udiyagiri, Nellore, Karnúl, Coimbatore, Kistna, and Godávari. The style of work differs more or less in each District. Dr. Bidie states that "the designs are floral and mythological and worked out with great minuteness, and are really more remarkable as examples of patience than as works of art." The Mysore carvings are reported as "elaborate and minute, representing figures in Hindu mythology, skilfully encircled by intricate foliage, with figures of animals in relief. The details are grouped with quite an eastern skill, and form an exceedingly rich ornamentation. Prices depend entirely on the workmanship, for where a box by one man may be bought for R5, a box of the same size and pattern from another man is not obtainable for R20." Flappers, called *chauris*, are made of sandalwood in imitation of yak's tail, which are used to drive away flies. A long piece of sandalwood is divided lengthwise into numerous slices, each slice is as fine as hair, and the whole resembling a *chauri* made of yak's tail. A small part of the wood on the other end is left entire, which is carved and made into a handle. Such *chauris* when waved before the face or behind a man in order to drive away the flies emit the fine fragrance of sandalwood. A *chauri* of this kind has been supplied for the Glasgow International Exhibition by Diwan Raghu Náth Ráo, late of the Indor State. Fans, combs, paper-knives, and other small articles are also made of sandalwood. Rámpurá, a town within the Indor State, is noted for its sandalwood *chauris*, pen-holders, and fans. The price of a *chauri* is R80, and that of a fan R30. *Chauris* are also made at Bhartpur and other Native States. Rosaries, combs, and other small articles are made of sandalwood at Ajmir, which are purchased in large quantities by pilgrims who resort to the *Dargah Khwaja Sáhib*, the tomb of a Muhammadan saint.

Inlaid Woodwork.

Wood is inlaid with ivory, horn, brass, and silver. In Bengal the art is very little practised. Only in Monghyr ivory and horn are sometimes inlaid on furniture or small articles made of ebony wood. The demand for ivory-inlaid ebony work is very small and is apparently diminishing. There are only six or eight carpenters now in Monghyr who follow the profession of furniture making and inlaying on wood. A large number of men who used to do this work is now employed in the East Indian Railway, an occupation that has been found more lucrative than the indigenous industry of the town.

As stated before, the Naginá wood-carvers, in the North-Western Provinces, decorate their more elaborate and expensive work with silver and mother-o'-pearl mounts as a set-off to the black of the ebony of which the articles are made. But the most noted inlaid woodwork in the North-Western Provinces is the *Tárkashi* work of Mainpuri. The articles are made of *Shisham* (*Dalbergia latifolia*) wood, on which foliage and geometrical designs are most minutely formed by hammering in fine brass wire. The surface is then polished, and the article then presents to the eye an intricate maze of golden patterns running into all directions in endless profusion, though with the usual regularity and symmetry of an Indian handiwork. The art was all but extinct a few years ago, when it fortunately attracted European attention. Though not yet in a prosperous condition, it is, however, slowly reviving, and the last few Exhibitions have done it much good. It can be introduced with good effect for pannelling doors, picture framing, &c. The following account of the mode of manufacture and the present state of the industry has been supplied by Mr. A. H. Pirie, Honorary Secretary, Provincial Museum, Lucknow:—

"This is a work pecular to Mainpuri itself, on which about 35 different men find employment. Hard wood, generally *Shisham*, is used. It must be well seasoned. The brass wire is let into the wood in the following way. A diagram is first drawn in pencil on the wood; then with a sharp knife incisions are made along the pencil marks and the wire put into the incisions and then beaten down to a level with the surface with an iron hammer. The process requires considerable time and labour. Thus a plate of 12 inches in diameter takes one workman 20 days. The best workman makes a profit of R20 per mensem and the others make from R10 to R15 per mensem for the whole year. The manufacture is certainly flourishing and the number of workmen is increasing to some extent every year."

A collection of Mainpuri *Tárkashi* ware has been sent to the Glasgow International Exhibition. A typical collection would cost about R200. The following may be put down as the price of ordinary specimens:—Stationery case, R15; plate, R18; ladies' work-box, R18; octagonal box, R25; box for papers,

R30; picture-frame, R35; book-stand, R5. Originally *Tárkashi* work seems to have been chiefly employed in the ornamentation of boxes and wooden sandals, so largely used in the country in former days. Sandals are still decorated with wire-work in Pilibhit, a town in the North-Western Provinces at the foot of the Himalayas. The work done there is, however, inferior to that of Mainpuri. A flower bud, in imitation of that of the pomegranate, made of wood coloured red or of blood stone, is inserted on the sandal, which people wearing it firmly hold between the big and the second toe. In walking, the bud opens with the pressure of the foot as each step is taken and shuts when the foot is raised for the next step.

Panjáb is celebrated for its ivory and brass inlay on wood. Ivory inlay is extensively carried on in Hushiárpur, and brass inlay comes from Chiniot in the District of Jhang. Small square wooden seats, called *chaukis*, almirahs, wall-brackets, tables, chairs, boxes, desks, rulers, picture-frames, cabinets, and other household articles made of *Shisham* wood are inlaid with ivory at Hushiárpur. A small edging of blackened wood is occasionally introduced to set off the ivory. The industry has only been lately revived, and it is specially practised by workmen who reside at the village of Ghulám Husain Bassi near Hushiárpur. They now drive a considerable trade. Several workmen combine in the work. Mr. Kipling after writing about "word-carving," as practised in Hushiárpur, makes the following remarks on the subject of this industry:—

"Of equal and, indeed, superior importance as an industry which may be expected to support skilled workmen, is the wood-inlay of ivory and brass of the District. The extension of this trade to articles of European use is mainly due to the efforts of Mr. Coldstream, C. S. For many years pen-cases, walking staves, mirror-cases, and the low *chauki*, or octagonal table common in the Panjáb and probably of Arab introduction, have been made here in *Shisham* wood inlaid with ivory and brass. The patterns were very minute and covered nearly the whole of the surface with an equal spottiness. Mr. Coldstream procured its application to tables, cabinets, and other objects, and during recent years a trade has sprung up which seems likely to grow to still larger proportions. The faults of the inlay are a certain triviality and insignificance of design and its too equal and minute distribution. At various times some of the inlayers have visited Lahore, and have been shown at the School of Art examples of good Arabic and Indian design, and they have frequently been furnished with sketches. When the blackness and ugliness of an Indian village are considered, it is really matter for surprise that decorative invention survives in any form. There are numbers of artisans, many of whom are in the hands of a Hindu dealer, who is naturally but little concerned in the artistic quality of the wares he sells. The ivory used is generally the waste stuff left by the turners of ivory bangles and by comb-makers and is worth from R1 to R2 per ℔. It is frequently alleged that bone, especially camel bone, is used as well as ivory, but both ivory comb-makers and turners make a good deal of waste, which is quite large enough for the small details of the inlay. Blackwood, the old heart-wood of the *Kinum* (*Diospyros tomentosa*), incorrectly called *abnús* or ebony by the workmen, is occasionally used both as a ground and, in combination with ivory, as an inlaying material, especially in the familiar herring-bone pattern. Brass is also employed, but with less effect, for when foliated work in small patterns is worked in brass, it is necessary that the metal should have a better surface than it generally receives in the Hushiárpur work."

Brass inlay is also practised at Hushiárpur, but the best work comes from Chiniot. The brass is cut into thin plates before being inserted on the wood, which is done with great precision and neatness. Woods of colours are also employed in inlaying. Mr. Kipling writes :—

"Wood inlay is understood to a limited extent by nearly all the more skilful *mistris* or carpenters of the Panjáb. They employ box and other white woods upon *Shisham*, or the latter upon the yellow *Deodár*. But very few specimens are, however, to be seen surpassing the artistic work of the Mayo School of

Industrial Art. Rám Singh, the head carpenter there, has done some beautiful work."

At Chiniot brass inlaying is chiefly practised in the decoration of camel-panniers called *Kajáwá*, of panels, windows, &c. A panel would cost from R5 to R10, a window R40 or R45. The price of a typical collection of Hushiárpur ivory inlaid work may be as follows:—A table R45, wall bracket R15, picture-frame R6, wall-shelf R35, box R25.

Work similar to that done in Hushiárpur is made at Etawa, a town in Kota, Rajputana. The wood used is that of *Shisham*, which is inlaid with ivory and mother-o'-pearl. The Kota screen at the Colonial and Indian Exhibition was made in this style of work. The industry is confined to two or three families belonging to the *Khati* caste, who turn out their work very slowly, though it is, as a rule, carefully and strongly executed.

In the Madras Presidency the art of inlaying on wood is chiefly practised in the well-known Vizagapatam work. Work-boxes, card-cases, inkstands, chess boards, and other knick-nacks are made here, chiefly of sandal-wood, which are decorated with ivory fret-work, tortoise-shell, horn, &c. Dr. Bidie writes:—

"The surface of the ivory is generally adorned with etchings in black of mythological figures very well executed, or with floral forms in light and shade, which are copies of European designs. The workmanship of the articles is usually superior, and although expensive, they are much in demand as drawing-room ornaments."

The prices of the Vizagapatam sandalwood articles may be put as follows:—Sandalwood and ivory ink-stand, R50; watch-stand, R25; chess-board, R55; blotting book, R40; box, R135; picture-frame, R10.

Cabinet work and furniture of ebony wood are inlaid with ivory in the town of Mysore. The work is done in the old conventional Carnatic and Mughul patterns. A teapoy inlaid with ivory is sold for R50, a chair for R100, and minor articles for a price down to R2. "A door 6′ × 12′ manufactured for the Bangalore palace cost R1,500, and was awarded a gold medal at the Calcutta International Exhibition. The ivory inlaid doors at Tippu Sultan's tomb are very beautiful."

On the Bombay side work-boxes, glove-boxes, and other articles are minutely decorated by inlaying on the surface small pieces of ivory, stag-horn, tin, glass, &c. This work is done at Surat, Baroda, Ahmadabad, Kach, and Bombay. Sir George Birdwood makes the following remarks on the subject of this industry :—

"A good deal of ornamental furniture is also made in 'Bombay inlaid work,' so familiar now in the ubiquitous glove-boxes, blotting-cases, book-stands, work-boxes, desks, and card-cases which go by the name of 'Bombay boxes.' They are made in the variety of inlaid wood-work, or marquetry or tarsia, called *piqué*, and are not only pretty and pleasing, but interesting on account of its having been found possible to trace the introduction of the work into India from Persia step by step, from Shiraz into Sind, and to Bombay and Surat. In Bombay the inlay is made up of tin wire, sandalwood, ebony, sappan (brazil) wood, ivory white and stained green, and stag-horn. Strips of these materials are bound together in rods, usually three-sided, sometimes round, and frequently obliquely four-sided, or rhombic. They again are so arranged in compound rods as, when cut across, to present a definite pattern, and in the mass have the appearance of rods of varying diameter and shape, or of very thin boards, the latter being intended for borderings. The patterns commonly found in Bombay, finally prepared for use, are *chakar-gul*, or 'round bloom,' *katki-gul*, 'hexagonal bloom,' *tinkoniá-gul*, 'three-cornered bloom,' *adhi-dhar-gul*, 'rhombus-bloom,' *chorus-gul*, 'square (matting-like) bloom,' *tiki*, a small round pattern, and *gandirio*, 'plump,' compounded of all the materials used; also *ekdáná*, 'one grain,' having the appearance of a row of silver beads set in ebony; and *pori lihur, jafrán marapech, jeri, baelmutana, sankru hansio*, and *prohansio*, these eight last being bordering patterns. The work was introduced into Sind from Shiraz about a hundred years ago."

In Nepal very little inlay work on wood is carried on. It is almost entirely confined to the ornamentation of *Hukkas*, the stems of which are sometimes inlaid with brass and iron, ivory, or mother-o'-pearl,

---

Lacquered Ware.

The art of lacquering wood is practised all over India, the Province of Panjáb being the most noted for its manufactures of this kind. The art consists in coating an article of wood with lac of different colours, and often cutting out patterns on it with a chisel. The wood is first turned into an article of the required shape and size, and when thoroughly smoothed and cleaned, it is ready to receive the lacquer. This is done by setting the article on the turner's frame, and as it is made to revolve, the coloured lac-sticks are hard pressed upon it. The heat produced by the friction softens the lac and makes it adhere to the wood. Layers of red, green, black, and other colours, as may be required, are thus put one after the other. The patterns are cut by hand with a chisel, always going down to the depth of the colour required. For instance a leaf may be produced by cutting down to the green layer, and a flower by cutting down to red, and so on. The following more detailed description of the process has been taken from Mr. Baden Powell's "Pánjab Manufactures":—

"When about to apply the sticks of lacquer colour, the wooden article, duly smoothed and clean, is set on the turner's frame and made to rotate. If the colour to be produced is an uniform surface of lac colour, the lac-stick is pressed rather hard against the wood and the colour comes off as the heat produced by the friction is sufficient to soften the lac and detach a portion. When enough colour has been applied, the article looks dull and streaky, but a piece of bamboo is taken and a fine edge put on it with a chisel; this is skilfully rubbed over the surface of the article till the colour has evenly spread, and by skilful manipulation a polish begins to show on the surface, which is enhanced by a gentler application of bamboo edges, and finally completed with oil and a rag. To produce the mottled appearance so much admired, the sticks of colour are selected of a rather harder composition, and less easily softened by heat. The article to be coloured is set revolving, and the workman, holding the colour-stick against it, very lightly allows a point here and a point there of colour to attach itself; the wood soon appears to be sprinkled over with coloured dust.

"The workman takes another colour and repeats the process, moving the stick up and down along the revolving block, when by his skilful manipulation the second colour adheres at points which the first colour has left blank; sometimes a third colour is touched in in the same manner. When enough colour is on the surface, the different points of colours are rubbed together and combined into a mottled or marbled appearance by rubbing, as before described, with a bamboo edge, and finishing with a rag and oil. The prettiest mottle is that of crimson and black, crimson and white, and blue and black. Around the rim of a box or lip of a cup, a border is often put on, with a flower pattern on it, which is done in a different way.

"The article is again set spinning on the frame, and colour applied where the desired border is to come, in a uniform hand, and well rubbed in and smoothed with bamboo; a coating of red is always given first, over the red, a coating of green is applied till the red disappears, and over the green black.

"The flower pattern is produced by hand with a small sharp chisel; so delicately does the workman adjust the force and depth of his cut, that he will, for the flower, let us say, make it appear red by cutting away the black and green coats and exposing the red layer, for the leaves he will scratch down to the green one, and for a white line he will cut down to the wood. A mistake seems never to be made in this work; a slip of the tool would of course spoil the whole."

A writer in the *Journal of Indian Art* in comparing Japanese and Indian lacquered work is of opinion that the word "lac-turnery" should be substituted for "lacquer" as it is practised in India. He writes :—

"The word 'lacquer' as applied to Japanese varnish and Indian shellac is somewhat misleading to the untechnical mind. We are in the habit of describing the ordinary shellac coloured wood turnery of India and the Burmese ware with a basket work basis as lacquered. A lacquer would seem to mean a fluid varnish applied with a brush and set aside to harden, either in a stove, as in Birmingham, or in a damp press as in Japan. Indian lacquer, so called, is merely the surface obtained by pressing a stick of hard shellac coloured *ad lib.* to a rapidly revolving wooden object. The friction developes heat sufficient to make it adhere irregularly. The end of a dry palm leaf stem cut chiselwise, and applied in the same way, melts it still more and spreads it equally, while a drop of oil applied with further friction with a bit of rough muslin polishes the surface, which is as hard and good after ten minutes' work as it can ever be. It lasts, too, fairly well; but being only shellac and colour after all, it is not to be compared with Japanese lacquer, in some specimens of which, it is credibly reported, water can be boiled without injury to the vessel, and which never seems to scale or peel off. It might be worth consideration whether some confusion would not be avoided by the adoption of the phrase, 'lac-turnery,' to distinguish the common Indian ware from the lacquered or varnished surfaces. Sind boxes are turned and covered with shellac, while the decorated trays and panels of Haidrabad, Deccan, are lacquered in the true sense. At present Indian catalogues describe most glossy surfaces as lacquered."

In comparing Japanese lacquer work with that produced in India the same authority makes the following remarks :—

"India is behindhand in most painting and varnishing processes. It is perhaps not generally recognised that in this respect the arts of the East generally are in the state of those of Europe before the time of Van Dyck. The ordinary powers of linseed oil are unknown, and painting, whether pictorial or decorative, is in water-colour, protected by resin varnishes. But, while the Japanese possess a varnish of unique properties, the Indian artisan is limited to sundras or East Indian copal, mastic, rosin, and shellac; and, except when working under English coach-builders, it has not entered into his mind that many successive coats of varnish may be laid, rubbed down, and polished until a fine surface is attained. If some of the best Calcutta carriage work had only an English climate to withstand, it would probably last as long as that of Long Acre; but it is done under European superintendence; while if left to himself the native artificer is content to apply his *raugan* with the palm of his hand, and to leave it with its natural sheen, so that from the Japanese or English mechanic's point of view it is more of a smear than a polished body of varnish. The preliminary processes before the application of varnish are those in use everywhere. Wood surfaces to be painted in water colour are treated with a ground of brick-dust or inferior white earth (there is no good whiting in the country) and glue or tinfoil levigated with glue or covered with shredded hemp or cloth, while embossed work for gilding or treatment with tin and yellow varnish to simulate gold is loaded up with a brush in glue and white earth. The old ceiling work of the Panjáb, the lacquered panels of Haidrabad, Deccan, and the beddings of Rajputana and Delhi are examples of this last method. There is never any rubbing down of the varnish, though stones are used with water to smooth glue or gum laid grounds. There is, however, one notable exception to the general rule of ignorance as to Japanese processes, which is so curious that it is mentioned here in the hope that further research may bring out other examples. Mr. Walter Lawrence, C.S., writes:—'In Sháhpurá, a small Rajput State of the Sesodia family, there are made some very beautiful lacquered shields by a family of artisans at the capital. Old workmanlike shields which have done duty in the desert of Marwar are bought up for three rupees a piece and brought over to Sháhpurá, where they are carefully soaked and worked up for the lacquer process. It is said that some 60 coats of varnish are applied to each shield, and that it takes a year to finish one. The people of Sháhpurá know little of how the ancestor of the lacquer family came to their city, but they have a legend that he came from the East, and that he was not a countryman of Hindustan.'"

Very little lacquering work is now done in Bengal, Murshidabad and Patna being the only places where the industry is practised on a limited scale. It is said that good lacquered ware is made at a place near Sirájganj, but no specimen of the work has yet been brought for show.

In the North-Western Provinces, lacquered wooden

articles are made in many places, notably at Bareilly, Agra, Lucknow, Fatehpur, Sháhjahánpur, Benares, and Mirzapur. Chairs, tables, and other furniture articles are made at Bareilly; boxes, plates, and small articles at Agra; legs for bedsteads at Lucknow, Fatehpur, and Sháhjahánpur; and toys at Benares and Mirzapur. Each District has a style of its own different from its neighbour. The art of lacquering is, in the North-Western Provinces, more applied to the decoration of bedstead legs than to any other article. Toys made at Benàres, Fatehpur, and Mirzapur are more remarkable for their cheapness than beauty. Packs of native cards are made at Fatehpur of thin woòd, painted and lacquered, and also nests of boxes, in the construction of which considerable ingenuity and skill are shown. A collection of North-Western Provinces lacquered ware can be obtained for R100.

In the Panjáb, the *Kharádi* or wood-turner is found in nearly every town and village, but Pákpattan, Derá Ismáil Khán, Firozpur, Sahiwál, and Hushiárpur have acquired a particular reputation for their lacquered-wares. Pákpattan articles were hitherto considered the best, but of late other places have equalled, if not surpassed, the Pákpattan manufactures. Bed-legs, frames of rope bedsteads, boxes, sticks, chairs, &c., are made in this place. "The work has a fine polish and generally a marbled or mottled appearance, often in two or three colours, and the article finished with a flowered border, which latter is done by a species of handiwork different from the rest, and certainly affording a good instance of the delicacy of native handling." Mr. Kipling has supplied the following information with regard to the industry as carried on in other places of note:—

"Bed-legs, water-vessels, goglets, boxes, rulers, and toys are made at Hushiárpur. The Hushiárpur lacquer differs from that of Pákpattan in the use of metallic (tin) ground under transparent colour, and in addition to the scratched work of colour, figures of a mythological character are boldly painted and covered with transparent lacquer. Ornamental boxes, trays, globular boxes, teapoys, &c., are made at Derá Ismáil Khán. The lacquer of Derá Ismáil Khán is unique in character. Very few colours are employed, and the pattern is usually of fern-like scrolls of almost incredible minuteness and delicacy of execution, mostly wrought or rather scratched by women. The caskets, tables, &c., are lavishly ornamented with ivory studs, flowers, and similar projecting ornaments. A workman of Firozpur has almost raised lac-turnery to the dignity of fine art by his skill in pattern scratching. He uses the wood of the tamarisk or *Pharwán* for his wares, and not, as elsewhere, *Shisham* or poplar. This wood, though used in Sind, where wood of any kind is scarce, is seldom touched by the Panjáb workmen. His work is the best of its kind in the Province. Chessmen, tables, toys of various kinds, plates, teapoys, &c., are made at Sahiwál in the Sháhpur District. The lac-turnery of Sahiwál differs from that of other places in being more crude in colour and simpler in execution. A particularly unpleasant aniline mauve is used, but there is a better class: vases, plates, and toys are made in two colours, red and black, or red or yellow or black, or either. The scratched patterns are bolder and larger than elsewhere."

In Rajputana, wooden chess-boards and men, painted and gilded and lacquered, somewhat in the style of the Surat work, are made in Jaipur. In the School of Art at Jaipur a large quantity of incised lacquered ware, like those of the Panjáb, is produced. These consist of bottles, betel-boxes, vases, cups, plates, *Lotás*, *Suráhis*, *Abkorás*, &c. A series of teakwood panels, painted with scenes from the *Razam-námah* (Persian version of the *Mahábhárata*), and then lacquered, intended to serve as book covers or panels for cabinets, were sent to the Colonial and Indian Exhibition. These panels were copies of originals done by the best artists in the time of Akbar (A.D. 1588). They were done in the Kashmir style under the instructions of Dr. Hendley. About the manufacture of lacquered ware at Jaipur Dr. Hendley writes:—

"Wood is turned into round shapes, boxes for tobacco or

opium, bedstead legs, rulers, staves, &c., and then lacquered in bands of pure bright colours or in variegated designs by the application of the lac as the article is rapidly turned on the latter, the whole being concluded with good polish. At Khandelá, moreover, wooden toys are carved, coloured and varnished with lacquer. The small quaint figures of elephants, deer, camel, &c., are sold as low as 32 per rupee."

Lacquered playing cards of leather are made at Siwái Mádhopur. Lacquered slates were sent from Jaipur to the London Exhibition. Large quantities of lacquered cups are made at Indragarh, a small town in the Kota State. The wood used to make the cups is that of *Khirni* (*Mimusops indica*). Earthen *Suráhis* are also lacquered at Indragarh. The lac is melted and put on the *Suráhis* with a small piece of iron. Lacquer on pottery is also practised in Bikánir. Coloured lac is put on articles of common China. It is also practised on stone, glass, ivory, and wood, and the Bikánir work receives additional effect from the plentiful use of gold leaf in the decorations. The Bikánir screen at the Colonial and Indian Exhibition was made in this style. The process of manufacture is described as follows:—

"On the surface of the wood, which had been previously well scrubbed with liquid clay and allowed to dry, the outlines of a flower pattern are stencilled with a bag of powdered charcoal through perforated paper. Successive layers of liquid clay are then applied with small squirrel's hair brushes within the outlines of the pattern, each layer being allowed to dry before the next application, until a raised surface bringing out the stalks, leaves, and petals with sufficient distinctness is produced. The whole surface is then fixed by a coat of paint, and when this is dry gold leaf is applied over all."

The price of lacquered jars and vases made at Bikánir is R2 to R5. Lacquered shields are made at Sháhpur, the price being R25 or R38, including cost of boss and grip. Lacquered glass *Lotás*, *Hukka* stems, bed-posts, and several sorts of ingenious toys with delicate and neat shades of colour are made in Karauli. In Jhallawar, the turners of Bakain make a variety of toys, boxes, &c., and carry on a large business in them. One article peculiar to the place is the lacquered cocoanut shell bracelets. Trays, writing boxes, and bed supports are made at Mandáwar and Rájgarh in Alwar, but the work is not so fine as that of the Panjáb. Bedsteads and Indian clubs are made at Dholpur.

In the Madras Presidency the lacquer work of Karnúl has long been famous. Dr. Bidie writes:—

> "Some of the old specimens are superior to anything which can now be produced, both in design and execution. The patterns are floral and in slight relief, and the colours very bright, with much gilding."

Articles generally made are tables, boxes, and fans. Besides Karnúl the other places where lacquered articles are made are Vizagapatam and Nossam in Cuddapah District. In the last place, dish-mats made of leather are painted with pictures, which are packed in boxes, of a kind of lacquer ware. The lacquer patterns on these boxes are floral. Native playing cards are also made here, which are put in similar boxes, oblong in shape, and covered with mythological figures in brilliant colours. The boxes do not appear to be made of wood, but of layers of paper and cloth. Fans made of palm-leaf or of paper and cloth are lacquered and painted in brilliant colours at Chitvail and Nossam in Cuddapah District. An inferior kind of lacquered work, consisting of trays, tables, &c., is done at Nandyál. Toys are made at Vellore "out of a light pale-coloured wood, called *Vepále*, which turns out well, and is probably that of *Holarrhena antidysenterica*. The articles are in the shape of miniature cups, goglets, pots, and other domestic utensils, and are covered with a beautiful coloured varnish or lacquer, which does not suffer from immersion in water, or come off when the toy is put in a child's mouth. The lacquer is composed of lac as a basis, with pigments of different kinds to give the colours."

Toys, vases, boxes, &c., are made at Chennapatna in Mysore. These toys have a reputation in that part of the country. They are of two or three colours, and are highly polished. A set of sixty articles sells for R 10. Chess-men and chess-boards are also made, as well as large shields representing the face of a giant, which are carried by pilgrims to Tirupati.

Beautiful lacquer work is made at Bainganpalli, a town in the Raichur District of Haidrabad (Deccan), and is used in the ornamentation of articles of domestic use. Like the inlaid metal-work of Bidar, a set of lacquered articles is given as a wedding dowry. "The work is of two kinds, one embossed and the other plain, and called, respectively, *Munábathi* and *Lajawardi*. The embossing is produced by a tedious process. Shells or slags from the forge are finely ground with some glutinous substance, which is kept a secret, and layer upon layer of this ingredient is put on with a brush till the requisite height is attained. The whole is then covered with gold leaf, the designs are picked out in paint, and the article varnished. The prices charged are about R8 per square foot for *Munábathi* and R4 for *Lajawardi*. The work would be cheaper but for the levying of a heavy blackmail—a right which few landlords (*Jágirdárs*) fail to exercise."

Lacquered ware is extensively made in the Bombay Presidency, from the small wooden toys of Sáwantwádi to the rich lacquered work of Haidrabad (in Sind), "with hunting scenes in outline, delicately tinted on a rich brown ground." Besides toys, articles of a higher order are also made at Sáwantwádi. These consist of ware brilliantly coloured, and illustrating subjects from Hindu mythology. The following account of the industry as carried on in the Bombay Presidency has been supplied by Mr. B. A. Gupte :—

"The Sind workers are Musalmans, who state that they came originally from Zanzibar. They are very indolent, irregular in their habits, and poor, and the capital they require is borrowed from dealers. From August to November the demand is brisker than during any other time of the year, although the Huzur Deputy Collector, Haidrabad, reports that of late the demand for Sind lacquered ware has decreased and that the industry is declining. The annual outturn in Haidrabad is only about £100 to £130. At Sáwantwádi there are only half a dozen workers in lacquered ware, four of them being *Sutars* (carpenters) and two *Chitaris* (painters) or *Jingars*. One has capital of his own, while the others either receive advances from customers, or obtain the raw material on credit. The demand is reported by the Political Superintendent to be decreasing, trade in lacquered ware having been replaced by European and Chinese toys. The annual outturn of lacquered ware at Sáwantwádi is said to be about £200, and the articles are sent to Bombay, Poona, Belgaum Baroda, Dharwar, Satara, Kolhapur, Goa, and several other places."

Lacquered articles made at Haidrabad (Sind) consist of cigar-cases, boxes, flower-vases, &c. A collection would cost about R80. The Sáwantwádi State has contributed a collection of lacquered ware to the Glasgow International Exhibition. These consist of cabinets, tables, brackets, trays, toys, &c. A collection of smaller articles would cost about R50. Playing cards with ten incarnations of Vishnu are made at Sáwantwádi. Articles made of cocoanut shells are also ornamented with lacquer work.

Wooden toys are made in Sylhet (Assam) by four Musalmans. They are lacquered and quaintly coloured with various patterns, and are sold in sets of one hundred pieces. A Muhammadan of Sylhet also makes another curious lacquered article, *viz.*, the blow-pipe. "The pipe is of bamboo and lacquered with effective colours. The arrows, one hundred of which are sold with each pipe for R3-2, are made of small strips of bamboo, 8 or 9 inches long, tipped with iron and winged with an inverted cone of paper."

The following account of lacquering industry in Burma has been supplied by Mr. Tilly:—

"The lacquer-ware used in British Burma is of two kinds—(1) that in which the article is made of basket-work lacquered over; (2) that in which the article is made of wood. With regard to shape alone a distinction might be drawn between things used in ordinary life and those which are dedicated to the service of the monastery. The census tables do not distinguish between makers of, and dealers in, lacquer-ware, but 676 persons were returned under both heads, of whom by far the greater portion are dealers only. All the lacquer-ware made on a basket-work form comes from Upper Burma, where it is a very important trade. In British Burma the trade is confined to the production of wooden articles lacquered over, such as the large round platter with a raised edge, in which the family dinner is served, round and square boxes, and bowls. Another set of artists produce richly-gilt boxes used in the monasteries for holding palm-leaf manuscripts, the bowls with a pagoda-shaped cover used for carrying food to monasteries and pagodas and shrines on which to place images of Gotama. The coffers referred to appear as if covered with pictures drawn in black on a gold ground, and the effect is so good that a small demand for tables, panels, and bowls of the same work has sprung up. The process of manufacture is as follows:—A deep red lacquer is made by mixing the sap of the *Melanorrhœa usitatissima* with vermillion in the proportion of $12\frac{1}{2}$ parts to 10 parts. The sap or *thitsi* is used alone when a black lacquer is required. The wooden bowls, platters, &c., are scraped down with fine steel scrapers to make the surface as smooth as possible before laying on the lacquer. All cracks, holes, and chipped edges are filled, and built up as it were with a putty made of the lacquer itself mixed with teakwood sawdust. The articles are then put away until the putty is dry and quite hard. The lacquer, the raw *thitsi*, is now rubbed all over the article with the bare hand, so that the least particle of sand or stone may be detected and the article put by in a cool and airy place to dry, not in the sun, however, as the lacquer would crack or blister. In about three or four days they are quite dry, and they then receive a thick even coating of *thayo* made up of *thitsi*, rice-water, and paddy-husk ashes. Again the article is put away to dry and harden; when the lacquer is quite dry and hard, it is smoothed down with water and paddy-husk ashes and stone polishers of graduated fineness from sandstone to a smooth pebble. This process removes all gloss or polish, and the last coating or *a youngtin*, is given to the article, either black or red, as a polish. The grounding is invariably black and only the last coating red if red-coloured ware is required. The above process in lacquering bowls, &c., is gone through in preparing gilt tables and boxes for keeping Buddhist palm-leaf manuscripts. The boxes are generally coated with red lacquer, the tables invariably with black. After the boxes have been well washed and smoothed down, a coating of lacquer, red or black as the case may be, thick in body, is laid on and the articles put by for a day or two. This coating is to act as a gold size. When the size has sufficiently hardened to permit touching without smearing the fingers, the worker proceeds to paint the design which he wishes to produce on the box or table, the lines standing up above the surface. The paint used is made from sulphide of arsenic or orpiment, which the worker rubs with a little water on a sandstone palette. To this he adds a small quantity of powdered gum arabic, so as to make the paint adhere to the size. The outline must, however, be finished before the *thitsi* groundwork on which he is painting has become too dry to be serviceable as a gold size. The drawings being finished and the paint dry, the process of gilding begins. The gold leaf is laid on over the whole surface, over the size and over the drawings or tracings; the gold adheres to the size but not to the paint. The article is then put away, always in a cool and airy place, until the gold has firmly adhered to the size. The tracings, or rather the paint which rises above the level of the general surface, is now washed away with cotton-wool and water, and the design stands out prominently against the gold ground in red or black lines according as the lacquer beneath the gold is red and black. Some of the panels are decorated in bas-relief by attaching beadings; figure and foliage work made by mixing *thitsi* and finely powdered bone-ash, and taking a cast from a mould cut out in a soapstone slab: a panel so treated looks as if it were made of polished ebony. The shrines and the priests' begging bowls are first carved or turned in wood and afterwards covered with gold leaf and ornamented with pieces of green and red glass and looking-glass. Gilt lacquered ware is comparatively cheap, and the artists do not do more than earn enough for a livelihood.'

VII.—Art manufactures in Stone.

The art of stone-carving has already been noticed under the head of "Decorative Stone-carving as applied to Architecture." All that now remains to be done is to give an account of the smaller objects of stone-carving turned out in different parts of the country, and of the inlaid marble work done at Agra.

Stone-carving.

Wherever stone is found, plates, cups, and other household objects as well as images of deities and toys are made. In Bengal, such things are made in Monghyr, Gya, Sasseram, all over Chota Nágpur, and the Tributary States of Orissa. A collection of stone manufactures was sent to the Colonial and Indian Exhibition from Gya, Bardwán, Mánbhúm, and Monghyr. But the Bengal manufactures have not much artistic merit. "The images made in Bardwán and Gya are evidently copies of forms that have been handed down from father to son, and have, as would be expected, lost any artistic feeling they may once have possessed. The images of animals are but little better than those of deities. The Gya and Mánbhúm vessels are better, but the former are being spoilt by a tendency to cover them with gilding." The Gya articles are, however, the best made in Bengal. The material is a sort of black marble, and the articles consist of plates, cups, deep oval basins, jars, figures of deities, mendicants and animals. They are largely purchased by pilgrims, who go there in all seasons, for every good Hindu is bound to place a prescribed offering on the sacred foot of Vishnu there in the name of his dead ancestors, which act is believed to free them from purgatory. The District of Mánbhúm in Chota Nágpur produces good soap or pot-stone articles. Plates and other articles are made at Monghyr by Messrs. Ambler & Co. In the North-Western Provinces large quantities of household articles are prepared of sandstone at Mirzapur, which are sold to pilgrims both at Benares and Allahabad. By far the most important of the North-Western Provinces stone-carving are the articles formed of soapstone at Agra. Boxes, plates, paper-weights, and other small articles are made. The floral and perforated patterns are particularly good. The local names of patterns are given as—*Phulchamas Jáliká*, *Bhogli-ká-choliathmas*, *Kamrakhi*, *Athmas-jálidár*, *Manobat-ki-choli*, *Angur*, and *Dabás-u-chol-choli*. The articles are cheap, prices varying from R2 to R15. A collection can be had for R50. Stone-carving is rare in the Panjáb. A few toys are made at Delhi and Lahore. Book-stands, chairs, and vessels of various sorts are carved to a limited extent at Amritsar, Lahore, Chiniot, and Delhi. The workshop attached to the golden temple at Amritsar has some good Sikh carvers, who can produce excellent work. In the Central Provinces some stone-carving of merit is carried on in the town of Chanda, and in a village named Kanheri, in the Bhandárá District, where small vessels are made of a soft stone which is quarried there. "They are not intended for ornament but for use, since there is not the same scruple about using them more than once at meals as exists in the case of earthenware vessels. They are also used for keeping preserves, which would be likely to acidify in metal vessels." Jaipur is famous for its marble figures of deities, men, and animals all over India. Dr. Hendley states:—

"Jaipur supplies most of Bráhmanical India with idols in white marble, plain or coloured and gilt; in red or black marble; and in Dungárpur chlorite, a soft and easily worked stone, which turns black when well oiled, rubbed with lamp-black and charcoal, and polished. The purest white marble is brought from Makráná, a short distance from the Jodhpur side of the Sambhar Lake, but a much liked white marble, often veined with blue, of a cheaper kind, is obtained from Raialo on the Alwar border, and is especially worked at Dausa. The stone masons prepare in the summer enormous stocks of images, which are bought by the brokers from Gujrát (Bombay) and elsewhere after the rains and then sold by retail in the winter. The Makráná marble is worked at Jaipur, though sometimes very large idols are roughly hewn at the quarries to lessen expense of carriage. Baldeogarh on the Alwar border yields black marble, of which figures of animals, besides great idols, are made. The red marble from the same place is usually cut into the forms of camels and plates. All these marbles are employed in architecture, and in addition of late green marbles from Ajmir. The boys learn to carve by making small images from soapstone. These sell readily among the poor."

The *Chiteras* or painters colour and gild the images. Jaipur marble figures are generally sold from R1 to R10. A good collection cannot be had at less than R200. Both at Jaipur and at Makráná, plates, trays, boxes, chess-boards, and other articles are carved of marble, which are sent to Agra to be inlaid with coloured stones. Rough marble is also largely exported from Makráná. Cups, saucers, and paper-weights are made at Jasalmir. "These are of yellow limestone, blended with red ochre-like substance, and of other stones." The articles are well polished. They are sold at R2 to R4 a piece. Stone bowls, idols, and figures of animals are carved in Karauli. The bowl called *pathrotá* is used for storing coin in. They are made of the red and white sandstone found in the State. The execution is rough. Figures of Hindu deities and toys are made of red sandstone in Bikánir. Plates, cups, and grindstones are carved at Bhartpur of sandstone from the local quarries. Soapstone cups, bottles, boxes for betel-leaves, and other articles of a similar nature are made at Bijáwar, Chhatrapur, Orchhá, and Alipurá in Central India. They show considerable skill and taste. In the Madras Presidency, common soapstone articles are made at Tinitani and Chandragiri, North Arcot District; Salem; Kistna; Madura District; Cuddapah; and Vizagapatam. Small idols are produced at Hallal, Bellary District; Saidapuram, Nellore District; Anantpur; Palladan, Coimbatore District; Cuddapah; Gudiyatum, North Arcot District; Trichinopoly; and Tanjore. Among the objects sent from the Madras Presidency to the Colonial and Indian Exhibition were an image of Gautama Roya in sienitic granite, being a copy of the colossal monolithic statue at Karkala in South Canara; and a model in soapstone of the altar on which the sacred basil (*Tulsi, Ocimum sanctum*) is grown in the courtyard of Hindu houses. Images of Hindu deities are carved of soapstone in Mysore. Many sacred objects, cut in this stone, centuries old, are now found in a perfect state of preservation all over the State. The price of an idol, two feet high, is R25, and a smaller one may be had for R5. Cooking vessels are made of soapstone at Nullur. At one time Nullur ware had a considerable export trade to other Provinces, but the demand at present is limited to local requirements. In Colonel LeMessurier's opinion "this industry would be capable of indefinite extension by reducing the cost of production and improving the shape of the vessel." Very little stone-carving of this kind is practised in the Bombay Presidency. The only objects sent from this part of the country to the Colonial and Indian Exhibition were a pair of carved plates from Dhrangadara. A collection of stone toys were sent from the same place to the Calcutta International Exhibition. Carving of idols is practised to a small extent in Baroda, Bhavnagar, and Kach.

Inlaid Marble of Agra.

The mosaic work of the Tájmahal is now employed in the decoration of plates, cups, boxes, and other small objects. The art consists in inlaying on white marble ground coloured stones, such as jasper, heliotrope, carnelian, chalcedony, &c., in exquisite arabesques. Mother-o'-pearl has recently been introduced in the work, but not with good effect. It is supposed by many that the mosaic decorations of the Tájmahal were of Italian origin. This supposition is based on the fact that one Father Da Castro, who lived in Lahore at the time when the Táj was under construction, told Father Manrique, who arrived in India in 1640, that this celebrated edifice was designed by a Venetian architect named Geronimo Verroneo, and that the internal decorations were executed under the superintendence of a Frenchman, Augustin de Bordeaux. On the other hand, there is a tradition in the country that one Isa Muhammad Effendi, a Turk sent to the Emperor Sháh Jahán by the Sultán of Turkey, was the designer of this magnificient mausoleum. In a paper contributed to the *Indian Journal of Art* (I, p. 61), Sir George Birdwood has, however, conclusively proved that mosaic work is of Eastern origin and that it never flourished in the West. Besides, a close observation of the Italian work of the time has convinced him that Western hands could not have executed the mosaic decorations in the Táj. "From the Orpheus, which is traditionally held to be a likeness of Austin himself, to the pictorial representations of fruits and birds, they are nothing more than clumsy attempts to directly copy oil and fresco paintings in an unsuitable material; and it is quite impossible that the men who devised such artistic monstrosities could have been the same as those whose hands traced in variegated *pietra dura* the exquisite arabesques of the Táj, informed in every undulating line, and drooping bud, and bursting flower, with the true principles of inlaid decoration." The following may be quoted as the prices of the Agra mosaic:—A table from R300 to R600; box, R30 to R100; plate from R10 to R50; chess-plate from R100 to R200; model of Táj, R500.

VIII.—Lapidary's Work.

The lapidaries of India have been celebrated from very early times for their skill in cutting and polishing stones. Mr. Ball in his Geology of India, Part III, states:—

"It is probable that the polished and cut pebbles of India have been spread over the world to an extent of which few people are conscious. It is said that the pebbles which the tourist or visitor is induced to buy at many well-known sea-side and other resorts in Europe, as mementos of the place, have not only been originally produced but have been cut and polished in India. If it be so, the trade is a more creditable one than that which sends sham jewels to Ceylon, because the stones are really what they pretend to be, true pebbles, and they are often extremely beautiful objects. It has sometimes been thought that in the name 'brooch' the source of the pebbles which were first employed for the purpose is recorded, but the derivation is said to be from the French broche, a spit or skewer. From Barygaza, the modern brooch, the famous onyx and murrhine cups of the early Greeks and Romans were obtained, it is believed.

"Nero is said to have paid 300 talents or £55,125 for one of the small cups made of the murrhine or carnelian (?), which was probably not very different in any respect from those to be obtained in Bombay at the present day."

The polisher of stones is found in small numbers in most of the principal towns. In Calcutta they cut and polish stones for rings, and there are also a few diamond cutters in the metropolis of India. Lapidary work in Bengal is, however, unimportant. In the North-Western Provinces, agates are found in the bed of the river Ken in the District of Banda, which are made into brooches, studs, knife-handles, paper-weights, &c., chiefly for European use. Knife-handles are sold at R5 to R12 per dozen, sleeve-links and buttons at R3 per dozen; paper-weights at Re. 1 each; necklaces, R3; moss agates at Re 1. A collection has been sent to the Glasgow International Exhibition. Good work in seal engraving is done at Agra and Lucknow and is still largely patronised by the wealthy classes.

At Bherá in the Panjáb, caskets, paper-weights of sorts, whip and stick-handles, knife-handles, *Hauldilis* or necklaces are largely made of false jade. Necklaces of all sorts, small trays and toys, stones for rings, bead-bracelets (*Ponchis*), and other articles are made at Amritsar. Mr. Kipling writes :—

"The green, jade-like stone used at Bherá has not yet been assigned its proper name,; it is not true jade, nor do authorities on the subject admit it to be plasma. It is said to be found near Kandahar and to be brought down the river Indus on rafts floated with inflated skins to Attock, whence it is carried to Bherá. Other stones resembling serpentine and purbeck marble are used as handles and also in the fashioning of toys and small objects, as paper-weights, by the lapidary cutlers of Bherá. There is a larger production than finds profitable sale."

A collection of Bherá *jade*-handled cutlery has been sent to the Glasgow International Exhibition by Imám-ud-din, Muhammad Din, and Khuda Bakhsh. Knives and forks are sold at R1 to R4 each, daggers at R7 to R15, a box at R30. Necklaces, knife-handles, sleeve-links, paper-knives, &c., are made and sold at Amritsar by Kashmiris who have settled in that town. These are mostly of carnelian, agate, and jade. Mr. Kipling states that this trade received a great impetus from the Calcutta International Exhibition, to which they were sent in large numbers and nearly all sold. It is suspected that many of the articles are imported and not made at Amritsar; possibly the carnelian articles are from Cambay in the Bombay Presidency. The prices vary from R5 to R15 a piece. A little of this work is done at Lahore and Delhi also.

The pebble-work of Jabalpur in the Central Provinces has acquired some reputation. It consists of knife-handles, paper-knives, studs and other ornaments neatly cut from agates and other stones found in the bed of the Narbadá. The manufacture is precisely similar to the one carried on at Banda in the North-Western Provinces. Under this head Mr. J. B. Fuller mentions the onyx beads "which are to be found at some places in the Narbadá valley. They are bored and have evidently been used in former days as ornaments, but are now found detached, and, as a rule, buried a little depth below the surface of the ground. They are known (among the Muhammadans) by the name of *Dáná-Sulaimáni*, having, according to common belief, fallen from the throne of Solomon when passing over the Narbadá valley in one of its ærial flights."

The garnet work of Jaipur is an important industry. The best garnets are found near Rájmahal on the Banás river in Jaipur territory. They also come from Udaipur and Kishangarh States. The matrix in which the stones are embedded is mica chist or serpentine, and the crystals are usually of dodecahedral form. The colours vary from yellow with a brown tinge to purple; the latter are the most valuable, and are the real almandine or noble garnets. Dr. Hendley writes:—

"The Rajputana garnets are similar to the Pegu or Syriam stones, or the commonly called amethystine or oriental garnets. According to Pliny, the dull-coloured *Carbunculus* of India used to be hollowed out into vessels that would hold as much as a pint, but such large specimens are certainly not found in the present day, though, perhaps, if the Rájmahal quarries were properly worked, good pieces of some size might be obtained, for it is stated at Jaipur that clean stones were formerly not uncommonly discovered up to a weight of 2·4 ounces. The rough stones are sold by the diggers to dealers on the spot, or to the lapidaries in Jaipur or Sarwar. The best are cut *en cabochon* or into tallow shapes, that is to say, as carbuncles or stones hollowed out into a concavity underneath, like half-plums; these are largely exported to Switzerland, Germany, England, Italy, Austria, and France, to be used for ornamental purposes, and as jewellery. The violet stones, or alamandine garnets, are much admired in France. The commoner rough stones are also exported in considerable quantities for watch-making purposes. They are valued at from 6 annas to R1-8 per pound at Jaipur. The better stones, worth from R5 to R75 per pound, are all cut *en cabochon* by the lapidaries."

Garnets are cut as carbuncles or with facets in Jaipur and are strung in a great variety of ways as bracelets, necklaces, or set in ornaments. The Jaipur garnets are in great demand throughout India and Europe, and are so cheap and superior that they have practically driven the produce of other mines out of the market. R10,000 worth of Jaipur garnet jewellery has been sent to the Glasgow International Exhibition. The prices may be quoted as follows:—One dozen facet cut ring stones R3; cabochons of very fine colours, R6-8 each; silver necklace, set with garnet, R37; one pair silver bracelets, set with garnets, R18; garnet and crystal necklace with pendants, R26. At Jaipur crystals are also cut into beads, necklaces, bracelets, and also for the handles of daggers known as *Peshkabz*. Some of the handles are carved in the form of a horse's head and are much admired by Rajputs.

Knife-handles, paper cutters, paper weights, crosses, brooches, necklaces, and other ornaments are made at Cambay, in the Bombay Presidency, of agates, bloodstones, carnelians, and stones of different colours. The supply is obtained from Ratanpur in the territory of the Rájá of Rájpipla. The following account of the industry has been compiled from Mr. J. M. Campbell's *Bombay Gazetteer*:—

The stones are brought from the mines to Ratanpur, the village of gems, and made over to the contractor, who has purchased by auction the right of working the mines for the year. He "divides the stones into two classes, those which should and those which should not be baked. Three stones are left unbaked : an onyx, called *mora* or *bawa-ghori*, the cat's eye, called *chashamdár* or *dolá*, and a yellow half-clear pebble called *rori* or *lasaniá*. These stones are found in different shapes, and are seldom more than one pound in weight. Except these three varieties all Ratanpur pebbles are baked to bring out their colours. . . .

"By exposure to sun and fire, among browns the light shades brighten into white, and the darker deepen into chestnut. Of yellows, maize gains a rosy tint, orange is intensified into red, and an intermediate shade of yellow becomes pinkish purple. Pebbles in which cloudy browns and yellows were at first mixed are now marked by clear bands of white and red. The hue of the red carnelian varies from the palest flesh to the deepest blood-red. The best are a deep clear and even red, free from cracks, flaws, or veins. The larger and thicker the stone, the more it is esteemed. White carnelians are scarce. When large, thick, even-coloured, and free from flaws, they are valuable. Yellow and variegated stones are worth little. Four agates—the common, the moss, the Kapadvanj, and the veined—rank next to the Rájpipla carnelians. The common agate is of two kinds—a white half-clear stone called *dolá* or *chashamdár* and a cloudy or streaked stone called *Jamo*. The colour varies, but is generally a greyish-white. Both kinds come from North-East Kathiawar near Mahedpur in Morvi, 3 miles from Tankara. Of the stones, which lie in massive blocks near the surface, the most perfect do not exceed five pounds in weight, while those of inferior quality, in many cases cracked, weigh as much as sixty pounds. These stones are brought to the Cambay dealers by merchants, who, paying a royalty to the Morvi Chief, hire labourers, generally Kolis, to gather them. When worked up, the common agate is a greyish-white, and being hard, brittle, and massive, it takes a high polish. Like the common agate, the moss agate, *Suabhaji*, comes from Bud-Kotra, 3 miles from Tankara in Morvi. Found in the plain about 2 feet under the surface in massive layers, often cracked, and from half a pound to forty pounds in weight, they are gathered in the same way as the common agate. When worked up, they take a fine polish, showing, on a base of crystal, sometimes clear, sometimes clouded, tracings as of dark-green or red-brown moss. Besides, from the town of Kapadvanj in Kaira, where, as its name shows, the Kapadvanj agate is chiefly found, this stone is brought from the bed of the river Majam, between the villages of Amliyara and Mandava, about 15 miles from Kapadvanj. It is found on the banks and in the beds of rivers, in round kidney and almond-shaped balls from half a pound to ten pounds in weight. Picked up by Bhils, they are sold to a Mandava Bohara, who disposes of them to the Cambay stone-merchants at from 6*s.* to 24*s.* for forty pounds (R3 to R12 a maund). When worked up, the Kapadvanj agate takes a high polish. It varies much in colour and pattern. In some cases they are variegated; in others they have forms of finely-marked plans grouped into landscape and other views. The trade names of the chief varieties are *khaiyu*, *agiyu*, and *ratadiyu*. The most valued Cambay agate, the veined agate, *dorádár*, comes from Rámpur, in Ahmadabad. Found near the surface in pebbles of various shapes, not more than half a pound in weight, they are gathered in the same way as moss agates, and when worked up take a high polish, showing either a dark ground with white streaks, or dark veins on a light background. Of other Cambay stones the chief are the jasper or bloodstone, the chocolate stone, a variegated pebble known as *maimariam*, crystal, the lapis-lazuli or azure stone, the obsidian or jet, and the blue stone, *pirozá*. Of these the first four are found in Gujrát. The rest are foreign stones brought from Bombay. The jasper, heliotrope, or bloodstone comes from the village of Tankara in Morvi, about 20 miles north of Rájkot, found on and near the Fort of Bhag hill, in massive layers of from half a pound to forty pounds; it is gathered in the same way as the agate. When worked up, it takes a high polish, varying in colour from *liláchhantdár*, a green variety with red streaks or spots, to the finer *patoliá*, whose green base is more equally mixed with red and yellow. The chocolate stone, *rathiá*, comes from Tankara in Morvi, found on the surface, or a few feet under ground, in masses of from one to eight pounds; it is too soft and earthy to take a high polish. *Maimariam* is a liver-brown, marbled with yellowish marks of shells and animalculæ. Dug in blocks of considerable size at Dhokavada on the Ran of Cutch, about 60 miles north of Disa; it is too soft to take a high polish. Cambay crystal, *phatak*, comes from Tankara in Morvi, where it is found in masses of from one to twenty pounds. As clear as glass, it takes a high polish. The best Cambay crystal comes from Madras, Ceylon, and China. Lapis-lazuli, or azure stone, *rajavarat*, is deep-blue with a sprinkling of silvery or golden spots; a foreign stone, coming to Cambay through Bombay; it is found in rounded balls in Persian and Bokharan river-beds. It is too soft and earthy to take a high polish. Jet or black stone, *kálá phatar*, is also foreign, coming through Bombay from the hills of Bassora and Aden, where it is found in large blocks. Like glass in fracture, it is not very heavy, and takes a high polish (it is probably obsidian). The Cambay jet trade has almost entirely ceased. The Cambay blue stone is not the true *pirozá* or turquoise, but a composition imported from China in flat pieces of not more than half a pound in weight. Like blue glass in appearance, though soft, it takes a good polish." The rough stone generally passes through three processes in order to make it into the required article, *viz.*, sawing, chiselling, and polishing. "Cambay agate ornaments belong to three classes, those suited for the Chinese, the Arab, and the European markets. For the Chinese market carnelian ornaments only are in demand. Of these there are two kinds—flat stones named *muglaigul*, and beads called *dol*. The flat stones, oval, square, and like watch seals, are worn in China as armlets and dress ornaments. Plain polished round beads are made into necklaces of fifty stones each. For the Arab markets, the stones most in demand are Rámpur agates, Ratanpur carnelians, cat's-eyes, and bloodstone. These are wrought into both plain and ornamental ring stones, necklaces, wristlets, and armlets. Of necklaces there are those made of cut beads, *peludár dol;* of diamond cut beads, *gokhendár dol;* of almond-shaped beads, *bádámi dol;* and of spear head-shaped beads, *chamkali dol.* Again, there are necklaces of these stones, called *madali* or *tavit*, and of plain round beads used as rosaries as well as necklaces. Of armlets and wristlets there are those of two stones, *motá madalia* worn either on the arm or wrist, wristlets of seven round flat stones, *patiá*, wristlets of several flat stones, *ponchi*, armlets of one stone cut into different fanciful devices, *báju*, and single stones in the shape of large flat seals, *nimgol.* Rings, *anguthi*, and stones for setting as rings, *naginá* are also made of carnelian and cat's-eyes. For the European markets, the articles most in demand are models of cannon with carriage and trappings, slabs for boxes or square tables, cups and saucers, chess-men, flower vases, pen-racks, card and letter racks, watch-stands, inkstands, knife-handles, rulers, paper-cutters, pen-holders, necklaces, bracelets, brooches, paper-weights, crochet needles, silk-winders, marbles, brace and shirt studs, seals, and rough stones polished, on one side. Within the last thirty years (1851), part of the trade with Arabia lay through Veraval in South-West Kathiawar. At present (1878), except a very small supply for the Sind and Kabul markets taken by the horse-dealers and other Afghans who visit Cambay, the whole produce is bought by Bombay merchants, chiefly of the Bohara caste, and by them sent from Bombay to China, Arabia, and Europe."

In Burma, precious stones except diamonds are polished in the large towns. In Rangoon, there were 14 lapidary establishments in 1885.

IX.—Ivory, Horn and Shell Manufactures.

Ivory-carving.

A graphic account of Indian ivory-carving has been contributed by Mr. Kipling to the *Journal of Indian Art* (I, p. 49). Mr. Kipling is of opinion that the art in India never arrived at the same stage of development as "the ivory and gold work of Greece, the carving of the later Roman Empire, or that of mediæval times." In this he differs from other authorities on the subject, for many hold that ivory-carving as an art was very skilfully practised in ancient India, although the articles turned out might not have been so good as those of ancient Greece and Rome. According to *Brihat Sanhitá* it was considered the best material for bedsteads. That sacred book directs that the legs of a bed should be of solid ivory, and the frame-work made of some choice wood to be inlaid or veneered with thin plates of the same material. "In selecting ivory about two thicknesses at the root of the tusk, which is hollow, should be rejected, if the animal from which it is taken come from the plains; but if it be a mountain grazer, somewhat less." Mr. Kipling saw an elaborately carved ivory coach in the possession of the Mahárájá of Patiálá, a modern work, made by the carvers in the employ of the State. Whatever the position of the industry might have been in ancient times, ivory-carving is not in a flourishing state at the present day, if the preparation of ivory for inlay work is excluded from the account. Ivory ornaments and the inlay of ivory on wood have already been noticed separately. Carved objects in ivory are worked in very few places, the most noted being those made at Murshidabad and in Travancore. Ivory in large quantities is brought to Bombay from Africa. A portion of it is reshipped and the rest kept to meet the demand for it in India. There is also a local supply from the herds of elephants that roam in the jungles of Assam and South India. This supply has, however, become very small now, owing to the stringent regulations passed by Government for the protection of wild elephants. The articles generally carved out of ivory are figures of gods and goddesses, men, animals and other toys, combs, ornaments, *Chauris* or fly-drivers, mats, caskets, &c.

Specimens of ivory-carving were sent to the Calcutta International Exhibition from Murshidabad, Gya, Dumráon, Darbhángá, the Tributary States of Orissa, Rangpur, Bardwán, Tipperah, Chittagong, Dacca, and Patna. The Murshidabad manufactures are perhaps the best in India, fully displaying in them the finish, minuteness, and ingenuity characteristic of all true Indian art. They are remarkable also considering the simple and rough nature of the few tools by which they are made. The industry is, however, declining, and it is said that the number of artizans engaged in the work is not now one-fourth of what it was twenty years ago.

Many of the chiefs of Orissa and the wealthy landlords of Behar have artists in their pay who are able to turn out good articles of carved ivory. Specimens of their handiwork were sent to the Calcutta Exhibition. Thus, the Mahárájá of Darbhángá sent a mat made of strips of ivory, which cost R1,325. Pictorial ivory cards, toys, figures, images of gods, flappers, chessmen, combs, fans, bangles, &c., were sent from other places. Ivory bangles and other personal ornaments are made at Murshidabad and Cuttack. Ivory mats were a specialty of Sylhet, where they are now made in very small quantities. A good collection of Murshidabad ivory work may be had for R500. The following are the prices of typical specimens:—Image of Durgá, R60; Image of Káli, R30; elephant with seat, R60; bullock cart, R16; plough with ploughman, R16; a camel, R12; a boat, R40; a man, R8.

Ivory-carving is now very little practised in the North-Western Provinces. The Mahárájá of Benares employed one or two ivory-carvers, and in the District of Gonda in Oudh there are a few men who follow the trade.

In the Panjáb ivory-carving is practised to a limited extent in Amritsar, Delhi, Patiálá, Sháhpur, Multan, and Lahore. Combs, paper-cutters, card-boxes, and bracelets are generally made at Amritsar. In addition to these articles, figures are also made at Delhi. Chessmen and little toys are made at Sháhpur; bracelets and toys at Multan; and combs, bracelets, and toys at Lahore. Mr. Kipling remarks:—

"Ivory carving is not an art which flourishes in the Panjáb. At Amritsar great quantities of combs are made and also paper-cutters and card-boxes ornamented with geometrical open work patterns of some delicacy of execution, but no great interest in design. Figure work is but seldom wrought in this Province, owing to the predominance of Musalman notion. The ivory carvers in the Dariba at Delhi reproduce the work of Murshidabad in all its variety, but seem to produce nothing of local origin."

Among the articles sent from the Panjáb to the Colonial and Indian Exhibition was an elaborately carved *Bartáná,* an instrument for adjusting and smoothing the edge folds of a turban of a person of quality. A model of a garden was also sent from Amritsar.

In Rajputana two or three men at Jaipur do some

ivory-carving, but there is no great demand. Bangles, boxes for holding antimony, salt-cellars, and trees of ivory inserted in a glass bottle are made at Bikánir. Price of such articles varies from R1 to R30. Beautiful *Chauris* (flappers or fly-drivers) of ivory are made in Bhartpur. These cost from R5 and upwards. Besides bangles noticed in a previous page, *Surmádáni* or antimony-boxes are made at Páli in the Jodhpur territory. At the Colonial and Indian Exhibition Alwar exhibited an ivory elephant with riders. The trappings were enamelled. The other objects of ivory sent from this State were an antimony-box with pearls set round the upper surface of the cover, a perforated screen-work, and a scent-box. Figures of animals are made at Rewa, in Central India, which are sold at about R5 each. Paper-cutters, sword hilts, paper clips, combs, &c., were received for the Colonial and Indian Exhibition from Ratlám, Dhar, and Alipurá. The Ratlám work shewed minute carving. Prices of small articles from 8 annas to R1-4-0.

In the Madras Presidency ivory is chiefly used in the decoration of the Vizagapatam work already mentioned. Travancore is, however, an important seat of ivory-carving. Mr. Kipling states that "a throne with foot-stool made in this place and sent to the 1851 Exhibition, as a gift to Her Majesty the Queen-Empress, is one of the most notable productions from this region." Mr. Purdon Clarke, C.I.E., mentioned to me of an extremely beautiful casket sent to the Exhibition of 1851 from Travancore. A good collection of Travancore work was sent to the Colonial and Indian Exhibition consisting of picture-frames, glove-stretchers, hand-mirrors, combs, paper-cutters, and paper-weights with figures of various objects on them, *e.g.* an elk on the coils of a boa-constrictor, a hermit, a bird's nest, an areca-nut tree, a hare and a snake, a woman and child, &c.

In the Bombay Presidency ivory-carving is practised only to a little extent. "Ivory figures are made in Bombay and Surat by Parsi work-box makers, but of late they have taken to using stag-horns instead. Combs are made of ivory at Poona, where there are half a dozen shops opposite the temple of Ganapati in Kasbá Peth. Two of them belong to Sonárs, and the rest to Marhattas. Almost all the original workers have left the trade for want of support. The comb-makers have no capital and raise money by borrowing it at R1-8-0 per cent. per mensem and R1-8-0 per cent. commission on the sale-proceeds." For the Glasgow International Exhibition, two sets of ivory wristlets have been obtained from Broach, and the Thákur Sahib of Bhavnagar has presented a handsome collection of ivory manufactures, consisting of rose-water sprinklers, boxes, a whistling top named *koyal* after the Indian cuckoo, &c. A figure of Krishna with the flute, called *Muralidhar*, was sent from Poona to the Calcutta International Exhibition, the price of which was R50, and a jewel box from Kach, valued at R385.

In Assam, ivory-carving is carried on to a small extent at Jorhát. Mr. Darrah writes :—

"A few carvers in ivory still remain amongst the descendants of those who worked for the Assam kings, but the handicraft appears to be dying out, as there is next to no demand for the articles produced. These are mainly spoons and forks, combs, and sometimes chessmen. The favourite patterns represent a crane in the act of preening, and a crocodile with a fish in its mouth."

Ivory-carving is done in many places in Burma, chiefly at Moulmein and Rangoon. Mr. Tilly thus describes the industry :—

"Foliage and figure work is generally combined in such objects as *dáo* or sword-handles, paper-knives, table ornaments, &c. Figure work is met with by itself in images of Gotama. The

Census Report of 1881 does not distinctly mention any ivory-carvers. It is known that there are three master-carvers in Moulmein, two or three in Rangoon, and a few more scattered throughout the country. There is only one man at present known whose work approaches the excellence of that of the wood-carvers. This man is Maung Nyaing, of Moulmein, and his work is well designed and very well executed. The productions of other men are inferior, the curves of thin foliage are interrupted, and their figures are out of proportion. A curious and intricate effect is obtained by Burmese workmen for *dáo*-handles and table ornaments. The outside of the specimen is carved with foliage and flowers, through the interstices of which the inside is hollowed out nearly to the centre, where a figure is carved *in situ*. The figure looks as if it had been carved separately and inserted into a flowery bower, but closer examination shows that this is not the case, and the men may at any time be seen carving the figure through the opening of the tracery. The Moulmein carver often executes orders for the king of Siam and did the same for the late king of Burma and for Shan chiefs. These articles consist of chairs or thrones, entire tusks carved with images of Gotama. He also made an ivory mat for the late king of Burma, which might be rolled up. The elephants' tusks are obtained from Upper Burma and Siam and are sold at from R7 to R15 a *viss*. If a pair of tusks weigh more than 25 *viss*, the higher price is given. There is no fixed rate for this kind of work, but it is not considered as remunerative as that of the other artists of Burma."

In Nepal ivory-carving is carried on to a limited extent, as the raw material is scarce and expensive. The articles made are figures of divinities, combs, dice, dominoes, chopsticks, and *Kukri* or dagger-handles. Dominoes, almost exactly resembling those in use in Europe, and chopsticks are made for export to Tibet.

Horn Work.

In ancient times, water vessels, cups, combs, and musical instruments were made of horn. Knife and dagger handles were also made and arrows tipped with it. A cup made of rhinoceros horn is considered a very pure article by the Hindus. Horn is now largely exported in its raw state, and articles are made of it in very few places now-a-days. In Bengal, Sátkhirá, Cuttack, and Monghyr are the three places where small articles are made of horn. A box made of buffalo-horn was sent from Sátkhirá to the Calcutta International Exhibition. Its price was R10-8. Scent-bottles, cruet stands, and *hukka* mouth-pieces were sent to the above Exhibition from Cuttack. They were well made and cheap; the price of a scent-bottle being R2 and of a cruet-stand R3. These are executed in the hill States of Orissa. Monghyr prepares ornaments mentioned in a previous page. Buffalo-horn combs are produced in many places. They are strong and are therefore preferred to the vulcanised India-rubber combs imported from Europe. In Jaipur, "bows are made of buffalo-horn and strung with silk threads. They are painted with diaper ornament and lacquered. Shields are also made in horn and enriched with metal bosses, but many more are manufactured from leather or *papier maché.*" Powder horns inlaid with ivory are made all over Rajputana. In Madras, horn is largely used in the Vizagapatam work, which is decorated with a delicate fret-work of ivory. Snuff-boxes, walking sticks, umbrella-handles, pen-holders, and similar small articles are made of horn in Mysore. A snuff-box is sold for R2, a pen-holder for R5, and a walking stick for R18. A mango-shaped snuff-box was very much admired at the Colonial and Indian Exhibition and Professor Reauleux, Privy Councillor of the German Empire, informed me that it is possible to create a demand for it in Germany. In the Bombay Presidency, articles are made of bison horn at Viziadrug, Jaitapur, and Málvan in the Ratnagiri District. Mr. Gupte states that "about thirty years ago the only articles turned out were trays and caskets for the worship of idols, but of late cups of various shapes, lamp-shades, animals, notably snakes, are made to order for Europeans, which fact has given a start to the industry." A collection consisting of flower-stands and miniature models of camels, antelopes, and snakes have been sent to the Glasgow International Exhibition. Prices of articles made at Viziadrug are as follows:—A candlestick ornamented with cobra snakes, R50; a casket to keep idols, called *Sampusht*, R1-8; a snake, 6 annas; a tray, R3-8; a pair of cows, R8. The ornamental boxes made in Surat and Bombay are decorated with patterns of cut stag-horn, as described in a previous page. Water-vessels, cups, *Arghas*, and rings are made of rhinoceros horn in Nepal. The water-vessels hold water for oblations to gods and manes, as the water held in them is considered particularly pure. The cups are for drinking. The *Argha* is a shallow cup carved round the edge, used in religious ceremonies.

Shell Manufactures.

Ornaments made of conch-shell have already been described under the head of Jewellery. Mr. Locke, in his list of articles contributed to the Vienna Universal Exhibition of 1873, writes:—

"The *Sánkháris* or shell-workers at Dacca distinguish the several shells and their various qualities by the names *Titkuri*, *Páti*, *Lálpáti*, *Alabelá*, *Dhalá*, *Kulai*, and *Shurti*, the *Titkuri*, being the best in quality of grain, lustre, and suitability for fine cutting and delicate finish. There is considerable variety in the patterns of these *Sánkhá* bracelets, from the rude broad flat ring, to the thin delicate annulet, rounded, or with notched or beaded edges, carved with tigers' heads, enriched with ornamental incising, and illuminated by touches of tinsel, lac-colour, gilding, &c.";

To the above information Dr. Rájendra Lála Mitra adds:—

"It should be noticed, however, that those bracelets which are made of entire pieces, or annulets cut out of the shell, require the last-named species, which from its size yields rings just large enough for the human wrist. The first two varieties are too large for such annulets, and their chips and cuttings are therefore used only in inlaying. Their superior density and gloss adapt them well for this purpose. It should be borne in mind, also, that the different species vary greatly in size, according to age, and it is often difficult to identify them in the dry state."

Small articles are also made of *Kauri*, conch and tortoise shells, but in very small quantities. In Bengal, small toilet baskets covered on the outside with *Kauri* shells and lined with red cloth are employed by Indian ladies to keep vermillion and other knick-nacks. The use of such baskets is diminishing year by year, but well-made articles of this description are very curious. In Jaipur, Aqua marina shells found in the State are carved into ornaments. Tortoise shell is largely employed in the Vizagapatam work. A jewel box was exhibited at the Calcutta International Exhibition which was considered the finest work of this kind ever exhibited. "The interior of the box was carved with ivory fret-work, rivalling lace in the delicacy of the tracery and elaborate nature of the patterns, which embraced floral and mythological figures. The fret-work was laid on a background of tortoise shell, and the ivory, instead of being etched as usual, was carved out to the minutest detail with great skill and fidelity." Tortoise shells are worked into ornaments in Gujrât and Bombay.

X.—Pottery.

A more learned account of Indian pottery has not been written than that by Sir George Birdwood in his "Industrial Arts of India." All lovers of Indian art should read it in order the better to appreciate the value of Indian pottery. Sir George Birdwood has there pointed out how in India precedence is always rightly given to the shape of the vessel, and the decorations, if any, are always subordinated to the shape. "Nothing can be in worse taste, nor, in an æsthetic sense, more wasteful, than to hide a lovely form under an excess of foreign ornament," observes Sir George Birdwood. He further states:—

> "In the best Indian pottery, we always find the reverent subjection of colour and ornamentation to form, and it is in attaining this result that the Indian potter has shewn the true artistic feeling and skill of all Indian workmasters in his handiwork. The correlation of his forms, colours, and details of ornamentation is perfect, and without seeming premeditation, as if his work were rather a creation of nature than of art; and this is recognised, even in the most homely objects, as the highest achievement of artifice."

Unglazed earthen pottery has been made in India from time immemorial. *Kalasa* or water-jar, *Kapála* or cooking vessels, *Pátra* or platters, *Saraká* or goglets, and *Páriká* or cups were the earliest forms of earthen utensils made in the country. The practice of throwing away the pots in use, and obtaining fresh ones on prescribed occasions that prevailed in the country, gave great impetus to the trade of making earthen vessels. Every large village in India has its potters, and baked pottery for everyday use is made all over the country. The art of making glazed pottery seems to have come to India from China by way of Persia. The most notable places where artistic pottery is now made are Khulná, Dinájpur, Sewán, and Ránigan j in Bengal; Azamgarh, Lucknow, Sitápur, Rámpur, Aligarh, and Khurjá in the North-Western Provinces; Delhi, Multan, and Pesháwar in the Panjáb; Jaipur; Burhánpur in the Central Provinces; Madras, Madura, Salem, and other places in the Madras Presidency; and Bombay and Hallá in Sind in the Bombay Presidency.

In Bengal the Sewán pottery early attracted the attention of Europeans. It is of the same style as that made at Azamgarh in the North-Western Provinces, which has been characterised by Sir George Birdwood as "generally feeble and rickety in form, and insipid and meretricious in decoration." The colour of the vessels is either black or white, decorated with the hand, after baking, by white patterns made of a mixture of mercury and tin. The unglazed vessels of Dinájpur and Khulná have attracted some attention of late, chiefly for their elegant shapes. Within the last few years, Messrs. Burn & Co. of Calcutta have established a pottery work at Ránigan j. The pottery made there is no doubt the best in Bengal, but it is mostly in the European style both in shape and design. A collection of Sewán pottery can be had for R10, of Dinájpur, R5, and Khulná, R15.

In the North-Western Provinces, the pottery made at Azamgarh has already been mentioned. The vessels are generally jet black in colour with silvery floral patterns, which give them an appearance of *Bidri*-ware. The process of manufacture is a family secret, but Sir George Birdwood supposes that the black colour is obtained by baking the ware with mustard oil-seed cake and the "silvery ornamentation is done by etching the pattern, after baking, on the surface, and rubbing into it an amalgam of mercury and tin." *Suráhis*, plates, and other articles are made at Lucknow. The shapes and colours of Lucknow vessels are good. The pottery of Rámpur is generally of a blue, white, and claret colour. The shapes and the colours were much admired at the Colonial and Indian Exhibition. But the pottery produced at Khurjá, a town in Bulandshahr, received the greatest attention at the above Exhibition, and all the articles found a ready sale. In the Khurjá ware there is a greater range in colour and shapes than is found in that of Rámpur. A small quantity of pottery of a peculiar glaze is manufactured by one family at Dewa, a town in the Bárabánki District of Oudh. The process of manufacture is a family secret. A peculiar kind of unglazed pottery is made at Aligarh. The articles are in plain black or slate colour, with raised ornamentation. Extremely thin and light earthen vessels with silvery patterns are made at Amrohá, but these are so brittle that it is with difficulty they can be safely taken to a distance. Such thin ware is known by the name of *Kágazi* or "paper-like." There are men in India to pay for such idle curiosities. In the *Suráhis* and plates made at Saháranpur a heavy gilding is used as an outward decoration. Ordinary jars, vases, &c., of extremely graceful shapes are made at Atraulá in Gonda, and Sitápur, on which quaint patterns are painted with the hand. Prices of the most noted North-Western Provinces pottery may be stated as follows :—Azamgarh—flower vase, 10 annas, cup with cover, 6 annas, *Hukka* 4 annas, *Suráhi* with plate 5 annas, *Abkhorá* with plate 6 annas, *Lotá* 5 annas. Lucknow—jug 2 annas, sprouted *Lotá* 2 annas, *Suráhi* 2 annas, sugar-basin 2 annas, milk jug 2 annas, cup and saucer 2 annas, flower vase 11 annas. Rámpur—vase R1-4, *Suráhi* R1, flower vase 12 annas, bowl 12 annas, cup 10 annas, plate 3 annas to R1-8. Khurjá

—*Suráhi* R2-8, jar 3 annas, *Lotá* 8 annas, flower vase 8 annas. Aligarh—*Lotá* 6 annas, *Suráhi* 8 annas, flower vase 8 annas. Sitápur—jar 8 annas, pot 8 annas. Atraulá—jar R1-8, flower pot R1-4, *Suráhi* 6 annas.

Panjáb has acquired a great reputation for its pottery. Not only does this branch of art-ware, but also the other handicrafts of the Province, largely owe their prosperity—and in some cases even their very existence—to the able and learned way in which they have been brought to the notice of the European public by Mr. Baden Powell and Mr. Kipling. North-Western Provinces owe the same debt of gratitude to Mr. Growse and Mr. Rivett Carnac, Rajputana to Dr. Hendley, Madras to Dr. Bidie, Bombay to Mr. Griffiths, and India in general to Sir George Birdwood, Sir Edward Buck, and Mr. Purdon Clarke.

The following account of the Panjáb pottery has been supplied to the Government of India by Mr. Kipling:—*Suráhis*, plates, *Abkhorás*, *Lotás*, tiles, &c., are made at Delhi. This ware is believed to be the only true porcelain in India. It is really a *porcelaine tendre*, and in a few highly vitrified examples resembles very closely old Persian ware. The paste or body is powdered felspar, held together for the purpose of working with a mucilage or gum. Everything must be made in a mould, as the material has not the elasticity of ordinary clay. The finer kind is vitreous and semi-transparent. The coarser sorts are identical in texture with the tiles used for the external covering of mosques, &c. At Agra, Delhi, and Lahore (*Kashi* work) the colours now used in its decorations are a blue from cobalt and a turquoise from copper. Red and yellow are being attempted, but hitherto with imperfect success. Multan glazed pottery, which in Europe would be called a faience, has a red or yellowish earthen body covered with an opaque white enamel in which flint is a large ingredient, painted in two colours, dark blue and turquoise. The work is usually completed at one firing, *i.e.*, the enamel and painting are done on the unburnt clay. The art was originally confined exclusively to architectural details, chiefly tiles for wall linings, finials, tombs, &c. There is now a great demand for this pottery in the form of vases and other ornaments all decorated in a strictly conventional way, with no trace of Hindu fantasy. Peshâwar glazed pottery is a rough faience; a common reddish yellow (earthen) body or paste, covered with a soft lead glaze, is chiefly made in the form of plates. Scarcely anywhere else in India is glazed pottery employed in this manner. The ware, considered as pottery, is decidedly poor. But there is a quality of colour in its very simplicity which is pleasing to artists. Of late years an attempt has been made to adapt it to European requirements, such as tea sets, &c., but with only moderate success. Lahore glazed pottery generally consists of sweetmeat jars called *Martbáns*, smoking bowls, cups, &c. An examination after rain of the great mounds of brick-burning refuse, which are the only hills Lahore can boast, shews that glazed and coloured pottery must at one time have been more common than it is now. There are signs that it may again come into favour. The price of a good *Chhilam* (smoking bowl) is a pice and of a *Martbán* or jar four annas. Specimens of coloured and enamelled tile work of unusual excellence are produced at Jallandhar. Muhammad Sharif, the artist, to whom these works are due, is a striking example of a common form of oriental secretiveness. He can make all the colours and glazes of the old Mughul tile work as seen on the Nakodar tombs in this District and many other places in the Province. He has been persuaded from time to time to send a few samples of his craft to various Exhibitions; but as he works without any assistance, they have to be priced at rates which prohibit their use on any large scale. Unglazed pottery is made in various places in the Province. In addition to the ordinary *Bhande* or unglazed ware in common use, there are many characteristic local varieties, *e.g.*, the thin paper-like *Kágazi* pottery made at Gujránwálá and Bháwalpur, the painted water-coloured pottery made at Hushiárpur, the *Adrak* (ginger) smeared ware of Jhajjar (Rohtak District), the black painted red ware of Pind Dádan Khán, and in most places water-colour painted toys and images for festive occasions, fairs, &c.

The prices of typical specimens of the most important of the Panjáb pottery may be stated as follows:—Delhi—large jar R2, small cup 2 annas, flower-stand 8 annas, *Surdhi* 12 annas. Multan—*Surdhi* R4, flower pot R3, large flower vase R10, small flower vase R1-4, cup and saucer 12 annas, plate R1-4, square tile R1. Peshâwar—1 dozen plates R3, jar 8 annas.

In Rajputana, Jaipur has lately acquired great celebrity for its pottery. They are practically the same as those made at Delhi, and in shape and colours they somewhat resemble the old Egyptian ware. Jaipur pottery is mostly made at the School of Art, or by students, or former employés in the school who have set up independent business in the town. Plates, vases, water-bottles, pierced tiles, and panels are the things generally made.

"The articles are made in moulds and glazed with felspar and starch. The colours chiefly employed are blue from oxide of cobalt, and green from oxide of copper; both ores are found near Bhagor and Khetri in the north-east portion of the Jaipur State. Some of the pottery is semi-translucent, and in addition to blue and green a few other colours have been sparingly employed, specially a canary yellow, a dark blue and brown for vases of one colour. Most of the best examples are hand-painted with conventional floral or arabesque patterns, and sometimes with figures of animals."

Of unglazed pottery made in Jaipur, the most interesting are the *Hukkas*, vessels, and plates, manufactured at Bassi. The vessels are black or red in colour, thin and well-polished, and are very popular amongst the people, who purchase large quantities at the Bassi railway station. Pottery of a similar description, but of a lighter colour, is prepared in a village called Lálsot. Some porous pottery is made at the School of Art from white clay obtained from the Bochárá hills near Jaipur. Vessels known as *Bataks*, of coarse clay but of peculiar shape, like rounded pilgrim bottles, are brought to Sambhar from a place called Gudha on the opposite side of the Salt Lake, where they are produced. Glazed pottery, consisting of water-bottles, cups, smoking bowls, &c., is made at Bikánir and other large towns in the State. Prices are cheap, ranging from half anna to four annas a piece. Alwar turns out quantities of *Chhilams*, *Suráhis*, betel-boxes, cups, and other articles of ordinary unglazed pottery. They are light and durable, and are generally ornamental.

In the Central Provinces Burhánpur pottery has an old reputation. It is an ornamental glazed earthenware of a brown ground colour diversified with decorations in light yellow lines. The secret of glazing is confined to a single family, and the amount of work turned out is therefore very small. Taken as a whole the pottery is not altogether wanting in artistic merit. Specimens of glazed pottery were sent to the Colonial and Indian Exhibition from Indor, Mudasaur, and Chhatrapur. Central India pottery was never shewn before at any Exhibition. Some of the red and black pottery, though very rude, might under encouragement develope into good work.

The following account of pottery manufactured in the Madras Presidency has been supplied by Dr. Bidie:—

"The ceramic ware of Southern India consist usually of plain terra-cotta. The colour is generally red, and the articles well and uniformly fired and of very graceful shapes. In some places the ware is ornamented by simple surface decoration, executed while the clay is moist, or by etching after it has been fired. Some of the vessels found in ancient cairns and cromlechs are of great size and excellent finish. One in the Museum is 3 feet 6 inches in depth, and 8 feet 9 inches in circumference at the bilge. Antique pottery articles are found to vary greatly as to shape, some being flat and broad, others more or less globular, some pear-shaped, &c. In some cases the amphora-like pear-shaped vessels have feet, like those figured by Dr. Schliemann in his 'Ilios.' The clay of which the ancient pottery is made is of very superior quality, and the articles are often ornamented with incised linear and other patterns, very much in the same manner as the pottery found in barrows and cromlechs in Europe, and in the ruins of the ancient city of the Trojans. In some cases the external surface of the pottery has a varnished appearance, which was produced by rubbing it with the seeds of *Gyrocarpus Jacquini* and burnishing. Some of the small cup-like vessels of the cairns are covered in the interior with a black lacquer-like varnish. A similar appearance was observed in the pottery found by Dr. Schliemann, varying from a dull black to a rich resinous colour. Professor Virchow is of opinion that the most common mode of producing a simple black colour was to fire the articles slowly in shut-up places to produce much smoke, which entered into the clay and impregnated it. In the case of the vessels with rich lustrous black coating, Professor Landerer believes that a coal-black colour was produced by smearing the vessels with tar, or the pissa asphalt of Herodotus, before baking, and that, when fired, the resin was changed into the fine black varnish. No doubt some processes of this kind were also known and practised in India. In some modern pottery a species of ornamentation is attempted by covering the red clay with a white ground colour, and laying on a sort of floral decoration with powdered micaceous earth, which becomes yellowish. This kind of decoration is not fired and can be easily washed off. In the North Arcot District a white kind of clay is used for making pottery, and yields a very porous and clean-looking ware. At Karigeri, Gudiyatum Taluk, this soft pottery receives a pretty green glaze, and is made in various handsome shapes, some of which are imitations of Delft ware and other European manufactures of the fifteenth and sixteenth centuries, patterns having been introduced by collectors. The colour of the glaze is of different shades of green, and it often has a marbled or shaded appearance. The ornamentation is entirely surface decoration, carried out in the plastic clay before the glaze is put on, and consists of various floral and other patterns. Some of the water-bottles are double, the outer shell being pierced so as to allow air to circulate around the inner. According to Mr. Cox (North Arcot Manual) great care is taken in preparing the clay for this pottery. After being fashioned on the wheel it is dried for ten days in the shade and two in the sun, and is then baked for twelve hours in a close oven. To produce the glaze, equal parts of (*Zangala pachi*), verdigris and bangle-earth (*Soudu-man*, an alkaline earth) are fused in a furnace till they form a green glaze. 'This being powdered and mixed with water is painted over the vessels, which are then dried in the sun and baked as before. If half a part of white lead be added to the verdigris and bangle-earth, a yellow glaze is produced. In either case, when the baking has been too prolonged, the glaze assumes a blackish colour.' The localities of manufacture are Sivagangá, Madura, Timmangalum, and Periyakulam, Madura District; Udiyagiri, Nellore District; Cuddapah; Vizagapatam; Gudiyatum, North Arcot District; Salem; Anantpur; Uppinanguda; South Canara; Kistna; Trichinopoly; Malabar; Godávari; and Tanjore."

Pottery in the European style is manufactured in Kurg. There is a European factory in Mercara employing about 60 hands. Tiles, flower-pots, pipes, &c., are produced. Ordinary potters number about 250 in the little Province, who make water-vessels, cooking pots, tiles, goblets, &c.

In the Bombay Presidency, Sind has long been famous for its beautiful glazed pottery, and, as in the Panjáb, the art was brought to the Province by Muhammadans from Persia, although there is a tradition that the industry was introduced direct from China by a Chinaman. Sind pottery is now manufactured in

Bombay under European supervision in the "Wonderland Art Pottery Works," established by Mr. Terry, formerly of the School of Art in that city. Mr. Gupte writes on the subject of pottery produced in the Bombay Presidency:—

"Glazed pottery is made at Hallá and Tattá in Sind, where glazed tiles of lovely colour and design were in former days extensively produced for tombs and mosques. The Sind potters claim their descent from a naturalized Chinaman who was induced by one of the Mirs or Rulers of the Province to settle in Haidrabad. As Sind pottery is at present not much in demand, the manufacture is said to have undergone a certain deterioration. It is, however, admitted that some of the specimens received for the Glasgow International Exhibition are very beautiful, good in design and effective in colouring, ranging from a light golden yellow to a dark rich brown. The rich blue on white ground is also much appreciated. From the pottery works in Bombay carried on under the supervision of Mr. Terry, a retired Educational Officer, a large and very fine collection has been secured. The forms and colourings of Mr. Terry's ware are more numerous and varied than those of the Sind ware, although the head Potter is a Sindi, and Mr. Terry does not interfere with the designs and shapes selected unless they are European. The adaptation of some of the ornamental decorative designs from the Ajantá Caves to the ware is most effective. A variety of pottery, remarkable more for the quaint shapes than for the paint or glaze, can easily be distinguished from the Sind and Bombay ceramic ware. It comes from Pattan in the Baroda territory. Though primitive in character, it is very effective for decorative purposes."

Pottery of the ordinary kinds is made all over Burma. Salt-boiling pots are made almost in every District where salt is manufactured. Small water-vessels are produced in Shwegyin, Rangoon, Moulmein and other places. The large water-pots, commonly known as Pegu jars, are chiefly prepared at Twant. Bassein makes an ornamental pottery. About the manufacture of this ware Mr. Tilly writes —

"The working season is the dry weather, *i.e.*, from November to the following May. To every two parts of earth one part of fine sand—sea sand is the best—is added and the mass mixed with water till it is soft enough to work. A lump is then taken up and moulded by hand into the form of a cylinder, which is set upon the centre of a wooden wheel revolving horizontally, and the clay is fashioned by the hand as the wheel is worked round. When turned the pots are left for a day to dry: the glaze is then given by the application of a mixture of galena and rice water, and the pots are at once put into the kiln, where they are burned for three days. The kilns are of masonry and vary in size; an ordinary one is about 20 feet long by 12 feet broad and 10 feet high in the centre; the roof has much the appearance of a large unkeeled boat turned upside down. Many of the pots, owing to defective workmanship, crack and break in the burning; sometimes as many as a 100 out of 250 in the kiln. In one season two men could turn out about 1,200 pots of different sizes. In some of the salt-manufacturing Districts the pot maker exchanges with salt-boilers for salt at the rate of 365lb of salt for every 100 salt-boiling pots sold. The other kinds of pots are usually brought down for sale to the markets in Rangoon and other large places, an ordinary-sized pot costing about 2 annas."

XI.—Glass Manufactures.

The manufacture of glass was known in ancient India. As early as eight hundred years before Christ, *i.e.*, at the time when the *Yajur-Veda* was composed, glass was one of the articles of which female ornaments were made. It is also mentioned in the *Mahâbhârata*, and in another old book called the *Yuktikalpataru* the effects on the human system of drinking water out of a glass tumbler are stated to be the same as those of drinking out of a crystal cup. Dr. Rájendra Lála Mitra supposes that glass in India was formerly made of pounded crystal. But at present the material mostly used for the manufacture of glass is an impure carbonate of soda, called *Reh*, an efflorescence that has of late laid waste large tracts of country in Upper India. The manufacture of glass in India is still however in its most primitive state, the indigenous production being a coarse blue or green glass full of flaws and air bubbles. This is produced by melting the *Reh* soil over a strong fire. Or, where *Reh* is not procurable, quartzose pebbles ground and mixed with an equal quantity of an alkaline ash is the material commonly used. This seems to be the substance which, according to Pliny, the Greeks employed for glass-manufacture. The glass thus obtained is chiefly used in the manufacture of bangles, beads, and crackle ware for perfumes. White glass is obtained by melting broken pieces of European ware, of which small vessels are sometimes made. But glass-ware is now almost entirely imported from Europe. Glass vessels of Indian manufacture produced in a few places have, however, recently attracted European attention, and some of them have been highly admired for their graceful shapes and beautiful colours. Patna in Bengal has acquired such a reputation. The articles made in this place were first noticed during the Calcutta International Exhibition, and they sold extremely well at the Colonial and Indian Exhibition. A good collection consisting of *Lotás, Abkhorás, Suráhis,* plates, flower-pots, cups, &c., can be had for R50. It is supposed that the sale of these articles will increase when they become better known to the public. In the North-Western Provinces crackle ware is largely made in the Bijnor District. These mostly consist of bottles or flagons, which are sold to pilgrims who come from a long distance to bathe in the holy water of the Ganges, and who always carry back to their homes a bottle-full of the sacred water. Raw glass is also exported to other places for the manufacture of bangles and small bottles, in which scented oils and perfumery are sold retail. Small flasks and glasses are made at Deoband, a town in the District of Sahāranpur. These are in various colours and are very effective. Prices are extremely cheap. Walking sticks of glass are made at Lucknow. Bangles and lamp chimneys are made at Delhi and Lahore in the Panjáb, globes and pear-shaped carboys at Karnál, and small wares at Hushiárpur. Mr. Kipling writes:—

"This art as yet is quite in its infancy. The Hushiárpur workman is almost the only one who works independently with his own materials,—independently, that is, of foreign aid; for a few glass-blowers at Lahore collect fragments of white European glass and melting them down blow cheap lamp chimneys and bottles. At Karnál the glass globes are made, which, when silvered inside, are broken up into the small mirrors used in *Shishádár* ornamental plaster-work for walls, and sewn into the embroideries known as *Shishádár Phulkáris.*"

Bottles and beads, both white and of various colours, are made at Jaipur chiefly in the School of Art. One or two private men in the bazar also do the work.

The colours produced are cobalt blue, Indian red, marbled and dark green, &c. Bangles of various colours are made both in the town of Jaipur as well as in many other places in the State. They are chiefly worn by Musalman women. Plaques of frosted glass are made at Gwalior, the patterns being chiselled on the glass. A piece four inches square is sold for R5. Bangles of various colours and designs are made in Indor.

In the Madras Presidency the manner in which glass is made has already been described under the head of Glass Bangles in the Chapter devoted to Jewellery. Small quantities of glass-ware are made at Salem, Trichinopoly, and Anantpur. The colour of the glass is usually various shades of green and claret. Dr. Bidie states that "owing to imperfect annealing the few articles of glass usually made are too brittle for use. They consist of balls, which are hung up as ornaments, small cups, and bottles." In Mysore bangles, rings, and phials for scents are made in large quantities at Mattod and Chinnapatna. There is a large local demand for such articles. The bangles are red, green, yellow, black, and blue in colour, and are sold at one anna for a dozen.

In the Bombay Presidency glass-ware is manufactured in very small quantities. Mr. B. A. Gupte writes:—

"Very little glass is produced in the Presidency, and that principally is manufactured at Kapadvanj in the Kaira District and is remarkable for iridescent properties and good colour resembling old Venetian. The shapes too of the little vessels and cups are very quaint and beautiful. At Kapadvanj the workers are Musalmans, numbering about 70, who have been following this craft for several generations. Most of them are poor and have frequently to borrow money for the purpose of carrying on their work. The materials for making glass are—*Us*, an alkaline earth obtained locally, impure carbonate of soda (*sajikhár*), and a variety of dark flinty sand from Jaipur.

The glass is made in large earthy furnaces, in form like huge slipper baths, the floor sloping towards the holes prepared to receive the melted glass. The materials are mixed together in certain proportions, placed in the furnaces, and when raised to a white heat the molten mass is run into a trench, where it remains till it is cool. It is then broken up into small pieces, re-melted and shaped into bangles and small vessels, which are mostly used as toys."

On the subject of glass-manufacture in India Mr. Kipling makes the following general remarks :—

"It has often been remarked that in this country there is abundance of material for glass-making, and certainly there is no lack of soda. Flint sand is also to be had, nor are lead or borax prohibitively dear. But the difficulty in this, as in so many industries, is the lack of fuel. It would probably be cheaper to carry such glass-making materials as are to be found in the Panjáb to the hearths of Staffordshire, and bring them back made up into glass, than to attempt the manufacture on a large scale here. Nor is there any use for glass in the native scheme of life, except to contain *Itrs*. At all Panjáb fairs one of the most popular toys is a glass tube terminating at each end in a bulb and enclosing a small quantity of water. The tube is narrowed in the centre by a ring of thread, and the slow procession of air bubbles that ensues on reversing the tube is the point and interest of the toy. Not one in fifty of these brittle tubes survives the journey home; but such trifles as this, with bangles and rings, are the only uses to which this beautiful material is put."

XII.—Leather Manufactures.

One of the earliest materials of which primitive man made his household utensils is the skin of animals. Siva, the Great Destroyer in the Hindu Triad, is clothed in a tiger's skin, and deer skin was used as a seat by the Bráhmans of ancient India. In the *Rig-Veda* leathern bags to hold water have been mentioned, similar to those used in India at the present day. Leathern bottles were also made. Straps and bands were manufactured of leather and hide, and sails were also made of the same materials. In those days hides and skins do not seem to have been held impure, nor any articles made out of other animal substances. The feeling against taking life and using animal products either for food or for the manufacture of dress, shoes, and domestic articles, originated in a later age, when the Aryans had fairly settled down in the hot plains of India and retained only a faint tradition of those cold, bleak and hungry regions beyond the high mountains from which their ancestors originally came, and when living in the midst of a profuse abundance of grains, vegetables, and fruits they could well afford to extend to the brute creation the benefits of mercy and charity. The feeling gradually deepened, and when the time was ripe it culminated in Buddhism with its most sacred injunction—*Thou shalt not kill!* Even after the reaction against the stern philosophy defined and promulgated by the great Gautama, which led to the re-establishment of modern Hinduism in India, the belief in the sanctity of life retained its firm hold in the mind of the Indian people, and the bolder sects of Bráhmans of those times, who were instrumental in bringing back the old religion, often shocked the public by their reckless disregard of the general opinion on the subject. Thus it was that the five holy men, the ancestors of the modern Bráhmans of Bengal, who came from Kanauj about one thousand years ago, dressed in trowsers and coats and with sacred threads made of deer skin, were refused audience by the then king of Bengal until they had proved their Bráhmanical power by reviving a dead piece of wood by blessing upon it. Since that period powerful protests were made from time to time against the practice of killing animals either for sacrifice or for food. Such a protest took the shape of a tremendous religious upheaval in Bengal about four hundred years ago, which had well-nigh driven a fifth of the population from the fold of Hinduism, but for the circumstance that the leader of the movement was himself a Bráhman. In such struggles, however, when the mundane interests of men came into collision with religious ordinances, religion has always to give way. Laws were made in India making apologies and exceptions for the use of animal substances. Sankha and Likhita declared that water raised from wells in leather buckets is pure and wholesome, and the sage Atri was made to say that "flowing water and that which is raised by machinery are not defiled." Oleaginous substances were also allowed to be kept in leather vessels, because they had to be transported from place to place and earthen jars would not be strong enough. At the present day, besides shoes and saddlery, these bottles and buckets are the chief manufactures of leather in this country.

Shoes and boots were in use in ancient India. When Ráma went to exile for fourteen years, at the desire of his step-mother, to allow his step-brother Bharata to ascend the throne of Oudh, Bharata refused to do so, but persisted in leading a hermit's life like his brother in the forest, and in managing the kingdom in the name of Ráma by placing his shoes on the throne as a symbol of the rightful authority. Bharata's address to Ráma on the subject, when his expostulations failed to bring him back to his home and kingdom, has been beautifully rendered by Mr. Griffiths in his translation of the *Rámáyana* :—

> "Through fourteen seasons will I wear
> The hermit's dress and matted hair ;
> With fruit and root my life sustain,
> And still beyond the realm remain,
> Longing for thee to come again.
> The rule and all affairs of state
> I to these shoes will delegate.
> And if, O tamer of thy foes,
> When fourteen years have reached their close,
> I see thee not that day return,
> The kindled fire my frame shall burn !"

Shoes have also been mentioned in other ancient books, and they can also be seen in the statues in the old temples. Shoes and slippers in ancient India were made of buffalo hide as also of bovine leather. Slippers with an upturned front were mostly in use like those still worn in South India and the Bombay Presidency.

In Bengal country shoes have almost gone out of fashion, and English shoes of black or patent leather, either imported or made in the country, have taken their place. Country-made slippers of brown leather, tanned according to native process, are, however, extensively worn by the people. In Upper India country shoes are still universally used. These are made of a reddish leather with a curled front, low sides, and covering the feet only up to a little above the toes. They are often lined with red or green velvet, and ornamented with tinsel and gold or silver embroidery. The slippers made for ladies are often very fine and artistic. Patna, Benares, Lucknow, Rámpur, Agra, Delhi, Lahore, and Jaipur are the principal seats of manufacture. Delhi exports large quantities of such shoes to other parts of India. Agra exports shoes not so ornamented. About the trade of Agra in this article the Provincial Officer writes :—

"The trade in shoes is carried on in the muhallas of Nakhasá, Kándhári, and Maithas, and gives employment to about 500 *Chámárs* (cobblers). The price of a plain pair of shoes is 12 annas, and that of embroidered work is as much as R10. There is not, however, a large sale of the more expensive kinds, as these are imported from Delhi, where they are sold cheaper because of the gold and silver being more or less alloyed. Un-embroidered shoes are exported from Agra to different parts of India. The average profit is said to be about 3 per cent., and the wages of the workmen are about 2 annas a day. The *Chámárs* work up the leather part of the manufacture, while the embroidery is done by the Muhammadans. The trade is not flourishing. Shoes from Jalesar, in the Eta District, are remarkable for their lightness combined with durability. This latter class of shoes is not to be had ready-made. They are prepared to order."

About the Delhi industry of making ornamental boots Mr. Kipling makes the following remarks :—

"Connected with the gold and silver wire trade, about to be noticed in detail, is the considerable trade in embroidered shoes, for which Delhi has long been celebrated. The variety of patterns and shapes is remarkable, even in a country where fantasy runs riot. Nothing could be prettier or more dainty than some of the slippers made for native ladies' wear, embroidered with seed pearls, usually false, with spangles and every variety of gold and silver thread, and inlaid with red, black, or emerald green leather in decorative patterns. Gilded and silvered leather are also used. Sometimes gold and silver embroidery is worked on cloth over a basis of leather. Men's shoes are often no less elaborate. In 1864, according to Mr. B. H. Baden Powell, Delhi exported shoes to the value of four lakhs of rupees yearly. It is probable that the trade has greatly increased since that time, for the railway has opened new markets, and shapes unknown in the Panjáb are now made, *e.g.*, the Marhatta shoe with a heavy cleft, broad toe, much turned up. English forms are creeping into use. No sumptuary regulation to restrain extravagance in gilded shoes, and enforce the use of plain black leather, could be half so potent as the unwritten ordinance which permits an oriental to retain a pair of patent leather boots on stockinged feet, and requires him to doff shoes of native make when in the presence of a superior. In time, perhaps, the preference for European forms, consequent on this ordinance, may tell on the Delhi shoe trade; but hitherto it cannot fairly be said to have done it much harm."

Both ornamental and plain shoes are made at Jaipur and all over Rajputana of the same patterns as those of Delhi and Agra. A collection of Jaipur shoes has been sent to the Glasgow International Exhibition. In the Central Provinces the town of Chanda is famous for its embroidered shoes.

Slippers are generally used in South India. They are made of a soft white or red leather, with the front slightly turned. These slippers are often embroidered with silk thread dyed red.

In Haidrabad (Deccan) Ráichur is famous for its shoes and slippers. They are generally made of leather dyed red, and sometimes gilt or silvered. The slippers are embroidered with gilt copper, and are commonly used by the middle classes, men and women, specially dancing girls.

In the Bombay Presidency the shoes worn are divided into three classes, called *Jodá*, *Jutá*, and *Váhana*. "The Deccan tribes generally call their shoes *Jodá*, of which there are two varieties, made with the heels turned in, named *Shiroli* or *Bráhmani*, or those with single broad rounded toes, and *Marhatti*, or those with the double toes divided down the centre. The Gujrátis, Bhoras, Musalmans, and Parsis, call their shoes a *Jutá*, which has a pointed toe and standing heel. The shoes worn by Musalman women are also called *Jutás,* but they differ from the others in being like slippers, without heels, open at the back. Poona is noted for the *Shiroli* or *Bráhmani* shoe and Ahmadnagar for the *Marhatti* or two-toed shoe."

Sandals are made in many places in the Panjáb, Rajputana, and Bombay. The sandal or *Chapli* worn in Northern India is of many forms, but none of the varieties resemble the classic shape with a separate stall for the big toe worn in Bombay. In parts of the Himalayas and Kashmir an elaborately laced sandal encloses a sock in soft deer-skin, and forms one of the most comfortable foot-coverings known. The Pesháwar sandal is generally embroidered with silk. Embroidered sandals of this kind of unusual excellence are made in Derá Gházi Khán. Bannu, another frontier District, makes pretty gold-embroidered buskins, in soft red leather. Sandals are extensively used all over Haidrabad. They are sometimes ornamented.

Of other art-manufactures in leather may be mentioned small bottles, often of very good shapes. These are used to hold water, scented oils, and other liquid substances. They are mostly made in Rajputana. In Gorakhpur in the North-Western Provinces, fancy articles of embroidered leather are produced, which have of late found favour among Europeans. These generally consist of table and teapoy covers and are prepared from antelope (*sambhar*) leather. The prices range from R10 to R50 a piece. Small leather boxes, cigar-cases, and book-covers, ornamented with quill-work, are made chiefly in Biláspur, a hill State in the Panjáb Himalayas. "Black leather is first made into boxes and other forms, then decorated with circles or patterns of green or red leather, or leather covered with foil, fastened on in the manner of applique work, and then the whole sewn in designs of white, with thin strips of the tough and flexible quill of the peacock." A Biláspur box costs about R10. Another very curious leather-manufacture in the Panjáb is the *Hukka* bottom decorated with brass. Green leather and silver studs are also sometimes employed in the ornamentation of such articles. Mr. Kipling supposes that "the idea of this work was doubtless suggested by the brittleness of the earthen *Hukka* vases, when required to be moved from place to place; and the costliness of brass or silver vessels." Country saddlery is generally made of cotton, silk, and velvet, the better kinds of which are often embroidered; but ornamented leather saddlery, trappings and stirrup fastenings are sometimes made in Upper India and Rajputana. Chanda in the Central Provinces produces a very superior kind of leather saddle cloth. The Provincial Officer writes:—"Chanda was once a town of very large size and is surrounded by a massive stone wall seven miles in circumference. It was formerly the capital of a dynasty of rulers representing one of the oldest races in the Provinces—the Gonds. City and race have now alike greatly declined in importance. The greater part of the area within the Chanda wall is now under cultivation, and the town has now only 16,000 inhabitants. The embroidered leather work of Chanda is the only industrial relic of its past magnificence." Ornamented camel trappings are made at Khetri in the Jaipur State. Camel saddles, water-bottles, lacquered or plain, pipes, silver-mounted and lacquered, embroidered bridles and belts, cuirass leather, powder flask and pouch are made of leather in Bikánir. Saddlery of leather, in the European fashion, are largely made at Cawnpore. Leather is also employed in making mule trunks (*Yakdans*), water-bags (*Massaks* and *Purs*), and other articles for ordinary use.

Shields have been made of leather from pre-historic

times. It was made all over the country, but its ornamental forms were chiefly to be found in Upper India and Rajputana, and latterly in the Bombay Presidency when the Marhattas acquired the sovereignty of India. In this part of the country "the manufacture of leather shields from the hide of rhinoceros and the blue bull was one of the most important industries during the old fighting days. At Ahmadabad alone about one hundred families were engaged in the trade. As shields are no longer required for warfare, the demand for them practically does not exist. A few however are made to supply the European demand for curios." Ahmadabad shields are sold for R25 to R35. Shields are also made at Baroda.

Skins of deer, with the hair intact, are beautifully tanned in Kangra and Hushiárpur with the leaves of *Rhus Cotinus*. They are thus formed into a fine soft skin of a greenish buff colour and are made into trousers, coats, leggings, and gloves. Afghan sheepskin jackets, called *Postins*, are also made with the wool intact. They are often embroidered. Ornamental belts are made in the North-Western Provinces, the Panjáb, and Rajputana. They are largely to be found at Pesháwar and go by the name of "frontier belts." They "form part of the equipment of every fighting man on the frontier, and they are also worn by those who follow peaceful avocations. Many are embroidered with coloured silk, some with filaments of quills." A collection of such belts was received for the Colonial and Indian Exhibition from Pesháwar, Bannu, and Kohát. Derá Gházi Khán also sent a very complete specimen, to which were attached embossed leather powder flasks, cartridge pouches, sword slings, &c., all excellent in design and colour. Sheep skins are prepared in a very superior manner at Salem, Trichinopoly, Malabar, Kistna, Godávari, Vizagapatam, and Periyakulam in the Madras Presidency. At Ráichur leather with metallic gold and silver appearance is manufactured. A sort of indigenous saddle is made at Karnúl of European baize and gilded leather. The Nossam dish mats are made of thin leather, hand-painted. Figures of men and women grouped into the form of a horse or elephant are painted upon these circular pieces of leather. Native playing cards are made of leather in many places. Sometimes they are made of fish scales. Playing cards made of leather are often covered with figures. Very good leather cards were made at Jaipur, but the best artist in the place has lately died.

XIII.—Basket ware.

From very old times, bamboo, rattan cane, reeds, grasses, notably *Munj* (*Saccharum Munja*), palm leaf, and date leaf were employed in India in the preparation of basket ware and mats. These materials are still employed for the same purpose, chiefly in the seaboard Provinces, where canes, reeds, and grasses are abundant. In Bengal oval boxes called *Petárás*, are made of rattan cane, which are sometimes covered with leather, and are used to keep clothing and all sorts of family valuables. They are light and strong, and well-fitted for travelling purposes. These boxes are now going out of fashion, and leather portmanteaus and steel boxes imported from Europe are now taking their place. Formerly oblong boxes, called *Jhámpis*, were made of thinly sliced bamboo, in which valuable documents were kept. Tin and wooden boxes have now taken their place. Baskets of rattan and bamboo canes are made all over the country and form an important feature in the domestic economy of a Bengal household. But these have no artistic merit in them. Ornamental baskets and braids are made of palmyra leaves in Diamond Harbour near Calcutta. They are similar to those of China and Japan. Of late they have found some favour among Europeans. Near Calcutta long round boxes are made of date leaf. The leaves are gathered when young, and in drying they assume a satin-like glossiness, which imparts to the boxes a very effective appearance. Small ornamental table mats are made in Monghyr, which are chiefly purchased by Europeans. They are made of *Siki*, *Sar* or *Munj* grass. The prices are:—basket 4 annas, straw hat for ladies and children 8 annas, fan 8 annas, a set of table mats R1-8. These table mats and fans found a ready sale in the late Exhibitions. Basket wares of the same material are made by Bráhman women in Darbhángá. They are not sold; a collection has, however, been obtained for the Glasgow Exhibition through the Magistrate of the District. No good basket ware is produced in the North-Western Provinces, except some curious specimens turned out by women in Bahraich and other Sub-Himalayan Districts. These are made of *Munj* grass and ornamented with red thread and *Kauri* shells. Tiffin baskets and chairs are made of *Munj* culms in many Districts, but they possess no importance in an artistic point of view. Panjáb is equally poor in basket manufactures. Baskets of tolerably good quality are made at Chanda in the Central Provinces, but they are more of economic than artistic interest. In the Jaipur State, cups, water-bottles, and betel-boxes are made of the scented root of *Khaskhas* grass (*Andropogon muricatus*).

In the Madras Presidency, besides coarse baskets for ordinary household work, finer kinds are made in two places, *viz.*, at Kimedi in Ganjam and Palikat in Chingleput District. Dr. Bidie writes:—

In the case of the Ganjam manufactures, some energetic local officer has evidently endeavoured to effect what he considered improvements on the old simple native productions, and the result is a vile imitation of the commonest and most inferior basket-work of Europe. And as if this were not enough, the manufacturers have also been put in possession of, and taught how to use, aniline colours, with unspeakable results. The objects produced now-a-days in the new style show how native artistic talent may be led astray and degraded by the efforts of gentlemen who mean well but are utterly destitute of æsthetic taste. Some of the nested baskets which are not after a European muster and the mats are of pleasing patterns, and would be pretty but for the profusion of aniline colours with which they are daubed. Those made at Palikat are all very much of the same pattern of work, and generally nested. Until of late years the makers of these baskets used country dyes of sober colours, but now they have taken to the use of aniline pigments with a pertinacity which nothing will stop until the public taste is sufficiently educated to induce them to refuse to buy such trash. Unfortunately the chief purchasers are passengers and crews of home-going steamers, who buy them as curiosities, regardless of all defects. So fond are the makers of the baskets of the aniline colours, that it was only with the special aid of the Collector that a few articles stained with indigenous dyes could be got for the Calcutta Exhibition.

The collection of basket ware sent from Madras to the Colonial and Indian Exhibition was not an important one. The Palikat ware is made of the leaves of the palmyra palm (*Borassus flabelliformis*), and cigar-cases are also made of the leaves of the date palm (*Phœnix sylvestris*). The other places where basket ware is made in the Madras Presidency are Tenkasi in Tinnevelly District; Anantpur, Periyakulam in Madura District; Salem, South Canara, Shiyali in Tanjore District; Tanjore, Godávari Cuddapah and Vizagapatam. Baskets, boxes, cradles, &c., are made at Shimoga in Mysore. Rattan boxes, square and round, for keeping clothes, cradles, shields, and other articles are made in Kurg.

In the Bombay Presidency, bamboo baskets lined with cloth and decorated with lacquer, and baskets, boxes, and fans, made of *Khaskhas* root and ornamented with lace and beetle wings, are the specialties of Sáwantwádi. Poona also turns out similar articles in imitation of the Sáwantwádi ware, but they are inferior in workmanship, being made of cow-dung and paper coated with a layer of the fragrant *Khaskhas* (*Andropogon muricatus*) root. At Sáwantwádi there are only eleven and at Poona ten or twelve, who make *Khaskhas* baskets and fans. They are saddlers by trade, but as the demand for native-made saddles has declined, they have taken to *Khaskhas* work, there being a considerable market for articles in this material. At the Yerrowda, Thánà, and Ratnagiri Jails, baskets, chairs, and other articles are made of cane, and in the city of Bombay itself several Chinamen carry on an extensive business in such manufactures. The prices of basket ware depend upon the kind and quality of the materials used.

Assam produces a varied assortment of basket work, chiefly made of bamboo and rattan cane. A fine description of bamboo hat, called *Jhámpi*, is worn by the people as a protection against sun and rain. The Assam screen at the Colonial and Indian Exhibition was constructed chiefly of very fine basket work of bamboo and rattan cane. The different panels were of different designs, on which were inserted intricate figures of very fine cane-work.

Mats are made all over India of bamboo, reeds, and grasses, rattan cane, aloe fibre, screw pine leaf, palmyra leaf, and date leaf. Bamboo mats called *Darmá* are largely employed in Eastern Bengal for the construction of walls of houses. Palmyra and date palm mats are used as a bed by the poorer classes on which they sleep in the night. In an artistic point of view two kinds of mats are only important, *viz.*, those made of *Mádur* grass (*Cyperus tegetum* and *C. Pangorie*) and of *Sitalpáti* grass (*Maranta dichotoma*). *Mádur* mats are employed all over Lower Bengal as a bed by the middle and the poor classes. Floors of European houses are covered with this kind of mat. A very fine kind of *Mádur*, called *Masland* mat, is produced in the District of Midnapur. The finer the culms of the grass are sliced the softer and the more delicate becomes the mat. It is often striped red with sappan wood-dye, and sometimes ornamented with silk and face work. *Masnad* is the seat of honour among oriental nations, and this fine mat being often spread over other rich floor-cloths on account of its coolness, it is called the *Masland* mat.

The culms of the sedge are sliced into fine strips by men of the *Báiti* caste, which their women subsequently weave into mats. Similar mats are made at Pálghát and Tinnevelly in the Madras Presidency. Dr. Bidie writes :—

"Several species of sedge appear to be used for mat-making, but the one from which the finest sorts of mats are manufactured at Tinnevelly and Pálghát is *Cyperus Pongarie.* Tinnevelly mats of the first quality are generally uncoloured, or with one or two simple bands of red and black at each end, and they may be made so fine that a mat sufficient for a man to lie on can be rolled up and packed into the interior of a moderate sized walking stick. The strips of the split sedge used in the Pálghát matting are not so fine as those employed in Tinnevelly, and the article is therefore heavier, coarser in texture, and not so flexible. The Pálghát mats are also usually coloured with black and red in geometrical patterns. Both these, as well as the Vellore mats, are made in a rude kind of loom, the warp consisting of cords of common twine separated more or less according to the quality desired. The woof consists of strips of the split sedge dyed, or of the natural hue. The black colour is produced by iron, gall-nut powder, and the pods of the *Babul* (*Acacia arabica*). A red dye is got by boiling the split sedge in water with the wood of *Varthangi* (*Cæsalpinia Sappan*) and the leaves of *Kasan* (*Memecylon edule*). For yellow, which is not so often used, the colouring ingredient is turmeric."

Another fine mat made chiefly in Eastern Bengal is the *Sitalpáti* or "cool-mat." It is made of the culms of *Maranta dichotoma,* which are split into very fine slices lengthwise. These are then well scraped and the glossy parts remaining under the rind are made into thin and narrow strips, which are woven into mats. The superior quality of a *Sitalpáti* is judged by its glossiness, smoothness, and fineness of texture. It is said that the best kind of *Sitalpáti* is so smooth that a snake cannot run over it. At any rate these mats are very cool, and for that reason well-to-do people spread a *Sitalpáti* over their bed in the hot season. Faridpur, Bákarganj, Tipperah, and Chittagong are the Districts where

Sitalpáti mats are mostly made. The industry is almost entirely confined to women. Parents receive a heavy compensation from the men who marry their daughters, the amount being proportioned to their skill in making *Sitalpáti* mats. Good *Sitalpáti* mats are made in Sylhet in Assam by a caste known as *Dás*. A *Sitalpáti* mat sells from R5 to R100. Ivory mats are also made in Sylhet and Burma.

Aloe fibre matting is manufactured in some places, notably in the Hazáribágh, Lucknow, and Allahabad jails. It is strong and well suited for covering floors of houses, or saloons and passages of steamers. Coir matting is an important manufacture in Madras and Bombay. It is very strong and is now being largely employed as a cover for floors and brush door-mats. Those made in the Midnapur jail in Bengal are very superior in quality. Matting made of *Munj* grass is produced in the Allahabad, Lucknow, Benares, Delhi, Ludhiáná, Ambala, Siálkot, Gujrát and other jails. The culms are reduced to a fibrous stuff by beating with a mallet, which is then dyed and woven in patterns into a thick fabric suitable for floor-cloth. It is cheap and ought to find favour outside India.

In the Madras Presidency mats of various kinds are made in many places, such as Salem, Kistna, northern parts of Udiyagiri, Nellore District; South Canara; Madura and Timmangalam, Madura District; Wandiwash, North Arcot District; Pattamadai, Tinnevelly District; Ellore, Godávari District; Pálghát, Malabar District; Shiyali, Tanjore District; Chitvail, Cuddapah District; Porto Novo, South Arcot District; Malabar; Cuddapah; and Tanjore. Various substances are used, the most important being bamboo, rattan, palmyra leaf, date palm, screw pine and sedges. A considerable industry in plain and coloured mats is carried on at Wandiwash in the North Arcot District.

Fans are made of palm leaf, bamboo, the sweet-scented *Khaskhas* root (*Andropogon muricatus*), *Munj*-grass, date leaf, peacock feathers, ivory, and talc. Palm leaf fans are made all over Bengal and Madras, both large and small. The larger ones are waved before or behind a rich man by his servant, and formed the sole means of obtaining air in the hot season before the present *Pankhá* was invented by a Dutchman in Chinsura. The smaller ones are the usual hand-fans. Both are often ornamented. Bamboo fans are of the common kinds and are not ornamented. Fans are made of the *Khaskhas* root on account of its sweet odour, and as they are generally used after being wetted, they impart to the air a cool fragrance. *Khaskhas* fans are often highly ornamented. They are made with ivory handles at Reni, in Bikánir; the prices range from R1 to R20. In the Bombay Presidency they are, however, made on a more elaborate scale. The materials used are the *Khaskhas* root, gold lace, tinsel, satin, peacock feathers, silk, cotton cloth, gold spangles, silver spangles, &c. A bamboo frame is first made, on which the fan, formed of velvet, satin, cotton cloth and *Khaskhás* root pasted together, is firmly fixed. Various devices are then worked upon it with gold thread, tinsel, beetle-wings, &c. A fringe of peacock feathers is also put round. When complete, the fan is removed from the frame. The handles are made by carpenters and are either lacquered or painted. Similar fans are also made in Mysore. They are fringed with the *Khaskhas* root, instead of peacock feathers, but that material is used for ornamentation, on which gilding and coloured silks are also employed. The handles are sometimes elaborately carved. Such fans are usually made by Bráhmans serving in temples. Prices range from R3 to R15 according to size, without the carved handles, which cost R10 to R25 each. Peacock feather fans are made at Jhánsi, Etawa, and Agra in the North-Western Provinces and exported in large quantities to Calcutta. In the Madras Presidency fans are made of painted palm leaves at Chitvail in Cuddapah and elsewhere, but those made in Tanjore are better in quality. They have a talc border and silk fringe and the handles are ornamented with bits of coloured glass in imitation of precious stones. Ornamental fans, apparently of paper covered with a thin cloth, are made at Nossam, a town in the Cuddapah District. "They are furnished with ribs of bamboos radiating from the handle in imitation of the ribs of palm leaf, from which doubtless they were originally made. The surface of the fan is covered with some pigment so as to give a body to work on, and then the final pattern is laid on with gilt and brilliant colours, which give it somewhat the look of lacquer work. The decorations on one side consist of the eyes of the peacock feathers in their natural colours, and on the other of a floral pattern." Good talc fans of exquisite patterns were formerly made in Tanjore, but the work has greatly degenerated of late years. Cloth fans with tinsel ornaments were also made in Tanjore. In Dr. Bidie's opinion, fan industry in this place has declined probably from want of encouragement. Fans are also made at Kálikot in the Ganjam District. According to Hindu medicinal books fans made of different materials possess different properties. Fans made of palm leaf, cane, cloth, or peacock feathers are said to correct irregularities in the three humours—heat, bile, and phlegm, and those made of bamboo to increase the secretions. Umbrellas are also made of bamboo and palm leaf, which are sometimes highly ornamented. This industry has, however, been practically destroyed since the introduction of English umbrellas.

XIV.—Textile Manufactures.

Cotton Fabrics.

Even in its present moribund state the production of textile fabrics, made of cotton, silk, wool, and hair, in the old primitive method of weaving, forms such an important and comprehensive industry in India that it will not be possible to give in this work any but a very general account of the manufacture as carried on in the different Provinces. Neither tradition nor history gives any precise information about the time when cotton first appeared as an important article in the domestic economy of an Indian household. But as geology has preserved traces of early forms of life upon earth, so has Indian society preserved in its different strata the manners and customs of pre-historic ages side by side with the highest type of modern civilisation. The trousers and coats made at the present day of the bark of *Sterculia urens* in the north and of *Antiaris succedanea* in the south shew as much the kind of raiment worn by our forefathers, as the charm written on the thin epidermis of the *Betula Bhojpatra* suggests the material on which they inscribed their sacred songs after writing was invented. These, together with the leaf garment still worn by the Jowangs of the Orissa hills and the sheep-skin clothing of the north-west frontier, were evidently the early forms of dress known in India. *Gárhá*, *Gazi*, and other coarse descriptions of cotton fabrics point to the first epoch of cotton manufactures in the world, while its highest development was the muslins like the "Running Water" (*Abrawán*) or the "Evening Dew" (*Shabnam*), which, notwithstanding their Persian names, were woven in India when Egypt built her pyramids, Solomon reigned in Jerusalem, Romulus founded Rome, and Harun-al-Rashid went his nocturnal rounds in Baghdad. Notwithstanding the extent of their present production, cotton manufactures in the old style are in their last gasp. The few small pieces of wood and bamboo tied with shreds of twine and thread which the weaver calls his loom, and which he can as easily make himself as buy from his neighbour the village carpenter, can no more compete with the powerful machinery worked in Lancashire than a village cart of western Bengal can run a race with the "Flying Scotchman." Yet the wonder is that cotton fabrics can still be manufactured with the old primitive loom all over the country. In one sense it is a misfortune that it should be so; for it shews the low value of human labour in India. Machinery, with all its modern improvements, seems to contend in vaih with a moribund industry, that must linger on as long as the worker in it has nothing better to do than to produce from it fourpence a day as the joint earnings of himself, his wife, a boy, and a girl. Those that wield the machinery should lay their heads together and devise means to teach the people how better to employ their hands in other crafts. Another reason why Indian looms can still compete with Lancashire goods is that the European process of manufacture has not yet been able to give to the fabrics that strength for which native manufactures have a reputation. Nor has machinery yet been able to make those gossamer fabrics for which a wealthy Indian always paid a fabulous price.

Thus cotton is still woven all over the country—Plain cloths, from the thickest carpet, called *Dari* or *Satranji*, to the thinnest one-threaded *Malmal* or *Eksuti;* striped cloths, called *Chárkháná*, *Susi*, and *Lungi;* cloths with diagonal patterns like the *Khes;* and damask cloths with patterns poetically described as the *Bulbul chashm*, like the *Gháti* and *Chádar* of the Panjáb. In Bengal the most important cotton manufactures are the *Dhoti*, *Chádar*, and *Sári*. *Dhoti* is a piece of plain cloth with a coloured border, generally five yards long by one and a quarter yards wide, worn by the men. *Chádar* is a wrapper or sheet three yards long by one and a half yards wide. And *Sári* is a cloth like the *Dhoti*, with a broader border, worn by women. Large quantities of all the three cloths are imported from England, but those turned out by the native loom, though much dearer, are preferred for their greater durability, their finer quality, and the air of respectability they give to the wearer in the estimation of his countrymen. But all these fabrics are woven of English twist. Chandernagore, Simla at Calcutta, Kalmi near Howrah, Baránagar in the Twenty-four Parganás, Sátkhirá, Sántipur, Pabná, Dogáchi, &c., are the places where *Dhotis* and *Sáris* are chiefly made. A kind of cloth called *Kokti*, made of a naturally dyed yellowish cotton (*Gossypium herbaceum*, Var. *Religiosum*), is woven in the Darbhángá District. The Bráhman women of Tirhut excel in making thread of the finest description from this cotton. There are different varieties of the cloth, the coarsest pieces selling at prices from R5 to R6 each. The size of a piece is generally from 32 to 40 cubits long by 2¼ to 2½ cubits wide. These self-coloured cloths are extensively used by the Bráhmans of Tirhut in the shape of *Dhotis*, *Sáris*, winter *Chádars*, and coats. Until lately they were highly valued not only in Tirhut but also in the adjoining Districts. Imported goods have, however, greatly injured the manufacture.

By far the most important of Bengal cotton manufactures in an artistic point of view are of course the Dacca muslins. The value of the Dacca muslins consists in their fineness, to attain which an incredible amount of patience, perseverance, and skill were formerly displayed both by the spinners and weavers. One way of testing their fineness was to pass a whole piece of muslin, twenty yards long by one yard wide, through the small aperture of an ordinary sized finger ring. Another test was the compass within which a piece could be squeezed. Tavernier relates of a Persian ambassador in Bengal having on his return home presented to his monarch a piece of Dacca muslin turban, thirty yards long, placed within a highly ornamented cocoanut shell, not larger than an ostrich egg. No one who ever wrote about Dacca muslins forgot to mention this incident as an incontrovertible proof of the delicate texture of the fabric, but an ostrich-egg is not a small thing and there does not appear to be anything so very astonishing in the fact of thirty yards of fine muslin going within the space inside its shell. The best test, however, was the weight of the cloth proportioned to its size and number of threads. It is said that two hundred years ago a piece of muslin, fifteen yards long by one yard wide, could be manufactured so fine as to weigh only 900 grains. Its price was £40. Dr. Taylor, writing in 1840, stated that in his time a piece of cloth of the same dimensions and texture could not be made finer than what would weigh 1,600 grains. The price of such a piece of muslin would be about £10. It is generally believed that the artists of the present time have lost that manipulative skill and the delicate touch of hand by the aid of which such gossamer web was formerly produced. Three years ago I was informed by one of the manufacturers of Dacca muslin that the generation of women who spun the yarn of which the finest fabrics were made has all passed away, except two very aged beings, who with their defective eye-sight earned but a precarious livelihood at Mánikganj, a town near Dacca. It has also been stated that the long-stapled cotton which alone could produce the thread of which Dacca muslins were made has also disappeared. It may be all true, but there is no doubt that if a demand arises the finest fabric ever made at Dacca can still be made there. The thread used for the best kind of muslins can no doubt be still spun by the women of Dhámrái, a village 20 miles north of Dacca, if they are sufficiently paid for their labour. R50 per ounce is not a heavy charge for such yarn. A piece of cloth ten yards long by one yard wide cannot be woven in less than five months, and the work can only be carried on during the rains, when the moisture in the air prevents the thread from breaking. It is only an oriental who can feel a pride in the possession of an article of such exquisite fineness, and an oriental alone can spend money for the purchase of a cloth of such ethereal texture. The decline of the Dacca industry is the natural result of the decline in the power and prosperity of oriental nations in Asia, Africa, and Europe. *Malmal* is the general name for all fine plain muslins, both Indian and European, and the special names of the finest qualities made at Dacca are *Shaugáti* or "Presentation," *Sharbati,* or "Sweet like a Sherbet," *Shabnnam,* or the "Evening Dew," and *Abrawán* or "The Running Water." Dr. Taylor mentioned that some thirty-six different kinds of cloth were made in his time (1840), but he must have included in the list many of the patterned and loom-embroidered cloths. The chief difference by which the several qualities of Dacca muslins are distinguished at the present day consists in the number of threads in the warp, the finest qualities having 1,800, the second 1,400, and so on, the threads being finer in proportion to their greater number. The warp contains more threads than the woof, the proportion being generally 9 to 11. A series of interesting experiments conducted by Dr. Forbes Watson established the superior fineness of the Dacca muslins to similar fabrics made in Europe. His final conclusion on this point was:—

"However viewed, therefore, our manufacturers have something still to do. With all our machinery and wondrous appliances, we have hitherto been unable to produce a fabric which for fineness or utility can equal the 'woven-air' of Dacca—the product of arrangements which appear rude and primitive, but which in reality are admirably adapted for their purpose."

Messrs. Nitái Charan Basák & Co. of Dacca supplied large collections of fabrics both to the Calcutta International and the Colonial and Indian Exhibitions.

Muslins are also made at Behar and at Jahánábád, near Patna. Various kinds of checks, striped cloths, mosquito curtains, known by the names of *Photá*, *Magná*, *Nimjá*, *Lungi*, *Chárkháná*, *&c.*, are made in Rangpur, Dinájpur, and the Eastern Districts of Bengal.

In the North-Western Provinces, muslins of a fine quality are made at Sikandrabad in the District of Bulandshahr. These are usually fringed with gold and are used for turbans. Handkerchiefs of fine muslin cloth are also made here. Ladies' handkerchiefs made of Sikandrabad muslin, plain, are sold at R2-8 per dozen, while those with golden borders at R3-8; gentlemen's handkerchiefs, plain, at R3-6; with gold border, R5-8. *Dopattás* or sheets, worn by women as shawls, are also made at Sikandrabad. *Dopattá* muslins are of very fine quality, and there is a great demand for it in the Provinces. Plain and striped muslins are made at a place called Mau in the Azamgarh District, which are chiefly exported to

Nepal. Lucknow also makes large quantities of plain and striped, bleached and unbleached muslins, which are preferred to European cloths for purposes of *Chikan* embroidery. They are also used by Indian gentlemen for turbans and summer shirts. Most of the Lucknow muslins are made at Mahmudnagar, and are known by the name of *Sharbati, Malmal, Adhi*, and *Tarandam*. Striped ones are called *Doriá*. Muslins with damasked patterns are made at Benares and Jais in the Rái Bareli District; those woven in the former place almost equal in delicacy fabrics of the same kind produced at Dacca. They are largely used in the manufacture of country caps. Muslins made at Jais had formerly a great reputation, but the industry has declined since the fall of the kingdom of Oudh. Good muslins were made at Tándá in the Faizabad District, and they had a great sale when Oudh had a court of its own. Rámpur produces a superior cotton damask, called *Khes*, either plain or with borders in coloured thread or interwoven with gold thread. It obtained a gold medal at the Calcutta International Exhibition. The Provincial Officer writes :—

"Rámpur *Khes* and *Lungis* are not surpassed by any hand-work in India for their fine weaving and cotton. To work on silk is much easier, but it requires great art to make the embroidery on cotton so durable and soft. It is not so good as is done in Benares and the Panjáb, but it is proof against water, and will stand any amount of washing and knocking up by the washerman."

Cotton cloths of different kinds are woven at Moradabad, Pratábgarh, Cawnpore, Lalitpur, Sháhpur, Misáuli in Rái Bareli District, Aligarh, Mau in Jhánsi District, Mau in Azamgarh District, Sahåranpur, Meerut, &c. Agra turns out large quantities of check and striped cotton cloths, the industry giving employment to more than one thousand men. "The thread is made at Agra. There is a considerable wholesale export trade and a large local trade in it. The average profit is about 3 per cent. The wages earned by the workmen is about 2 annas a day. Both Hindus and Muhammadans are employed in it, and it has been carried on in Agra for centuries. The trade received a very great impetus by the opening of the railway." Coarse cloths, called *Gárhá, Gazi*, and *Dhoti-jorá* are made all over the Provinces, which the peasantry prefer to English cloths for their durability. Large quantities of these cloths are printed and used for female dress.

In the Panjáb, muslins were formerly made in large quantities at Delhi. Mr. Baden Powell in his "Panjáb Manufactures" stated that "these muslin turbans are manufactured in great quantities, of Chinese cotton; about two lakhs of rupees worth are annually imported." The industry has declined in competition with European manufactures, so that no specimens could be seen at the Colonial and Indian Exhibition. At present turbans are made at Hushiárpur, Sirsá, Jallandhar, Ludhiáná, Sháhpur, Gurdáspur, Patiálá, and other places, but these are not of fine quality. The only place where fine muslins are now woven in the Province is Rohtak. *Tanzeb,* as fine muslin is called here, is mostly used for loose summer shirts. *Gháti* or a highly glazed longcloth is made at Jallandhar. Before the introduction of European goods it was the material of which the dress of an Indian gentleman was prepared. *Gháti* cloth is either plain or damasked or diapered with the *Bulbul-chashm* or "Nightingale-eye" pattern. It is needless to state that the industry has declined. The most important of the Panjáb cotton manufactures are now the *Lungi, Khes, Susi,* and the coarse cloths known as the *Dosuti, Gárhá,* and *Gazi.* The *Lungi* is a long piece of cloth with a short width, chiefly used for a turban. Mr. Baden Powell writes :—

"This is a long scarf. They are made everywhere, but specially in the Pesháwar Division, where they are woven of exquisite fineness, and with most beautiful borders, in which coloured silk and gold thread are often tastefully introduced. The *Lungi* is universally worn by the inhabitants of the Pesháwar and Deráját Divisions. The long ends with the coloured borders hanging down present a very elegant and picturesque appearance. When the *Lungi* is not worn as a turban it is used as a scarf, being cut in half and the two pieces sewn together. A *Lungi* is either plain cloth of any colour, oftenest white or dark blue, or else a small check like the Pesháwar *Lungi*."

Lungi is made at Pesháwar, Ludhiáná, Gugairá, Kohát, Lahore, Hushiárpur, &c. A collection of *Lungis* have been sent to the Glasgow Exhibition by Attai and Ghaffar, weavers of Kohát. It is made both of cotton and silk, and the prices vary from R15 to R50.

The following description of *Khes* and *Susi* have been given by Mr. Kipling :—

"*Khes* is the name by which a stout fabric, woven in coloured chequer patterns, is known in the Panjáb. The loom for *Khes* weaving is wider than usual, and the cloth is prized for winter wraps. It is suitable for some European uses. Dark red, dark blue, and white are the usual colours. Newer combinations, though often tried, are seldom agreeable in effect. R19 per hundred yards is an ordinary price, but there are several qualities. These cloths are something like the ginghams and checks of England. They are mostly woven with imported yarn either English or Bombay mill-spun. *Susi* is the popular name for a peculiar quality of striped cloth (loom coloured), which is in great favour for women's *paijámás* (drawers) and other articles of dress. Printed imitations of *Susi* are now imported from Europe, but the English cloth, compared with that of native make, is of such poor substance that it does not seriously compete with native cloths. Lines of silk are frequently introduced in warp."

Good *Khes* is made at Muzaffargarh, Lahore, Siálkot, Firozpur, Karnál, Jhang, Derá Ismáil Khán, and Patiálá. A *Khes* sells at R5 to R7 each. *Susi* is woven in many places, notably at Jallandhar, Gurdáspur, and

Siálkot. A piece of *Susi* sells at R3 to R5. Another kind of check cloth, largely made at Ludhiáná, is called *Gabrun* or *Gamrun*, or better known by the name of "Ludhiáná cloth." It is largely used by Europeans for summer clothing.

In Rajputana, *Susi*, *Gárhá*, *Gazi*, and *Dosuti* are produced in Jaipur. Muslins are made at Kota by a number of Hindu and Muhammadan weavers from thread imported from Europe. These are mostly turban pieces, of which R25,000 worth are turned out annually, the most part of which is exported to Nimach and other places out of the State. The price of a piece 12 yards long varies from R4 to R15. *Susi* and coarse cotton fabrics are made at Ajmir, Bikánir, Karauli, Jaipur, Jodhpur and every other place of note in Rajputana.

Chanderi, in the Gwalior territory, produces a superior quality of muslin. It is usually left white, but bordered with exceedingly handsome silk and gold lace. In some cases the silk border is coloured differently on either side. Fine muslins in tasteful colours with silk and gold borders are made at Indor. These are only second in quality to those of Chanderi. Cloths of a fine texture, turbans, *Dhotis*, and female dresses are woven at Sarangpur in the Dewas state. These are made of thread spun from the naturally-dyed yellow cotton, the product of *Gossypium herbaceum*, var. *Religiosum*, commonly known by the name of Nankin cotton. These cloths are mostly bordered with silk and they have a great reputation in Central India for their excellence. Turbans and other head-dresses of a fine kind of muslin are made at Orchhá. Check muslins are produced at Gwalior.

Central Provinces have long been famous for their cotton manufactures. "The weaving of fine cotton cloth is the most characteristic manufacture of the

Nágpur, Bhandárá, and Chanda Districts; the cloths of Úmrer (in Nágpur) and Pauni (in Bhandárá) being considered especially good. The art of spinning thread of great fineness is one for which these Districts have long been well known. In 1867 a piece of Chanda thread was exhibited at a local Exhibition of such fineness that a pound's weight of it would reach a distance of 117 miles. The best compliment to its excellence was paid by some gentlemen in the cotton trade, who, notwithstanding that the public were particularly requested not to touch the specimens, succeeded in snipping off pieces of it to carry away as curiosities. The importation of English yarn and the competition of the machine-made yarn of the Nágpur Cotton Mills is reported to have resulted in a great decline in the art of hand-spinning. The weaving industry has not suffered so greatly from this competition, partly because of the intrinsic excellence of the goods manufactured and partly because of the prejudice in favour of wearing them which exists among the better class of Marhattas. The greater part of the woven goods turned out consists of turbans and *Dhotis*, which are distinguished by bearing a border of (generally) dark red silk, on the breadth of which the value of the fabric in great measure depends. These borders are often woven in intricate patterns of different shades of colour. But the manufacture has fallen off under the competition of English-made goods; and it is now not uncommon to attach a locally made silk border to cotton cloths imported from Bombay. The Deputy Commissioner of Bhandárá writes that the cotton-weaving industry has declined very considerably during the past ten years. Not only is the number of articles now turned out much less than formerly, but the value of the goods is very much lower. Pauni used to be especially famous for the finely woven broad-bordered and richly ornamented turbans and *Dhotis* which it produced. Bhandárá, too, used to produce a plentiful supply of turbans and waist-cloths of considerable value. Quantity and quality have now fallen off at both places. The opening of railway communication with Bombay has therefore had the same ill-effect on local weaving as on brass-working, and has greatly harmed the two principal indigenous handicrafts of the Provinces. It is fair, however, to add that it is only the production of fine cotton cloth which appears to have suffered, and that the weaving of the coarse cotton stuffs worn by the agricultural classes seems to have greatly increased in some places. The Deputy Commissioner of Hoshangabad reports that the number of weavers in that town has increased from 116 to 216, and the officer in charge of the Harda Subdivision of the same District writes that the weaving industry was thought to be dying out, but this is not the case. The coarse fabrics which are made are preferred to imported goods by the labouring class for their greater strength and durability."

In the Madras Presidency, the finest muslin is woven at Arni. At present the demand, however, is very small, and the industry is all but extinct. Specimens are now made only to order. The following account of the mode of manufacture adopted in preparing the yarn and in weaving and bleaching the muslin has been supplied to Dr. Bidie by a native of the place:—

"Paruthi cotton, from an indigenous plant, five years old, should be made use of, as, if new cotton be used, the threads will be too thick. The people of Chingleput do not know how to spin this five-year old cotton. The Telugu Parayas of Cherivi Irugalam, Kolladam, Pondava Kham, Chettulpakham of the Trivellor Taluk, and Kannavaram and Timparantakapuram, of the Kalahastri State, are employed in spinning the yarn. The *modus operandi* is as follows: They pull the cotton with the fingers, collect it into a heap, and beat it exactly as common cotton is beaten by cotton-beaters. The dust is collected, placed on a dry rind of the plantain stem, one cubit long, rolled, tied in four or five places with ropes, and laid by. The whole of the cotton is thus dealt with, and kept tied up in bundles in the rind of the plantain stem. They then spin it by means of wheels. These wheels are similar to the ordinary ones, but their spokes and axles are small. A spindle is attached to the wheel, the cotton kept tied in the rind of the plantain stem attached to the spindle, and the wheel put in motion, when the yarn winds itself on the spindle. Four hundred and eighty cubits of yarn are formed on each spindle, and this is a full day's work. Six sticks are pared off thin planks and fixed in the ground, and the yarn on the spindle is wound round these with an instrument called *Pandai* (a reel-like instrument), and then they are formed into *Sidus* (skeins or knots). *Sidus* are of six sorts, the price of the lowest quality being one anna and of the first quality 6¼ annas each. Thus far the Parayas do the work. Their work ends with forming *Sidus*. The subsequent work is performed by the weavers. Six hundred of the *Sidus* are required to manufacture a piece of muslin. What is called a piece of muslin is 16 yards long and 1½ yards broad. The aforesaid *Sidus* are wound upon a *Pandai* and starched. While the yarns are still wet, they are wound upon another *Pandai*, and when dry, they are again starched, and the starching process is thus repeated five times. The starch used is rice starch. This should be filtered through a tight cloth, diluted with fresh water, and then applied. Then skeins are fixed for a distance of 16 yards, and the *Sidus* that have been starched are run into warps. They are then attached to the frame and set in a delicate loom and woven. This is called a *Padugá*. The articles connected with the loom are similar to those used in the manufacture of ordinary cloths. The whole of the apparatus used in weaving the muslin is thin and fine. Starch is not applied to some of the *Sidus*, which are wound on a *Pandai* and then transferred to a dry reed, as long as a finger (this is called a *Kandai* or reel). This unstarched yarn is used as weft. The reel is put into a shuttle made of bamboo and then used in weaving. Three hands are required for weaving the muslin : one should work at the loom, and the other two should stand one on each side of it, and pass the shuttle through. If in the said manner the three persons attend solely to this work, they can weave a cubit a day. To make a *Padugá* and attach it to the loom will take twenty days. The weaving can be completed in a month or thirty-two days. Like the *Sidus*, there are six sorts of muslins, the price of the lower quality being ₨25 and the finest quality ₨200 per piece. Only a few of the weavers at Arni can perform this weaving; all of them cannot. Bleaching is done in the following way:—Muslins of the first, second, and third sorts should not be beaten on stones in washing them. They should be beaten on sand, bundled in the shape of a stone in strong cloth. They are washed in water from springs excavated in river beds. After washing the cloth in the aforesaid manner, it is put into a pot containing a mixture made of half a measure of the juice of *thumbai* (*Leucas aspera*) plant, four measures of water, and five *pollams* of limestone, and boiled for a *jamam* (7½ Indian hours). This is called the process of boiling or steaming. All this work is done by the washermen, but the weaver is present and gives directions. After the cloth is boiled, it is taken out, dipped in water, again beaten on a bundle of sand and left to dry. When it is a little dry it should again be wetted. After this process is repeated for two days, the cloth should again be boiled. In doing so, the *thumbai* juice and the limestone are not necessary, but fresh water should be made use of. The cloth should again be taken out, and steeped for one whole day in four measures of lime-juice. On the following day, it should be taken out, dipped in water, again beaten on a bundle of sand, and alternately allowed to dry, and wetted. If the muslin is subjected to this process for ten days, it becomes white. Thus far the work is carried on by means of the washerman. After this the weaver applies starch to the cloth. On the first day it is dipped in starch and dried. On the following day it should be starched and dried in the same way. After doing this for five days, on the sixth day starch should be applied to it little by little by the hand and allowed to dry. After thus starching the whole of the cloth, it is folded and kept. Twenty days is the time taken up in bleaching the muslin in the aforesaid manner."

In Haidrabad (Deccan) brown-coloured (*khâki*) and other coarse muslins are made at Ráichur. They are very comfortable in the hot weather and are used by the men in making their loose jackets and by the women for wraps. Finer muslins are made at Nandair and other places; they are always salmon coloured.

Dhotis or waist-cloth for men, *Sádis* or women's garments, *Khâns* or bodice pieces, *Lungis* or scarfs, *Susi* or striped fabrics, *Sarpos* or bed-covers, turbans, and other cotton cloths are largely woven all over the

Bombay Presidency. Ahmadabad is noted for *Sádis* and *Dhotis*, Yeolá for *Sádis* and turbans, Sholápur and Ahmadnagar for *Sádis* and *Kháns*, and Karáchi for *Lungis*, *Susis*, and *Sarpos*. Hand-spinning is now practically extinct, and almost all the yarn of which these fabrics are woven is obtained from the Bombay Cotton Mills or from Europe. At Ahmadabad about 900 families follow the trade of weaving, and at Yeolá about 900 looms are at work for the manufacture of *Sádis* and 1,000 for turbans. *Sádis* have generally a border of gold, silk, or coloured cotton thread, and turbans have gold ends. Pieces of cotton-plaids known as the Thána cloth are woven at Thána, a town near Bombay.

In Assam spinning and weaving are done at home, and almost every household has its own spinning wheel and its own loom. Both spinning and weaving are done by women. As in the other Provinces of India, in Assam too English yarn is rapidly taking the place of home-spun thread, except when coarse and particularly durable cloths are required. The cotton grown in the Province is, however, still largely used for domestic purposes. *Dhotis* or waist-cloths, *Chádars* or sheets, wrappers, and shawls—locally called *Barkápars*, *Khaniá-kápar*, *Chelengs*, and *Paridiá-kápar*—napkins called *Gámochás*, scarfs called *Rihá* and a species of petticoat called *Mekhlá* are the articles usually manufactured. *Dhotis* are not generally ornamented, but occasionally coloured patterns are woven on the border. *Chádars* are always plain, except the superior kinds woven by women of respectability for private use, which equal fine muslins in the delicacy of texture, and which are generally embroidered at home. *Bar-kápar* is coarsely woven, but it is a very durable cloth. It is worn by both sexes in the same way as a shawl is worn in Europe. *Khaniá-kápar* is a very finely woven cloth, worn like a shawl, and is elaborately embroidered. *Cheleng* is a similar cloth, but is smaller in size. *Paridiá-kápar* is the finest of all cloths made in Assam.

In the little State of Manipur, on the north-east frontier of India, cotton cloths are woven at home as in Assam.

"Almost every description of cotton cloth is made in this little principality, from fine muslins down to coarse *Daris* or carpets. All classes of women weave, from the wives and daughters of the Mahárájá down to the poorest in the country. Little girls begin to learn at a very early age, and soon attain to great skill. Amongst all but the highest classes the women not only supply their families with cloth, but make for sale also. As a rule, coarse cloths are far cheaper than in British territory, but the finer descriptions are much dearer. The latter are generally made from English thread, which for the better fabrics has almost superseded that of native manufacture. Even for the better class of petticoats English thread is now used. This doubles the price. The cheapness of Manipuri cloths is entirely due to the fact that every woman in the valley employs her spare time in making them instead of in idleness. The Nágá tribes, who utilise their women for field work, are ceasing to manufacture cloth. They buy it instead from the Manipuris, who are now beginning to imitate the Nágá tribal patterns. The Manipuri cloth manufacture is thus artificially kept up by the want of an occupation that pays better."

Like Assam and Manipur, weaving is a home-industry in Burma. The cotton used is almost exclusively that grown in the Province, which, after being cleaned by the aid of a very primitive apparatus, is spun into thread with a spool and a wheel in much the same way as used to be done in Europe. It is then woven into fabrics in a machine exceedingly simple, not unlike the hand-machine formerly in use in Europe. The fabrics woven usually are—*Patsos* or waist-cloths worn by men, about 15 feet long by 3½ feet wide; *Tamein*, worn by women, a sheet of two portions sewn together, 4½ feet long by 5¼ feet broad; *Thindaings* or coverlets; and *Saungs* or thick sheets.

These home-made fabrics are rough, but more durable than the imported fabrics, which latter, however, are preferred by the younger generations and the gay people of the towns for their gaudy colours and ornamental designs.

Silk Fabrics.

Silk, though it might have been originally discovered in China, did not take long to make its way to India. No mention of it is, however, made in the *Vedas*, but it was common at the time when the great epics, the *Rámáyana* and the *Mahábhárata*, were composed. Fabrics are made of the mulberry silk (*Bombyx mori*, &c.), of *Tasar* silk (*Antheræa mylitta*), of *Eri* or silk produced by worms fed upon castor-leaf (*Philosomia ricini*), *Mugá* silk (*Antheræopsis assama*), *Cricula* silk (*Cricula trifenestra*), and Burma silk (*Attacus atlas*). Under the East India Company large quantities of mulberry silk were produced, chiefly in Bengal, and exported to Europe. The industry gradually declined since the abolition of the Company's filatures, and only a few years ago it was in an extremely deplorable state, owing, it is said, to the deterioration which Bengal silk has undergone in quality of late years. The Government of India is now making strenuous efforts to revive the trade by removing the causes of its decline, and if it ever goes back to its former prosperous condition, India will owe a lasting debt of gratitude to Mr. Thomas Wardle of Leek, Staffordshire, for the great exertions he has made in this direction. Mr. Wardle was in this country three years ago, and he was surprised to find that India purchases large quantities of China silk for the more valuable fabrics made in India. He writes:—

"One thought is somewhat saddening with regard to silk in

India at the present time. I have recently travelled over the greater part of India, and I have everywhere found, in all the silk centres, that for the more ornamental silk fabrics Indian silk is not used, but that the manufacturers procure their supplies from China on the one hand and Bokhara on the other. This ought not to be. Bengal is capable of producing silk to a vastly extended degree, not only enough for all the requirements of India, which are really very great, both for weaving, embroidery, and minor purposes, but for a greatly increased export trade. Under European careful supervision the native Indian works beautifully. He cares more for patient manual labour and real handicraft traditional work than he does for progressive thought or invention, and it is not to be wondered at that it has been left to the quicker brain and the desire for development that characterises the people of the West to produce results which find a readier market than his own unaided and unguided efforts can secure."

In Bengal the alluvial Districts in the Ganges valley are the home of the mulberry silk. Maldah, Bogra, Rájsháhi, Murshidabad, Birbhum, and Bardwán have long been famous for their silk manufactures. Sir George Birdwood states that "there is on record that in 1577 Shaikh Bhik, of Maldah, sent three ships of Máldáhi cloth to Russia by the Persian Gulf." Large quantities of silk fabrics are also made in Bánkurá and Midnapur. The hilly tracts in the west of Bengal; chiefly the Districts of Mánbhúm, Singbhúm, and Lohárdágá, form the centre of *Tasar* silk manufacture, while *Eri* has found a congenial home in the Sub-Himalayan regions of North Bengal and Assam. The *Mugá* silk is only produced in the last-named Province. A piece of silk, unbleached and unwashed, is called *Korá*, and a bleached and washed cloth is called *Garad*. *Dhotis* or waist-cloths, *Chádars* or sheets, *Sáris* or cloths worn by women, handkerchiefs, scarfs, gown pieces, *Lungis*, and cloths of different patterns bearing different names form the chief silk manufactures of Bengal. Similar fabrics are also made of *Tasar* silk. *Eri* cloth is coarse when new, but it gets soft and smooth by wear. *Mugá* silk, though rough, is considered the strongest of all silks known in India. A white mulberry silk, 8 yards long, would cost about R20; a twilled gown piece, R20 to R40; one dozen handkerchiefs, R6 to R12; a piece of *Tasar* cloth, 12 yards long, R10; ditto twilled, R20; ditto flowered, R25. Cloths made of pierced mulberry cocoons are called *Matká*, which are considered a purer article than the ordinary silk fabrics, for in the manufacture of it the moths inside the cocoons are not killed. It is therefore largely purchased by the *Jainas* and the *Vaishnavas*, who have the greatest aversion for the destruction of animal life. Midnapur has a reputation for its white mulberry silks. In fact, the silk produced by the worms in March, known by the name of March-*band* or the "March produce," is more glossy, more white, and more soft than that spun in other seasons.

In the North-Western Provinces, silk fabrics are manufactured at Benares and Agra. Benares embroidered silk *Sáris* have a great reputation all over India. Of plain cloths the most important are the yellow waist-cloths called the *Pitámbars*, *Sáris* or cloth worn by women, *Dopattás* or sheets worn like shawls chiefly by women, *Mashru* or cloth with an admixture of cotton worn by Muhammadans, *Sangi* or silk piece for female under-garments, *Gulbadan* or silk piece used for trousers, *Rumáls* or handkerchiefs, scarfs, &c. Striped and check silk cloths called *Susi* and *Gulbadan* are largely manufactured at Agra, where about 300 men and women are engaged in the industry. The raw silk is obtained either from the Panjáb or from Bengal, and the manufactured cloths are exported to other parts of India. Agra silk-weavers are all Muhammadans, who get about 3 annas a day as their wages. The trade is declining owing to competition with European goods. Silk girdles or *Izárbands* are largely made at Agra and are imported to Rajputana and Central India. The industry is many centuries old, but is now falling off.

Silk fabrics are made in many places in the Panjáb, notably at Lahore, Patiálá, Bháwalpur, Multán, Amritsar, Mullári, Pesháwar, Kohát, and Jallandhar. At Lahore a better quality of silk was formerly made than what is manufactured now-a-days. Although the industry has greatly declined, there is still a demand for the inferior fabrics now produced. Striped cloth, called *Gulbadan*, and a self-coloured silk called *Dariyái* are generally made. The silk is made to wash, and lustre is not indispensably necessary. Lahore silk sells from 5 annas to R1-8 per yard. Large quantities of silk are woven at Patiálá, chiefly *Gulbadan* and girdles or *Izárbands*. Bháwalpur, however, is the chief centre of silk-weaving in the Panjáb. Bháwalpur silks are generally striped. They have good substance, but little lustre, and the colours are not always good. "In Multan and Bháwalpur, almost exclusively, the variegated silks are produced; the patterns are checks or stripes with various sprigs or herring-bone patterns on the stripes; gold thread is frequently introduced. The *Shuja-kháni* is a silk of this character. . . . . Commercially speaking, the Bháwalpur silks seem the most likely to be attractive; they are certainly well adapted for curtains and the finer class of hangings, but the cost is somewhat high." *Gulbadan* cloth is largely made at Amritsar. The quality of the fabric has very much deteriorated since the subversion of the Sikh rule in the Panjáb. The Sikh chiefs of former days liked a fabric with a web of 2,400 threads, but what is made now is poor in texture and narrow in breadth, which Mr. Kipling considers "the surest sign of poverty." As stated before, lustre is not a necessary qualification for a good silk, but a stiff, thick silk, with a downy feel on the surface, is what is sought for. *Gulbadan* cloth is always striped; green and crimson, lilac and scarlet, and yellow and crimson being the favourite combinations. Mulléri has long had a reputation for its silk fabrics, and for a mixture of silk and cotton. At Pesháwar, Kohát, Sháhpur, and Bháwalpur and many other places silk *Lungis* are largely made. They are of various colours, and often with golden thread interwoven. *Lungis* are chiefly used for turbans, and "are extensively worn on the Panjáb frontier, and are often adopted by southern folk as handsomer than the ordinary white turban. Some of the arrangements of stripes are, like the Scottish tartans, distinctive of various *Khels* or clans." A smaller turban, called the *Kallapech*, is also made in these Districts. It is worn wound round the conical gold cap called *Kalla*. It is said that there are upwards of one hundred looms at work in Jallandhar for the manufacture of silk fabrics, which are exported to other places. "A dove-coloured, lustreless *Lungi* or *Palas*, with gold border and ends, may be taken as a type of Jallandhar silk-weaving, but other colours are also woven." *Lungis* and other silk fabrics made at Jhelam are highly spoken of. *Khes*, described under cotton fabrics, is also made in silk, mostly in patterns, sometimes plain. Mr. Baden Powell writes:—

> "The *Khes* is also woven in silk, either check pattern in squares, or plain silk, with a gold border, and edged with some fancy pattern edging on either side of the gold; beautiful thick scarlet *Kheses* of the kind are made at Lahore, and are much sought after."

Specimens of wedding dress for Muhammadan bride and bridegroom, made at Batálá in the Gurdáspur District, were sent to the Colonial and Indian Exhibition, "to show one of the rustic uses of the local silk manufactured." Specimens of Chenille work (on wire) were sent to the Colonial and Indian Exhibition from Wazirabad in Siálkot District, consisting of cushions, cigar-cases, boxes, balls, &c. Mr. Baden Powell writes:—

"The Chenille or thin velvet piping is, I believe, imported, and the art consists in arranging lengths of it, as required, in circles, loops, lines, and patterns (the colour and form being according to the taste and design of the workman) on some surface, either of cloth or wood, so as to form a pattern. In this way, the workman will produce on a cushion beautiful groups of flowers and leaves, all made of pieces of Chenille or shades sewn on, the groundwork being filled up uniformly with rows of black Chenille. If the work is on cloth, as for sofa cushions, the Chenille is delicately sewn on silk; if on wood, as is often done with trinket boxes, glove boxes, and also on leather shoes, the Chenille work is stuck on with gum or glue."

It is said that the art was introduced at Wazirabad by an English lady many years ago, and that articles of Chenille work have become very popular with educated natives of India and the Eurasians, although it has no sale among the lower classes of the people or the upper classes of Europeans. Of smaller articles of silk made in the Panjáb are the *Izárband* or netted silk girdles for fastening the trousers; silk cord and tassels called *Sejband*, used to tie the four corners of a bed-sheet to the posts of the bedstead; *Parandá*, a silk pendant or *queue*, consisting of a cluster of silk threads with tassels and ornamented with gold thread and beads, which are worked into women's hair fringes; and buttons and loops for *Chogás*, &c. These are mostly made at *Siálkot*, Gurdáspur, Lahore, Patiálá, and Delhi.

Very little silk is woven either in Rajputana or Central India. A few specimens of silk fabrics, used for the dress of native ladies, coloured in deep crimson on one side and green on the other, were, however, sent to the Colonial and Indian Exhibition from Chanderi, a town within the Gwalior territory. Large quantities of *Tasar* silk are produced in the Central

Provinces, chiefly in the Districts of Seoni, Biláspur, Sambalpur, and Chanda. *Tasar* is woven into fabrics at a number of places in Sambalpur, notably at Barpali. Good cloth is also made in the town of Biláspur, where a colony of weavers was settled some years ago by Mr. Chisholm, when he was Deputy Commissioner of that District. In the Chhattisgarh District *Tasar* silk is very largely used for *Dhotis* or waist-cloths and for coats. Fabrics of mulberry silk are largely woven in Burhánpur. The cloths turned out are similar to those made at Ahmadabad in the Bombay Presidency. Silk borders for cotton *Dhotis* are made at Burhánpur and Nágpur. "The fine cotton cloths made at Pauni and Andhargáon in the Bhandárá and at Umrer in the Nágpur District bear, as a rule, a border of silk, which is generally of a plain dark-red colour, but is occasionally made up in varied colours and patterns. Silk-weaving is therefore, in these places associated with cotton-weaving, and is carried on by the same caste of men (the *Koshtás*). The dark-red colour is obtained by cochineal (*Dánákirmáni*), and the colour produced at Umrer is considered to be the best, mainly, it is said, on account of some peculiar property in the water used there, which gives a brilliancy of tint unobtainable elsewhere. Under ordinary circumstances then, silk-weaving in these places is restricted to the weaving of borders, but if plain silk fabrics are required they can be readily made up to order."

In the Madras Presidency, silk fabrics are made N Salem, Periyakulam in Madura District, Gudur in atellore ·District, Karnúl District,· Conjeveram in Chingleput District, Barhampur in Ganjam District, Trichinopoly, Bellary, Kistna, Arcot, Cuddapah, Vizagapatam, Tanjore, Iyempet, in Tanjore District, and Wallaja in North Arcot District. Fine silk cloths are made at Bellary, which are used to make jackets for women. "The patterns of these, with perhaps a few exceptions, are purely native, and generally in excellent taste, although the colours are very brilliant. White silks, plain and figured, are also made at Conjeveram, and very superior gold-bordered cloths at Madura, Chingleput, and Tanjore. The gold wire used in decorating the Madura cloths is either prepared locally or imported from Europe; the latter is the more brilliant when worked up, and possibly more durable. The gold is most commonly introduced as warp in the borders or spots in the body of the cloth, but when gold ends are wanted, it is worked in as weft."

Silk cloths were in former days largely manufactured in Mysore, and Mysore silk had a reputation for its durability. The industry has, however, declined owing to a silk-worm disease. Most of the villages have still their mulberry gardens, and in Colonel Le Messuriers's opinion, there is an indication of a revival. In the Haidrabad territory silk *Sáris* are made at Ráichur, which are largely used by the better classes. A superior kind of satin-like mixed cloth, called *Mashru*, and an inferior kind called *Sangi*, like those made at Benares, are largely made in Haidrabad. These are used for trousers by Muhammadan ladies and Parsi gentlemen. Silk *Sáris* and bodices are made at Indúr and Zelgandal. Aurangabad has long been noted for its flowered silks, of which one variety known as the *Himru* is largely used by noblemen for coats and by women for bodices.

The following account of silk manufacture in the Bombay Presidency has been furnished by Mr. B. A. Gupte:—

"Silk fabrics, either plain or mixed with gold-thread, are chiefly woven at Yeolá, Poona, Ahmadabad, and Surat, and silk fabrics without any admixture of gold are woven at Tháná, Sáswad, Belgám, Revadándá in Kolaba, Kaládgi in Bijápur, and Sholápur, each containing only a few looms. *Sádis* or dresses for women and *Pitámbars* or dresses for men, which are held purer than cotton, are the chief articles of trade. *Sádis* are cut into pieces 24 to 30 inches long and sold as bodice-pieces or *Kháns.* The silk manufactures of Yeolá are one of the most important of Násik industries, and are estimated to support 4,000 families. *Paithanis* (female silk garbs), *Pitámbars* (sacred cloths for males and females), *Lugdis* (silk *Sádis*), *Phadkis* (female scarfs), and *Kháns* (bodice-pieces) from Yeolá are in considerable demand among the higher classes of natives, not only among the wealthy, who daily wear them, but also among those who appear in them only on festive occasions. The establishment of the industry at Yeolá, which now contains about 925 looms, dates from the beginning of the eighteenth century (1155 H.), when one Raghoji Náik, a relation of the present Patel, by the promise of a monopoly, induced a certain Shámdas Valji, a Gujráti Baniá, to bring silk-weavers to settle at Yeolá. The monopoly was continued by the Peshwá's Government, and new-comers could not start silk looms in Yeolá except by paying the original settlers a fee of £35. Of this amount, 2*s.* 6*d.* went to the Kázi, £1-5*s.* to the Peshwá's Government, and the remainder to the Gujráti silk-weavers for a caste dinner. Under the British rule the monopoly was at first respected. In 1837 the petition of a Northern India-man named Bápu, for leave to open reeling and spinning machines in Yeolá was rejected by the Assistant Collector, and his decision was, on appeal, upheld by the Collector. A further appeal to the Revenue Commissioner was more successful, and in September 1845 Bápu gained leave to set up a machine in Yeolá. On the 26th of January 1848 the Gujrátis filed a suit in the Civil Court for damages. The point was decided in their favour, but on appeal the High Court upset the decision (24th June 1864) and put an end to the monopoly. Since that time many classes of outsiders have taken to silk-weaving, and now there are 250 Khatris, 300 Koshtis, 200 Sális, and 25 Musalmans. All the silk used at Yeolá is imported in the raw state. It is received from three places—China, Bengal, and Persia, through Bombay. The dealers, who are men of means, with capital ranging from £500 to £40,000, make raw silk over to the twister or *Rahálkari*, also called reeler, in whose establishment it is sorted, reeled, and twisted. Silk in the twisted state is called *Sheriá.* It is then handed over to the dyer (*Rangári*). Finally it goes to the weaver (*Mágwála*), by whom it is warped, sized, and woven. The patterns in these fabrics are mostly taken from objects in nature and of daily use, such as *Katári*, from the dagger of that name; *Bugdi* from the gold ornament with pearls worn by women in the ear. At Poona there is a large silk-weaving industry, which has to a great extent competed successfully with Yeolá. Four or five hundred looms are at work; of these nearly two-thirds are owned by Musalmans and the rest by Hindus. Among the Musalmans there are two sub-divisions,—Momins and Julahás,—and among the Hindus there are three—Khatris, Koshtis, and Sális. The dyers of Poona are all Hindus; they have come from Paithan about four or five generations ago. These people invariably use aniline dyes, and this, together with the inferior and cheaper quality of the silk used, give the Poona silk traders a decided advantage over the silk traders of Yeolá. Poona silks are sold to the local traders, who send them to Bombay. Demand for Poona silks is steadily on the increase. Weavers are paid 1*s.* to 2*s.* 6*d.* a yard for the fabric woven according to the pattern. The weavers say that they earn about £1 10*s.* to £2 10*s.* a month each. At Thánå there are only twelve looms at present in the place of about 4,000, which have been noted by early travellers."

A few pieces of bridal dress, called *Patolás,* were sent from Surat to the Colonial and Indian Exhibition. This garment is given to the bride as a present from her maternal uncle. The *Pitámbar* is a piece of silk cloth dyed yellow, and often with a border of some other colour. It is worn by the Hindus when worshipping as well as during the different meals. Silk fabrics are also made at Haidrabad and other towns in Sind. The articles made in that part of the Presidency resemble those of the Panjáb.

The *Eri* and *Mugá* silk fabrics are the specialties of Assam. *Eri* is the produce of the worm which feeds on the castor plant leaves, and *Mugá* of a worm which feeds on the leaves of forest trees, chiefly of that called *Som* (*Machilus odoratissima*). It has not yet been found possible to reel *Eri* cocoons; the yarn is therefore made by spinning. It is uneven and coarse, but the cloth, though rough, is exceedingly durable, for which it is prized by the poorer classes.

Eri fabrics made are—*Barkápar*, the commonest kind of cloth, being a sheet 21 feet by 5 feet, universally worn by men of the peasant class during the cold weather; *Gámochá*, a towel or napkin; *Dukathiá,* a wrapper used by women and children; and *Mekhlá*, worn as a species of under-garment or petticoat by women, usually 7 feet by 4 feet or 6 feet by 3 feet in size. No woman of respectability would willingly engage in the manufacture of *Eri* cloths. They like the *Mugá,* which is as common amongst the rich as *Eri* is among the peasantry. *Mugá* silk is amber in colour, has much more lustre than the *Eri,* and its cocoons can be reeled. It is manufactured by women of all ranks. *Mugá* fabrics generally are—*Dhotis* or waist-cloths of various sizes; *Mekhlás* or an under-garment or petticoat for women, often sewn up like a pillow case with one end free and a hole on the other for the head to slip through; *Rihás*, a scarf for women, often elaborately ornamented by gold and silver embroidery; *Gámochá*, used as a handkerchief; *Erá Barkápar*, a warm wrapper worn by the peasant women in the cold season, made of thread spun from the floss of *Mugá* cocoons and pierced *Mugá* cocoons which do not admit of reeling: it is necessarily a coarse cloth. [See also "Mixed Fabrics," "Dyeing and Calico-printing," and "Brocades."]

Woollen Fabrics.

In India, artistic decorations have never been so profusely lavished on manufactures of sheep-wool as on cotton and silk fabrics. *Pashminá*, of which Kashmir shawls are made, is not sheep-wool, but a soft down found on the goat in Tibet and Central Asia. Sheep-wool has never been in high estimation as a material for clothing. The climate of the plains is unfavourable for the production of sheep-wool of a superior quality, suitable for the manufacture of fine fabrics. Nor do woollen fabrics keep in good preservation in this climate. Mr. Baden Powell noticed it as remarkable that—

> "in the plains during the cold weather natives do not like woollen goods; it is only the poorer classes who resort to the *kambal*, or blanket. Every one who can afford it much prefers wearing several thicknesses of cotton cloth, and coats padded with cotton wool are universally worn."

The reason why the people of India do not largely use wool for winter clothing is because it is neither cheaper nor a better protection from cold than cotton. A common saying goes among up-country people that once there was a dispute between Cold and Wool. Cold bragged to Wool, "However thick you may be I can pierce you." Cotton, who sat there listening, at length asked—"Can you do the same to me?" Cold said in reply—"No, I have nothing to say to you." In the opinion of the people no amount of thick wool can be as warm as quilted cotton.

The chief centre of woollen manufactures in India is of course the Panjáb. Of sheep-wool the most common stuff is the blanket. Indian blankets are not like those made in Europe, and very little attention is paid to softening or felting them. They are coarse and rough. Blankets are not only made in the Panjáb, but also in Rajputana, North-Western Provinces, and more or less in other parts of the country. In the Panjáb they are chiefly made at Lahore, Rohtak, Sirsa, Kasúr, Firozpur, Hushiárpur, Gujránwálá, Ráwalpindi, Jhelam, Núrpur, &c. Among finer stuffs, good blankets and shawls were formerly made of a soft sheep's wool obtained from Rámpur or Basáhir, a hill State in the Panjáb. Considerable quantities of woollen stuffs are now made in the Himálayan States, where the cold demands a warmer clothing than in the plains. Among the woollen clothing made in the hills, "a striking example is to be found in the quaint dress of the Chamba 'gaddi' or mountain shepherd. It is of coarse but stout and warm grey wool, the ample coat or blouse being secured at the waist by a long girdle of dark-brown wool rope felted till all trace of plaiting disappears." Blankets are made at Jaipur, Ajmir, Bikánir, and Jodhpur in Rajputana. In the Ajmir District, blankets made at Todgarh are considered the best. In the North-Western Provinces good blankets are produced in the western Districts, chiefly in Meerut and Muzaffarnagar. Bahraich in Oudh is noted for its woollen manufactures. Coarse blankets are prepared at Arrah, Gya, and Sitámarhi in Bengal. *Loi* is a superior kind of sheep-wool fabric largely used in North-West India as a winter wrapper. It is chiefly made at Lahore, Sirsa, Ludhiáná, and Amritsar. *Pattu* is a woollen cloth of the Panjáb Himálayas used for trousers and coats by the hill people. Gloves, stockings, neckties, *Namdás* or felts, saddle-pads, &c., are made of sheep-wool in the Panjáb. Cloaks are manufactured of this material in Jaipur, and *Sáris* in Ajmir, which the Ját women wear as an under-garment. Bikánir serges are considered the best in Rajputana. Jodhpur makes wrappers and petticoats of sheep-wool. These are prepared by Ját and Vaishnava women in their leisure hours, chiefly at Alai, Khajwáná, Indáná, and other places. Of late they have been largely purchased by Europeans.

In an artistic point of view, the fabrics prepared of the wool or down formed under the hair on the skin of the goat in Tibet and Central Asia are the most important. This wool is called the *Pashminá*, and of it are made the celebrated Kashmir shawls. Besides the regular shawls, which are elaborately embroidered either in loom or by needlework, other kinds of plain fabrics are made of this stuff. Of these the most noted are the *Alwán* or *Yáktárá*, a plain unfelted shawl cloth, of thin twisted thread, and the *Rámpur Chádar*, a plain soft shawl largely purchased by Europeans. *Rámpur Chádar*, or, as it is called by Europeans, *Rámpur shawl*, "is of thin, plain, single thread or twist *pashm* in white, red, and other colours. It may or may not have a shawl border or embroidered corner pieces. The value varies according to quality, and as people are in the habit of demanding cheapness, the use of a soft wool called *wáhabsháhi*, imported from Kabul to adulterate or replace the real shawl wool, is not uncommon. The name 'Rámpur,' is derived from the fact that in former years some fine blankets or shawls made of the soft sheep's wool of the Basáhir Valley (Upper-Satlej, capital Rámpur) used to be sold at Ludhiáná, and the *Pashm Chádars* now sold are an improvement on this, but have kept the name." Another kind of goat-wool cloth is called the *Malidá*. "When *Pashminá* cloth is carefully felted and softened by repeated working and treading with water saponified by soap-nut (*Ritá*, *Sapindus trifoliatus*) it shrinks, felts, and softens, and is called *Malidá* (literally, rubbed fabric); this is used for a variety of articles, and forms the groundwork of the silk-embroidered *Chogás*, capes, jackets, neckties and other embroidered fabrics so common in Kashmir, Amritsar, and Ludhiáná." Besides Kashmir, the chief centres of *Pashminá* manufacture in the Panjáb are Amritsar, Ludhiáná, Lahore, Simla, Núrpur, and Tiloknáth in Kangra District, Jalálpur in Gujrát District, and Dinánagar in Gurdáspur District. The industry is in the hands of the Kashmiris, a large number of whom have settled down in all these places. *Lungis*, scarfs, gloves, stockings, neckties, and other smaller fabrics are also made of *Pashminá* wool. Camels have an inner wool similar to that of the goat, which is made into shawls and *Chogás.*

Goat and camel hair is made into bags, coarse cloths, mats, and ropes, both in the Panjáb and Rajputana. Beyond the frontier, varieties of "bark" and "Urmak" and other camel-hair cloths are made. Blankets of goat hair are produced in the hill Districts of the Panjáb, plain or with check pattern, and ornamented with borders and fringes of cotton often of a pleasing design. Blankets of goats' hair are made by the hill tribes of Nepal, chiefly by the Magars.

Mixed fabrics.

Fabrics of silk and cotton mixed are woven in many places in Bengal. A cloth called *Garbhasuti*, a mixed fabric of cotton and *Tasar* silk, is made in the Districts of Bánkurá and Mánbhúm. A piece 15 yards long would cost about R12. *Garbha-suti* is, however, the general name of mixed fabrics where the warp is cotton and the weft silk. Another mixed fabric known in Bánkurá is the *Asmáni*, which is woven of coloured silk and cotton threads. Bhágalpur is famous for its *Báftá* cloths, which are soft and glossy and largely used for wrappers and coats. *Báftá* means "woven" applied to a plain fabric of silk and cotton mixed. Jute and cotton are mixed in the Rangpur District, and woven into a female garment called *Mekhli*. In Dacca, muslins called *Azizulla* or *Ajiji* have stripes of *Mugá* silk. Various kinds of mixed silk and cotton fabrics are manufactured in the Maldah District. A favourite pattern among the weavers of this place is that called *Serájá*, probably a corruption of Shiraz, the town in Persia of that name, from which place the pattern might have been originally brought. Other designs are often supplemented with the *Serájá* in the same piece of cloth. A very good collection of mixed fabrics was obtained from Maldah for the Melbourne International Exhibition of 1880. Among these the following were the most prominent patterns: *Sádá Serájá*, white ground with crimson *Machhlikántá* or fish-bone stripes; ditto, white ground with orange stripes; *Lál-serájá*, red ground with fish-bone stripes; *Asmáni Serájá*, green and purple ground with fish-bone stripes; *Sabzi-katár*, green ground with fine stripes of checkered crimson and yellow, and having figures resembling the dagger called *Katár* between the stripes; *Lál-katár*, red ground with stripes and figures of *Katár*; *Bulbul-chashm*, gold ground with diamond patterns poetically compared with the eye of the nightingale; *Lál-kadam-phuli*, red ground with flowers in gold colour, resembling those of *Anthocephalus Cadamba*; *Sádá-kadam-phuli*, white ground with crimson flower stripes; *Sáda-bel-phuli*, white ground with figured stripes in crimson, blue and white, and flowers resembling that of *Jasminum Sambac*; *Kálá-pátádár*, purple ground with fish-bone stripes alternately of crimson and white and crimson and yellow; and *Lál-pátádár*, crimson ground with broad fish-bone stripes of gold colour edged with purple and white. The names of other patterns were *Sarbár Serájá*, *Sádá-bara-kadamphuli*, *Safed-kárdár*, *Kálá Machhlikántá*, *Lál-kárdár*, *Kankini*, *&c.*

In the North-Western Provinces, the cloth known as the Azamgarh satinette has of late acquired a good reputation. It is of two kinds,—*viz.*, cotton and *Tasar* mixed, called *Sangi*; and cotton and mulberry silk mixed, called *Gutter*. The industry is old, its origin dating so far back as 1565 A.D. Only six or seven persons are engaged in the weaving of these satinettes, and it is said that, working with the ordinary country loom, they can turn out fabrics to the value of three or four lákhs in a year. The cloth called *Mashru,* already noticed under the head of silk fabrics, is made at Benares and other places. *Mashru* is a cloth of cotton and silk mixed, made specially for the use of the Muhammadans, for it is not lawful for them to wear pure silk. This mixed fabric is also made in the Panjáb, and another kind called *Shujá-khání* or *Sufi.* The last-named fabric is chiefly manufactured at Bháwalpur. Mr. Baden Powell describes it as "exactly like *Gulbadan* (or sometimes *Susí*) pieces, striped on coloured ground; but the fabric is of silk and cotton mixed, the warp being cotton: it is rather stiff and hard, and is glazed with a mucilaginous emulsion of quince seeds." *Khes* is also made of silk and cotton mixed. Flannels and striped sheets of cotton and wool are made in Kashmir. *Sáris* of silk and cotton mixed are commonly woven at Burhánpur in the Central Provinces. They are of great softness and texture, and are made up in a large variety of patterns and colours. *Mashru* cloth is largely made at Ahmadabad in the Bombay Presidency. Mr. Gupte writes:—

> "The word '*Mashru*' comes from Persia and means 'cleverly woven,' a name applied to show the dexterity with which the cotton warp is completely covered with the silk weft so as to render it quite invisible. It is much used by the Musalmans, who are forbidden from wearing unmixed silk fabrics. One variety of this fabric, which is a brocade on a purple ground, is known as *Nawábi-himru,* from the fact of the pattern being exclusively used for the last four generations for the dresses of the Nawábs of Surat."

In Upper India the commonly accepted meaning of *Mashru* is "permitted,"—*i.e.*, being a mixed fabric, Muhammadans are permitted to wear it. Another kind of mixed cloth, called *Iláichá,* is made at Surat of cotton and silk, of which the Bhorá women make their *Barkás,*—*i.e.*, the long muffler with which they cover themselves from head to foot when they go out. Silk and cotton *Sádis*, shot with shades of red and green, are made at Belgám. Mixed *Sádis* are also made at Surat. Of other cotton and silk fabrics may be mentioned the *Chandrakalá* and *Lugde Sádis*, turban cloths, *Kháns* or bodice pieces, *Dhotis* or waist-cloths, *Garbh-suti* cloths, *Lungis*, *Dopattás* or sheets, *Susis*, &c., made at Yeolá, Kaládgi, Ahmadabad, Surat, Poona, and other places.

Dyeing and Calico-printing.

Until recently this was an important industry in many parts of India. It has, however, suffered greatly in competition with European goods. Plain dyeing is practised by a class of people called the *rangrez*, and printing by the *chhipi* or *chhipigar*. The dyers and printers are mostly Muhammadans. The dyes principally used in India are as follows: *Acacia arabica* or *Bábul*, bark and pods; *Acacia catechu*, cutch, extract obtained by boiling the wood; *Adhatoda vasica*, leaves; *Anogeissus latifolia*, leaves; *Areca catechu*, betel-nut, extract from the nuts; *Bixa Orellana*, seeds; *Butea frondosa*, flowers; *Cæsalpinia sappan*, sappan wood; *Carthamus tinctorius*, safflower; *Cedrela toona*, flower; *Coccus cacti*, cochineal; *Coccus lacca*, lac; *Crocus sativus*, saffron; *Curcuma longa*, turmeric root; *Datisca cannabina*, flower; *Indigofera tinctoria*, indigo; *Lawsonia alba*, leaves; *Mallotus Philippinensis*, *Kamilá* powder; *Morinda citrifolia*, *A'l* root; *Nyctanthes arbor-tristis*, *Harsinghár* flower; ochres, red and yellow, called *Multáni*, *Geru*, and *Hirmji*; *Oldenlandia umbellata*, roots; *Phyllanthus emblica*, fruit; *Pterocarpus santalinus*, red sandal-wood; *Punica granatum*, rind of fruit; *Quercus infectorius*, gall-nuts; *Randia dumetorum*, fruit; *Rubia tinctoria*, madder root; *Semecarpus anacardium*, nuts; *Terminalia belerica*, fruit; *Terminalia chebula*, fruit; *Woodfordia floribunda*, flower; yellow arsenic; sulphate of iron; &c. Black may be obtained in conjunction of the following substances: (1) *Morinda citrifolia*, sulphate of iron; *Terminalia chebula* (myrobolam) and alum. Or (2) safflower, sulphate of iron, and myrobolam. Or (3) indigo, sulphate of iron, and myrobolam. Or (4) red earth, sulphate of iron, and myrobolam. Or (5) red earth, sulphate of iron, myrobolam, and alum. Or (6) *Acacia arabica*, pods and black earth. Or (7) sulphate of iron, myrobolam, and alum. Grey is obtained from indigo and oak-galls combined. Lavender—Safflower, oak-galls, and alum. Purple—Indigo and safflower. Maroon—Indigo and safflower in proportions different from the above. Blue—Indigo, vitriol, and lime. Green—Indigo, *Butea frondosa*, and *Nyctanthes arbor-tristis*; or sulphate of iron, turmeric, pomegranate rind, and alum; or turmeric and blue vitriol. Yellow—Turmeric, *Nyctanthes arbor-tristis*, *Butea frondosa*, lime, and acidulated water; or turmeric, pomegranate rind, and alum; or yellow orpiment; or yellow ochre. Orange—Turmeric, safflower, and acidulated water. Pink—Cinnabar. Red—Safflower, madder, myrobolam, and alum; or sappan-wood, myrobolam, and alum; or only lac. Brown—Sulphate of iron, catechu, and myrobolam; or lac and sulphate of iron.

In calico-printing the first process is the washing, which is done by the washerman. The cloth is then bleached by a low-caste people called the Chámárs and washed again. A mordant consisting of myrobolams, galls, and *Acacia arabica* legumes is then applied to the cloth, which when dry is placed on a flat block of wood and beaten with a club to obtain an evenness of surface. The cloth is then printed with different kinds of prepared dyes by means of wooden stamps on which the patterns are cut.

Very little dyeing and printing is done in Bengal. A few dyers and printers from Behar and the North-Western Provinces have opened shops in the principal towns of the Province, especially in Calcutta. Besides Calcutta, the only places in Bengal where cloth-printing is carried on to some extent are the Districts of Patna, Darbhángá, and Sáran. The specimens sent from Patna to the Colonial and Indian Exhibition shewed that in that place fabrics are only stamped in colours. But in Calcutta, the cloths, after being stamped, are boiled in a dye solution that imparts to them a reddish tinge which is a fast colour. Tinsel-printing is largely done in Calcutta. The art consists of stamping on the cloth, by a hand-block, a preparation of gum, and then fixing, upon the patterns thus formed in gum, false gold or silver leaf. Before stamping, the cloth is always dyed a plain colour. Gold foil is generally applied on a violet ground and silver on red. The patterns are either floral or geometrical, but always bold, striking, and tasteful. Tinsel cloths may be denominated as mock embroidery in gold or silver.

In the North-Western Provinces dyeing and calico-printing is carried on on a more or less extensive scale in most of the towns. Farukhabad, Kanauj, and Lucknow are, however, the chief centres of this industry. At Lucknow printing is generally done on English cloth, while Kanauj and Farukhabad chintzes are of coarse rough cloths, called *Gazi*, *Gárhá*, and *Dhoti-jorá*, woven in the country. Good prints are also made at Jahángirabad in Bulandshahr and Jafarganj in Fatehpur District. Printed cloths are generally known by the name of *Fard* and *Razái*, sheets worn as shawls in the cold weather, quilted or not; *Liháf*, a night cover in the cold weather, quilted, and used as a substitute for blankets; *Toshak*, quilted and made into a thin mattress; *Pálangposh*, or bed-cover, thrown over the bed during the day, to keep off dust, with which the atmosphere of India is laden for the greater part of the year; *Jázim* and *Farsh*, printed coarse cloths, spread on the floor; *Shámiáná*, used for awning; *Chhint Zardá*, cloth dyed with yellow ochre, made into tents. Many of these printed cloths are suited for curtains and dados in European houses, specially the yellow prints of Lucknow and the cloths dyed with *A'l* (*Morinda citrifolia*) and country sulphate of iron in Bulandshahr. The coarse printed cloths of Farukhabad and Kanauj would make good dados. At present Lucknow and Farukhabad export large quantities of their stamped fabrics to other Provinces.

As an illustration of the different kinds of prints manufactured in the several towns of the North-Western Provinces, a list might be given of the fabrics turned out in a few taken at random: Lucknow—*Fard*, *Razái*, *Liháf*, and *Pálangposh*, mentioned above. Farukhabad—*Fard; Liháf; Bund-udi*, used for petticoats, chiefly by village women, patterns of red on a reddish ground; *Bund-surkh*, a similar cloth; and *Chhint-Zardá*, cloths with yellow patterns used for tents. Kanauj—*Chhint-Kandi*, on English cloth, used for female dress by the Márwáris; *Chhint-Butedár*, made into shirts and coats; *Pálangposh; Liháf; Toshak;* and *Fard*. Tirwá Thatiá in Farukhabad District—*Fard*, fast; *Fard*, fleeting; and *Chhint-Momi*, for female dress. Bishangarh in Farukhabad District—*Chhint-Nimser*, used for female dress. Mau-Ránipur in Jhánsi District—*Kharuá*, country cloth dyed red with *Morinda citrifolia* (*Ál* root), used for mattresses and pillows; *Nathni*, *Chapetá*, and *Chhint-Agrewar*, printed country cloths, used for female dress. Órái in Jalaun District—

Golbuti, on country cloth, used for shirts and female dresses; *Shámiáná*, for tents and awnings; *Toshak*, for mattresses; *Jázim*, for floor-cloths; *Dhoti-jorá-Zanáná*, for female cloth; *Angochhá*, for napkins; and *Sálu*, a fine English cloth dyed red, or the turkey red of India. The names of other towns where the industry of calico-printing is more or less an important one are—Káshipur in Tarái District; Aligarh and Atrauli in Aligarh District; Agra; Muttra and Brindában in Muttra District; Mainpuri; Allahabad, Soron, Phulpur, and Mandá in Allahabad District; Fatehpur, Kaliánpur, and Jafarganj in Fatehpur District; Cawnpore; Chándpur and Najibabad in Bijnor District; Sháhjahánpur; Mirzapur; Muzaffarnagar; Deoband in Sahåranpur District; Khurjá and Jahángirabad in Bulandshahr District; Bágpat in Meerut District; Etawa; Banda and Pailáni in Banda District; Jaunpur; Benares; &c.

Of plain dyed cloths, the *Kharuá* and the *Sálu* are the most important, as there is a large export trade in these fabrics. They are both red, dyed with *Ál* root (*Morinda citrifolia*), colour fast, the former in coarse country cloth, used for mattresses and pillows; the latter in fine English cloth, used for turbans, winter quilts, &c. *Sálu* is sometimes dyed a fleeting colour with safflower. English turkey red is gradually ousting the *Sálu* from the market.

Besides stamping with blocks, another process of dyeing and producing patterns in colours followed in these and other Provinces is that of making knots on the cloth to be coloured. It is known as the *Bandháná* process, and the spotted cloth produced by it is called the *Chunri* cloth. The process has been described as follows:—

"Cloth to be dyed is first of all washed, and the places on which spots are to be made are marked out with red earth.

The spots are produced by isolating these places from the dye in which the cloth is dipped, and this is done by tying them up in knots—a process requiring considerable ingenuity, generally done by females. In this way not only can white spots be produced on a coloured field, but spots of one colour on a field of another. The whole is, for instance, first dyed yellow; the knots are then tied, and it is then dyed red. This will give yellow spots on a red ground. Instead of spots, lines are often made, and in the spots themselves there is a great variety, since they may be of any shape and any size. The borders are often dyed in different colours from those of the spots or field, which gives the cloth a very picturesque appearance. The *Chunri* is worn by women only; the place where it is chiefly manufactured is Muttra, and large quantities are sold at the July festivals of that sacred city in honour of the birthday of its patron deity, Krishna. The principal dyes used in colouring *Chunri* are oil, madder, safflower, and sappan-wood."

Calico-printing is as extensively practised in the Panjáb as in the North-Western Provinces. The chintzes turned out are about the same, and there is little or no difference in the materials used and in the process followed. Mr. Kipling writes:—

"There are few crafts more widely practised than cotton-printing, which is found in the small villages of remote Districts as well as in large towns. At Kot Kamáliá in the Montgomery District and Sultánpur in the Kapurthala State, two comparatively insignificant places, the best work is produced. The printing is done, of course, entirely by hand, and the dyes used are indigenous in nearly all cases. The patterns vary considerably. Those of the Ambala District on narrow widths are 'all-over' diapers or stripes and are principally sold in the hills. The Sultánpur work is often in two colours only, a terra-cotta red on a salmon or ivory ground, and is eminently suited for wall hangings, *dados* or *dewargirs*, as they are called by native workmen. Other examples are from Lahore, Multan, Hassan Abdal, Siálkot, Amritsar, &c. In Kot Kamáliá *pardás* are made partly of hand brush-work, aiding the black in the production of a large tree, as in the hand-painted *persiennes* of a hundred years ago imported from Persia. The chief native use of cotton print is in the form of an *abra*, a large oblong quilt, which, wadded with cotton, forms a winter wrap. It is now, however, largely used for lining the walls of European houses, and no other means of decoration produces so warm and rich an effect at so cheap a rate. The dyes used in the printing protect the cloth from insects, and when tightly stretched they are not found to harbour dust. The trade has greatly improved of late years, and received an impulse from the Panjáb Exhibition of 1881-82.

"Another variety eminently suited for decorative purposes is the gold and tinsel printing done at Delhi, Kangra, Rohtak, Lahore, and other places. This is printed with wooden blocks in a *massála*, chiefly composed of glue, which serves as a gold size, on which gold, silver, or tinsel-leaf is applied. Fabrics of this kind will not, of course, bear washing. The natives use them for wedding gear, but they are coming into favour for *portieres*, curtains, and panelling in English houses. Another curious variety, which, though not cotton-printing strictly speaking, may be conveniently noted here, is the lac and colour painting on red and blue cotton fabrics produced in the Peshâwar District. Blocks are not used, but red, yellow, and other colours in a thick sticky pigment are applied in bold semi-barbaric patterns, on which, as they dry, *abrak* or powdered talc is sprinkled.

"It should be noted that, contrary to common belief, few of the colours used in native cotton-printing are permanent. The red from madder, blue from indigo, turquoise from copper, and black from iron, are often fairly fast, while greens and yellows are fugitive. No glazing is applied to coloured work as in Persian, Masulipatam, and English chintzes. The white *Gháti* or 'long cloth' of Rahon, Jallandhar, on the other hand, is very highly glazed."

The average price of printed cotton in the Panjáb is ten annas per square yard. Hand-painted cloths for use as *Abras* or winter quilts are made at Firozpur, and they are described as "curious examples of a very elementary kind of decoration." In connection with hand-painted fabrics may be mentioned what is known as the "Afridi lac cloth," produced in the Pesháwar District, already noticed in Mr. Kipling's account quoted above. It is described as the only instance in which linseed oil is used in the art of colouring.

"This work is not peculiar to the Panjáb frontier, but is practised by Hindus at Ahmadabad and Morvi, in the Bombay

Presidency. At Násik a perforated stamp at the end of a tube full of colour produces a pattern on a similar principle to the perforated cylinders used to make patterns in front of thresholds, but in one case the colour is a dry powder, and in the other it is mixed with linseed oil. As the paint dries, powdered mica is sprinkled over it. The Pesháwar work is all traced with a stick, no stamps or tubes being used, and the original colours, before the attention of tradespeople was drawn to it, were always good. The work is more durable than might be supposed, and some specimens received from Bannu for the Colonial and Indian Exhibition were really fine in colour. Much of the Pesháwar work is very poor."

Kashmir printed fabrics have suddenly acquired a well-deserved reputation both in India and in England. It is said their introduction in England for decorative purposes is due to Mr. Purdon Clarke. They are made at Sambar, a small town at the foot of the hills, some thirty miles south of Jammu. "The demand for them has recently been so great that the Kashmir Government has practically made a monopoly of the sale, and now charges R14 a piece for them, the old price having been from R9 to R10."

In Rajputana, Sángánir in Jaipur is famous for its printed fabrics. Both English and country cloths are used for the purposes of printing, but largely the latter. *Ál* root is extensively used as a dye. There is an export trade in Sángánir calicoes. Jaipur itself, as well as Bagru, another town in the State, produces a quantity of chintzes. Knot-dyeing is also practised in Jaipur to a large extent. Barar, a town in the Kota State, turns out large quantities of dyed and printed fabrics. The industry gives employment to 108 families of the Khatri caste. Knot-dyed cloths of very intricate patterns, often consisting of pagodas, trees, animals, and birds, are produced in two or three different colours. Prices vary from R4 upwards. A coarse country cloth, called *Takri*, like the *Gárhá* of Upper India, is largely employed in Ajmir for purposes of printing. Female garments, bed-covers, and floor-cloths are extensively made of it. Colours are chiefly derived from *Ál*, madder, or *Majith* (*Rubia tinctoria*), indigo, and turmeric. Calicoes printed at Nayánagar are the best in the Ajmir District. Cloths are dyed and printed at Sambhar, Jodhpur, and other towns in Marwar. Coarse calicoes are printed at Gwalior, Ratlám, Ujjain, Mundasur, Indor, and other towns in Central India. The dyed cloths of Gwalior are of many varieties, and some of the pale shades are very pretty. Ujjain and Mundasur stamped cloths also shew a considerable variety of patterns. Printing in mock silver and gold leaf is extensively practised in Rajputana and Central India. Chanda in the Central Provinces turns out large quantities of printed fabrics, on coarse country cloths, in colours chiefly derived from *Ál* (*Morinda citrifolia*). They are generally used for female garments, druggets, curtains, and bed-quilts. Sambalpur makes a coloured cotton cloth, called *Lugá*, of a very curious design. These are worn by the women of Orissa.

Chintzes are made in many places in the Madras Presidency, chiefly at Wallaja, Arcot, Mederpauk, Timpur, Anantpur, Kumbakonum, Salem, Chingleput, Cuddapah, Coconada, Trichinopoly, and Godávari. Dr. Bidie makes the following general remarks on the subject :—

"Amongst Hindus everything connected with clothing is more or less regulated by the ancient and rigid laws of caste, so that the articles in this class also possess more or less of an ethnological interest. The brilliancy of the colours and their grouping in Indian textile fabrics are generally very different from European conceptions, but it will be found that some of their most characteristic designs are, so far as the choice and arrangement of colours are concerned, copies from nature, and therefore not unpleasant. The results, however, are often so remarkable that no European would venture to wear articles presenting such combinations, although on a dark-skinned people they do not seem at all out of place, and often have a most picturesque effect. As India is the botanical source of the cotton plant, so from remote ages her people have used its fleecy wool in the manufacture of cloth. From India the art of cotton manufacture travelled to Egypt and Assyria. In the thirteenth century the Italians were making attempts to imitate Indian cotton goods; but it was only in the end of the seventeenth century that the art found a footing in Scotland and England. Various allusions are made in the works of travellers to the cotton manufactures of Southern India. Tavernier, a dealer in precious stones, who travelled in India about the middle, and Dr. Fryer who visited it in the end, of the seventeenth century, both speak of the common cotton manufactures as *Calicuts*—a term derived from the place at which they were originally made. Tavernier ('Travels in India,' page 126) says: 'Chites or painted Calicuts, which they call Calmendar—that is to say, done with a pencil—are made in the kingdom of Golconda, and particularly about Masulipatam. These chites serve for coverlets for beds, for sofas or table-cloths after the country fashion, pillow-covers, handkerchiefs, but more specially for waistcoats, as well for the men and women in Persia.'"

The *Calmendar* (*Kalmdár, i.e.*, made with a pen) of Tavernier is the celebrated Madras Palampore. As its name implies, Palampore is used as a bed-cover. Stamped cloth made to serve the same purpose is called *Pálang-posh* in Upper India. Palampores were made formerly in a much more artistic way than at the present day, both as regards the composition of their complex patterns and their colouring. The most interesting point in the Palampores is the mythological scenes with figures in the Dravidian style, and their descriptions in the vernacular language. Dr. Bidie writes:—

"In some cases the figures are printed on the cloth with wooden blocks, but all the finer Palampores are prepared by stencilling and hand-painting. The stencil plates are made of stout pieces of paper. On these the outlines of the pattern are first traced in ink and then perforated with minute holes in the most accurate manner with a fine needle. The stencil is then complete, and when in use, is placed on the cloth and covered with charcoal in very fine powder, which is rubbed so as to make it pass through the minute perforations and leave a tracing. The rest of the work is done entirely by hand, and thus considerable scope is given for the exhibition of individual taste in the selection and grouping of colours. The Kalahastri Palampores contain mythological scenes, and are full of descriptions of these in the vernacular. Some of the more expensive Masulipatam-made Palampores are virtually hand-painted pictures on cloth. The principal places of Palampore manufacture are Eleimbedu in Chingleput District; Karnúl, Kalahastri, and Wallaja in North Arcot District; Anantpur and Tirupapiliym in South Arcot District; Jammalamadugu and Cuddapah in Cuddapah District; Kistna, Masulipatam, and Godávari." A hand-painted Palampore costs R15 to R20.

In the Bombay Presidency, calico-printing is carried on at Ahmadabad, Kaira, Baroda, Broach, Malegám, Kach, and in some of the Kathiawar States. *Sádis*, or the cloths worn by women, are printed on fine English fabrics, and *Jázims* or floor-cloths on coarse country stuffs. *Jázims* are well suited for use as dados in European houses. "At Kaira 400 Hindu and 150 Musalman families are engaged in calico-printing. The printing is remarkably well done, clear, and not blurred, and is superior to that of either Ahmadabad or Broach."

Wool and silk fabrics are generally dyed in plain colours; they are rarely stamped like chintzes. The superior fabrics made of these materials are mostly woven of coloured threads, plain, or with patterns brought out in the loom or wrought by needle embroidery. Silk fabrics are generally preferred dyed. The shot silks known as *Dhup-chháyá* or "sun and shade" and *Mayurkanthi* or "peacock's neck" are much admired by Indians, though not liked by Europeans. Other names of dyed silk fabrics to be found chiefly in Bengal are *Beguni*, a violet colour like that of the fruit of the egg-plant (*Solanum Melongena*); *Lál ásmáni* or "red sky;" *Mauj-lahar*, or "chequered ripple;" *Chánd-tárá*, or "moon and stars"—*i.e.*, of a spotted or powdered pattern ; *Suti-phulal*, or "flower-threaded ;" *Panchpát*, or "five-leaved ;" *Narunsi*, or "nail-cutter-like"—*i.e.*, with stripes or lines as fine as the edge of a nail cutter ; *Phulal* or "Flower-like ;" *Jhilmili*, "barred" or gauze-like ; *Chauphuli*, or "four-flowered ;" *Lahariá*, or "wavy ;" &c., &c. Wool is dyed with galls, sulphate of iron, indigo, turmeric, lac, cochineal, *Butea frondosa* flower, &c. The dyes used to colour silk are *Kamilá* (*Mallotus Phillipinensis* powder), cochineal, turmeric, *Akalber* (*Datiscus cannabinus*), *Harsinghár* (*Nyctanthes arbor-tristis*), indigo, *Asbarg* (*Delphinium ajacis*), sulphate of iron, gall-nuts, &c. A substance called *Tezáb*, being a distillation from saltpetre, sal ammoniac, sulphate of iron, and alum, is largely used in dyeing wool. English chemicals, such as sulphuric acid, sulphyndilic acid, &c., are also used. Aniline dyes are now being extensively employed both in dyeing silk and wool. The ease, the small cost, the rapidity and the simplicity of working, with which dyeing can be accomplished by the use of aniline colours, have recommended them to the dyers, and the brilliancy of tints they produce has recommended them to the ordinary consumers. In Bengal, wherever silk is produced and woven, silk-dyeing is carried on. Both mulberry and *Tasar* silks are dyed. Undyed *Tasar* silk is, however, preferred. Weaving of coloured silk thread into patterned fabrics is done by machine at a place called Ultádingi, in the suburbs of Calcutta. The enterprising proprietor of the establishment, Kasim Ali Sahib, hails from Surat. He has brought the machines from Europe. The fabrics made here are for use in Burma, the people of which country prefer brilliant colours yielded by the aniline dyes to sober hues derived from vegetable substances. Aniline colours are therefore used here. Large quantities of undyed fabrics are also woven in this mill, some of which are afterwards hand-printed by blocks made of tamarind wood. The patterns are floral, designed by the proprietor himself, and the blocks are prepared by men in his employ. Patterns have frequently to be changed as fashion changes in Burma. A kind of printed silk made and sold in Bengal is called *Námábali* or silk sheet on which names of deities have been stamped all over with a wooden block. It is worn as a wrap by old Hindus. Silk handkerchiefs and scarfs were in former days extensively dyed by the *Bandháná* or knot-dyeing process for export to Europe. Such articles are not now in fashion. In the North-Western Provinces, silk-dyeing is practised both at Benares and Agra,—*i.e.*, wherever weaving of silk fabrics is carried on. So in the Panjáb. In the Central Provinces and Bombay, fine cotton cloths have, as a rule, a silk border, generally of a plain dark-red colour, but occasionally made up of varied colours and patterns. The dark red is obtained from cochineal, and the colour produced at Umrer near Nágpur is considered to be the best, "mainly," it is said, "on account of some peculiar property in the water used there, which gives a brilliancy of tint unobtainable elsewhere." In the Bombay Presidency, among other fabrics, the *Patolá*, or bride's garment, of differnt patterns, is woven of coloured silk threads. Mr. Gupte has supplied the following information about the manufacture of this silk cloth :—

"It is woven with warps and wefts which have been separately tied and dyed by the *Bandháná* or knot-dyeing process. The dyer takes a small bundle of the warp after it has been dyed in the lightest colour, and draws in pencil across it some lines at measured distances, according to the design to be produced. His wife then ties the silk, along the spaces marked, tightly round with cotton thread, through which the dye will not penetrate. It is then dyed with the next darker colour found upon the warp, and the process is repeated until the darkest colour is reached. The weft is then treated in the same way, being so tied and dyed that, in the loom, when it crosses the warp, each of its colours may exactly come in contact with the same colour in the warp. The little bundles of warp have next to be arranged in the loom by the weaver, who then takes the little bundles of weft one at a time, using each in its own place through the design."

Patolá cloths are largely made in Surat, Baroda, Cambay, Ahmadabad, and Broach. The *Pitámbar* or the yellow waist-cloth, though, strictly speaking, should be of natural yellow, the usual colour of the mulberry silk, is now artificially dyed, not only yellow, but also red, green, purple, orange, or black. Bi-coloured *Pitámbars,—i.e.*, yellow on one side and crimson on the other—are made at Yeolá. A specimen of this was sent to the Colonial and Indian Exhibition. Mr. Gupte states that the yellow dye withstood the sun perfectly throughout the whole of the summer, and it was declared by experts that the crimson was also beautifully dyed.

Wool is dyed for shawls and carpets. The process of *Pashminá* wool dyeing for shawl manufacture, as formerly practised in Kashmir, is described as follows by Mr. Moorcroft, quoted by Mr. Baden Powell in his "Panjáb Manufactures":—

"The dyer prepares the yarn by steeping in clean cold water. He professes to be able to give it sixty-four tints, most of which are permanent. Each has a separate denomination, as for instance—the crimson is termed *Gulánár* (pomegranate flower); the best kind is derived from cochineal, imported from Hindustan; inferior tints are from lac and *Kirmis* (Chermes), distinguished as *Kirmisi*, *Kirmdana*, and *Kirmisi* lac, or cochineal or lac chermes: logwood is used for other red dyes; blues or greens are dyed with indigo, or colouring matter extracted by boiling from European broadcloth. Logwood is imported from Multan and indigo from India. Safflower and saffron, growing in the Province, furnish means of various tints of orange, yellow, &c. The occupation of a dyer is invariably hereditary. The whiter and finer the fibre of the wool, and the finer the yarn into which it is made, the more capable, it is said, to be of receiving a brilliant dye, and this is one reason why the fine white wool of the goat is preferred to that of the sheep."

Aniline dyes are now largely employed in colouring wool, specially that used for carpet-weaving.

Lace, Borders and Edgings.

The preparation of gold and silver wire and of *Kálábatun* has been described under "Manufactures in Metal." Gold and silver wire is used in lace-making, and *Kálábatun* in the weaving of brocades and cloths of gold and silver, also in embroidery. *Lace*, as understood in Europe, was not known in India. Its manufacture has only been lately introduced into the country, chiefly among the native Christians of Madras. Specimens of white lace, black silk and gold lace, and purely gold lace, were sent from Madras to the Calcutta International Exhibition. They were made by Indian girls in the Christian Mission Schools, and the work was admirably good. All were of European patterns. Dr. Bidie is of opinion that "the industry, if conducted under suitable guidance and with good thread, promises to become of some importance, as labour is comparatively cheap in India, and this sort of work admirably suited for the patient and neat-handed Hindu." That the manufacture of lace can be made a profitable industry in India seems to be beyond any doubt. Great Britain annually imports more than a million's worth of lace from Holland, Belgium, and France. Her poor people of India might with a little encouragement get a share in this important trade. There are thousands of high-caste widows in this country who would gladly employ their dexterous fingers from morning to evening to earn only a penny a day. If carefully advanced, any measure to teach the people to make lace for

European use will be no doubt gladly accepted by the people themselves. In Upper India, lace for European use is made at Delhi, Agra, and Lucknow. The word has been transformed into *Lais*. It is made on a warp of yellow silk, with gold or silver wire for woof. This lace is used for military and civil uniforms, but European lace is now largely employed for the purpose.

Lace, ribbons, borders, and edgings for Indian use are known by the names of *Gotá*, *Kinárá*, *Anchal*, &c. They are of various breadths and patterns, and are woven in a tiny loom with silk thread for the warp and gold or silver wire for the woof, or *vice versâ*. Dacca, Murshidabad, Patna. Benares, Lucknow, Agra, Delhi, Lahore, Jaipur, Burhánpur, Haidrabad in Sind, Surat, Ahmadabad, and Aurangabad are the chief centres of Indian lace manufacture. *Gotá* and *Kinárá* are chiefly used as borders for female garments. If gold wire is twisted with red or orange silk thread, the *Kálábatun* is known by the name of *Surkh* or *Sunheri*. If silver wire is twisted with white silk, the *Kálábatun* is called *Sufed* or *Rupali*. The lace made from each bears the same name. The narrowest ribbon is the *Dhanak* and the widest the *Anchal*, which is used as a border for that side of the *Sári* which is thrown over the left shoulder. Intermediate breadths and patterns are numerous. *Lachká*, *Patri*, *Bankri*, *Pathá*, *Kiran*, *Paimak*, &c., are well-known names. *Gokhru* and *Gangá-Jamuná* are favourite patterns in lace manufacture. Other patterns, chiefly of gold lace for European use, are known by the names of Bunch Pattern, Folding Pattern, Grape Leaf Pattern, Lion Pattern, Tree Pattern, Diamond Bunch Pattern, Horse Pattern, Peacock Pattern, &c. A collection of these patterns was sent to the Calcutta International Exhibition from Lucknow. At Agra lace-making has been carried on from time immemorial. It gives employment to about 6,000 persons. Thin gold-woven ribbons, called *Sarpech*, are worn on the head by bridegrooms, as also plumes made of finely-cut silver leaf. The distinction of wearing *Sarpech* belongs by right to the King, but as in the East the bridegroom is considered the king of the day, he is allowed to bedeck himself with the royal robe. Large quantities of spurious lace, of the same colours, breadths, and patterns as the real ones, are made of imported tinsel. These are mostly used in the decoration of caps. Borders for *Dhotis* and *Sáris*, either of dyed silk, plain or patterned, or of silk and gold, are woven at Umrer and Burhánpur in the Central Provinces, and at Ahmadabad, Surat, Yeolá, and Poona in the Bombay Presidency. These go by the name of *Kor*, *Kinárá*, *Tás*, *Lappo*, *Phit*, and *Pallav*. The borders are sewn on to cotton or silk fabrics woven in the country, sometimes on English cloths. The designs are of many kinds and are known by different names. For instance, *Kor* was received from Ahmadabad for the Calcutta International Exhibition with *Keri Khajuri ne toran* pattern, or mango pattern, diamond-shaped, with three-lobed pendants; pea and mango pattern; jasmine pattern; peacock pattern; &c. The variety of patterns in the Surat borders is equally interesting. Shawl borders, called *Kinárá*, or *Háshiá*, of different breadths, colours, and patterns, are woven in Kashmir, as well as in all those places in the Panjáb where shawls are manufactured. Peacock feather ribbons and trimmings are now made at Jhánsi, but the work does not seem to be getting into favour.

Brocades and Cloths of Gold and Silver.

Silk fabrics with raised patterns are called brocades. Gold or silver cloths—*i.e.*, silk woven with gold or silver thread—are known in India by the name of *Kinkhábs* (kincob). Silk brocades are made wherever silken stuffs are manufactured on an extensive scale. Murshidabad, Benares, Bháwalpur, Multan, Ahmadabad, Surat, Yeolá, Poona, and Aurangabad are the places most noted for silk brocades. *Sáris*, made at Báluchar near Murshidabad, with flowers and figures, were a short time ago highly appreciated by Bengal ladies, but these have now very nearly been ousted from the market by cheap "pine-apple" cloths imported from England. Benares *Sáris* still maintain their old reputation, but it is the fabrics with gold and silver flowers that are mostly sought after. Panjáb patterned silks are known by the name of *Shujákháni*, noted under "Mixed Fabrics." In the Bombay Presidency *Sádis* and bodice pieces are generally made with patterns. Aurangabad still maintains its reputation for flowered silks. A patterned silk called *Himru*, already noticed under "Mixed Fabrics," is largely used by rich men for coats and by ladies for bodices. Some good *Himru* silks have been sent to the Glasgow International Exhibition from Surat. Mr. Gupte describes them as brocades of great beauty and interest. He states:—

"They are much worn by rich Arabs, who import them from Surat. The colourings are of great delicacy, and the designs very characteristic. Much taste is shown in the use of the various colours, not only in their disposition in the designs, but in their respective tones, in which there is thorough harmony. They are all studies and are exquisite stuffs. With regard to the designs, they may be described as of Arab or Muhammadan forms, chiefly geometrical, for even in those of the more floriated treatment there is more or less of geometrical spacing."

Gold and silver wire and *Kálábatun* thread are often introduced in the manufacture of the more valuable fabrics. Sometimes a few bands of gold are put at the end of a cotton muslin or a silk fabric. Panjáb

Lungis, even the common ones, bear a few bands of gold just at a little distance from the ends. But the ends of the more costly ones are entirely woven in gold, and as these are chiefly used for turbans, one end with the gold is allowed to hang behind, with an effect at once picturesque and becoming. In Bombay, Central Provinces, and the whole of South India, gold is almost invariably introduced as a border into superior fabrics made of cotton or silk. In the *Kinkhábs*, however, gold or silver is worked on a silk basis all through the piece, practically forming it in all appearance into a cloth of gold or silver. By gold is meant the silver wire with a gold coating, as described under the head of "Manufactures in Metal." Silver brocades are made with silver wire without the gold coating. False gold and silver *Kinkhábs* are made of copper wire gilt, mostly imported. *Kinkhábs* were in former days extensively used by rich men for their dress, but English education is rapidly modifying the tastes of the people, not only of those who can afford to wear such costly cloths, but of those too who are expected to look upon such gorgeous apparel with admiration and awe. The one by choice would now prefer simplicity and sobriety in personal appearance, while very probably the other would stare at a shining dress with a contemptuous sneer. The demand for gold and silver cloths is now decreasing, as of many other Indian art-manufactures, among the people themselves. Besides dresses for wealthy people, gold and silver brocades were formerly used for elephant and horse trappings. In Bengal, gold and silver brocades are made at Murshidabad, but in Northern India Benares is the chief seat of this manufacture. Its embroidered silks and brocades have long been famous all over the world. The varieties of brocades woven at Benares are numerous. Some are rose-coloured, some purple, some black, and some white. The patterns in some are spangled, which are known by the name of *Butedár,* while through others run scrolls of foliage and flower. These are called *Beldár.* Then there is the hunting pattern called *Shikárgah.* Other patterns are known by the names of *Janglá*, *Miná*, *Jáldár*, &c. It is estimated that upwards of 2,750 workmen find employment in the manufacture of silk fabrics and gold and silver brocades in Benares. Balbhadra Dás is the principal brocade merchant in this city. Lucknow also makes some brocades, but the industry there is not so important as in Benares. As Benares is in the north, Ahmadabad and Surat are in the south of India famous for their *Kinkhábs*. Sir George Birdwood mentions a piece belonging to the Prince of Wales "as one of the most sumptuous ever seen in Europe. It is of Ahmadabad work, rich with gold and gay with colours, and was presented to the Prince by the young Gaikwar of Baroda." About 500 to 600 looms are at work at Ahmadabad for the manufacture of *Kinkhábs,* while in Surat 900 to 1,000 looms are engaged to weave the same material. At Ahmadabad, "*Kinkháb* with the woof either of gold or silver only is woven, while at Surat the variety with gold and silver thread, as well as that with silk alone, is manufactured." A gold brocade thinner than the *Kinkháb* is called *Khand.* Both at Ahmadabad and Surat, *Kinkhábs* and *Khands* of various patterns are manufactured. The pattern *Chánd-tárá*, *i.e.*, "moon and stars," so named from the representations of heavenly bodies figuring on the cloth, was noticed by Sir George Birdwood. On the *Kinkhábs* of Ahmadabad and Surat the patterns commonly seen are *Chasamphul* or "eye-flower," *Mohorbuti* or "gold coin," *Keri* or "mango," &c. *Khands* are also made of many patterns. Aurangabad in the Haidrabad State has long been famous for its gold cloth.

Embroidery.

Embroidery is either worked in loom or wrought by needle-work. On cotton fabrics the patterns are made of cotton, silk, or gold or silver wire twisted with silk thread called the *Kálábatun.* Coloured wool imported from Europe is sometimes interworked with cotton. Silk fabrics are embroidered with silk, wool or *Kálábatun* thread, and woollen fabrics with the same materials. Some of the best gold embroidery is done on a velvet ground or on English broadcloth. Velvet is not made in India, but is imported. The heaviest kind of gold embroidery is known by the name of *Kárchob.* It is done by fixing the fabric to be embroidered on a frame-work. The patterns are first lightly painted or printed on the fabric with some kind of coloured material, and which the embroiderer follows in laying the *Kálábatun* thread. Lighter gold and silver embroidery is called *Kárchikan.* Gold and silver embroidery on cotton is called *Kámdáni.*

Besides plain and striped muslins, embroidered fabrics of different patterns are turned out at Dacca, the embroidery being either worked by hand in the loom or done by needle. Of those hand-embroidered in the loom, the *Jámdáni* muslins have acquired great celebrity. The process of manufacture is described as follows :—

"The long warp threads being arranged, the weaving is begun as in the case of a piece of ordinary cloth, and a pattern of the embroidery drawn on paper is pinned beneath. As the weaving goes on, the workman continually raises the paper pattern to ascertain if his woof has approached closely to where any flower or other figure has to be embroidered, and when the exact place is reached, he takes his needle (*i.e.*, a bamboo splinter), and as each woof thread passes through the pattern, he sews down the intersected portion of it, and so continues until it is completed. When the embroidered pattern is continuous and regular, as in the usual *Sári* border, the weaver, if a skilful workman, usually dispenses with the aid of a paper pattern. Two persons generally work together at a piece of *Jámdáni*, by which a great saving of time is effected."

Jámdáni is of many patterns. One is the *Karelá*, or patterns having the shape of the fruit of *Momordica Charantia*, eaten as a vegetable. The fruit is of an egg-shape, somewhat tapering to a point at each end. In the patterns it is often accompanied with leaves and flowers, the whole forming either a diaper or are worked in detached bunches. The last form is called *Torádár*. When small flowers or sprigs are powdered over the fabric, it is called *Butidár*. Dacca weavers frequently make the patterns run obliquely across a piece. It is then called *Terchá*. When the patterns run like a net-work over the fabric, it is called *Jálaár*. Another pattern of the *Jámdáni* cloth is the *Panná-hazárá,—i.e.*, a "thousand emeralds," so called when the patterns in a *Butidár* fabric are connected with each other by horizontal bands of closely set, irregular, quatrefoil spots. Gold thread is often introduced among the *Jámdáni* patterns to heighten their effect. Other patterns of *Jámdáni* cloth are known by the names of *Duriá* or striped, *Gendá* or marigold, *Shaburgá* or spotted, &c. *Jámdáni* muslins were in very general use, but the demand for them is decreasing. Both cotton and silk are employed in the needle-work of Dacca. Embroidery with cotton thread is known by the general name of *Chikan-dázi*. *Mugá* received from Assam is chiefly employed to silk-embroider the cotton fabrics of Dacca. *Mugá*-embroidered cloth is known by the name of *Kasidá*. Another kind of Dacca embroidered cloth is the *Jháppan*, which takes its name from that of the vertical loom in which the fabric is made. *Jháppan* is embroidered both with cotton and silk. . The patterns are very beautiful, sometimes consisting of a "square chequer (diagonal) diaper of green double lines, the larger squares being charged with the figure of a split pomegranate, in maroon and gold colour; the smaller squares at the intersections of the double lines of the chequer bands have 8-foiled rosettes of alternate green and gold colour petals, the intervening band-spaces being filled with green (conventional) foliage." Others shew "a very singular 'all-over' scroll arabesque of birds, insects, foliage, flowers, and fruit (pomegranate)." *Jhabbá* is another embroidered cloth of Dacca. The striped cloths called *Duriá* and *Chárkháná* are also embroidered. *Kasidá* is a favourite cloth among the Arabs, Persians, and Turks, specially the patterns called *Mugá-chárkáná-kasidá*, *Kátá-rumi-kasidá*, and *Nilá-chárkháná-kasidá*. They also take *Chikan* work known by the names of *Badan-khás-háshiá*, *Samudralahar*, *i.e.*, sea-wave, &c. An embroidered cloth called *Azizulla* is also a favourite fabric among these people. The prices of Dacca embroidered cloths may be put as follows: *Jháppan* piece $4\frac{3}{4}$ yards long by 34 inches in breadth, R15 to R60. *Kasidá* $5\frac{3}{4}$ yards long 39 inches broad, R12 to R30. *Jámdáni* cloth, $11\frac{3}{4}$ yards long 34 inches broad, R30 to R90. Dacca embroidery, in gold or silver on velvet or silk fabrics, is called the *Kálábatun*, *Kárchob*, or *Kárchikan* work. A collection of such embroidery has been sent to the Glasgow Exhibition. It is made in the form of lace ornaments; price R5 each. Specimens of embroidered ornaments consisting of necklets and dancing bracelets were sent from Dacca to the Colonial and Indian Exhibition. Caps are largely embroidered with gold-work.

Large quantities of cheap embroidered cotton cloths are brought to Howrah. These are of various colours and of various patterns, and are well suited for curtains in European houses. They are mostly *Sáris* worn chiefly by women of the poorer classes.

Finer kinds of similar fabrics are made at Sántipur, of which the Howrah cloths seem to be a coarse imitation.

In Calcutta, large quantities of cotton embroidery, called *Chikan*, are sold among Europeans. Handkerchiefs, ladies' dresses, and clothing for children are so embroidered by men residing in the neighbouring Districts. *Chikan* work is also done at Lucknow in the North-Western Provinces. It was introduced into that town from Bengal, and now gives employment to upwards of 1,200 persons, chiefly women and children of good families impoverished since the abolition of the Oudh Court. The muslin used is manufactured at Lucknow. *Chikan* workers also embroider silk and *Tasar* fabrics with silk thread, and they also make cotton and silk edgings of different patterns.

Soznis or quilted bed-sheets with needle-embroidery are made at Maldah, Rájsháhi, Nadiya, Puri, and other Districts of Bengal. The needle-work is done by females. *Soznis* are made in a different way in Bombay. The process of manufacture followed there is thus described:—

"*Soznis* are cotton and silk fabrics stuffed with cotton to serve as quilts, and the manufacture is a specialty of Broach, the invention being attributed to Hasanbhái Karimbhái, a resident of Mundaphia. The peculiarity of the work consists in each little square bag being woven and united by the loom to its fellows. The operation is peculiar. The weaver sits with his feet in a pit in which there are eight treadles corresponding with and governing the action of the eight heddles above. There is a double layer of fibres in the work, one white and red, and the other green and red, and they are arranged one above the other. By raising with a hook and string treadles numbered 1 and 3, he opens the set of red square compartments for stuffing them with cotton wool, and by raising those numbered 6 and 8 he opens the set of green compartments. When the red warp is on the top of the green, the weaver works his treadles alternately by raising first those numbered 1, 4, 6, and 8, and then those numbered, 2, 3, 5, and 7, while when the green is uppermost, he raises those numbered 1, 4, 5, and 7, and then those numbered 2, 3, 6, and 8."

Soznis are also made at Shikárpur (Sind) in imitation of those brought to India from Bokhara. Bokhara *Soznis* are embroidered with brilliantly coloured silks in bold patterns. Beautifully wrought *Soznis* are also produced in Kashmir.

Gold and silver embroidery or *Kárchob* work is done with *Kálábatun* thread in Murshidabad and Patna. Elephant-*jhuls*, horse-trappings, canopies with fringes, *Pálki*-covers, gowns, jackets, dresses, bodices, prayer-carpets, caps, slippers, money-bags, belts, &c., are embroidered with *Kárchob* or *Kárchikan* work. A canopy with fringe was sent to the Colonial and Indian Exhibition by Maháráni Swarnamayi of Murshidabad, the price of which was R1,518, and a *Pálki*-cover, the price of which was R2,000, both richly embroidered. Pillow-cases are also embroidered in this way, of which specimens were sent to the Colonial and Indian Exhibition from Sáran. At Calcutta itself dresses for dancing girls and turbans used by itinerant theatrical players are embroidered with *Kálábatun* work. A collection of gold and silver embroidered fabrics, fringes, crowns, turbans, caps, wreaths, embroidered *Hukka* pipes, &c., was sent from Calcutta to the Colonial and Indian Exhibition. *Hukka* pipes called *Nalchás* are adorned with lace, embroidery, and glass-beads, in all the large towns of Upper India. False-lace is employed for the common ones. Agra is the chief centre of *Nalchá* pipe manufacture.

In the North-Western Provinces large quantities of velvet caps embroidered with silk are made at Lucknow, Benares, and Agra. Lucknow is, however, celebrated for its gold and silver embroidery. These are known under the names of *Kámdáni* or muslins hand-embroidered in gold wire, and *Zardozi* or velvet cloth embroidered with gold and silver thread. Lucknow exports its embroidered fabrics to all parts of India. *Sáris,* sheets called *Dopattás,* coats, mantel-fringes, saddle-covers, bags, hangings, caps, and shoes are articles generally prepared. The materials for embroidery made at Lucknow, *i.e.,* gold and silver wire, *Kálábatun* thread, &c., have lately found great favour in the Continent of Europe, where they are employed on embroidery for church purposes. Gold and silver embroidered banners are made both at Lucknow and Benares. Caps, belts, and *Hukka* pipes are extensively embroidered at Agra. False lace and gilt wire-threads are largely used for the decoration of cotton caps. Whips and walking sticks are ornamented with embroidered work at Fatehpur.

Panjáb is celebrated for its varied kinds of embroidery. Mantel-pieces, table-covers, chair-covers, tea-cosies, and cushions, embroidered with floss silk at Delhi, are largely purchased by Europeans. Woolen (*Malıdá*) *Chogás* embroidered with silk at Amritsar and Ludhiáná are used by Europeans as a morning dress. Table-covers, screens, cushions, tea-cosies, mantle-piece covers, brackets, chair-covers, panel screens, and other articles of a similar nature are embroidered in gold at Delhi chiefly for European use. Caps, *Chogás,* coats, *Dopattás,* or sheets worn as a shawl by women, are worked in gold for the use of the Indian people.

But the most famous of all the Panjáb embroidery are the celebrated Kashmir shawls, which, besides Kashmir itself, are more or less worked at Amritsar, Ludhiáná, Núrpur, Gurdáspur, Siálkot, and other places in the Panjáb, where a large number of Kashmiri immigrants have settled. Kashmir shawls are of two kinds—(1) Those woven in the loom, called *Tiliwállá*, *Tilikár*, *Kánikár*, or *Binaut*; (2) Needle-worked shawls called *Amlikar*, in which "the ground-work is a plain *Pashminá* piece, and the pattern is entirely due to minute and most elaborate needle-work in *Pashminá* thread all over the whole surface." Mr. Kipling has made the following remarks regarding the present position of the shawl industry in the Panjáb:—

"The Kashmir shawls are of two kinds: the first is the loom-woven, in which the pattern is produced in the loom itself by the aid of a vast number of small bobbins carrying the coloured *Pashm*, the shuttle and cross-threads being only used to secure the whole fabric; the second is the cheaper kind, in which the whole of the pattern is embroidered with the needle. The shawls are made in traditional forms, the *Doshálá* or long shawl in pairs, the *Rumál* or square shawl, and the *Jámiwár*, or shawl always in broad stripes of alternate colour, green and white, red and blue, &c. The shawl trade is a very fluctuating one. As a rule it may be said that the fabric is too costly in proportion to the appearance it makes. The exports for Kashmir were in value—1880, R21,50,000; 1881, R10,88,000; 1882, R11,31,000. The introduction of the aniline dyes has done a great deal to injure the design and appearance of shawls, especially the coarse crimson known as magenta shawl. Weaving is carried on in Amritsar, where, however, the Chángthán stout wool is obtained, and not the first quality, which never leaves Kashmir. In Gujrát a little coarse shawl weaving is done, and at Núrpur also, but here, and occasionally at Siálkot, shawl edging only is made. The edge of the shawl has to be stiffer and stronger than the shawl itself, and is woven on a silk ground. There is some likelihood that the *Kinárá* or edging by itself may become an article of trade, as it might be used for dress trimmings and other purposes."

In Kashmir itself shawl manufacture is now in a deplorable state. The value of the trade was in former days estimated at half a million pounds, but, now the industry is well nigh moribund. "Unless means are taken by Government to preserve it, the art of weaving the finest shawls will probably be extinct. The warehouses of London and Paris are full of shawls which find no purchasers, and their value in Kashmir has consequently fallen to a third of what it was ten years ago (1876)." As an instance of the present deterioration in the value of Kashmir shawls may be cited the price put upon a specimen sent to the Colonial and Indian Exhibition. In former days it would have cost R800 to R1,000. The price put upon it at the Colonial and Indian Exhibition was R300. *Alwáns* and *Rámpur Chádars* have already been mentioned under the head of plain woolen manufactures. Rámpur shawls or *Chádars* are largely purchased by Europeans.

Another important embroidered fabric of the Panjáb that has of late found great favour among Europeans is the *Phulkári* cloth. It is a silk embroidered coarse cotton cloth originally wrought by the peasant women in many Districts of the Panjáb and Rajputana. The Ját women used these embroidered cloths for *Orhnis* or shawls, bodices, petticoats, &c.; they are now made into curtains in European houses. Specimens of *Phulkári* cloths were sent to the Colonial and Indian Exhibition fron Amritsar, Siálkot, Montgomery, Ráwalpindi, Firozpur, Hazárá, Bannu, Hissár, Lahore, Karnál, Kohát, Derá Ismáil Khán, and Rohtak. Those made in Hazárá are probably the best, as there the traditional patterns are strictly adhered to. Mr. Kipling writes :—

"Since the Panjáb Exhibition of 1881 a considerable trade has arisen at Amritsar, where, and in the neighbouring villages, women of nearly all castes occupy their leisure in this work. The best *Phulkáris* are wrought on cotton cloth of country manufacture, dyed in various shades of dark to light red or in indigo to black. The silk used would be called *filoselle* in England, and the colours are usually black, gold, orange, lac, red, somewhat crude green, and recently some raw and unpleasant aniline mauve and magenta hues. There are no curved forms in the patterns, and the stitch, a long and straight one, is carried across the field in diapers, herring-bones, chequers, and zigzags in such a way that it is unnecessary to trace the pattern first; the spacing being done by eye, and in fine work by counting the stitches of the ground. English Turkey red is occasionally worked upon, but the fineness of the cloth is rather a disadvantage than otherwise; one of the points of this work being the contrast of the lustrous silk with the deep, rich texture of the country-made cotton fabric. None of the modifications indeed which have been tried by people in search of some trivial novelty of treatment have turned out improvements. Industrial and Mission Schools have succeeded in producing Europeanised versions of the *Phulkári* of quite astonishing hideousness, and it may be broadly said that the more primitive the District the better the work. In some cases the whole field is hidden by a diaper of gold or orange coloured silk with admirable effect. In others, gold-coloured lozenges with red flowers are thinly powdered over the dark ground. The variety of pattern, however, is practically as endless as the kaleidoscope, and it is no wonder that this agreeable and comparatively cheap material is greatly in favour for decorative purposes. The *Shishádár* (looking-glass) *Phulkári* has small, circular, slightly convex mirrors sewn in the pattern, which produce a quaint and fantastic effect. The same work is applied to feminine garments, as in the bodice, drawers, and petticoats. Pretty bags are embroidered in the Hazárá District, but as the work is there an exclusively domestic occupation, it is not always easy to procure them. In judging a *Phulkári* for texture and workmanship, as it is worked from the back, the back should be examined for evenness and fineness of stitch. No frames are used, and the darning, so to speak, should be without buckle or stretch. At Amritsar the work can be procured on any size or shape of cloth for special uses, if ordered through such firms as Devi Sahái and Chambá Mal, or Devi Sahái and Prabhu Dayál. The silk varies much in quality, and should be carefully examined by the purchaser. The prices range from R5 to R20 for the ordinary *Chádar*. The *chop*, a variety with a deep border and plain field, is effective for some purposes. In the Hissár and Sirsá Districts curious and characteristic *Phulkári* work is wrought on a rough, country-made, woolen fabric, dyed red, woven in narrow widths and joined down the middle with an open work stitch. The patterns are quaint and archaic, and worked in sampler stitch. Occasionally creatures and objects are attempted in squares and triangles, but simple chequered patterns are more common. These primitive and unpretentious fabrics are in a good tone of colour, and have a quality of design in which more ambitious work often fails."

The embroidery known as Chambá *Rumáls* are peculiar to Chambá and Kangra. A specimen of this embroidery wrought in the household of one of thė Ránis of Chambá is kept in the Indian Museum at South Kensington. Gold and silver embroidery is wrought to a certain extent in Derá Ismáil Khán and Patiálá. In the former place caps called *Kallas* are made, round which the Afghan and frontier turban is wound. Horse and saddle cloths, table-covers, and mantle-borders are made at Patiálá. In Gurgáon, woolen cushions or pads, on which the water jar is carried by women, are decorated with shells. In the Derá Gházi Khán District saddle-bags, horse and camel gear are worked by the women of the pastoral tribes.

It is said by a competent authority that "the art of embroidery is nowhere carried to a greater perfection than in Kashmir, taking into consideration execution, colour, design, and price." The specimens sent from Kashmir to the last two Exhibitions were however few. Those displayed at the Colonial and Indian Exhibition consisted of a waistcoat, collar and cuffs for ladies' dress, and were the finest work procurable. They were silk embroidery on wool.

Corsets or breast-cloths, caps, handkerchiefs, veils, bags, babies' robes, and anti-maccasars embroidered in silk were sent to the Colonial and Indian Exhibition from Jaipur. Specimens of work performed by the Jaipur Girls' School, consisting of table-mats, napkins, &c., were sent to the same Exhibition, as also caps, slippers, anti-maccasars, embroidered in gold. At Shergarh in Kota, a small State in Rajputana, English broadcloth is embroidered with floss silk and made into saddle-cloths and elephant trappings. These are done by two families of *Muchis* or shoe-makers. Saddle-cloths are the only articles for which there is any great demand in that place, and they are generally made for local sale. Prices from R20 upwards according to the size of the cloth to be embroidered. At Ajmir there is one establishment, employing about fifteen persons, engaged in embroidery work. It makes articles of dress and edgings for garments, but the work is not so good as of Delhi or Lucknow. Bikánir sent specimens of hair embroidery to the Colonial and Indian Exhibition. This ornamentation is employed on articles of dress for both men and women, and the prices vary from R1 to R65 for each garment according to the quality of materials used. Bodices, jackets, shawls of dancing girls are embroidered with gold at Bikánir. Embroidery in coloured silk and gold thread is executed in Jodhpur : such embroidered work is tied over the turban and is in great demand in the State. Meo sheets and the dress of Ját women are embroidered with silk in the Alwar State. It is practically *Phulkári* work. Gold embroidery of all descriptions is also done in this principality. Alwar embroidery is much admired for its superior designs and for the fineness of workmanship. The work, however, differs little from that made at Delhi.

In Central India, Ratlám turns out horse-trappings embroidered with silk and wool, and Datiá makes chess-boards ornamented with cotton. Chess-boards are embroidered in gold at Charkhári It is a handsome old style of work. Gold embroidered scent-stands, caps, sword-belts, mats, and bags are made at Dhar. Ratlám works handkerchiefs and *Hukka* mouth-pieces in imitation gold and silver. Handkerchiefs and caps are wrought in handsome gold embroidery at Datiá. Pouches and gun-cap holders are silver-embroidered at Alipurá. It has already been noted that Burhánpur in the Central Provinces produces large quantities of embroidery materials, chiefly the *Kálábatun* thread. Burhánpur also turns out a quantity of embroidered stuffs, of which handkerchiefs made of flattened wire and silk are characteristic of the place. *Pardás* or curtains are also made. Besides specimens of these articles, a *Chogá* was sent to the Colonial and Indian Exhibition. It was prepared of cloth of gold, richly embroidered, and was a very fine sample of Burhánpur work.

About embroidery work as carried on in the Madras Presidency, Dr. Bidie, in sending specimens of the art to the Calcutta International Exhibition, made the following remarks:—

"Some styles, such as those used for adorning the hangings of temples, are no doubt of very ancient date in India; but the arts of embroidering muslin, silk and cloth, as now practised, seem to be of comparatively recent origin in the south, and to have been introduced by the Muhammadans. The Madras work of this kind may be classed as follows:—(*a*) muslin embroidered with cotton thread; (*b*) net embroidered with silk thread; (*c*) net embroidered with silver thread; (*d*) net embroidered with gold, or gold and silver; (*e*) net embroidered with gold and beetles' wings; (*f*) *Dungari* embroidered with floss silk; (*g*) woolen cloth embroidered with silk thread and gold. The embroidered *Dungari* is of very recent introduction, having been introduced by Mrs Carmichael with the object of affording poor Muhammadans occupation. The patterns which originally came from Northern India were got from South Kensington. Embroidery is an art in which the people of India particularly excel owing to the deftness of their fingers, good taste in flat patterns, and great patience, and it is very desirable that the work should be encouraged."

A very fine specimen of Madras embroidery, *viz.*, a cover for an idol, was sent to the Calcutta International Exhibition. It was a fine example of old Dravidian art. The pattern was characteristic of South India, and was worked out, regardless of expense, with gold lace and pearls. A large collection of embroidered stuffs was sent from Madras to the Colonial and Indian Exhibition, but they were mostly worked under European supervision. In his report to the Government of India, Dr. Bidie states:—

"The embroidery industry is chiefly carried on by poor Muhammadans, and as it now exists, seems to have been introduced by them. Some of the more costly styles, such as gold embroidered silk and velvet, can only be got to order; and as there is little or no demand for such expensive articles, the art must shortly die out. White muslin and black lace are also embroidered with gold scroll and beetle's wing covers, the *elytræ* of one of the *Buprestidæ*."

The places where the art of embroidery is practised in the Madras Presidency are North Arcot, Palanakatta in Tinnevelly District, Trichinopoly, Godávari, and Tanjore. In Travancore gold and silver embroidery is practised to some extent. A collection was sent to the Colonial and Indian Exhibition, which included among other things a gold collar and cuffs, gold coiffure and fichu, as well as silver fichu, coiffure, and cuffs. Aurangabad in the Haidrabad territory has long been famous for its valuable embroidery work. *Sáris*, coats, caps, handkerchiefs, turbans, saddlecloths, tray-covers, and cushions are heavily and richly embroidered in this place. Embroidery in gold and beetle-wings is in great demand among Europeans for ball dresses. The effect produced by dresses worked in this way is very lovely, specially by lamp light. "The glint of the pieces of the gold-beetles' wings adds considerably to the richness even by day, and forms a relief to the otherwise monotonous effect of the gold." Imitation gold and silver embroidery is also produced with gilt copper. Gulbargá, another town in Haidrabad, turns out a quantity of embroidered stuffs, but it cannot compete with Aurangabad.

In the Bombay Presidency "embroidery is principally carried on at Shikárpur and Haidrabad in Sind, in Kach, in Surat and Bombay, and is executed in various materials, such as silk on cotton, as the *Soznis* of Shikárpur, silk on silk, as the *Odhne*, a square sheet worn by the women of Kach; silk, gold and silver thread used singly or together on cloth or satin for various articles of dress, and also for table-cloths, cozies, cushion-covers, &c., as those of Haidrabad. Another kind of embroidery, heavy in character, called *Bharát-kám* (literally 'work filled in'), where the ornament is first worked in relief in a coarse cotton thread and afterwards covered with gold or silver thread, is extensively made for caps, coats, *Masnads*, saddle-cloths, &c." A species of embroidery made of gold and silver spangles and twisted gold wire is produced in Kathiawar. It is said that the art is undergoing a marked deterioration, notably in Sind, "in design, colour, and mode of execution. The designs are ill-composed; there is a want of balance in the distribution of the masses; the colouring is staring, owing to the introduction of aniline dyes; and the execution is poor when compared with old work." A collection of embroidered caps was sent to the Calcutta International Exhibition from Surat. The patterns in them bore the names of *Hire-bandi* or "Diamond-set," *Ardha-buti* or "Half-foliaged," *Kothani* or "Fortified," &c. Prices ranged from R1-8 to R4-8. A quantity of *Kor* or silk embroidered borders was also sent from this place both to the Calcutta and the Colonial and Indian Exhibitions. The work on them is called *Reshmi Bharát-kám* and is a speciality of Surat. "In former days, these borders were much used by Parsis and Gujrátis for their women's dresses, but of late the introduction of foreign silks has replaced this practice to a great extent." Another kind of embroidery extensively practised at Surat is called *Badláni*, in which the design is worked in flattened gold or silver wire, and is done by women.

The art of embroidering dresses forms one of the chief domestic industries of the women of Kach. A specimen of patch-work in which pieces of silk were most skilfully stitched without any kind of pattern by the tailors of Bhavnagar was sent to the Colonial and Indian Exhibition. It is used as a cover for bullock-carriages, called *Raths*. These *Rath*-covers are also worked in gold. About the embroidery work in the Bombay Presidency Mr. Gupte has furnished the following information :—

"Among the natives of Kach and of the Kathiawar peninsula almost all the women wear embroidered bodices, petticoats, and scarves; among the Venjaris of the Khandesh District a similar practice prevails. The women of the higher classes of Hindus in Maháráshtra or Marhatta-speaking Districts occasionally wear embroidered bodices or have the outer ends of their *Sádis* similarly decorated. Among the Gujrátis and Parsis, the borders of the *Sádis* or scarves of their women and those of the shirts for their children always used to be embroidered in former days, but of late in several instances in or about Bombay this practice has been dropped and replaced by a free use of French and Chinese silks. Among men the Meman residents of Kathiawar, Kach, and Gujrát wear much more embroidery than the males of any other community in the Presidency. Next to the Memans are the Musalmans of Surat and Bombay. The Marhatta men sometimes wear a narrow strip of embroidery on their long coats near the neck, and the bags known as *Batwas* and *Chanchis* used by them for keeping the ingredients of betel leaf are occasionally embroidered. The Europeans in India are now the principal buyers of embroidered articles and chiefly of such as are suitable for the drawing room. Embroidery for household use is practised to a large extent by the women of Kach and Kathiawar and to a small extent by those of Gujrát and Maháráshtra; but for commercial purposes it is worked mostly by men (though sometimes by women) at Shikárpur, Rohri, Karáchi, Haidrabad, Surat, Sáwantwádi, and Bombay. The embroiderers of Shikárpur and Rohri in Sind are called *Chikandaz* or *Kundidaz*. They are all Musalmans of the Suni sect, and number about 40 to 50. About six or seven generations ago the Shikárpur embroiderers were Hindus of the Bhatiá caste; and although they are now Musalmans, they have among them sects which do not intermarry. They believe that they are poorer than what they were formerly because the families of the Mirs and nobles of Sind, who were their great patrons, have become extinct while the number of workers has increased. English broadcloth or velvet, the material they have to work on, is supplied by the customer or local trader, but the coarse cotton stuffs for *Chádars* or bed-sheets they work entirely on their own account. The silk in use is imported by dealers from Bokhara, and then spun and dyed at Karáchi, Haidrabad, and Shikárpur. Embroidery in silk or cotton thread as practised in Kach and Kathiawar is done in 'chain,' 'back,' 'side,' 'button-hole,' 'cross,' 'ladder,' and 'loop' stitches, with bits of glass introduced at regular intervals and carefully worked in. The demand is steady all the year round, caps, shirts, petticoats, and bed-sheets being in much request in the local market. The value of a cap ranges from 2*s.* to 6*s.*; of a shirt from 4*s.* to £1; of a petticoat from £2 to £4; and of a bed-sheet from £2 to £3. Among articles for a European drawing room are table cloths £2 to £5 each; cushion covers 10*s.* to £1 each; slippers 2*s.* to 4*s.* each; doyleys 2*s.* each; and teapoy covers £1 to £3 each. The women sew the family clothes, but they give no aid to the men in their professional work. The embroiderers of Haidrabad differ from those of Shikárpur and Rohri in being able to work on the frame in silk, gold or silver thread, in addition to the hand-work for which these two places are specially famous. But they resemble the workers of those places in all other respects. Silver thread embroidery is from three to four times, and gold thread from six to eight times as costly as silk thread embroidery. As there are no gold and silver thread makers in Sind, the Haidrabad embroiderers bring these articles from Kabul, Bactria, and Agra. The Bactrian lace is considered the best. In the city of Surat there are about 650 men who earn their livelihood as embroiderers. They are mostly Musalmans, who have no tradition of having come to Surat from any other place. The gold, silver, or silk thread required for embroidery is supplied to them by the local merchants, who get the work done by employing them as labourers at a rate of 1*s.* to 3*s.* a day. The silk used in preparing the gold and silver thread for embroidery is called *Asára*, and the silk thread used in sewing the *Kárchobi* or frame-work embroidery is called *Nakh*. *Asára* means that which is spun on the *Asári* or reel, and *Nakh* means that which is spun through holes bored into the nail (*Nakh*). The second of these processes is quite obsolete, but the expression is still used to indicate the extreme thinness of the thread. The gold and silver thread used by the embroiderers is of local manufacture. The silk thread is also spun and dyed in the city of Surat. There are four chief varieties of embroidery, locally known as *Hátjári, Kárchobi, Badláni*, and *Reshmi-bharát-kám*. Of these, the second and the fourth require frames. There are at Surat 25 to 30 men who do the *Hátjári* work, literally hand-made gold or silver thread work; about 500 who do the *Kárchobi*, or work done on the frame; and about 100 who do the *Reshmi-bharát-kám*. It is curious to note that the Surat embroiderers in silk thread are called *Chikandaz*, a name also given by the Sindis to the embroiderers of Shikárpur, Rohri, Karáchi, and Haidrabad in Sind. The *Badláni* or work in flattened gold or silver wire is done by Bhorá women during their leisure hours. The *Kárchobi* work in gold and silver thread is sub-divided into five groups: (1) *Kasabtiki*, gold or silver thread spangles, which is peculiar to Surat; (2) *Jhikchalak*, from the twisted thread (*Jhik*) and the zigzag thread (*Chalak*); (3) *Bharát-karáchi* from its being in imitation of the Karáchi work, in which bits of card-board are used for giving a raised body to the designs; (4) *Jhik-tiki* from the twisted threads and spangles used; and (5) *Chalak-tiki* from the zigzag thread (*Chalak*) and spangles *Tiki*. *Reshmi-bharát-kám* is done in chain and back stitches. The first thing an embroiderer has to do is to print with gum mixed with chalk the designs required, which he does with carved blocks obtained from local carvers at 6*d*. to 10*d*. each, or with paper stencils. Very often he has only a small number of little blocks from which he produces many elaborate designs by varying their arrangement. The total value of the articles embroidered at Surat in one year is said to range from £700 to £1,000. The Sáwantwádi embroiderers are Hindus of the Jinger caste, who execute work only to order. In Bombay, embroiderers from Delhi have settled themselves, and one has opened a large establishment on the Kalbadevi Road, employing about 200 workers. Besides the Musalman embroiderers from Delhi there are a few establishments of Goanese native Christians, who embroider caps at 6*s*. to £1, slippers at 4*s*. to 12*s*., trousers at 12*s*. to £2, and coats at 10*s*. to £5 in gold and silver thread on velvet in '*Point de Plume*' stitches on a raised body consisting of card-board cut to sizes, with the help of paper stencils."

In Assam almost all the fine sorts of cotton and silk fabrics are elaborately ornamented, mostly in the loom, with patterns worked in cotton, silk, gold or silver thread. There are no professional weavers in Assam, and all this work is done by women of the household, even women of respectability. The patterns are of the most varied kind, "as fresh ones are constantly being invented. It is a matter of pride for a woman skilled in weaving to have a special pattern of her own." The superior kinds of cotton *Chádar* or sheet, which are sometimes as fine as muslins, are decorated with elaborately worked patterns of flowers, fruits, and birds in coloured thread, sometimes of silk and sometimes of cotton. *Khaniá-kápar* is a highly ornamented cotton shawl, "usually very finely woven and elaborately adorned along the borders with graceful designs of flowers and creepers. Sometimes the whole of the front sheet of the *Khaniá* is tastefully decorated with flowery spots. The ornamentation is usually made either with silk or coloured thread, or with a mixture of silk and gold or silver." *Cheleng* is another kind of cotton shawl, ornamented like the *Khaniá*, but seldom to the same extent. It is smaller in dimensions than the *Khaniá*. *Paridiá-kápar* is another kind of embroidered cotton shawl, very finely made and most artistically ornamented. "This article of clothing is made and worn only by the upper classes. It is the highest example of the art of weaving as known in Assam. A single *Paridiá-kápar* will cost from R40 to R200, according to the fineness of the material used and the nature of the decoration employed. The ornamenting thread is usually gold or silver twist, sometimes both, and the design, though generally confined to the border, spreads sometimes over the whole article. Representations of flowers and birds are the commonest species of decoration, but the pattern consists sometimes of nothing but graceful curves arranged symmetrically along the borders. Occasionally a *Paridiá-kápar* is made by attaching to a centre piece of very finely woven muslin-like material border pieces ornamented by a few Muhammadans who still retain a knowledge of the art of weaving with gold and silver thread." Of silk cloths, the *Rihás* or scarfs worn by women and *Erá-Barkápar* are generally ornamented in the same way as the cotton fabrics. Cloths made of *Eri* silk have seldom any kind of decoration except a coloured design at the two ends. Articles made of *Mugá* silk are generally elaborately worked.

"The materials principally used in loom embroidery are—*Asu*, an imported cotton thread dyed with various colours, chiefly yellow, red, and blue; *Mugá* thread, a species of silk very common in the Province; gold thread; silver thread. *Asu* is used for almost all articles, and *Mugá* thread is very generally employed also. For *Paridiá-kápar* gold or silver thread only is used.

"Besides the ornamenting done in the loom, a species of needle embroidery is also much in vogue. This kind of work is usually carried on by Muhammadans, the following embroidered cloth being the ones most commonly made:—*Kársipi-kápar*, a richly embroidered cotton cloth used as a wrapper. It is made of very fine material and decorated profusely with representations of butterflies, animals, and flowers worked in flattened gold wire. *Rihár-áchal*, the ends of a silk *Rihá* or scarf, commonly worn by women. The borders and ends are usually decorated with gold thread twisted with steel wire, or with gold thread alone. *Káparer-áchal*, the ends and borders of a cotton *Chádár*, ornamented in much the same way as the *Rihár-áchal*. *Garuchok*, the ends of a round pillow. The material is usually imported woolen broadcloth, but the decoration consists of flowery designs worked generally in cotton of different colours. The embroidered portion is usually 8 or 10 inches square. *Bátá-dháká*, the ornamental cover of a betel-tray decorated like the *Garuchok*. It is usually 18 or 20 inches square. *Talichá*, an ornamental cloth, usually 4 or 5 feet square, spread over an inferior cloth used for sitting on. The material and decoration are the same generally as for *Garuchok* and *Bátá-dháká*."

In Burma, at least in that portion of it hitherto known as British Burma, gold and silver embroidery is only practised to supply costumes for the theatre. In the decoration of such dresses gold and silver are freely used, as are precious stones, and the result is an exceedingly costly garment. A jacket of a very common work for a prince in a marionette company would cost about R150. Specimens of this work were sent from Prome to the Colonial and Indian Exhibition.

In connection with embroidery may be noticed the patch or *applique* work of Burma, called *Kalaga*, which has recently found favour among Europeans for use as hangings, screens, curtains, &c. It is made both of silk and cotton.

"The best *Kalagas* are made in Kemmendine, a suburb of Rangoon, where there are four or five families engaged in the work. Cloth (cotton) *Kalagas* are red hangings or *Pardás* about 10 or 12 feet long and 4 or 5 feet deep, on which are pourtrayed scenes from one of the mythological plays. The work is technically known as *applique* work, and is formed by cutting the figures and foliage of the picture out of vari-coloured cloths and sewing them on to the background. The result in Burma is a gorgeously coloured screen, which is used to decorate the house on festive occasions or to partition off a part of it for a guest. The *Kalaga* also forms a gay roof-covering for the bullock cart when the family travels to one of the large pagoda feasts. The process of manufacture is as follows:—Part of the red cloth ground is stretched by lacing it to the sides of a wooden frame. The leaves and the flowers of the border and the strips used to line out the divisions of the picture are marked out on the differently-coloured cloths with chalk and cut out with a pair of scissors. The border running round the edge of the *Kalaga*, which is about 15 inches broad, is first lined out with strips of cloth, and the leaves and flowers are then added. The detached pieces of the pattern are pasted on with rice paste and afterwards firmly sewn on with thread of the proper colour. When the border is finished the figures are placed in the centre. As is the case with all Burmese art-work, the designs are bold yet graceful, the grotesque element being specially good."

An ordinary cotton *Kalaga* may be bought at eight annas per square foot and a better quality costs ten annas. Silk ones are made in the same way, but the details are more carefully worked out, and the colours are so improved and arranged as to give the whole a very effective appearance.

Carpets.

Woolen pile carpets are known by the name of *Kálin*, *Kálichá*, or *Gálichá*. The original home of carpet manufacture was the wilds north of Persia—Kurdistan, Kirman, Khorassan, Ferahan, &c. The climate of India is unsuited for the production of that soft wool which could be made to glow with the richest tints and with which the best carpets were made in former times among the deserts of Central Asia. Nor is the moist atmosphere of this country favourable for the safe keeping of this magnificent product of art. An Eastern carpet should not be taken for a common floor-cover, but it must be looked upon as a rich tapestry on which the beautiful colours of nature are blended, as an oriental can only blend, into a soft serene atmosphere of dreamy refulgence. The manufacture of such carpets is now a thing of the past. There is now hurry in the world, all over from China to Peru. Art formerly belonged only to princes and their wealthy following. The princes of the East knew no hurry, but could wait and pay for a carpet like the one made at Warangul (in Haidrabad, Deccan) in the sixteenth or early in the seventeenth century, containing 3,500,000 knots on its entire surface, or 400 knots to the square inch, and the patterns on which were so complicated that a change of needle was required for every knot. This carpet belongs to Mr. Vincent Robinson and is now shewn in the Indian section of the South Kensington Museum. The public is now the patron of art, and the public can only afford to have the name, not the reality. So things for the most part are now getting to be made and sold not always for any intrinsic merit in them but in virtue of their traditionary reputation. For an account of carpets the reader is referred to Mr. Vincent Robinson's Work on Eastern Carpets and Sir George Birdwood's Work on Industrial Arts of India.

The manufacture of pile carpets was introduced into India by the Muhammadans, who, to whatever place they went, not only encouraged the indigenous arts but brought to it the handicrafts, and occasionally the craftsmen themselves, of Bagdad, Shiraz, and Samarcand. Persian carpets were, however, always preferred to those made in India, and princes and nobles of the Delhi Court when in its greatest splendour eagerly sought the stuffs woven at Hirat, or by the Sarrakhs on the Attrek, or the nomad tribes of Western Kurdistan. A few specimens of these carpets still remain in India, and these are now and then reproduced with more or less accuracy. For instance, a copy of the Hirati carpet that has been in the Jaipur family for over a hundred and fifty years was made in the Agra Central Prison and shewn at the Calcutta International Exhibition. The price put upon the copy was R1,000. Sir William Tyler thus describes it:—

"The original carpet, of which only a slip now remains, measuring some 20 feet by 12 feet, is woven from the finest *Pashm* wool, very similar to that employed in the celebrated Kashmir shawls, with a cotton foundation of twelve threads to the inch. The design of the border is entirely and purely Persian, consisting, as it does, of alternate medallions and flowers, with a fish on opposite sides. The design of the centre is evidently a mingling of the Afghan with the Persian and Arabic, as is shown by the geometrical outlines filled in with medallions and floral ornamentation. These are so beautifully and harmoniously intermixed that there is no clashing of style; in fact, so cleverly and neatly are the three classes of design intermingled that only a person thoroughly acquainted with the local peculiarities which, in ancient times, distinguished the patterns of one country from another could detect or separate them. The colours in the original carpet are purely Persian, and are as bright and as beautiful in tone today as they were when the carpet was first woven; the tints are, perhaps, a little mellowed by time, but this takes nothing from, on the contrary it rather adds to, their beauty. The deep red ground-work of the centre and dark green of the large border, as also the deep blue-green of the centre leaflets and flowers in the original, possesses a lustre making the wool forming the pile look, to the uninstructed eye, like silk. This is partly due to the description of wool used and partly to the ancient method of dyeing. The medallions in the centre of the carpet, with their connecting geometrical links, leaflets, and flowers, are, so far as design and harmony of colour are concerned, the most beautiful of any which I have yet seen. In the carpet now exhibited, and which was woven in the Agra Central Prison by the best weavers, the design has been most accurately reproduced; while the different colours, which blend together so harmoniously (and which have been so much admired by every one who visited the Jail while it was on the loom), have been accurately copied, great care having been taken to reproduce the exact shades employed in the original carpet. The best wool procurable, machine-spun and dyed with fast colours, has been employed in the formation of the pile, while the *warp* or foundation, which consist of twenty threads to the inch, is made of fine, machine-spun Nágpur cotton; in fact, no expense and trouble of supervision have been spared to render this copy as nearly as possible equal to the original. In weaving ordinary quality carpets, each weaver can with ease weave 72 square inches per day of eight hours; while with much difficulty, in the carpet now exhibited, each man could get through but 12 square inches, so closely and compactly has each line been beaten home. So well has this been done that the geometrical outlines appear almost as distinct as if drawn on paper with pencil and compass."

Carpets are now made in many of the jails of India by prison labour, notably at Bhágalpur in Bengal; Basti, Benares, Allahabad, Agra, Lucknow, Bareilly, and Fatehgarh, in the North-Western Provinces; Delhi, Lahore, Multan, Derá Ismáil Khán, Ráwalpindi, and Hissár in the Panjáb; Yerrowda, Tháná, and Karáchi in Sind in the Bombay Presidency. The example has been followed in Native States, and carpets are woven by prison labour in the jails at Rámpur, Jaipur, Alwar, Kota, Nábhá, Patiálá, and probably in other places. They are also made in the School of Art at Jaipur. The old Persian patterns are generally copied in the jails. At the Yerrowda Jail in Bombay the models followed are some old Persian carpets discovered in the Asar Mahal at Bijápur. New patterns are sometimes invented like the *Táj* and the *Parrot* patterns of the Agra Jail. The manufacture of woolen pile carpets as a private industry is carried on at Mirzapur, Bareilly, Moradabad, Bulandshahr, Bárabánki, and Jhánsi in the North-Western Provinces and Multan and Amritsar in the Panjáb. Wool and silk carpets are made by private persons at Warangul and Hammámkundá in the Haidrabad State, and at Adoni, Vadavedi, and other places in the Madras Presidency. It is said that the competition of jail manufactures with those of private firms has greatly injured and in some places destroyed the trade of the latter. But at the same time it is doubtful whether private parties would have the capital or the courage to make copies of old carpets like the one made at the Agra Central Prison. If the jails would only confine their operations to copy and preserve the most valuable examples of carpets and not make tawdry articles for a profitable sale, or make things already in the hands of private manufacturers, such as the cotton carpets called *Daris,* prison manufuctures would come into no competition with private industries. On the other hand they would set before the people models of good workmanship. Far from injuring the private trade, the jails have been instrumental in creating in many places the industry of carpet manufacture where it did not exist before. The best works of art, which it is impossible to produce in the ordinary course of trade competition, have always been encouraged, improved, and preserved by State interference. What is now required in India is a few prize appointments to be given as a reward to one or two highest experts in each branch of art. Their productions would be two high-priced to come into competition with the bazar manufactures in the same line, but they would serve as models by which the integrity of the art would be preserved. The mode of pile carpet manufacture is thus described by Sir George Birdwood :—

"The foundation for the carpet is a warp of the requisite number of strong cotton or hempen threads, according to the breadth of the carpet, and the peculiar process consists in dexterously twisting short lengths of coloured wool into each of the threads of the warp so that the two ends of the twist of coloured wool stick out in front. When a whole line of the warp is completed, the projecting ends of the wool are clipped to a uniform level, and a single thread of wool is run across the breadth of the carpet, between the threads of the warp, just as in ordinary weaving, and the threads of the warp are crossed as usual; then another thread of the warp is fixed with twists of wool in the same manner; and again a single thread of wool is run between the threads of the warp, across the carpet, serving also to keep the tags of wool upright, and so on to the end. The lines of work are further compacted together by striking them with a blunt fork (*Kangi*), and sometimes the carpet is still further strengthened by stitching the tags of wool to the warp. Then the surface is clipped all over again, and the carpet is complete."

The noted private carpet-manufacturers in Upper India are Babu Beni Prashád of Mirzapur and Messrs. Devi Sahái and Chamba Mal of Amritsar. Country wool is used at Mirzapur. It is said that the industry was in a bad state some years ago, but that its position has improved of late owing to large orders having been received from America and the European Continent. Babu Beni Prashád has sent a consignment of his carpets to the Glasgow International Exhibition. Carpets have also been supplied for the same Exhibition from the Bhágalpur, Allahabad, and Lucknow Jails. Carpet-weaving is practically a new industry in the Panjáb. It is said that carpets were woven at Lahore during the time of Akbar, but the industry died out long before the Sikh rule, "during which time, of course, there were absolutely no demands for the products of this purely Muhammadan craft." Amritsar carpets are woven by Kashmiris, and they strongly resemble ordinary Kashmir carpets. In writing about the carpet exhibits sent from the Panjáb to the Calcutta International Exhibition Mr. Kipling remarked :—

"It has been said that the Panjáb jails have injured the indegenous industry of carpet-weaving. It would be more like the truth to assert that they have created such as exists. It was not until the Exhibition of 1862 that the Panjáb was known beyond its border for the productions of carpets, and then only by the productions of the Lahore Jail executed for a London firm. There exists no specimens to show that the Multan industry, the only indigenous one of the Province, was of either artistic or commercial importance. The success of the Lahore Jail led to the introduction of the manufacture in other jails, and it is now taken up by independent persons. The series here shown by the Panjáb jails is of unusual excellence, and includes copies of Persian originals in the possession of the Jaipur State, and the more familiar patterns known as *Hirati*, *Shawl*, *Rumál*, and others. The qualities vary from the finest counts made to carpets of a cheaper kind. The Delhi Jail exhibits a reversible rug with a different pattern on each side. The Industrial Schools of Hushiárpur and Kasur display specimens of their production. Messrs. Devi Sahái and Chambá Mal, who have an extensive manufactory at Amritsar, show their own fabrics as well as importations from Bokhara. From Multan coloured carpets of great strength and solidity of texture are sent. The characteristic blue and white carpet, which seems peculiar to this indigo-growing centre, and is familiar both in woolen and cotton pile, is not, however, represented. A great improvement has taken place of late years in the Multan fabrics."

Wherever the manufacture of pile carpet forms an industry of an appreciable extent, wooleen rugs and small seats called *Asans* are made. Such articles are made at Mirzapur, Allahabad, Lucknow, Fatehgarh, Jhánsi, and other places in the North-Western

Provinces. Of these the rugs on which the Muhammadans sit to say their prayers, called *Jai-namáz*, are often most elaborately worked. Coloured felt rugs are made at Bherá, and in the Derá Ghází Khán frontier similar articles as well as camel bags are produced by Biluch women. Mr. Kipling remarks:—

"The texture is somewhat harsh, but the patterns are harmonious and good, and the fabric has great wear-resisting powers. Some of the camel trappings are decorated fancifully with white *Kauris*. Like other fabrics produced by pastoral people, as Central Asian carpets, they are sometimes apt 'to buckle,' *i.e.* they do not lie flat. The loom with the carpet on it is rolled up and carried away as the flocks are moved to fresh pastures. It may be noted that rugs and saddle-cloths, precisely similar in texture and pattern and in the use of shells as ornamental tassels and fringes, are found in the Balkans. In Central India and the Deccan the Banjárá women weave clothing and the pack-saddles of their bullocks in textures and patterns almost identical with this Biluch work."

Felts made in north-west Panjáb are largely used as floor-cloth. Two specimens of carpets made at Bannu were sent to the Colonial and Indian Exhibition. They were of a curious dingy red ochre colour, and are peculiar to that District.

The decline of the shawl industry has given a considerable impulse to carpet manufacture in Kashmir. "Numbers of shawl weavers unable to find employment in their hereditary craft are now employed in it. The best are made under the superintendence of M. Bigex, a French merchant." The price of carpets ranges from R4 to R20 per square yard. An embroidered rug, called *Gabhá*, is made at Kashmir. This is done "by cutting out forms in woollen cloths of various colours, which are inserted and counter-changed like the *opus consutum* of mediæval times, the edges and field being worked in a large 'broidery stitch in suitable colours." Felt rugs or *Namdás* are also made in Kashmir, which are ornamented with a bold outline pattern in coloured silk or wool. This work also adds to the durability of the felt.

Woolen carpets were sent to the Colonial and Indian Exhibition from Jaipur and Alwar in Rajputana, and from Rewa, Gwalior, and Jhánsi in Central India. One of the Rewa carpets was beautifully coloured—blue on a white ground. The workmanship was also excellent. It was much admired, and applications were made by private parties for copies. A rug was sent from the Datiá State. No carpets were sent to that Exhibition from Jabalpur in the Central Provinces. A few specimens were sent to the Calcutta International Exhibition from the Government School of Industry at that place. Jabalpur was once noted for its carpets, but the industry seems to have declined.

In the Madras Presidency carpets made at Masulipatam, Malabar, and in the neighbourhood of Coconada had a European reputation. According to Sir George Birdwood Malabar carpets "would seem to be the only pile woollen carpets made in India of pure Hindu design." The industry appears to be on the decline in all these places. The collections of carpets received from Madras in the Calcutta and the Colonial and Indian Exhibitions were not large. Carpets either of wool, silk, or cotton are still made in this Presidency at Kistna, Vridachellam, Adoni, Vadavedi, Karnúl, Bahavari, Wallaja, Ellore, Rájmahendri, Masulipatam, and Iyempett. In his report to the Government of India, Dr. Bidie states :—

"Some of the old colours are excellent, and the real old Madras patterns are of much merit. Carpets are made chiefly in wool and silk. Those made at Vadavedi in the South Arcot District are effective and interesting, as the patterns are evidently the outcome of some old designs in grass matting. The colours are black, white, red, and orange, and the general effect is quiet and pleasing. Carpets of the same class, but of better quality, are made in Adoni. In these the colours are in narrow stripes, plain or chequered, running across the piece, and rather glaring and inharmonious. Large numbers are made and sold, but although effective enough as a screen or table-cover in a remote corner of a room, they have a tiresome effect if constantly under the eye."

The patterns of the rugs displayed in the Madras Court of the Colonial and Indian Exhibition bore the names of *Kábul, Rám-Chandra Ráo-Khání, Bandar-Sháh-Nawáz Khání, Háshim Khání,* &c.

Bangalore in Mysore had a large export trade in woollen carpets. The trade has fallen off since the weavers took to dyeing the wool with aniline dyes. What are known as the "Bangalore carpets" are a specialty of the place. They are reversible, having the same pattern on both sides, and are noted for their durability. The price charged is R1 to R3 per square yard. Warangul, a town eighty miles from Haidrabad, has long been famous for its carpets and rugs. Sir George Birdwood writes:—

"The peculiarity of these rugs, of which several remain in the India Museum, was the exceedingly fine count of the stitches, about 12,000 to the square foot. They were also pefectly harmonious in colouring, and the only examples in which silk was ever used in carpets with a perfectly satisfactory effect. The brilliancy of the colours was kept in subjection by their judicious distribution and the extreme closeness of the weaving, which is always necessary when the texture is of silk. All this involves, naturally, great comparative expense, not less than £10 per square yard; and it is not surprising, therefore, that in the competition with the *Thug* carpets of the jails, the stately fabrics of Warangul, the ancient capital of the Andhra dynasty of the Deccan, and of the later Rájás of Telingana, have died out, past every effort to revive them."

The fine Warangul carpet lent to the India Museum at South Kensington by Mr. Vincent Robinson has already been noticed in a previous page. It does not appear that any carpets were sent from Warangul to the Colonial and Indian Exhibition, but some were sent to the Calcutta Exhibition of 1883-84, among which was a silken one (7′ 5″ × 5′ 2″) valued at R3,772. A woolen carpet of the same dimensions was priced at R950, and a cotton one slightly larger at R790. Carpets were received at the Calcutta Exhibition from Gulbargá and Hamámkundá, both in Haidrabad. Those from Gulbargá were made in the State Jail. Silk carpets are also made in that prison, of which two specimens were sent to the Colonial and Indian Exhibition.

It has already been stated that in the Bombay Presidency carpets are chiefly made in the jails. They are also produced by private manufacturers at Karáchi; and at Ahmadabad Mr. De Forest, an American gentleman, works a few looms under the management of his local agent. A carpet was sent to the Colonial and Indian Exhibition from the Sáwantwádi State, and a collection of pile carpets from the jails at Karáchi, Shikárpur, Haidrabad (in Sind), Thánà, &c. A similar collection has been sent to the Glasgow International Exhibition from Karáchi, Haidrabad, Shikárpur, Thánà, and Yerrowda Jails.

Daris or *Satranjis* are cotton carpettings or floor-cloths made by weaving thick strong cotton twists in the ordinary loom in the ordinary plain way. They have generally bands of blue in alternation with white, obtained by using coloured thread. Red, chocolate, and yellow stripes are also common, as well as cotton carpets with square and diamond shaped patterns. In the District of Rangpur in Bengal a peculiar design is brought out in blue on white ground which resembles in shape the foot of an elephant, hence called *Philpáyá*. *Daris* are made to a small extent at Gya, Bhabhuá, Champáran, and Behar in Bengal. But the chief centres of cotton carpet manufacture are Agra and Aligarh in the North-Western Provinces, from which places they are exported to other parts of India. They are made of different patterns and are of different qualities. Great care is often bestowed on the manufacture of the small carpets called *Jai-namáz*, on which the Muhammadans place themselves when they say their prayers. *Daris* are also made at Bareilly and Bulandshahr in the same Provinces, at Jaipur in Rajputana, Dharwar, Belgám, Ahmadnagar, Kaladgi, and Cambay in Bombay, and at Vadavedi, Adoni, and other places in the Madras Presidency. Cotton carpets are also made in almost all the jails where woolen carpets are manufactured. So far as is known, they are made in the jails at Baxar, Benares, Allahabad, Lucknow, Fatehgarh, Agra, Ambala, Hissár, Jhelam, Gujrát, Multan, Derá Ismáil Khán, Siálkot, Pesháwar, Ratnagiri, Gulbargá, &c. In a plain unartistic industry of this kind jail productions are likely to come into competition with private manufactures. An imitation pile carpet in coloured and uncoloured cotton is made at Mirzapur. It is called *Dulichá*.

INDEX.

(*Names of places as spelt in the map are shown within brackets, and figures against each line indicate page numbers.*)

A

D

G

H

J

K

L

M

N

O

P

Q

R

U

V

W

Y

Z

G. I. C. P. O.—No. 1022 R. & A.—18-7-88.—1,000.